EXPLAINING CREATIVITY

Explaining Creativity

The Science of Human Innovation

R. Keith Sawyer

OXFORD
UNIVERSITY PRESS

2006

OXFORD

UNIVERSITY PRESS

Oxford University Press, Inc., publishes works that further
Oxford University's objective of excellence
in research, scholarship, and education.

Oxford   New York
Auckland   Cape Town   Dar es Salaam   Hong Kong   Karachi
Kuala Lumpur   Madrid   Melbourne   Mexico City   Nairobi
New Delhi   Shanghai   Taipei   Toronto

With offices in
Argentina   Austria   Brazil   Chile   Czech Republic   France   Greece
Guatemala   Hungary   Italy   Japan   Poland   Portugal   Singapore
South Korea   Switzerland   Thailand   Turkey   Ukraine   Vietnam

Published by Oxford University Press, Inc.
198 Madison Avenue, New York, New York 10016

www.oup.com

Library of Congress Cataloging-in-Publication Data
Sawyer, R. Keith (Robert Keith)
Explaining creativity: the science of human innovation/R. Keith Sawyer
p. cm.
Includes bibliographical references and index.
ISBN-13 978-0-19-516164-9; 978-0-19-530445-9 (pbk.)
ISBN 0-19-516164-5; 0-19-530445-4 (pbk.)
1. Creative ability. I. Title
BF408.S284 2006
153.3'5—dc 22   2005012982

1 3 5 7 9 8 6 4 2

Printed in the United States of America
on acid-free paper

ACKNOWLEDGMENTS

I have been studying and teaching creativity for more than ten years, and have published several academic books on the topic. But when you write a book like this one, summarizing an entire field for the interested general reader, it's like learning the material all over again. It's been a wonderful experience! I begin by thanking Mike Csikszentmihalyi for introducing me to the field of creativity research. Then, I owe a debt to my students, who have helped me discover how best to explain creativity. I'd like to thank all of the musicians, actors, and artists who I've observed and interviewed through the years, for sharing with me their perspectives on creativity. I am grateful to Oxford University Press; the idea for this book was born in a conversation with Joan Bossert, and my editor Catharine Carlin ably managed the process. And I'd like to thank my wife, Barb, who made this book possible; I started working on it soon after our wedding, and finished it just after our son Graham was born.

CONTENTS

CONTENTS

Part IV Artistic Creativity

Part V Everyday Creativity

Part 1

Conceptions

CHAPTER 1

Introduction

Genius. Invention. Talent. And, of course, creativity. These words describe the highest levels of human performance. When we are engaged in the act of being creative, we feel we are performing at the peak of our abilities. Creative works give us insight and enrich our lives.

Creativity is part of what makes us human. Our nearest relatives, chimpanzees and other primates, are often quite intelligent but never reach these high levels of performance. And although advanced "artificially intelligent" computer programs hold the world title in chess, and can crunch through mounds of data and identify patterns invisible to the human eye, they still cannot master everyday creative skills.

In spite of its importance, creativity has not received much attention from scientists. Until very recently, only a few researchers had studied creativity. Most psychologists instead study what they believe are more fundamental mental properties—memory, logical reasoning, and attention. But in recent years psychologists—along with increasing numbers of sociologists, anthropologists, musicologists, theater experts, and art critics—have increasingly turned their attention to creativity. Because creativity is not a central topic in any of these fields, these scholars work without big research grants, and without a lot of attention from the leaders of their fields. Even so, their research findings have gradually accumulated, and our knowledge about creativity has now attained a critical mass. Perhaps for the first time, we hold in our grasp the potential to explain creativity.

By the 1990s, the science of creativity had converged on the *sociocultural approach*, an interdisciplinary approach that explains creative people and their social and cultural contexts. The sociocultural approach brings together psychologists, sociologists of science and art, and anthropologists who study art, ritual performance, and verbal creativity in different cultures. Scientists have discovered that explaining creativity requires understanding not only individual inspiration but also social factors like collaboration, networks of support, education, and cultural background. In this book, I explain creativity by bringing together psychological studies of individuals, sociological studies of individuals creating in groups, and anthropological studies of how people from different cultural and social backgrounds perceive and value creative products differently.

Why Explain Creativity?

Years ago, when I began to teach "the psychology of creativity" to college students, I discovered that the scientific study of creativity made some of my students nervous. Students often asked, "Isn't the whole project just a mistaken attempt to impose the analytic worldview of science onto the arts? Isn't creativity a mysterious force that will forever resist scientific explanation?" Some of the artists who take the class are worried that if they are too analytic, this new approach will interfere with their muse. We'll see that these worries are unfounded, and that explaining creativity is important for many reasons.

Explaining creativity can help us identify and realize every person's unique creative talents. Without explaining creativity, it's easy to fail to recognize and nurture individuals with important creative abilities. If we hope to solve all of the pressing problems facing our society and our world, we must take advantage of the creative talents of everyone.

Explaining creativity can help our leaders to respond better to the challenges facing modern society. Researchers have discovered that creativity is an essential skill for effective leadership (Bennis & Biederman, 1997; Simonton, 1994). Creative leaders have much more impact because they can motivate their teams more effectively. Creative leaders are especially effective at handling novel challenges that force them to go outside the typical routines. Changes in the modern economy have made creativity economically more important than ever (Florida, 2002). Increasing competition—due to deregulation and increased international trade—requires companies to innovate more rapidly. Rapid advances in technology demand more frequent and more substantial innovation. Technology and competition synergistically feed off each other; for example, the technology of the Internet makes it easier for companies to compete across national boundaries. Before the 1980s, creativity was thought to be only occasionally important to a corporation; but today most business leaders believe that creativity is critical to the survival of their organization.

Explaining creativity can help us all to be better problem solvers. We each face problems in our everyday lives that require creative responses. Our society faces challenges like pollution, poverty, and terrorism. Some of these problems can be solved simply by a single individual having a good idea; others will require groups of individuals to work together creatively as a unit.

Explaining creativity helps us realize the importance of positive, peak experiences to mental health. During peak experiences known as *flow,* people are at their most creative. Researchers studying *positive psychology* have discovered that flow and creativity contribute to a happy, fulfilling life (Csikszentmihalyi, 1990b). A better explanation of creativity can help people to achieve these positive, healthy experiences.

Explaining creativity can help educators teach more effectively. Educational psychologists are increasingly discovering the role that creativity plays in development and learning (Sawyer et al., 2003). In recent decades, psychologists have identified the step-by-step creative processes that underpin learning (Bransford, Brown, & Cocking, 1999; Olson & Torrance, 1996). Creativity is not only important to classroom learning but also to the critical informal learning that occurs in the preschool years—how to speak a first language, how to behave at the dinner table, how to make friends and engage in group play (Sawyer, 1997b).

Explaining creativity provides more than intellectual satisfaction; it will lead to a more creative society, and will enhance the creative potential of our families, our workplaces, and our institutions.

Beyond High Art

Many studies of creativity have been limited to those art forms most highly valued in the West. By limiting their studies to "high" forms—to fine art painting rather than decorative painting, graphic arts, or animation; to basic science rather than applied science, engineering, or technology; to symphonic compositions rather than the creativity of the violinist, the ensemble interaction of a chamber quartet, or the improvisation of a jazz group—these researchers have implicitly accepted a set of values that is culturally and historically specific. These biases must be discarded if we want to explain creativity in all societies, in all cultures, and in all historical time periods.

To explain creativity, we have to consider a broad range of creative behaviors, not only the high arts of Western, European cultures. In addition to fine art painting, symphonic performance of the European classical repertoire, and dramatic performance of scripted plays, a complete explanation of creativity must also explain comic strips, animated cartoons, movies, music videos, mathematical theory, experimental laboratory science, the improvised performances of jazz and rock music, and the broad range of performance genres found in the world's cultures.

Up until the 1980s, whenever psychologists studied creativity, they focused either on scientific innovation or on the high arts most valued in Western culture. But in recent years, the science of creativity has broadened to include creativity in non-Western cultures, and the creativity associated with the most influential contemporary developments in media and art—movies, television, music videos, multimedia, performance, and installation art.

This book is unique in that almost all scientific books about creativity have been limited to those expressions of creativity that are highly valued in Western cultures.[1] The bias in creativity research toward these fine arts is a little out of keeping with the times; postwar America has been characterized by its valorization of spontaneity and improvisation, not only in performance but even in writing and painting: Black Mountain and beat poets, bebop musicians, abstract Expressionists, modern dance, and installation art (Belgrad, 1998; Sawyer, 2000). The visual arts have been heavily influenced by the creative potential of performance art, resulting in installation-specific pieces and multimedia works that integrate video images or taped sounds. That's why in chapter 10 on visual creativity, I discuss not only fine arts painting but also movies and installation art. And in chapter 12 on musical creativity, I examine not only European symphonic composition but also the improvisational performances of jazz and of a broad range of non-Western cultures.

It's strange that psychologists of the late 20th century have been so focused on the fine arts; after all, within the arts themselves, such categories have increasingly been challenged and broken down since the 1960s (see Fry, 1970). In the 1960s, pop artists like Andy Warhol and Roy Lichtenstein broke the boundaries between high and low art, incorporating elements of advertising graphics and comic strips into their paintings. The Fluxus group began experimenting with performance and installation art, and in the following decades, installation art has become increasingly dominant within the mainstream art world. In the 1960s through the present, American popular music has experienced a flourishing of creativity that some believe is the historical equivalent to prior bursts of creativity in European symphonic music. In the 1970s, the New Hollywood era in film was a major creative break in movie production. In the 1980s, the advent of MTV and its music videos enabled a new burst of creativity among dance choreographers and film artists. Although audiences have been declining for the so-called high arts, the audiences for these new creative forms are huge and continually expanding. Any serious study of creativity in the early years of the 21st century must explain the full range of human innovation.

Performance and Product

Another distinctive feature of this book is that I consider performance creativity to be one of the most important examples of human innovation. High art usually is a created product that can be displayed, sold, or reproduced: a painting, a sculpture, a musical score. But performance creativity is ephemeral; there is no product that remains. The audience participates during the creation and watches the creative process in action; when the performance is over, it's gone, remaining only in the memories of the participants.

Recent overviews of creativity research have neglected performance entirely (for example, Winner, 1982; Simonton, 1999a; Sternberg, 1999). This is the first book about creativity that considers performance to be central to our explanation of creativity. When you add performance to the mix, you have to explain three important new things: improvisation, collaboration, and communication.

All performance genres include some degree of improvisation, defined as performance practice or variation under the control of the performer. Particularly in explicitly improvisational genres like jazz or comedy, the performer creates a lot of the performance on the fly, without advance planning and scripting. It's not like the fine arts, where the creative process is more compositional, and allows time for unlimited revision and contemplation.

Many genres of performance creativity are ensemble genres, and the creative process is unavoidably collaborative. One of the best examples of collaborative performance is jazz, where creativity comes from the musical interaction among the musicians. In a group improvisation, the creativity is essentially collaborative, and social interaction and collaboration must be a key part of the explanation.

And in performance, the audience is present and interacting with the creators during the creative process itself. This leads to the importance of communication; communication with an audience is more central in performance creativity than in the high arts.

Explaining performance creativity has changed the way scientists think about all creativity, because we now know that all creativity includes improvisation, collaboration, and communication.

The Goal . . .

In this book, I share with you what science has discovered about creativity. Every bookstore contains books about creativity, but almost none of them are based on solid scientific research. Instead of reporting scientific findings, they often give new words to old, unexamined beliefs about creativity—what I call *creativity myths*. In chapter 2, we'll learn about these creativity myths, and we'll see how uniquely modern and Western they are. The sociocultural approach takes us beyond these creativity myths, and gives us a scientific explanation of creativity.

My goal is to provide you, the reader, with the best explanation of creativity that current science has to offer. I've cast a broad net, and our journey will range far and wide—through psychology and sociology, through art history and literary criticism. So, keeping in mind that there is always more to learn—that science is, by definition, unfinished business—let's start our journey.

Note

1. We find this bias in many books on the psychology of creativity. Winner's 1982 book *Invented Worlds: The Psychology of the Arts* focuses on painting, music, and literature, and explicitly excludes what she calls "popular forms of art" such as television, jazz, and comic strips (p. 11). Wilson's 1985 book *The Psychology of the Performing Arts* focuses on "classical drama, music and opera" (p. i). Csikszentmihalyi's 1996 book *Creativity* is based on interviews with approximately 100 highly creative individuals; all of these individuals create in areas highly valued in dominant cultural groups in Western, European cultures: the sciences, the fine arts.

CHAPTER 2

Conceptions of Creativity

In his childhood in the 1930s, young Mihaly loved to climb the hills of his native Hungary, and the larger mountains just across the border in Czechoslovakia. Why does someone climb a mountain? The obvious answer to the question is "to get to the top," but Mihaly, like all mountain climbers, knew that he didn't climb mountains to get to the top. That's why mountain climbers answer the question with a half-joking reply, "because it's there." Mihaly climbed for the sheer pleasure of climbing.

Mihaly's family left Europe to escape the terrors of World War II. As he grew into a young man, these painful childhood experiences led him to choose a career in psychology (interview in http://mmp.planetary.org/scien/csikm/csikm70 .htm, accessed 2/19/2004). Mihaly Csikszentmihalyi found his way to the graduate school at the University of Chicago, the legendary but eccentric intellectual haven that's been called "a blend of monastery and Bell Labs" (DePalma, 1992, p. B11). Csikszentmihalyi studied with psychologist Jacob Getzels (1912–2001), receiving his doctorate in 1965 for his studies of MFA students at the famed Chicago Art Institute.

After seven years on the North Side of Chicago teaching at Lake Forest College, Dr. Csikszentmihalyi's successful research program led to a prestigious job at the University of Chicago in 1972, and he returned to the monastic intellectual community in the South Side neighborhood of Hyde Park. Along with Jacob Getzels, who was nearing retirement, he stayed in touch with those Master of Fine Arts (MFA) students from the early 1960s as they pursued their careers as artists. These studies resulted in the 1976 book *The Creative Vision*. *The Creative Vision* was a watershed in the contemporary study of creativity, the beginning of a whole new approach, an approach that has since blossomed into the most complete explanation of creativity yet offered by contemporary science.

In the 1950s, American scientific psychology was dominated by Harvard psychologist B. F. Skinner's behaviorist experiments with pigeons and rats. Everyone realized that creativity was difficult for behaviorists to explain. But among therapists, a new movement known as *humanistic psychology* was catching on. Abraham Maslow and Carl Rogers emphasized the importance of peak experience, inner motivation, self-actualization, and creativity. Creativity is one of the most positive, life-affirming traits of humanity, and people in all walks of life report that they feel at their peak and in flow when they are being their most creative (Csikszentmihalyi, 1990b). In grad school in the 1960s, Csikszentmihalyi was drawn to these theories because they had the potential to explain the pleasures he had always felt while climbing mountains (see figure 2.1). His research discovered that those artists who focused on intrinsic motivation in art school in the 1960s—the joy of the "flow" state—generated the most creative paintings. And ten years later, they had the most successful careers.

In the 1980s and 1990s, Dr. Csikszentmihalyi continued his studies of creativity, and helped to found the scientific approach that I call the sociocultural

FIGURE 2.1. Mihaly Csikszentmilhalyi mountain climbing in Colorado in 1992. Courtesy of Mihaly Csikszentmilhalyi.

approach. The sociocultural approach begins by attacking the heart of the problem: What is creativity? To explain creativity, we first need to agree on what it
is, and this turns out to be surprisingly difficult. All of the social sciences face
the task of defining concepts that seem everyday and familiar. Psychologists
argue over the definitions of intelligence, emotion, and memory; sociologists
argue over the definitions of group, social movement, and institution. But defining creativity may be one of the most difficult tasks facing the social sciences,
because everybody wants to believe he's creative. People typically use "creativity" as a complimentary term of praise. It turns out that what gets called creative has varied according to the historical and cultural period (Sass, 2000–2001,
p. 57). Psychologists have sometimes wondered if we'll ever reach a consensus
about creativity, and even whether it is a useful subject for scientific study at all
(Tardif & Sternberg, 1988, p. 429).

To understand the problem facing creativity scientists, let's conduct a
thought experiment. Imagine asking a group of typical American college students to define God. Most of them would be somewhat offended at the question itself. How can we define God? The Deity is a personal matter, and each
individual develops his or her own conception of God. It would not be appropriate, the students might respond, for them to come up with a single definition of God; there might be as many definitions as there are cultures, societies,
faiths. It's not for us to define religious belief, because any description would
exclude some beliefs. Ultimately, individuals decide for themselves what God
and religion mean to them.

When I ask my college students to define creativity, and to think of criteria that distinguish creative from noncreative behavior, some of them get almost as offended. They respond that it's not for us to judge whether or not
someone is creative; that's a personal matter. Creative expression represents
inner truth, the spirit of a unique individual. No one, they insist, can say a
person's mental processes or products aren't creative if that person believes
they are.

European Enlightenment humanism emphasized the divine nature of humanity; the human being became a sort of god. And if creativity represents the
purest expression of the spirit of the individual, it might capture the essence of
this divinity. When my students react as if I have asked them to define God, it
shows that they hold to these Enlightenment beliefs about creativity (Becker,
2000–2001). Robert Weiner has argued that globalization is expanding this
Enlightenment individualism beyond Europe, into a "global ideology of creativity" (2000, p. 113). Before we can explain creativity, we need to delve into
these conceptions of creativity, because they get in the way of the scientific explanation of creativity.

How Conceptions of Creativity Have Changed Over Time

Until the modern scientific era, creativity was attributed to a superhuman force; all novel ideas originated with the gods. After all, how could a person create something that did not exist before the divine act of creation? In fact, the Latin meaning of the verb "inspire" is "to breath into," reflecting the belief that creative inspiration was akin to the moment in creation when God first breathed life into man. Plato (427–327 BCE) argued that the poet was possessed by divine inspiration, and Plotin (204–270 CE) wrote that art could only be beautiful if it descended from God. The artist's job was not to imitate nature but rather to reveal the sacred and transcendent qualities of nature. Art could only be a pale imitation of the perfection of the world of ideas (Honour & Fleming, 1999). Greek artists did not blindly imitate what they saw in reality; instead they tried to represent the pure, true forms underlying reality, resulting in a sort of compromise between abstraction and accuracy.

Conceptions of the Artist

Most people who live in the United States share a common set of beliefs about artists. We think that most artists work alone. They're blessed with a special gift or genius. They have a uniquely valuable message to communicate, and generally have a relatively high social status. We believe that artworks should be signed by their creators; knowing who created a work is important to us. Art buyers seek out the best artists and buy their works. If you're one of the famous artists, your work will be collected by major museums. Imitations of your paintings are not valuable, no matter how skillfully executed they are.

But these beliefs about artists are extremely recent. For example, the idea that an artist works alone is less than 200 years old. In the ancient system of apprenticeship in studios, artists worked in hierarchically structured teams. To learn art, a child, sometimes as young as the age of seven, was apprenticed to a master. All products of the studio were attributed to the master, even though a great portion of the work may have actually been completed by his assistants. The master acted as a sort of artistic director, composing the overall picture and executing only the most difficult portions.

The idea that the artist has high social status is also less than 200 years old. In the nonnoble classes of Europe, status was based on economic success, and artists didn't make a lot of money. Artists were considered lower status than butchers and silversmiths, for example. This began to change during the Italian

Renaissance, as artists began to be recognized for their knowledge and their genius. Nobility began to value art, and they competed with one another to take the best artists under their wing.

The idea that artists have a unique message to communicate is also only a few hundred years old. For most of European history, artists were considered primarily craftsmen. When a noble contracted for a work with a painter, the contract specified details like the quantities of gold and blue paint to appear in the work, the deadline, and penalties for delays (Baxandall, 1972). A contract in 1485 between the painter Domenico Ghirlandaio and a client specified that Ghirlandaio would "colour the panel at his own expense with good colours and with powdered gold on such ornaments as demand it . . . and the blue must be ultramarine of the value about four florins the ounce" (quoted in Baxandall, 1972, p. 6). In some contracts, artists were paid by the time worked rather than a fixed price for the completed work. These contract details show us that art was considered to be a trade—a very different conception of the artist than we hold today.

The idea that the artist creates a novel and original work that breaks with convention is only a few hundred years old. Before the Renaissance, creativity was associated with the ability to imitate established masters, and to accurately represent nature (Becker, 2000–2001, p. 46). Although some people, including da Vinci and Vasari, argued that *genio* should not just be imitative, but should also incorporate originality, this argument did not become widely accepted until the late Renaissance (Lange-Eichbaum, 1930–1932).

The history of art reveals that our current conception of the artist only became widespread about 200 years ago (Heinich, 1993). What happened in Europe that brought about our modern conception of the artist? In the 15th century, the art of the portrait was born in Europe, a radical break with the prior tradition of painting only religious icons and scenes. Paintings and sculptures were increasingly signed by the artist in France, Germany, Flanders, and Italy. Consistent with renaissance thought more generally, this was the beginning of the idea that the artist was a unique individual with his own perceptions and abilities, and that his paintings and his conceptions were unique. By the 16th century, the artist began to be seen as a member of a prestigious minority, working apart from any court or church. This was the beginning of an idea that has continued through the modern era: that artists are independent from society's normal standards of taste, that artists are inspired innovators, and that the function of art is to communicate the inner insights of the artist to the viewer.

From the 16th through the 18th centuries, the institutions of the art world were first established throughout Europe: museums, a tradition of art criticism and the study of the history of art, an art market with dealers and patrons. Schools for teaching art—run by the government and apart from apprenticeship in a studio—were founded in Florence in 1563 and in Rome in 1577. These state run academies allowed aspiring artists to learn without apprenticeship to a master (see figure 2.2).

And finally, in the industrial revolution, economic changes led to the end of the studio system. For centuries, apprentices had to learn how to make their own paints from scratch materials, and also to make their own frames and paintbrushes; but after the 19th century industrial revolution, an artist could purchase paints, frames, and brushes that were mass produced. The 19th-century French impressionists are known for their radical new idea of painting outdoors, but this innovation would not have been possible without the invention of tubes of paint, which only became available in the 19th century. The modern concept of the artist—isolated, independent, inspired—could only emerge after all of these social and economic developments.

After several hundred years of broad social changes, during the 19th century Europeans began to see the artist as we conceive of him today: as a figure

FIGURE 2.2. Woodcarving of a painting academy from the early 17th century. Reprinted from Elkins, 2001, p. 17, Pierfrancesco Alberti Painter's Academy, early 17th century, Bartsch XVII.313.1. Used with permission of James Elkins.

balancing the tension between the conventions of academic quality and the demand for originality (Heinich, 1993). For example, in the 19th century, anti-academism emerged in France—one of the first artistic movements to explicitly reject academic convention. Delacroix, Corot, and Courbet rejected the conventional hierarchy of subjects that placed historical and heroic scenes at the top, and instead painted realistic, everyday scenes—an important early influence on impressionism.

Today, at the beginning of the 21st century, most readers are likely to hold to the modern conception of the artist—a unique and inspired individual who expresses and communicates his or her unique vision through the art work. Yet this conception of the artist is no more than 200 years old.

Rationalism and Romanticism

Over the centuries, conceptions of creativity have veered between two broad ideas: rationalism and Romanticism. Rationalism is the belief that creativity is generated by the conscious, deliberating, intelligent, rational mind; Romanticism is the belief that creativity bubbles up from an irrational unconscious, and that rational deliberation interferes with the creative process.

Over 2,300 years ago, Aristotle's view of art emphasized rationality and deliberation, and stressed the conscious work required to bring a creative inspiration to completion. The rationalist conception continued through the European Renaissance, when reason was valued above all. In 1650, Thomas Hobbes (1588–1679) called the invocation of the Muses the reasonless imitation of a foolish custom, "by which a man, enabled to speak wisely from the principles of Nature and his own meditation, loves rather to be thought to speak by inspiration, like a Bagpipe" (quoted in Smith, 1961, p. 24). Reason, knowledge, training, and education were considered necessary to create good art. When the term *originality* was first coined, it meant newness and truth of observation, not a radical break with convention. The most original artists were those who best imitated nature (Smith, 1961).

During the 18th century, the term *genius* was first used to describe creative individuals (Becker, 2000–2001; Tonelli, 1973), and this new concept of genius was primarily associated with rational, conscious processes (Gerard, 1774/1966; Tonelli, 1973). Genius was associated with both scientists and artists, and was thought to be based in imagination, judgment, and memory (Becker, 2000–2001, p. 47).

Only in the 1700s, with a growing rejection of rationalism, did writers in the English Romantic Movement begin to think that art might be created through nonrational processes (Abrams, 1984; Smith, 1961, p. 23). The Romantics believed that rational deliberation would kill the creative impulse (Abrams, 1953, p. 205). Instead of thinking rationally and deliberately, the artist should simply listen to the inner muse and create without conscious control. The Romantics argued that creativity requires temporary escape from the conscious ego and a liberation of instinct and emotion, "the spontaneous overflow of powerful feelings," in Wordsworth's terms (1800/1957, p. 116). Shelley called it "unpremeditated art" (Shelley, 1901, p. 381, "To a skylark," line 5) and wrote: "Poetry is not like reasoning . . . this power arises from within, like the colour of a flower which fades and changes as it is developed" (Shelley, 1965, pp. 70–71).

The Romantics were revolutionary; they valued the artist's imagination more than mastery of the traditions of the past. Romanticism was the birth of contemporary notions of creativity—the idea that the poet or artist has a privileged status as the epitome of the human spirit (Engell, 1981). As these Romantic conceptions spread through Europe, artists began to be thought of as more than craftspeople.

The Romantics believed that creativity required a regression to a state of consciousness characterized by emotion and instinct, a fusion between self and world, and freedom from rationality and convention. These ideas were not completely new; for thousands of years, scholars have connected creativity with altered or heightened states of consciousness. Plato used the term *enthousiasmos*, or "divine madness," to describe creativity. In ancient Greece, creativity was associated with demonic possession. A demon was a semi-deity and was viewed as a divine gift granted to selected individuals. Socrates, for example, attributed most of his knowledge to his demon (Becker, 2000–2001). Aristotle believed that creative individuals were *melancholic*, but this didn't mean he thought they were depressed; the word meant something different back then. In the Hippocratian humoral theory that held sway from ancient Greece through the Middle Ages, *melancholic* referred to one of four basic personality types, none of which were associated with mental illness (Wittkower & Wittkower, 1963, p. 102). Qualities associated with the melancholic temperament included eccentricity, sensitivity, moodiness, and introversion. Emulating melancholia became a fad among young men in 16th-century Europe (Wittkower & Wittkower, 1963, pp. 98–105).

Although both Plato and Aristotle associated creativity with heightened states of consciousness, neither of them actually believed that mental illness contributed to creativity. The belief that mental illness and creativity were related took its modern form during and after the Romantic era; the association of creativity with mental illness does not predate the 1830s (Becker, 2000–2001). The Romantics believed that clinical madness was an unfortunate side effect of extreme creativity. In the same way that melancholia became a trendy affectation in 16th century Europe, mental illness became so in the 19th century; many of the Romantic poets began to embrace madness, and some claimed to experience mental anguish and madness simply because they thought they were supposed to. This self-fulfilling prophecy continues into our own time: because we all share an ideology in which creativity and madness are linked, writers and artists sometimes behave eccentrically, and even voluntarily exaggerate these aspects of their personalities in psychological tests (Becker, 2000–2001). After all, many creative individuals believe that being normal is the same thing as being typical, and they're eager to distinguish themselves from the average person.

Romanticism dominated the 19th century, but by the end of the century, anti-Romanticism was growing. The 20th century saw a rebirth of rationalism known as modernism. Modernism is characterized by isolation, coolness, and detachment (Abrams, 1984, pp. 109–144). The French modernist poets Baudelaire and Mallarmé both emphasized the importance of dispassionate deliberation and conscious craft (Abrams, 1984). In the early 20th century, poets like Ezra Pound formulated a modernist aesthetic that rejected the "mushy emotivism" of "romantic subjectivism" (Sass, 2000–2001, p. 60). In the 1920s, Russian futurists and Czech formalists advocated a highly detached, analytic perspective on the world, one that stripped away the normal emotional and cultural associations of objects to instead focus on pure abstracted form (Sass, 1992).

Romanticism had one last burst in the predominantly rationalist 20th century, with 1950s postwar abstract Expressionism. The abstract Expressionists were said to create spontaneously from pure emotion and inspiration, unconstrained by planning, rational thought, or conscious filtering. However, even during the 1950s knowledgeable art experts were aware that this was a popular fiction. For example, Jackson Pollock's paintings—which in the popular conception simply involved flinging paint against canvas without forethought—were in fact carefully planned and composed. Pollack worked hard to master different techniques for dripping paint, experimenting with the results, and he composed his works in advance so that they would give the appearance of maximum spontaneity.

Within only a few years, the avant-garde of art had moved on beyond these neo-Romantic conceptions. The contemporary arts of the 1960s onward—sometimes called "postmodern"—represented a return to rationalism. Postmodern art is critical of our culture's conceptions of creativity—deconstructing notions of spontaneity, originality, and individual genius (Sass, 2000–2001, p. 61). Minimalism and pop art explicitly rejected Romantic-era beliefs about art; they could not have been more obviously unemotional, carefully planned and executed, and in fact reveled in their own artifice by noting the parallels with advertising, product design, and comic strips. Andy Warhol famously said "I want to be a machine" (quoted in Hughes, 1984, p. 48). Anti-Romanticism is prominent in postmodern art and theory, which rejects the ideals of authenticity, spontaneity, and personal engagement. This may be why the general public doesn't like modern art: Because the average person still holds to Romanticist conceptions of creativity.

Our Creativity Myths

European conceptions of creativity have changed over the centuries. And once you leave Europe, you find an even wider range of conceptions of creativity cross-culturally, as we'll see in chapter 8. The scientific explanation of creativity has found that many of our beliefs about creativity are inaccurate or misleading; that's why I call them creativity myths (Weisberg, 1986). These creativity myths are so widely believed that they sometimes seem obvious, common sense. When artists and scientists in European countries or in the United States are asked about their own creativity, they often repeat creativity myths, even though scientific studies of those same individuals later find that it didn't actually happen that way. Either they don't remember how they really did it, or they realize that they'll be seen to be more creative if their personal story fits in better with our culture's myths. Because the science of creativity often conflicts with our creativity myths, it's important to begin our explanation of creativity by first examining our own cultural conceptions.

Myth: Creativity Comes From the Unconscious

This idea originated in the Romantic movement and was fully explored by Freudian psychoanalysis. As one psychoanalytic therapist put it, "creative expression is a direct link into the unconscious of every individual" (Robertson, 1991, p. 191). The psychoanalytic conception of creativity has many similarities with the ancient belief in divine madness, because they both emphasize the passive role of the creator's mind. Rather than life breathed from God, the creative inspiration arrives from the unconscious. The spiritual undertones of such ideas were made explicit by Carl Jung, who connected Freud's notion of the unconscious with various forms of early 20th-century spiritualism.

In fact, creativity rarely comes in a sudden burst of insight. Instead, scientists have discovered that creativity is mostly conscious, hard work. For example, we now know that very few geniuses come up with one amazingly brilliant idea and then fade from the scene. Rather, in both the sciences and the arts, the most creative innovators also tend to be the most productive. For example, Simonton

(1988b, p. 77) discovered that Nobel laureates publish twice as much, on average, as other scientists who are nonetheless good enough to make it into *American Men and Women in Science*. Groundbreaking artists display a similarly high productivity; Picasso participated in the creation of cubism, but then continued to innovate for decades thereafter. Among acknowledged geniuses, it's hard to find one who was not highly productive. As a rule of thumb, half of all creative innovations in any given domain will be generated by 10 percent of the members of the field (Simonton, 1999b, pp. 149–150).

Creativity can be explained without invoking an unconscious muse. Rather than a mysterious unconscious force, the explanation of creativity lies in hard work and everyday mental processes. Throughout this book, I'll report on exciting new studies of the creative process that reveal that there is no mystery to creative inspiration. Creative originality and insight can be explained once you know the complex and intricate process that led up to the moment of insight.

Myth: Children Are More Creative Than Adults

Most of us have heard it said that all children are naturally creative, and that all adults would be, too, if formal schooling hadn't interfered and smothered our natural creative impulse. In the lead article in a 1992 issue of the *Utne Reader*, Anne Cushman wrote, "For most of us, the extravagant creativity of childhood is soon crushed by the demands of parents, schools, and society" (p. 53).

This myth originated in the 19th-century Romantic-era belief that children are more pure, closer to nature, and that society gradually corrupts them as they grow to learn its customs and ways. These ideas about childhood didn't exist before the 19th century. In the early 20th century, modern artists like Kandinksy, Klee, Miro, and Dubuffet looked to children's art and often imitated a childlike style in their paintings (see chapter 10). However, the scientific explanation of creativity shows that children aren't that creative. In this book, I'll show you why children aren't as creative as we think they are, and we'll discover the long and difficult path that adults take to become creative. Schools and society don't squash creativity; in fact, they make it possible (Sawyer et al., 2003).

Myth: Creativity Represents the Inner Spirit of the Individual

Prior to the renaissance, artists were thought of as craftspeople, not as visionaries with a special message to communicate. In the Renaissance, some scholars began to argue that creative art represented the inner spirit of the individual, and today, most Americans tend to think that creativity is the unique expression of some inner force of the individual. We often say that creativity is about saying something, and artists often talk about the message they are attempting to get across with their work. Yet the idea that creativity is primarily a tool for the creator to communicate with an audience is relatively new.

In painting, the artist's message has been a focus of graduate training in MFA programs and of the contemporary art world, with its emphasis on subversive, political, and message art. It's very difficult for artists today to be successful unless they can talk convincingly about their art—its meaning, their creative process, and their sources of inspiration. The artist's statement is a historically unique genre of writing that can make or break an artist's career—even though visual artists have never been known for their verbal skills (see chapter 10). Contemporary artists who simply paint or sculpt because they enjoy the process, or artists who just paint images that look cool to them, nonetheless have to come up with a message-oriented explanation to satisfy the market's demand for an artist's statement (Elkins, 2001).

We now know that you can't explain creativity as the expression of a person's inner spirit. Scientists have discovered that explaining creativity requires us to know a lot about the culture, society, and historical period. When we look at paintings from 500 years ago, we can tell that those paintings are 500 years old. And 500 years from now, when future art historians look at the paintings of today, they will just as surely be stamped with the characteristic markers of our culture and time period (see chapter 10).

Myth: Creativity Is a Form of Therapeutic Self-discovery

Another common conception of creativity in the contemporary United States is what I call the new age conception of creativity: that creativity is a form of self-discovery, therapy, and self-knowledge. Composer Aaron Copland said that "each added work brings with it an element of self-discovery. I must create in order to know myself, and since self-knowledge is a never ending search, each new work is only a part-answer to the question 'Who am I?' and brings with it the need to go on to other and different part-answers" (Copland, 1952, p. 41). As one classically trained singer said, "If you choose a musical life, you have to recognize that you're not setting up something that you are going to do, but you're cultivating and fulfilling something that you are" (quoted in Berman, 2003, p. 20). Artists with this conception of creativity often speak of the courage required to pursue creative activity; in a new age worldview, delving deep and discovering one's true self is one of the most highly valued endeavors, but it's also considered to be risky and difficult, a spiritual journey that results in personal transformation (see chapter 16). The new age conception of creativity is a return of the ancient idea that creativity is the result of divine inspiration.

There is some truth underlying the new age conception; researchers have discovered that engaging in creativity is one of the peak experiences in a person's life (see chapter 3). Some activities that we call creative are indeed therapeutic. Music therapy and art therapy successfully help many children and adults. In this book, I explain the therapeutic value of creative activities. But we'll also learn that therapy is not all there is to creativity; we need to go beyond this myth to explain creativity. For example, creativity is only occasionally a release of inner demons or life traumas. Most creative activity is conscious, skillful, guided hard work, and is incredibly enjoyable for the creator.

Myth: Creativity Is Spontaneous Inspiration

Today most of us believe that artistic creativity is spontaneous, not overly planned or organized, and that artists reject tradition and convention. We like to think of our artists as strong individualists, working in isolation, not influenced by the prevailing ideas taught in art schools or by stuffy white-haired museum curators. But like so much about our contemporary creativity myths, this idea only emerged in the 19th century. In the second half of the 20th century, the idea that the artist is a person who rejects convention took an even stronger hold on the popular consciousness. Ironically, at the same time, artists were entering art schools in increasingly large numbers to be trained in the conventions of the art world. In the United States today, a greater proportion of artists have the MFA degree than at any other time in history. Yet few of us are aware of the growing influence of formal schooling in fine art. In general, when the facts clash with our creativity myths, the facts are ignored—another reason why it's so important to begin our explanation by examining how these myths and conceptions are formed, and how they change over time.

But we don't need to be worried about the influence of formal schooling on artists. It won't squash their creativity or make them all traditionalists. The scientific explanation of creativity shows us that formal training and conscious deliberation are essential to creativity; as Louis Pasteur famously said, "Chance favors the prepared mind" (Dunbar, 1999; Seifert, Meyer, Davidson, Patalano, & Yaniv, 1995). In this book, we'll learn why formal training is important, and how it contributes to creativity.

Myth: Many Creative Works Go Unrecognized in Their Own Time and Are Only Discovered Decades Later

One of our most stubborn creativity myths is that unrecognized genius is quite common. I call this myth "stubborn" because it persists even though there is almost no evidence for it. There are remarkably few examples of works that were ignored during their creator's lifetime that are now thought to be works of genius. Writers on the topic tend to trot out the same tired examples repeatedly: we are told that Mendel's 19th-century work cross-breeding peas was not recognized as essential to modern genetics until 50 years later; or that the impressionists were considered such horrible artists that their works were never displayed in the French academy. But almost all of these examples, when examined more closely, end up failing to support the unrecognized genius view. Mendel's work, for example, was not rejected as inappropriate by his peers, and it was not rediscovered 50 years later; the Mendel story is a historically inaccurate myth (see chapter 14). And although the impressionists were excluded from the French academy, they quickly created their own network of galleries, patrons, and like-minded colleagues; they were avidly collected by rich Americans, and many of them died with money in the bank.

The sociocultural approach can help us to explain why our creativity myths persist even when there is no evidence to support them. In this book, we'll explain why creative works are almost always recognized in their own time, we'll examine how interpretations of creative works change over time, and we'll learn more about why our creativity myths persist.

Myth: Everyone Is Creative

The American ideology of democracy is the deep-rooted belief that everyone is equal (Menand, 1998; Rothstein, 1997; Stein, 1974). This ideology leads us to fear making value-laden distinctions, so we tend to believe that everyone is creative, and that no one should judge what counts as good art, or even what counts as "art" (Wallach, 1997; Weiner, 2000).

Science and art are incompatible with this cultural belief. Science succeeds only because of the active involvement of a national network of critical review by journal editors, grant reviewers, and department chairs. The art world also requires that distinctions be made, that criteria be applied, and that selection and evaluation take place. As Menand (1998) pointed out, "as long as 'art' is a term that confers value on an object (and there's no reason to have the term at all if it doesn't), people will mean something by it. . . . There is no exit from concepts" (p. 41). Rothstein (1997) critically considered how a government agency, the National

Endowment for the Arts (NEA), reconciles the ideology of democracy with the reality of the art world, and he examined how these tensions are reconciled within the agency. Not very well, it turns out; for example, funds must be equally distributed to each state and ethnic group, regardless of aesthetic merit. This results in "a vision of the arts that is pure pork barrel" (p. AR39).

In this book, I'll explain how creative works are evaluated, and how fields decide which works are more creative. The sociocultural approach explains why these critical selection processes are not opposed to creativity, but rather are a central part of all creative activities.

Myth: Creativity Is the Same Thing as Originality

In 1917, Marcel Duchamp submitted a new work to be considered for an exhibition in New York: a simple urinal turned on its back, and signed with a fictitious name "R. Mutt." The exhibition's judges rejected the work and it was not displayed; yet soon after, it was purchased by a wealthy collector, and today it remains one of the seminal works of 20th-century art, considered by some to be the origin of modern art. Duchamp's urinal challenged two aspects of our conception of art: that a work should be original, and that it should be unique. After Duchamp's shocking work, other artists began to experiment with the conventions of art itself, and art became reflexive, often commenting on itself and on the art world. The Dadaists experimented with many conventions of art: materials, techniques, durability, authenticity, even the importance of the "work" itself. They explicitly rejected any definition of art—as beautiful, tasteful, original, or spiritually inspired—and at times they tried to shock and disgust viewers.

In the United States, we tend to equate creativity with novelty and originality. But the high value that we place on novelty is not shared universally in all cultures. In performance, for example, we find that in almost all cultures—including our own—improvisation is allowed only in informal performances; in formal settings, in contrast, improvisation is not allowed. Formal performances must follow the movements of the dance, or the words of the script, verbatim. In most cultures, rituals forbid improvisation. This seems to be related to the power of ritual; a ritual can only perform its supernatural function if performed exactly, and a divergence from the appropriate dance or script would result in an ineffective ritual (see chapter 13). In a traditional U. S. Christian wedding, the religious official is expected to say "I now pronounce you husband and wife"; an unexpected creative improvisation such as "I exclaim that you are now joined for life" or even "From henceforth you will be married" would be disturbing, generally not welcomed by the participants and audience.

The idea that art should be original and should break with conventions is less than 200 years old. In the Renaissance, art was considered to be one of two kinds of imitation. The imitation of nature was original imitation; the imitation of other works of art was ordinary imitation (Smith, 1961, p. 18). When the term *originality* was first coined, it meant newness and truth of observation—not the sense of a radical break with convention as we mean today. The most original artists were those who best imitated nature.

Traditional cultures tend to produce aesthetic objects that we associate with "craft" rather than "art," in part because they are typically functional objects—clothing, baskets, water vessels, hunting weapons. These artifacts have often been collected in the West, but not always by art museums—more typically they're found in "natural history" museums. We don't value these objects because they seem to be mostly imitative, and our conception of creativity is almost exclusively focused on originality. But imitation is a long-established, deep-rooted form of cultural transmission, even in European fine arts (Delbanco, 2002; Gardner, 1973; Wicklund, 1989). For many centuries, and in many different societies, the ability to imitate and reproduce the acknowledged masters was highly valued; and developing this skill through practice was how one learned one's craft. Yet as Nicholas Delbanco, a director of an MFA program in writing, noted, "We've grown so committed as a culture to the ideal of originality that the artist who admits to working in the manner of another artist will likely stand accused of being second-rate" (2002, p. 59).

There are many creative domains that require the individual to insert as little of themselves as possible into the work. In translating a novel or poem to a different language, the translator is unavoidably creative; this is reflected by the fact that the translator receives attribution, and his or her name is published in the work next to that of the original author. But the ideal translator is one who most faithfully retains the creative spirit of the original, thereby keeping his or her own contribution to the translation as minimal as possible. Dubbing a foreign movie into one's own language requires that the translator develop a version of the original line that can most easily be spoken in the time that the foreign actor's mouth is moving, and it also requires the voice-over actors to match their delivery to the moving image. As with translation, the goal of the creator here is to keep his or her own contribution as minimal as possible. Although these are unquestionably creative activities, they are activities in which individual inspiration and originality are not valued, and in fact, are detrimental to the work. Our culture tends to consider such activities to be less creative—exactly because the creator is more constrained.

The sociocultural approach shows that all creativity includes elements of imitation and tradition. There is no such thing as a completely novel work. To explain creativity, we have to examine the balance of imitation and innovation, and the key role played by convention and tradition.

Myth: Fine Art Is More Creative Than Craft

Our culture is biased toward the fine arts—those creative products that have no function other than pleasure. Craft objects are less worthy; because they serve an everyday function, they're not purely creative. But this division is culturally and historically relative. Most contemporary high art began as some sort of craft (Baxandall, 1972; Harris, 1966; Martindale, 1972). The composition and performance of what we now call "classical music" began as a form of craft music satisfying required functions in the Catholic mass, or the specific entertainment needs of royal patrons. For example, chamber music really was designed to be performed in chambers—small intimate rooms in wealthy homes—often as background music. The dances composed by famous composers from Bach to Chopin originally did indeed accompany dancing. But today, with the contexts and functions they were composed for long gone, we listen to these works as fine art.

To take a famous example, photography is now considered an art. Photographs are in the collections of all the major museums. But when the technique of photography was first invented in 1839, it was considered a new technology and not a new art form. In 1844, the first major exhibition of daguerreotypes was not grouped with the artworks, but was in the Salon de l'Industrie Française. Between 1839 and 1890, photography was a mass market—focused on portraits—and there were very little aesthetic concerns (Denoyelle, 2002, p. 41). In 1852, the first exhibition of photographs with aesthetic intent was displayed at the Society of Arts in London; but these photographers remained marginalized—no market, no recognition—and photography, in the eyes of the art world, remained only a mechanical technique. In fact, artists of the time were convinced that photography could never become an art, because the photograph was not created by the hand of man, like painting or sculpture.

How did photography became an art? Our creativity myths would tell us that either those technicians working with the new tools gradually became more aesthetically skilled; or that established artists like painters and sculptors learned how to use the new technology and then applied their aesthetic abilities there. But what actually happened was that photographers themselves did not change at all; rather, the sociocultural system around them changed.

In 1890, Kodak introduced a cheap consumer camera that everyone could afford. This put the portrait studios out of business; the newly unemployed photographers needed a way to distinguish between what they did and this new popular photography. The movement of *pictorialism* was the response, with photographers attempting to imitate the artistic processes of painting; rather than reproducible photos, they worked directly on the negatives and other materials of the process. They presented their works in art galleries, next to paintings. The elements of an art world began to form: collegial groups called "photo clubs," a journal called *Camera Work*, and shows and openings. However, art photography remained marginalized; their were no markets, buyers, or collectors, and museums were not interested in adding photos to their collections. Pictorialism eventually died out with the onset of the World War I. An art form can't survive without a market, venues for display, and collectors.

After World War I, when some painters began to make photographs that we now think of as art, those painters did not themselves consider their photography to be art. Man Ray, who we remember today primarily for his photos, considered himself to be a painter. Brassaï, who wanted to become an artist, did not believe that his photography realized that desire. Although demand for photographic skill grew with the expansion of daily newspapers and the demand for wartime news, documentary photographs in newspapers often did not even have a signature.

It was not until 1960 that a market for photographic art began to form in the United States. This development coincided with a rejection of many traditional notions of art: that it was the work of the hand, that each work was a unique creation. Prices remained modest, but collectors began to emerge, and finally, in the 1970s, a true art market was established, with control over the originality and rarity of the works (limited edition prints), expositions, galleries, and museums. The most valuable prints are those where the negatives are lost; for this reason, some contemporary photographers destroy their negatives after making a predetermined number of prints. Where negatives remain available and unlimited prints could, in principle, be made, the market distinguishes between recent and "vintage" prints. Such a market requires experts that are able to look at a print and distinguish which year it was made from the negative.

In sum, it was not until the 1970s, well over 100 years after photography was invented, that photography took on the characteristics associated with art: the valuation of originality and uniqueness, the system of galleries, museums, and collectors, the supporting network of experts to evaluated value and confirm authenticity (Newhall, 1964).

Photography became an art only after the social system surrounding the activity became artlike, adopting the values and conventions of other established arts (Becker, 1982). Even today, the photos that conform more closely to the values of the art world are worth more—those made by the plasticians, who, like the pictorialists, produce unique prints by manipulating the developing process by hand (coloring a black and white photo, for example), and who create ephemeral scenes put together for the sole purpose of being photographed, only then to be disassembled.

The shift from craft to art happens over and over through history. It's always a social process, not a result of individual talent alone. Prior to the 15th century, painting was considered to be a craft and not an art, though this viewpoint shifted in the 15th century (Baxandall, 1972). To explain changing conceptions of creativity, we have to consider social, cultural, and historical factors.

How Scientists Define Creativity

Scientific studies of creativity have found that all of these myths are misleading, and many of them are downright wrong. Although there may be exceptions— those occasional cases of creativity that seem to support one of the myths—for the most part, creativity doesn't work that way. And we have to be careful about anecdotal stories that fit too well with our myths, because creators themselves are often misled by them.

But if our myths are wrong, then how should we think about creativity? Scientists have used several different definitions of creativity, but they all fall somewhere between two camps. In one camp are definitions that require that some socially valuable product be generated before the act or the person is called "creative." Only solutions to extremely difficult problems, or significant works of genius, are recognized as creative. This is sometimes called "big C" Creativity. In the other camp are definitions that don't require anything socially valuable; rather, the act of creativity is itself enough, even if nothing recognized as socially valuable is generated. Any and all works are considered creative, even those of a beginning student that will not be remembered after the end of the semester. In contrast to big C Creativity, this is called "little c" creativity. Little c creativity includes activities that people engage in every day: modifying a recipe when you don't have all of the ingredients called for; avoiding a traffic jam by finding a new way through side streets; figuring out how to apologize to a friend for an unintended insult. A person's dreams or a child's block tower could be creative under the second definition, but not under the first.

The sociocultural definition of creativity is in the first camp. Socioculturalists define creativity as a novel product that attains some level of social recognition. First of all, a creative idea or work must be novel. Yet novelty is not enough, because a novel idea may be ridiculous or nonsensical; many dreams are novel but rarely have any impact on the world after breakfast. In addition to novelty, to be creative an idea must be *appropriate*, recognized as socially valuable in some way to some community. This concept of "appropriateness" has taken many forms in scientific studies of creativity, and exploring what it might mean will be a constant theme through the chapters of this book (but it's most directly addressed in chapter 7).[1]

There's a problem with including appropriateness as a criterion for creativity: because a work's appropriateness can only be defined by a society at a given historical moment, it becomes hard to distinguish creativity from worldly success and power. In fact, the influential creativity researcher Dean Keith Simonton, a professor at the University of California at Davis, accepted the appropriateness criterion and then argued that only eminent people can be said to be creative (1999b). Due to the power of our creativity myths, many of my readers are likely to prefer a definition that allows us to incorporate unrecognized genius, people who are ahead of their time, or works that are simply so innovative that they are rejected as bizarre by the society, and thus do not meet the appropriateness criterion.

Although appropriateness may seem offensive to some readers at first glance, in this book we'll learn that it's not as bad as it may first seem. In fact, creativity can't exist, even in principle, without appropriateness. For example, almost all musical compositions use the 12-tone Western scale—the notation system that all musicians learn in training—and are composed for instruments that are widely manufactured, distributed, and taught. Just because a work conforms to these conventions doesn't mean that we would say it's not creative. To be creative, you don't have to compose a work for a 42-tone scale, using instruments that don't exist and that no one knows how to play.

In fact, composer Harry Partch (1949) spent his career writing such music, inventing and constructing his own unique instruments to perform his compositions (see chapter 12). Certainly no one would disagree with the novelty of this work, nor that it failed to satisfy criteria of appropriateness. And because it doesn't meet the appropriateness criterion, it's almost impossible to perform; it could only be performed if Partch himself guided a process that typically took about a year. First, Partch had a group of students build his instruments. After several months of construction, they would spend a few months learning Partch's idiosyncratic notation system and learning to play the instruments. After seven or eight months of work, the ensemble was ready to perform a few hours of music. Contrast this lengthy process with the eight or so hours of rehearsal it would take a trained symphony orchestra to perform a new composition that followed the usual conventions, and we see the problems that face creators whose work is not appropriate—it's hard to display, disseminate, or perform.

Certain genres of music have an even more closely specified set of constraints; a sonata must have a certain form, or else it can't be categorized as a sonata at all. And just because all sonatas share many characteristics doesn't mean that all of them are the same, or that a new sonata is somehow only a mere copy of all of the other sonatas. Defining how different a work has to be to be considered a novel work is a complex issue facing critics and experts in many creative domains. For example, folklorists typically expect there to be some variation in the performance of traditional songs like Appalachian mountain tunes or Southern gospel songs, and even with performance variation, most of the audience would consider all of the variations to be instances of the same song, even though they are not exactly the same.

Individual style provides another set of constraints that don't seem to be antithetical to creativity. Many listeners who are not connoisseurs in a certain musical genre have had the experience of thinking "it all sounds the same." Among my friends, I've heard this said of several rock bands including the Grateful Dead and R.E.M., of all bluegrass music, and of anything played on the accordion. Many people probably feel this way about the harpsichord compositions of Bach and of bebop jazz. Just because a painter generates a painting that is recognizably in a certain style or genre doesn't lead us to say that it's "the same" painting as every other one in that style. Many painters' careers are characterized by first discovering a new style and then continuing to explore that style, for years or even decades. Many popular bands continue to play in the same familiar style for their entire careers. In both painting and music, one can point to the exceptional rare individual who develops a new style every few years, for example, Picasso and Madonna. These individuals are rare because art markets and galleries pressure artists to continue working in the same recognizable style, so that they will generate a known product and thus develop a reputation and a market for that work. Record companies are infamous for insisting that popular bands under contract for multiple albums continue to produce albums that sound like their first big hit, because they know that fans become loyal to a band in part because they can count on consistency and reliability in style.

Scientific studies of creativity focus on big C Creativity, and its definition based on novelty and appropriateness. In part, that's because little c creativity is almost impossible to define; anything we do throughout the day that isn't completely scripted involves some amount of creativity. But as we learn about big C Creativity throughout this book, I think you'll agree with me that this study ultimately helps us to understand everyday creativity, as well.

Who Creates?

We tend to associate creativity with the human mind, and the study of creativity with psychology. We often think of creativity as a personality trait, like intelligence or extroversion. And when we look for the creator of a created product, we instinctively look for a person (Kasof, 1995). All of these ideas are related to those creativity myths that focus on the individual and neglect the social and cultural context. But creativity doesn't only emerge from human minds; many natural and social processes can generate appropriate novelty. Our exploration of human innovation can gain many insights from these other sources of creativity.

Natural Creativity

The foundational insight of the Darwinian revolution is that all of the species in the world were created through natural processes of evolution—variation, selection, and retention. There was no intentional designer; rather, nature itself is the creator.

Prior to this foundational discovery of the nineteenth century, for centuries humankind believed that all species must have been created by a divine creator. The famous "watchmaker" argument for the existence of God originated in the mechanistic era of the seventeenth century. William Paley (1743–1805) began by noting that an object as complex as a watch must have an intelligent designer. Why, then, when faced with the even more extreme complexity of an animal, would one not also assume that there had been a creator? Yet Darwinian biology shows that natural species, although they were "created" in some sense, were not created by any intentional being; rather, they were created through unintentional natural processes. In this sense, nature itself is creative (see chapter 5).

Group Creativity

When we see a created product, we assume that a single person created it. In this, we aren't that different from those theologians of the seventeenth century who assumed that a complex object like a watch or an animal must have had a single intelligent creator (Skinner, 1968). But many created products are created by groups, organizations, and entire societies. In fact, in the modern era of mass production, the wristwatch is not created by any single individual, but by a complex organization involving computer-aided design systems, microchips, factories in third-world countries, and international systems of distribution, manufacturing, and trade.

A jazz performance requires an entire jazz ensemble—for example, a drummer, a bass player, a pianist, and a horn player. The performance emerges from the interactions of four individuals working collaboratively; there's no way that such performance could be created by a single, solitary individual. Of course, we can speak of the creativity of the drummer or of the saxophonist, but we can also speak of the creativity of the ensemble as a unit. And the group's creativity is not a simple sum of the creative talents of the individual members; the group's performance is greater than the sum of its parts. Some combinations of musicians work well, and others don't; the same drummer might sound brilliant in one ensemble, yet only mediocre in another. To explain group creativity, we can't limit our focus to individual creativity; we must also consider group dynamics.

Theater performances are ensemble performances, with an entire cast of characters. Although the cast is performing from a script written by a playwright, and has been guided by a director through countless rehearsals, the quality of each night's performance varies due to the group dynamics among the members of the cast. This group dynamic is carried to an extreme in improvisational theater, when the actors do not begin with a script or a plot, but rather create all of these dramatic elements on stage in front of a live audience. In this kind of group improvisation, no one can predict in advance what will happen. Even the best groups, filled with extremely talented actors, fall flat much of the time; a brilliant performance on Friday night might be followed by a dud on Saturday.

Jazz and theater performances are created by groups, not by individuals. To explain group creativity, we have to focus on the processes of collaboration among group members.

Societal Creativity

Who created the systems that underlie the United States economy—the trading mechanisms of the stock market, the legal system and the government oversight organizations that administer the market, the surplus capital that feeds the market? This is a trick question, because no single person created these complex systems. Not even a single group or team created them; the systems emerged over decades and centuries, with contributions and modifications throughout by countless individuals and groups. The United States economy is a creation of the entire society, and it emerged over many lifespans.

Cultural historians have attempted to explain why some societies, in some historical periods, seem to be more creative overall than others. In Renaissance Florence, an incredible creative explosion resulted in novel products that we still admire today, in architecture, sculpture, painting, and science. Why did this occur in Florence, and not Paris or London? No one thinks it's because Florence just happened to get lucky, and suddenly had a lot of children born who were naturally brilliant. We can't explain the Florentine Renaissance with our

31

individualist creativity myths. Explaining it requires a consideration of many complex societal factors: the economic and political strength of Florence, the cultural values of the community, the system of patronage that emerged among the wealthy, the apprenticeship systems that were established to train new artists (see chapter 9). In cases like these, we could say that an entire society is the creative force. To explain societal creativity, we have to draw on social sciences like sociology, economics, and political science.

Conclusion

Through the centuries, Europeans have held to different conceptions of creativity. Artists have been thought of as poorly paid tradespeople, and as divinely inspired geniuses. Creativity has swung between rational and Romantic conceptions. There hasn't been a single historically continuous definition of creativity. The message for us today is that our conception of creativity is not universal; in fact, our own society may change its conception of creativity in the future. A science of creativity should be able to rise above these historical limitations, and take us beyond our creativity myths.

A second more subtle lesson to be drawn from this chapter is that these changing conceptions of creativity aren't random and unpredictable; they can be logically derived from broader properties of the society. The conceptions of art that a society holds follow logically from the styles and techniques of art, the social organization of the work, and the functions that art plays in that society. The deeply religious Europe of the Middle Ages associated creativity with the divine. Several broad shifts associated with the Renaissance led to a change in the conception of art. First, economic developments resulted in a demand for a new form of secular art—portraits and scenes of everyday life commissioned by the new business and trading classes. Second, during the Renaissance, the movement toward humanism led to an increasing emphasis on the uniqueness of the individual, and this resulted in a conception of the artist as uniquely inspired and talented, with a message and an insight to communicate that might not necessarily be divinely inspired. Third, the shift toward modern nonrepresentational art has often been interpreted as a response to broader social forces— the increasing mechanization of society or the maturing of photography as a more accurate representational medium in the late 19th century. Nonrepresentational art required yet another conception of creativity: creativity began to be conceived of as a break with conventions rather than as an imitation of nature, and art was reconceived as a way of experimenting with perception and representation.

Moving Ahead

We've now laid the groundwork to begin our explanation of creativity. We started by examining how conceptions of creativity have changed over the centuries. Then we examined our own conceptions of creativity, and I argued that many of them are creativity myths. Then I defined creativity as the emergence of something novel and appropriate, from a person, a group, or a society. A scientific explanation of creativity requires us to look critically at our own cultural assumptions about how creativity works, and scientific studies of creativity often fail to support our most cherished beliefs about creativity. But we should welcome the science of creativity because it provides light by showing us how creativity really works. Only with true understanding can we improve the creativity of people, groups, organizations, and societies. The goal of creativity research is to explain all of these forms of creativity—to move beyond creativity myths and develop a science of human innovation.

Thought Experiment

- Think of someone you know that you think is particularly creative.
- Why do you think so?
- Is it because of some distinctive behavior, lifestyle, or way of talking or dressing?
- Is it because you've seen one of his or her created works and you thought that it was creative?
- Do you think this person would be considered creative by people from other countries and other cultures? Or is there something uniquely American about his or her creativity?

Suggested Readings

Becker, H. (1982). *Art worlds.* Berkeley and Los Angeles: University of California Press.

Delbanco, N. (2002, July). In Praise of Imitation. *Harper's Magazine,* 57–63.

Honour, H., & Fleming, J. (1999). *World history of art* (5th ed.). London: Lawrence King.

Rothstein, E. (1997, October 26). Where a democracy and its money have no place. *The New York Times,* pp. AR1, 39.

Tardif, T. Z., & Sternberg, R. J. (1988). What Do We Know about Creativity? In R. J. Sternberg (Ed.), *The nature of creativity* (pp. 429–440). New York: Cambridge University Press.

Wallach, A. (1997, October 12). Is it art? Is it good? And who says so? *The New York Times*, pp. AR36.

Weiner, R. P. (2000). *Creativity and beyond: Cultures, values, and change.* Albany: State University of New York Press.

Weisberg, R. W. (1986). *Creativity: Genius and other myths.* New York: Freeman.

Note

1. Psychologists have always emphasized that true creativity required not only novelty but also appropriateness (MacKinnon, 1962): "Novelty or originality of thought or action, while a necessary aspect of creativity, is not sufficient. . . . It must to some extent be adaptive to, or of, reality" (p. 485). Stein (1961/1963, 1967, 1974) emphasized both novelty and *usefulness* at a point in time.

INTERLUDE 1

Defining Creativity

Psychologists began to study creativity in the 1950s, and right away, they had trouble defining it. In the 1950s and 1960s, psychologists searched for paper-and-pencil tests that could measure a person's creative potential. With a good test, they could simply have defined creativity as a high score on the test. However, this search was in vain; as we'll see in chapter 3, in spite of several decades of research, personality psychologists were not able to develop a test to measure creativity, and the effort was abandoned by the 1970s.

Also during the 1950s and 1960s, psychologists tried to develop ways to measure the creativity of individual works. For example, one common technique was to ask three expert judges to rate the creativity of a work and then to average their ratings. But this always seemed to be a little too subjective; how do we know the experts are good at judging creativity? What if they are thought of as experts only because they're attached to the old, dead, conventional ways of doing business? Then they would be exactly the wrong people to evaluate creativity. As a result of such worries, researchers have tried to develop more objective measures of the creativity of works. For example, Colin Martindale (1990) quantitatively measured the originality of poems with a computer program that counted the number of "unusual" words in the text, and measured the originality of paintings by asking college students to rate qualities like "representative of reality" and "otherworldly."

Without a rigorous definition, it's hard to engage in serious scientific study. By the 1970s, their failure to successfully define creativity had convinced many psychologists that creativity was not a distinct personality trait or mental process.

Instead, psychologists began to believe that creativity was just a word we used for products that were generated using common, everyday mental mechanisms that every person possessed. This shift to a more cognitive approach—the topic of chapter 4—led to the end of personality studies of creativity by 1980.

In part 1, we learned why psychologists have so much trouble defining creativity. It's because creativity—as we use the term in everyday language—is not a scientific concept; it's a culturally and historically specific idea that changes from one country to another, and from one century to another. That's why we had to start our explanation of creativity with an exploration of our conceptions of creativity—because otherwise, we couldn't begin to talk about what creativity actually is. No science can be based on something so variable, unless that science includes the cultural and historical contexts of creativity. In part 1, we've seen why the science of creativity has to be an interdisciplinary social science, incorporating findings from sociology, anthropology, and history. That's why psychologists alone can't define creativity.

The sociocultural approach to creativity was started in the 1980s by a group of psychologists who began to realize they needed the help of the other social sciences. In the next two parts of the book, I describe how the approaches of psychology, sociology, anthropology, and history all contribute equally to the new science of creativity. I'll begin with individualist approaches in part 2, because the study of creativity continues to be primarily associated with psychology, and we're particularly interested in the creative potential of individuals. But now that you've learned how our conceptions of creativity change over time and over cultures, you'll quickly see the limitations of the individualist approaches. I then turn to more contextualist approaches in part 3, and I show how these exciting new developments are beginning to work hand-in-hand with psychological research, resulting in a new science of human innovation.

Part II

Individualist Approaches

CHAPTER 3

Personality Psychology

As the applause swelled, Dr. Guilford took a deep breath, smoothed his tie and jacket, and began to walk to the podium. It was 1950, and Dr. Guilford was at the peak of his long and illustrious career. He had dedicated his life to psychological research. He'd played a key leadership role during World War II, helping the U.S. military carry out the most massive testing program in history. And now, he had attained the highest honor that the discipline of psychology could give—he had been elected president of the American Psychological Association.

Every year, at the annual meeting of the Association, the president gives the keynote speech, and this was Dr. J. P. Guilford's moment (see figure 3.1). Presidents traditionally use this opportunity to emphasize an important issue that they think deserves more psychological study. As Dr. Guilford began his talk, the hundreds of assembled psychologists in the room were shocked when they realized the topic he had chosen. The APA president had chosen to talk about creativity.

To understand why a professional psychologist in 1950 would be shocked to hear a speech about creativity from the APA president, you need to know a little about the field of psychology at the time. Since the 1920s, American psychology had been dominated by behaviorism—think of Pavlov's salivating dog and Skinner's experiments with pigeons. Behaviorists studied only behaviors they could see, and refused to consider anything that happened inside the brain. By the 1970s, this approach had been rejected by most psychologists, but 1950 was the heyday of behaviorism, and behaviorism didn't have much to say about creativity.[1]

FIGURE 3.1. J. P. Guilford. Courtesy of the University of Southern California, on behalf of the USC Specialized Libraries and Archival Collections.

A second prominent approach in 1950s American psychology was Freudian psychoanalysis. To a Freudian, creativity was a subliminal activity masking unexpressed or instinctual wishes; the people who chose to become artists were just redirecting unfulfilled sexual desires (Freud, 1917/1966, p. 467). That's why Freudians called the arts *compensatory phenomena*. The arts were based on illusion and the creation of a fantasy world, and were thought to be similar to a psychiatric disorder called neurosis.

A third reason that psychologists in 1950 didn't study creativity was that exceptional creativity was thought to be a by-product of high intelligence. Soon after World War I, Lewis Terman of Stanford University adapted Frenchman Alfred Binet's new intelligence test to the United States, and for decades after that, the study of talent and human potential was dominated by the study of intelligence.

Modern creativity research began with Guilford's influential 1950 APA presidential address (Guilford, 1950). After Guilford's stamp of approval at the national psychology conference, studies of creativity blossomed. During the years that followed Guilford's address there were almost as many studies of creativity published in each year as there were for the entire 23 years prior to his address (Getzels, 1987; Sternberg & Dess, 2001).

Of course, one evening's talk can't change an entire scientific discipline overnight. But Guilford's APA address was the right message at the right time. In the years after World War II, the United States was an economic powerhouse, a machine exporting its products around the world, generating jobs for everyone. But the booming economy of the 1950s was very different from the 1990s information technology boom; there were no start-ups, no venture capital, no NASDAQ. Instead, almost everyone worked for a large, stable corporation, and the work environments were much more structured than we're used to today. IBM was legendary for requiring each employee to wear a white shirt and a navy blue suit, every day. Businesses were organized into strict hierarchies—almost like the military—and everyone knew their place in the pecking order.

Like the military, these companies were extremely efficient. But many thoughtful commentators were concerned. After all, we'd just fought World War II to defend freedom, and our cold war adversary—the Soviet Union—was criticized as a restricted and controlled society. So it was disturbing that our society was beginning to seem increasingly constrained and regimented. By the late 1950s, people were increasingly worried about this "age of conformity," and a 1956 book called *The Organization Man* by William H. Whyte became a national best seller. Its theme—that the regimented economy was resulting in an America full of uncreative, identical conformists—was echoed in similar books through the early 1960s. The research psychologists that began to study creativity in the late 1950s and early 1960s were profoundly influenced by these nationwide concerns (as can be seen in transcripts of discussions at the influential Utah conferences on creativity in 1955, 1957, and 1959).

Like Guilford, many of the early creativity scholars got their start during World War II, evaluating personality traits for the military. For example, Donald MacKinnon and Morris Stein worked for the Office of Strategic Services, the predecessor to the CIA. They worked at the Assessment Center, a group that was charged with evaluating which people would best be suited for demanding roles overseas—irregular warfare, spies, counterespionage agents, and leaders of resistance groups—what we know today from CNN as "special ops." After World War II, these military psychologists founded several research institutes to study creative individuals. MacKinnon founded the Institute of Personality Assessment and Research (IPAR) at the University of California at Berkeley in 1949. Guilford founded the Aptitudes Research Project at the University of Southern California in the early 1950s. Stein founded the Center for the Study of Creativity and Mental Health at the University of Chicago in 1952.

Creativity research was a high-stakes game during the nuclear arms race: in 1954, psychologist Carl Rogers warned that "international annihilation will be the price we pay for a lack of creativity" (p. 250). Around that time, the government began to give research grants to psychologists studying creativity—funding research to identify creative talent early in life, to educate for creativity, and to design more creative workplaces. The goal of this research was no less than to better understand freedom and its place in American society; as Morris Stein wrote at the time, "To be capable of [creative insights], the individual requires freedom—freedom to explore, freedom to be himself, freedom to entertain ideas no matter how wild and to express that which is within him without fear of censure or concern about evaluation" (1961/1963, p. 119).

In 1950, the government created the National Science Foundation to provide fellowship funding to graduate students. The NSF's first priority was to develop a test to identify the most promising future scientists. Personality psychologist Calvin W. Taylor led that research effort from 1952 to 1954; when he stepped down in 1954, he drew on his NSF connections to get funding for a series of conferences at the University of Utah on the identification of creative scientific talent; the first one was held in 1955 (Taylor & Barron, 1963; Taylor, 1964). The Utah Conferences brought together most of the personality psychologists studying creativity. The fifth conference in 1963 even attracted Harvard professor and legendary LSD guru Timothy Leary (see figure 3.2).

FIGURE 3.2. Participants in the 1963 Utah Conference on the identification and development of Creative Scientific. Frontispiece from Taylor, 1964. Front row, left to right: Taylor, Torrance, Drevdahl, Clark, Leary, MacKinnon, Guilford, Sprecher, Wight; second row: Westcott, Jablonski, Hyman, Datta, Fiedler, Parnes, Gamble; third row: Roberts, McRae, Mednick, Levine, Holland, Beittel; fourth row: Astin, McPherson, Mullins, Brust, Barron, Elliott, Ghiselin.

Like Carl Rogers and Morris Stein, these creativity researchers believed they were defending freedom and helping to save the world from nuclear annihilation. Today, most people in the United States and Europe agree with Stein that liberal democratic societies are those most conducive to creativity (Weiner, 2000). At the first Utah Conference in 1955, Frank Barron of the Berkeley IPAR described the creative society; it had "freedom of expression and movement, lack of fear of dissent and contradiction, a willingness to break with custom, a spirit of play as well as of dedication to work" (1963, p. 152). By 1960, creativity scholars began to sound like they were writing the playbook for the Hippie era that came only a few years later. In 1961, Morris Stein argued that "A society fosters creativity to the extent that it encourages openness to internal and external experiences. . . . Societies that are full of 'don'ts,' 'shouldn'ts,' and 'mustn'ts' restrict freedom of inquiry and autonomy. . . . [Society] discourages creativity to the extent that social pressures to conformity are so intense that deviations are punished directly or indirectly through social isolation and ostracism" (Stein, 1961/1963, p. 130). In 1962, Donald MacKinnon advised parents and teachers "to encourage in their children and in their students an openness to all ideas and especially to those which most challenge and threaten their own judgments" (1962, p. 493). If you think parents were too permissive in the 1960s, you can't lay all the blame at Benjamin Spock's door (also see Hulbert, 2003).

As we learned in chapter 1, people's ideas about creativity are always influenced by their society and their historical time. So we shouldn't be surprised that postwar American psychologists emphasized a conception of creativity that fit exactly with a liberal democratic vision of society, one that contrasted the United States with the Soviet Union during the darkest years of the cold war.

Creativity and Intelligence

At the center of all personality measures stands the intelligence test. In the era of IQ testing that began with Stanford professor Louis Terman in the 1920s and ran through the 1950s, psychologists thought that creativity was strongly correlated with intelligence, so they tended to study intelligence rather than study creativity directly. And in fact, researchers have shown that creative adult artists, scientists, and writers get pretty high scores on tests of general intelligence (Barron & Harrington, 1981, p. 445).

Before creativity research could become its own area of study, psychologists had to prove that IQ and creativity were different traits and required different measures. By 1960, this goal had been accomplished; in summarizing the first three Utah Conferences on creativity, Taylor (1962) noted that one of the key results to emerge from the conferences was that creativity scores and IQ scores measured distinct traits. In research at the University of Chicago, Jacob Getzels and Philip Jackson (1962) studied 6th through 12th graders, and found that creativity and intelligence were statistically independent. This study was the source of the *threshold theory*: the theory that creativity requires a certain threshold level of intelligence, generally around an IQ of 120, but that above that threshold creativity does not increase with higher intelligence.[2] After World War I, Terman used his new IQ test to identify a group of extremely high-intelligence youths, all with IQs of at least 140, and he kept in touch with them for decades. In one of his last papers, Terman concluded that not more than one-third of these subjects, affectionately known as "termites," were noticeably creative (Rhodes, 1961, p. 307). A genius-level IQ is no guarantee that you'll be creative.

Divergent Thinking

One of the most obvious differences between intelligence and creativity is that intelligence requires *convergent thinking*, coming up with a single right answer, while creativity requires *divergent thinking*, coming up with many potential answers. During the 1960s, many researchers developed tests of divergent thinking, and studied the relationship between IQ scores and these new test scores. Dr. Guilford himself led the charge, at the Aptitudes Research Project at the University of Southern California.[3]

Guilford's Structure-of-Intellect model of the personality contained over 120 traits, and 24 of them were components of divergent thinking (Guilford, 1967). Guilford and his team developed a large number of influential tests to measure divergent thinking. Two of the most widely used measures of divergent thinking—the Torrance Tests of Creative Thinking (Torrance, 1974) and the Wallach-Kogan creativity tests (Wallach & Kogan, 1965)—are extensions of Guilford's tests. Torrance's tests were designed to satisfy one of the key goals of 1960s creativity research: to identify children with high creative potential so that they could be steered into careers requiring creativity, and to transform education to fully realize the creative potential of every student. Tests created by Guilford and by Torrance were widely used in the 1960s, particularly with young children.

Educational programs to teach creative thinking were popular during the 1960s; Torrance (1965) developed one of the most influential programs. But no one has ever been able to convincingly demonstrate that these programs actually increase creative ability. At first, researchers tried to prove their benefits by measuring students' divergent thinking abilities both before and after taking the creativity course. But these studies tend to have one big weakness: because the students were told the course would enhance their creativity, and because the students knew their divergent thinking was supposed to go up, they might have provided more answers on the post-test in a desire to conform to teacher expectations (Wallach, 1988).

There was an even bigger problem with measures of divergent thinking—high scores on these tests don't correlate highly with real-life creative output, as Guilford himself noted long ago (1970, 1971; also see the criticisms of Baer, 1993; Cattell, 1971; and Wallach, 1971). Barron and Harrington (1981) reviewed hundreds of studies; in some, divergent thinking was correlated with other measures of creative achievement, but in others they weren't (pp. 447–448). Most psychologists now agree that divergent thinking tests don't predict creative ability, and that divergent thinking is not the same thing as creativity. Creative achievement requires a complex combination of both divergent and convergent thinking, and creative people are good at switching back and forth at different points in the creative process.

Creative Personalities

Guilford's 1950 presidential address focused on scientific and technological creativity, and he later seemed remarkably prescient when the Soviets beat the Americans into orbit with the launch of Sputnik in October 1957. The American response was a mobilization in the schools to attempt to identify and nurture scientific talent and creativity. For psychologists in the 1950s and 1960s, creativity was pretty much synonymous with scientific creativity. Researchers worked hard to develop a test that could identify those children who were gifted and talented, so that schools could nurture their talent and target them for high-creativity careers in science and technology (e.g., Parnes & Harding, 1962). The formal name of the Utah Conferences was "The Identification of Creative Scientific Talent." Standardized creativity measures developed in the 1960s include the Barron-Welsh Revised Art Scale (Barron & Welsh, 1952; Helmstadter, 1972), the Gough-Heilbrun Adjective Checklist (Gough & Heilbrun, 1965), the Domino Creativity Scale (Domino, 1970), the Schaefer and Anastasi Biographical Inventory Scale (1968), and the Torrance Tests of Creative Thinking (Torrance, 1974).

In Berkeley, California, Donald MacKinnon's IPAR team was skeptical about the unproven stereotypes of the creative individual: "a genius with an I.Q. far above average; an eccentric not only in thinking but in appearance, dress, and behavior; a Bohemian, an egghead, a longhair . . . a true neurotic, withdrawn from society, inept in his relations with others" (MacKinnon, 1962/1978, p. 178). Their goal was to scientifically determine the traits of the creative personality. Researchers at IPAR studied successful architects, inventors, engineers, writers, and mathematicians (MacKinnon, 1978).

It's hard to measure creativity with a paper and pencil test. For one thing, it's hard to know if the test is really measuring creativity rather than some other trait. And even worse, a survey of several hundred tests of creativity showed that a person's score could be raised or lowered just by changing trivial things like the amount of time he or she was given to take the test, or the verbal instructions given to him or her in advance (Barron & Harrington, 1981, pp. 442–443). To get around these problems, IPAR developed a new method of personality assessment. They began by asking experts to suggest names of particularly creative people in their field. These peer-nominated creators were then invited to travel to Berkeley to submit to a battery of tests. Because these individuals were highly successful in a creative domain, their creativity was referred to as "big C" to contrast it with the "small c" creativity that we all possess in everyday life. The Berkeley researchers found that their highly creative subjects had the following traits (MacKinnon, 1978).

- Above average intelligence. Different professions scored differently on different submeasures of intelligence; writers scored highly on verbal intelligence, whereas architects scored highly on spatial intelligence. They found support for the threshold theory that exceptional creativity requires an above-average intelligence, but that above a certain level, additional intelligence does not result in additional creativity.
- Discernment, observance, and alertness. They can quickly scan ideas and select those that are relevant to solving their problem; they have a wide range of information at their command.
- Openness to experience.
- Balanced personalities. For example, creative males gave more expression to the feminine side of their nature than less creative men: creative men scored relatively high on femininity, even though they didn't appear effeminate and they seemed not to be homosexual.
- A relative absence of repression and suppression mechanisms that control impulse and imagery.
- Pleasant and materially comfortable childhoods, although they recalled their childhoods as not having been particularly happy. MacKinnon called this the theme of remembered unhappiness (1978, p. 182). MacKinnon hypothesized that their home life was no different from anyone else's, but that the difference was in their perceptions and memories; they're more likely to remember unpleasant experiences because of their reduced repression.
- A preference for complexity. They enjoy discovering unifying principles that can bring order to complex, unfinished phenomena.

Since the 1960s, a wide range of other studies has identified additional traits of creative people (Barron & Harrington, 1981; Feist, 1998; Tardif & Sternberg, 1988):

- articulacy (verbal fluency)
- metaphorical thinking
- flexible decision making
- the ability to internally visualize problems
- independence
- tolerance of ambiguity
- willingness to surmount obstacles and persevere
- willingness to take risks
- the courage of one's convictions
- high energy
- independence of judgment
- autonomy
- self-confidence, assertiveness, and belief in oneself as being "creative"
- ability to resolve and accommodate apparently opposite or conflicting traits within oneself

Many of these studies found that the most important characteristic of creative people is an almost aesthetic ability to recognize a good problem in their domain. They know how to ask the right questions. That's why highly creative people tend to be creative in one specific domain: it takes a lot of experience, knowledge, and training to be able to identify good problems. We'll explore these themes of problem-finding and domain specificity in chapter 4.

These characteristics don't support our cultural myths about creativity. For example, these are all habits of highly effective people, not of dysfunctional schizophrenics or alcoholics. Back in the 1960s, for example, IPAR didn't find any evidence to support the stereotype of the creative person as "a Bohemian, an egghead, a longhair . . . a true neurotic, withdrawn from society, inept in his relations with others" (MacKinnon, 1962/1978, p. 178). Creative people are happy, successful, and have well-balanced personalities.

Changes Over the Creative Lifespan

Developmental psychologists have studied how creativity develops and evolves over the lifespan of the creative individual, looking at the influence of birth order, family, and community.

Birth Order

Are you more likely to be creative if you are firstborn, or later born? Are only children more likely to be creative? Francis Galton (1874, 1962) was perhaps the first to observe that firstborn and only sons were overrepresented in science, and Havelock Ellis (1904) found the same pattern in other domains (see also Goertzel, Goertzel, & Goertzel, 1978; Torrance, 1962). In Roe's (1952a, 1952b) classic study, 39 of the 64 distinguished scientists were firstborn (15 of them were only children), 13 were second born, with only 12 remaining. Of the 25 who were not firstborn, five were the oldest male child, and two had an older sibling who died young. Firstborns typically represent more than half of the active scientists in any given discipline and have higher citation rates than later-borns. Csikszentmihalyi (1965) also found that the most original artists were more likely to be first born (p. 87).

But the birth order effect is controversial (see Schooler, 1972). In fact, Sulloway (1996) argued that firstborns are less likely to be innovative revolutionary scientists, because firstborns identify more with their parents and with authority, and are more invested in the status quo. Simonton (1994, 1999a) likewise argued that creative geniuses were generally not firstborns; he thought that firstborns and only children tend to make good leaders in times of crisis, but that middle-borns are better leaders in safe, peaceful times, because they are better listeners and compromisers.

Although these hypotheses are intriguing, the evidence is inconclusive. Based on current scientific knowledge, we can't say with any certainty whether first borns or later borns are more likely to be creative. It probably varies from one creative domain to another, and also with the type of problems facing the domain.

Family Influences

Studies of hundreds of eminent creative people have found that between one-third and one-half of them had lost a parent before age 21 (Simonton, 1999b, p. 115). This is called *the orphanhood effect*. How could such trauma lead to creativity in adult life? One hypothesis is that the loss of a parent produces a bereavement syndrome, in which children become high achievers to emotionally compensate for the absence of the parent. A second hypothesis is that loss of the parent forces the child to develop a resilient personality simply to overcome the obstacles that face a life with only one parent. If a person grows up in a happy, financially stable family, he or she may just have it too good in childhood to be driven to greatness (Simonton, 1999b, p. 114). A third hypothesis is that such a loss leads the child into a life that is less conventional than that of peers with a happy, normal family life.

Being a first- or second-generation immigrant and being Jewish are highly correlated with creative achievement. Nearly 20% of Nobel Prize winners have some Jewish background, far above their proportion in the world's population. These sociological and demographic factors may correlate with creativity because they result in a sense of marginality in the individual, and realizing that you're marginal may play a role in creative eminence (this argument was first made by Thorstein Veblen in a famous 1919 paper). Howard Gardner's creativity research led him to propose that the "exemplary creator" comes from the provinces, from the margins of power rather than the capital city (1993; also see Simonton, 1988b, pp. 126–129; 1999a).

These studies have revealed that significant minorities of creative people grow up in marginal communities, or have some early life trauma. But still, more than half of the most creative people say they grew up in stable, happy families. When Csikszentmihalyi (1996) studied 100 eminent creators, he didn't find any evidence of early trauma in childhood. And when the creative architects studied at the IPAR recalled their childhoods, they described the classic upper-middle-class, Protestant, liberal American lifestyle: fathers were effective in their demanding careers, mothers were autonomous and often had their own careers, religion was important but was not central or doctrinaire, families emphasized the development of a personal code of ethics, parents were not overly judgmental but encouraged the child's ideas and expressions, and the families moved frequently (MacKinnon, 1978). But ultimately, these findings can't be explained by personality psychology; these family characteristics demonstrate the ways that social class status reproduces itself across generations. Creative people are usually successful, and successful people generally have successful parents, as sociologists have known for decades.

Family and Community Values

The Flauberts steered Gustave into law, but he rejected their wishes and went on to write the famous novel *Madame Bovary*. Claude Monet's parents wanted him to enter their successful grocery business, but instead he became a painter. Wassily Kandinsky—the man who some say invented abstract painting just before World War I—was a professional lawyer and didn't begin painting until the age of 30. French painter Paul Gauguin moved with his wife to her native city of Copenhagen, where she joined forces with her family in the attempt to get him to give up his art and choose an occupation that would allow him to support his family. Ultimately the conflict could only be resolved by divorce.

These were strong personalities who were willing to go against their families' wishes; but other creative people who face such conflicts choose not to make a commitment to a creative career. Many adolescents internalize the practical value system of their families—the belief that creative pursuits are impractical, not suitable for a respectable person, and won't allow you to make a living and support a family. Many parents steer their children away from creative careers. There's a general cultural belief in many industrialized countries that creative pursuits are low status, not financially rewarding, and worst of all, selfish; after all, a responsible adult would choose to make money and support one's family. Other families don't want their children to become artists because they have conservative or religious value systems, and they reject the bohemianism of the art world.

To choose a creative career, a person has to believe that this life choice is morally worthy; the ambition to do great work is a driving force. Many creators first realize the necessity of this choice in adolescence. Every creator has to negotiate family and society: some lucky few have supportive, open-minded parents and relatives who provide all of the necessary support to nurture their creative talent; others are forced to rebel and to reject the practical value system of their families. The family dynamics involved in the career decision influence the creator for the rest of the career. These family issues are typically studied by psychoanalytic psychologists (e.g., Gedo, 1996).

Creative women face different societal forces than men. The pressure to be the breadwinner is still felt stronger in American men, for example, and this makes it harder for men to choose a creative career. Although women feel less pressure to be the breadwinner, there's still not much support in many segments of American society for women with independent, successful careers; they too are viewed as selfish when they pursue such paths. These cultural values probably contribute to the fact that large numbers of women enter art school, but professional artists are almost exclusively men (also see Guerrilla Girls, 1998).

The Lifespan Perspective

During his voyage around the world on the *Beagle*, Darwin kept exceedingly detailed notebooks on his observations. After returning to his study in London, he continued to keep daily notes as he reexamined his data. In 1974, creativity researcher Howard Gruber published the first detailed study of these notebooks (Gruber, 1974). By looking carefully through Darwin's day-to-day entries, Gruber realized that the theory of evolution by natural selection did not occur in a blinding moment of inspiration, an "aha" moment. Instead, the notebooks showed a more incremental process, a series of small mini-insights, each a key step in Darwin's theory. Darwin's creative inspiration was not the result of a single, isolated "aha" moment, but rather was constructed day-by-day over a long period of extended activity. Gruber argued that the insight of evolution by natural selection wasn't what made Darwin great; Darwin was a genius because he was able to build a conceptual framework within which evolution by natural selection would make sense. In fact, prior to Darwin, other theorists had proposed evolution by natural selection, but they're not considered the founders of modern evolution because they didn't successfully develop the conceptual framework within which that insight could be explained.

Gruber also discovered that creative people are successful because they always have multiple, overlapping, related projects under way at the same time (Gruber & Davis, 1988). He called this a *network of enterprises*. Gruber argued that what makes a person creative isn't a single insight or idea, but it's the bigger conceptual frameworks within which ideas emerge, are interpreted, and given life and elaboration. The network of enterprises doesn't happen in a sudden insight; it has to be built over long periods of time. Creativity is the work of a lifetime, and requires an extended biographical focus for understanding.

Lifetime Peaks

Lehman (1953) published a widely cited finding that individuals in different fields have their creative peaks at different ages. For example, physicists peak in their 20s or 30s, biologists and social scientists in their 40s, and writers and philosophers peak throughout the lifespan. This intriguing finding has recently gained additional support from studies by Simonton (1997a). Harvard psychologist Howard Gardner (1993) detected evidence for what he called the ten-year rule: that creative individuals tend to come up with major breakthroughs that are 10 years apart. He hypothesized that the 10-year delay was evidence for the importance of learning the domain—the language and conventions of a creative discipline. Under this explanation, the 10-year rule is yet more evidence of the importance of hard work, convention, and organized systems of knowledge in creativity.

Although there's some evidence for these career peaks, it doesn't mean you're all washed up if you're already past the average age for your career. After all, these are only averages. Dennis (1958) noted that highly original work occurs in most arts and sciences up to age 70 and beyond. Csikszentmihalyi's "Creativity in Later Life" study (1996) found that most creators remain productive long after retirement. There's still a lot we don't know about creative lives; creativity researchers need to do more studies of creativity over the lifespan.

Psychoanalysis

> An artist is once more in rudiments an introvert, not far
> removed from neurosis. He is oppressed by excessively
> powerful instinctual needs. He desires to win honour, power,
> wealth, fame and the love of women; but he lacks the means
> for achieving these satisfactions. Consequently, like any other
> unsatisfied man, he turns away from reality and transfers all
> his interest, and his libido too, to the wishful constructions of
> his life of phantasy, whence the path might lead to neurosis.
> —*Sigmund Freud (1917/1966, p. 467)*

Psychoanalysis has long associated creativity with access to more primitive, unconscious modes of thought—sometimes called *primary process thought.* Many schools of 20th-century art were influenced by Freud's psychoanalytic theories. Expressionism, dadaism, and surrealism were based in part on the idea that art involves the revelation of unconscious material. According to Freud, the creative insight emerges into consciousness from primary process thought. Freud argued that creativity involved the same mental processes as daydreams, fantasies, and full-fledged neuroses (1907/1989). Psychoanalytic theory explains the frequently noted connections between art, dreams, and children's play; they all involve regression to a more primitive developmental state.

Regression refers to a return to behavior patterns characteristic of an earlier stage of personality development. When repressed unconscious material is released, it usually causes psychological problems. By the 1950s, as creativity researchers discovered that most creative people were mentally balanced and not neurotic, psychoanalytic theorists modified this theory; they started to believe that creativity involved both primary processes and secondary processes. Creative people are able to partially control regression and can use it in service of a conscious goal; this "regression in service of the ego" is constructive rather than destructive (Kris, 1952). The creative person manages a sophisticated balance between primary and secondary process thinking, and this balance would be hard to maintain in the presence of mental illness. Psychoanalytic theorists no longer believe that creative people are more likely to be mentally ill (also see chapter 5, pages 83–90). For example, Rothenberg (1979) claimed that the creative process is "not only *not* primitive but [is] consistently more advanced and adaptive than ordinary waking thought" (p. 43).

The relationship between the unconscious and the conscious mind is still central to several influential contemporary theories—even those that are not psychoanalytic—as we'll see in the next chapter.

Motivation and Flow

> For the individual to find himself in an atmosphere where he
> is not being evaluated . . . is enormously freeing. . . . If
> judgments based on external standards are not being made
> then I can be more open to my experience. . . . Hence I am
> moving toward creativity.
>
> *—Carl R. Rogers (1954, p. 257)*

Personality research can help us to explain creativity, but not in the ways our creativity myths would suggest. Most psychologists today believe that innate creative talent is overrated. Most agree with Thomas Edison that "genius is one percent inspiration and ninety-nine percent perspiration" (Bartlett, 1955, p. 735). Researchers have discovered that creativity is largely the result of hard work. There is no magic, no secret. People who are willing to work hard tend to have certain personality traits, but not those we typically associate with creative types. There's no doubt that a special personality is required to make the choice for creativity, to knowingly choose the kind of lifestyle associated with the career, to be able to sustain the dedication and commitment to the work.

Psychologists have discovered that motivation plays an essential role in creativity. The most creative people are those who are intrinsically motivated— they're so motivated by their work that they often find themselves losing track of time. They focus in on what they are doing, forget about everyday problems, and are oblivious to distractions in the environment. For creative people, these are the peak experiences of their lives. The study of peak experience began in the 1950s with the humanistic psychologists Carl Rogers (1954, 1961) and Abraham Maslow (1954). Csikszentmihalyi (1990b) continued this tradition of work with his studies of the flow state—the sensation of peak experience that immensely talented people get from pursuing the challenge associated with cutting-edge creative pursuits.

In fact, decades of creativity researchers have found that external rewards can easily short-circuit the benefits of the flow state. It seems that when a person knows he or she will be rewarded for the quality of their work, they can't stop thinking about that reward, and they find it impossible to get into the flow state where they're doing the task simply because they like doing it. The potential interference of extrinsic motivation was a key emphasis of Torrance's method for teaching creative behavior; he called his method "unevaluated practice" (1965). In the 1980s, Theresa Amabile extended these early studies and found many situations where external reward interfered with the intrinsic motivation associated with flow. Amabile (1996) conducted a wide variety of studies showing that when subjects are told they are going to be externally evaluated or rewarded for creative work, their level of creativity (and their intrinsic motivation) declines. Creativity comes from intrinsic motivation, and externally motivating factors actively interfere with creativity.[4]

These studies emphasize the importance of extended periods of hard work, and the need for strong intrinsic motivation to provide the necessary level of dedication. They show that creativity can't be explained in terms of raw, innate talent or clever imagination. The most important predictor of creative output is hard work, dedication, and intrinsic motivation. And because motivation is so closely related to various factors in the social environment (Amabile, 1996; see chapter 7), motivation research has contributed to the rise of the sociocultural approach.

The Failure and End of Personality Psychology

Treffinger (1986) called the early hopes placed in first-wave creativity research the creativity quotient fallacy: the belief that researchers would develop an equivalent to the IQ test for creative potential, one that could be just as easily administered and scored using a pencil-and-paper test booklet. Treffinger's research team received the following letter from a school board official:

> Our school district is developing criteria for placement of students in programs for the gifted. We would like to consider creativity . . . an individual or group test of creative ability or a checklist of creative behaviors. Performance on these instruments must demonstrate creative thinking which is superior to that of children of similar age. . . . Naturally, we would prefer an instrument that could be administered quickly and easily and scored simply. (1986, p. 16)

This desire remains an impossible dream. Divergent thinking was quickly realized to be only one component of creative potential. And other types of tests were no more successful. In fact, different tests, each designed to measure creativity, often aren't correlated with one another (e.g., Alter, 1984; Baer, 1993). Another problem is that you can easily fool many of these tests by pretending to be creative; for example, if you know that divergent thinking is associated with creativity, when you're given a test you'll just write down different ideas as fast as you can think. Yet another problem is that even though some of these tests correlate with creative achievement, the tests might in fact correlate with *all* achievement. Rather than measuring creativity, they might instead be measuring success and social achievement more generally. By the mid 1980s, psychologists had given up on trying to measure creativity with a personality test (Cooper, 1991; Eysenck, 1990; Feist & Runco, 1993; Feldhusen & Goh, 1995; Nicholls, 1972; Rosner & Abt, 1974; Wakefield, 1991).

The personality psychologists working between 1950 and 1970 were an important first wave of creativity research. They made some important progress; they discovered that creativity requires hard work, dedication, motivation, and close attention to the work that has come before. Creative people are happy and productive, and tend to be quite successful—nothing like our myth of the tortured lone genius. But in the end, the personality psychologists didn't attain their ambitious goals—to find out what personality traits distinguish creative people from ordinary people, to develop a test that could identify exceptional talent early in life, and to design educational techniques that could improve a student's creativity. Part of the reason for this failure was that they were too willing to accept our creativity myths; personality psychologists weren't aware that their own conceptions of creativity were socially and historically unique (Raina, 1993; Stein, 1987).

Thought Experiment

- Think of one of your teachers or mentors—someone older than you that you have a lot of respect for.
- What words first come to mind when you try to describe what this person is like?
- Would you say that this person is effective and successful in life?
- Did this person work hard? Was he or she highly motivated?
- Would you say that this person is creative?

Suggested Reading

Barron, F., & Harrington, D. M. (1981). Creativity, intelligence, and personality. *Annual Review of Psychology, 32*, 439–476.

Feldhusen, J. F., & Goh, B. E. (1995). Assessing and accessing creativity: An integrative review of theory, research, and development. *Creativity Research Journal, 8*(3), 231–247.

Guilford, J. P. (1950). Creativity. *The American Psychologist, 5*(9), 444–454.

MacKinnon, D. W. (1962/1978). What makes a person creative? In D. W. MacKinnon (Ed.), *In search of human effectiveness* (pp. 178–86). New York: Universe Books. (Originally published in *Saturday Review*, Feb. 10, 1962, pp. 15–17, 69).

Piirto, J. (1999). A survey of psychological studies in creativity. In A. S. Fishkin, B. Cramond, & P. Olszewski-Kubilius (Eds.), *Investigating creativity in youth: Research and methods* (pp. 27–48). Cresskill, NJ: Hampton.

Stein, M. I. (1987). Creativity research at the crossroads: A 1985 perspective. In S. G. Isaksen (Ed.), *Frontiers of creativity research: Beyond the basics* (pp. 417–427). Buffalo, NY: Beary Limited.

Notes

1. Behaviorism's critics often pointed to the phenomenon of human creativity, and claimed that reinforcement methods couldn't teach creativity. Skinner realized the importance of this criticism, and repeatedly tried, although unsuccessfully, to respond (1968, 1972).

2. This theory has been criticized; Wakefield (1991) claimed there is little empirical evidence for the threshold theory; also see Runco and Albert (1986), who claimed the threshold effect is a psychometric artifact because they found different correlations using different intelligence tests.

3. In fact, the first divergent thinking test was developed by Binet, the originator of the IQ test, in 1896 (Barron & Harrington, 1981, p. 446)—a test of open-ended, multiple-solution items. These measures of "imaginative abilities" proliferated through the early years of the 20th century.

4. Note the meta-analytic critique by Eisenberger and Cameron (1996) who argued that the negative effects of reward are quite limited: to rewards on a single occasion that are given without regard to the quality of performance; the negative effects are not found when the reward depends on the quality of work, nor when the reward is presented repeatedly across multiple occasions (as is the typical case in schools; pp. 1162–1164).

In a cross-cultural study of this effect, Hennessey (2003) found that in a more collectivist culture (Saudi Arabia) the expectation of a reward did not undermine performance, suggesting that the effect might only occur in individualist cultures like the United States (see the discussion of individualist and collectivist cultures in chapter 8).

CHAPTER 4

The Second Wave: Cognitive Psychology

Guilford's 1950 APA address jump-started the modern era of creativity research. But soon after 1970, government funding dried up and studies of the creative personality slowly came to an end (Feist & Runco, 1993, p. 280). By 1980, it seemed clear that the first wave of creativity research—the 20 years of study into personality traits and creative potential in childhood—had failed to achieve its goals (cf. Feldman, Csikszentmihalyi, & Gardner, 1994).

But fortunately, in the 1970s a new group of psychologists began to study creativity in a new way, using a different approach that had even more potential to explain creativity. Research psychology was changing dramatically during the 1960s and 1970s. Cognitive psychology began to replace both the behaviorism and the personality psychology that had been dominant in American psychology after World War II. Instead of studying traits and personality differences, cognitive psychologists analyze mental processes that are shared by all individuals. Cognitive psychologists examine the representational structures of the mind, their interconnections, and the mental processes that transform them. Instead of studying the creative personality, cognitive psychologists shifted the focus to creative mental processes. They tried to explain creativity by showing how it emerged from ordinary, everyday mental processes—cognitive abilities that everyone has, the same ones that are used in noncreative activities.

The Stages of the Creative Process

Over the last century, philosophers have developed two competing theories about the creative process. Idealist theorists argue that once you have the creative idea, your creative process is done. It doesn't matter whether or not you ever execute your idea, or whether anyone else ever sees it; your creative work is done once your idea is fully formed in your head. This idea is often called the "Croce-Collingwood" theory, after two philosophers who promoted it in the 20th century (see Sawyer, 2000).

Action theorists, in contrast, argue that the execution of the creative work is essential to the creative process. Action theorists point out that in real life, creative ideas often happen while you're working with your materials. Once you start executing an idea, you often realize that it isn't working out like you expected, and you have to change what you had in mind. Sometimes the final product that results is nothing like your beginning idea. Perhaps the purest example of action creativity is jazz improvisation. Because it's improvised, musicians don't know what they'll play in advance; the notes emerge in the moment, from the complex give-and-take among the members of the ensemble. In improvisation, performers start playing without knowing what will emerge.

Scientific studies of creativity have shown that the idealist theory is false. Only an action theory can explain creativity. Creativity takes place over time, and most of the creativity occurs while doing the work. The medium of the artwork is an essential part of the creative process, and creators often get ideas while working with their materials.

In chapter 2 we learned that our creativity myths are more like the idealist theory than the action theory. We tend to think that ideas emerge spontaneously, fully formed, from the unconscious mind of the creator. If the idealists were right, it would be almost impossible to study creativity scientifically—because all of the action is in the head, the scientist can't observe it. We're lucky that the idealist theory is wrong, because action theories have a big advantage: they allow scientists to observe and explain the creative process.

Psychologists have been studying the creative process for decades. They have several different theories about how it works, but most of them agree that the creative process has four basic stages: preparation, incubation, insight, and verification (see figure 4.1).

- *Preparation* is the initial phase of preliminary work: collecting data and information, searching for related ideas, listening to suggestions.
- *Incubation* is the delay between preparation and the moment of insight; during this time, the prepared material is internally elaborated and organized.

- *Insight* is the subjective experience of having the idea—the "aha" or "eureka" moment.
- *Verification* includes two substages: the evaluation of the worth of the insight, and elaboration into its complete form.

Stage 1: Preparation

The holy grail of the first wave of creativity research was a personality test to measure general creativity ability, in the same way that IQ measured general intelligence. A person's creativity score should tell us his or her creative potential in any field of endeavor, just like an IQ score is not limited to physics, math, or literature. But by the 1970s, psychologists realized there was no such thing as a general "creativity quotient." Creative people aren't creative in a general, universal way; they're creative in a specific sphere of activity, a particular domain (Feldman, 1974, 1980; John-Steiner, 1985; Csikszentmihalyi, 1988b). We don't expect a creative scientist to also be a gifted painter. A creative violinist may not be a creative conductor, and a creative conductor may not be very good at composing new works. Psychologists now know that creativity is domain specific.

Most domains of creative activity have been around for many lifetimes—the centuries of European fine art painting, or the decades of empirical research in particle physics. Without first learning what's already been done, a person doesn't have the raw material to create with. That's why an important part of the creative process is first becoming very familiar with prior works, and internalizing the symbols and conventions of the domain. Creativity results when the individual somehow combines these existing elements and generates some new combination.

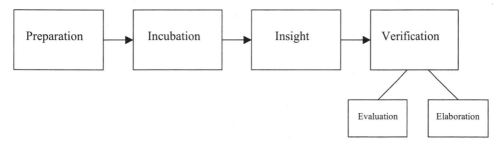

FIGURE 4.1. Stages of creative process (by author).

Some domain knowledge is internalized in a passive and direct way; the student of physics has to learn Maxwell's equations and Einstein's theories exactly. But some domain knowledge is creatively transformed even while it's being learned. When an artist walks through a gallery, she views paintings very selectively, looking for ideas or inspirations that can solve creative problems that she's currently working with. This can lead her to see something in a painting that its creator may not have intended. When a scientist reads a historical work by a long-dead theorist, he reads into the work whatever perspectives or issues he's currently working with.

No one can be creative without first internalizing the domain, and this is why scientists now believe that formal schooling is essential to creativity. After all, the function of schools is to pass on domain knowledge to the next generation. In modern science, for example, you can't even begin to work in a domain without first getting a PhD. However, the role played by schooling in creativity is complex; creativity isn't highly correlated with high grades in school and in college. Even in science, where schooling is perhaps more critical than in art, high grades are not strongly correlated with adult achievement (see Simonton, 1988b, pp. 118–126). And many eminent scientists begin to publish important articles before they receive their doctorate (Roe, 1972).

Some studies have found that creativity is an inverted U function of educational level; after a certain point, additional formal education begins to interfere with creativity. Figure 4.2 presents a curve derived from 192 creators from the Cox (1926) sample. In 1926, the education level corresponding to peak creativity was somewhere between the junior and senior years of college. Of course, these data are from an earlier era, and as the sciences have become progressively more complicated, this peak has shifted to the middle of graduate study (Simonton, 1984, pp. 70–73).

Up to college, formal schooling doesn't interfere with creativity; in fact, just the opposite. To participate successfully in a field, the young individual must internalize the domain. But the inverted-U pattern shows that there's some truth to the idea that schooling can get in the way. After getting just enough education to internalize the domain, further training can oversocialize a person, resulting in a rigid, conventionalized way of thinking.

Stage 2: Incubation

> Instead of thoughts of concrete things patiently following one
> another . . . we have the most abrupt cross-cuts and transi-
> tions from one idea to another . . . the most unheard-of
> combinations of elements, the subtlest associations of analogy;

in a word, we seem suddenly introduced into a seething
cauldron of ideas, where everything is fizzling and bobbing
about in a state of bewildering activity.

—*William James (1880, p. 456)*

William James was one of the first famous American psychologists. At a time
when almost all important science was being done in Europe, when aspiring
American scientists had to learn German and French to gain access to the domain, James was one of the first American psychologists to be widely read in
Europe. His writings on religious experience are still widely read today. In this
passage, James describes "the highest order of minds," the elevated level of performance that results in true creativity. Like James's "seething cauldron," many
creators use cooking metaphors to describe unconscious incubation: they talk
about "keeping things on the back burner," or "providing fuel for the fire," and
they say that creativity takes time to "stew" or "bubble up." James is describing
the incubation stage, when ideas and thoughts combine rapidly in an almost
undirected way.

The incubation stage is often below the surface of consciousness. It's the least
understood stage in the creative process. In incubation, mental elements com-

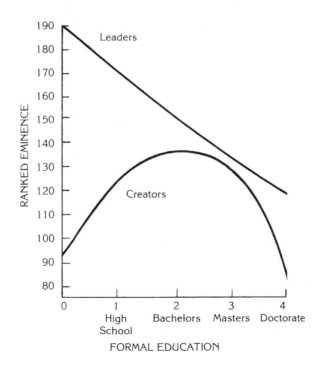

FIGURE 4.2. Curves of the relationship between formal education and ranked eminence for leaders and creators. Redrawn from *Journal of Creative Behavior*, volume 17, 1983. "Formal Education, Eminence, and Dogmatism," pp. 149–162, by D. K. Simonton. Reprinted with permission of Creative Education Foundation. Copyright 1983.

bine, and insight occurs when certain combinations emerge into consciousness. Einstein wrote in a letter to Hadamard that "the psychical entities which seem to serve as elements in thought are certain signs and more or less clear images which can be combined . . . .This combinatory play seems to be the essential feature in productive thought" (in Hadamard, 1945, p. 142).

Many creative people say they get their best insights during a period of idle time, when they take time off from their hard, focused work to engage in an unrelated activity—gardening, walking—or to work on another problem for a while. Former CEO of Citicorp John Reed, widely acknowledged to be one of the most innovative bankers, reports, "I do my best work when I have some alone time. It often happens when I'm sitting around a hotel room, I'm on a trip and nothing's going on, I sit and think, or I'm sitting on a beach . . . and I find myself writing myself notes." Physicist Freeman Dyson said that whenever he feels like he's not getting much done, he must be going through a creative period; his daily insights come while he's shaving or taking a walk. Economist Kenneth Boulding takes a 40-minute bath every morning, and reports that ideas often come to him while taking a bath (all quoted in Csikszentmihalyi & Sawyer, 1995).

In the last chapter, we learned that creative people multitask in networks of enterprise; they make sure that they're working on more than one project at the same time. While they're consciously attending to one project, the others are on the back burners. They know that good ideas require some incubation time, so they schedule their workday to accommodate this process. The unconscious mind seems to be able to incubate on many projects at once "in parallel," unlike the conscious mind, which can only focus on one thing at a time (also see Csikszentmihalyi & Sawyer, 1995).

Associations

Incubation can't start until the creative person has prepared by internalizing the products and conventions of the domain. But once the domain is inside the mind, incubation gets to work. During incubation, existing ideas bounce into each other, almost like atoms in a chemical soup. Some of the ideas will fit together into stable mental structures, whereas others won't fit at all. Some of these stable mental structures will somehow be striking enough to be noticed by the conscious mind.

The theory that new ideas are associations between existing ideas is one of the oldest theories in psychology; it's called *associationism*. Well over 100 years ago, psychologist Alexander Bain (1855/1977) first argued that in incubation, "the new combinations grow out of elements already in the possession of the mind" (p. 572). One of the first modern versions of the associationist theory of creativity was developed by psychologist Sarnoff Mednick (1962). Mednick identified several mental variables that contribute to the likelihood of having a novel association:

- the organization of an individual's associative hierarchy, the strength and structure of associations invoked by a given concept;
- the number of associations the individual has to the relevant elements of the problem;
- the individual's cognitive style;
- the ways that individuals select the creative combination.

And of course because the 1960s were the heyday of psychometric testing, Mednick developed a test to measure all of these things, the *Remote Associates Test* of creative potential (Mednick & Mednick, 1967). Mednick's associationist theory proposed that a more creative person has a flat associative hierarchy, allowing her to make large numbers of remote associations between seemingly distinct ideas. In contrast, average people have a steep associative hierarchy; they tend to have fewer overall associations, those associations are stronger, and they're between ideas that are more similar (see figure 4.3). In a flat hierarchy, more ideas are connected and their associations are not as strong; this results in a more interconnected mind that is better at generating groundbreaking interdisciplinary combinations (see also Simonton, 1999b).

Scientists have developed several different explanations for what happens during incubation. How do elements combine, and which combinations make it into conscious awareness? One hypothesis is that the combinations are random;

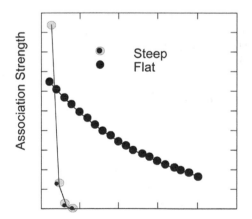

FIGURE 4.3. Steep and flat associative hierarchies according to Mednick's theory. From *Origins of Genius: Darwinian Perspectives on Creativity* by Dean Keith Simonton, copyright 1999 by Oxford University Press. Inc. Used by permission of Oxford University Press, Inc.

the creative person "just happened to be standing where lightning struck" (Campbell, 1960, p. 390). Simonton called these associations "chance permutations" (1988b, pp. 6–8, 1997a). Some researchers have suggested that nothing is going on in the subconscious mind; idle time results in insights because the person switches to a new environment and then has totally different experiences that can spark an insight (Seifert et al., 1995). But most psychologists believe that combinations are guided in some way beneath the surface of consciousness. For example, psychoanalytic theorists argue that the combinations are "active, directed forms of cognition in which the creator intentionally and in distinct ways brings particular types of elements together" (Rothenberg, 1979, p. 11); the elements are "integrated" rather than being "merely added or combined" (p. 12).

Cross-Fertilization

> All decisive advances in the history of scientific thought can be described in terms of mental cross-fertilization between different disciplines.
> —*Arthur Koestler (1964, p. 230)*

With their networks of enterprise, creative people work on multiple projects at the same time. While they're hard at work on one project, the other projects are incubating beneath the surface. In many cases, incubation brings together ideas from more than one project, and an insight results from the combination of two projects that the creator had originally thought were not related.

A lot of important scientific insights happen when scientists switch fields, introducing techniques or modes of thought that are already standard in another domain (Koestler, 1964; Simonton, 1988b, p. 127). Landsteiner's previous background in chemistry facilitated his isolation of blood groups; Kekulé's early desire to become an architect may have influenced the way he thought about the structural basis of organic chemistry; and Helmholtz acknowledged that his invention of the ophthalmoscope resulted from his interest in optics that predated his training as a physician.

Some researchers hypothesize that field-switchers have more novel insights because of their marginality. Because they're at the margins of the discipline, the thinking goes, they'll be more likely to have innovative ideas because they are less constrained by the domain (Black, 2000). But other studies have found no evidence that marginality contributes to creative output. Other researchers explain these multidisciplinary insights by appeal to analogical thinking, the idea that analogies between distinct domains allow the individual to perceive patterns in a way that would not be apparent to members of only one domain. The best explanation seems to be that if you have multiple projects and multiple domains internalized, you'll have a larger pool of basic ideas. As a result, your chance of having an interesting new combination during incubation goes up significantly (Simonton, 1988b, p. 128).

Cognitive Structures

> Our understanding of creativity cannot be complete without a detailed and rigorous treatment of the cognitive processes from which novel ideas emerge.
> —*Thomas B. Ward (2001, p. 350)*

Of all of the mental processes studied by cognitive psychologists, the ones thought to be most relevant to creativity are conceptual combination, metaphor, and analogy (Ward, Smith, & Vaid, 1997a, 1997b). It's creative to combine two concepts to make a single new one; for example, a "boomerang flu" is a flu that goes away and then returns. Many of us use novel metaphors in everyday speech, for example, saying that "children are sponges" to comment on how quickly they absorb new information. In analogies, some properties from one mental model are transferred to another; famously, de Mestral had the idea for Velcro when he began to wonder how burrs clung to his clothing (Hill, 1978).

The creative cognition approach explains creativity by examining how the mind combines concepts (Finke, Ward, & Smith, 1992). Creative cognition theorists hypothesize that a cluster of basic cognitive processes are used in creativity: generative processes that produce ideas, filtering processes that select among these ideas, and exploratory processes that expand on the potential of each idea. Generative processes include information retrieval, association, and combination. The mind then uses various properties of these ideas—novelty, surprisingness, aesthetic appeal—to evaluate which of them should be retained and explored. Exploratory processes then modify and elaborate the idea, consider its implications, assess its limitations, and even transform the idea.

For example, Wisniewski (1997) examined an everyday type of creativity as a way of better understanding conceptual combination: he examined cases when speakers combined nouns to make novel concepts, such as "car boat" to refer to a new kind of boat that is also a car, or "boomerang flu" to refer to a flu that goes away and then comes back. In such cases, the two component concepts themselves change when they are combined (the "car" that is a "car boat" is not exactly like any other kind of car); and this conceptual change is itself a form of creativity, as each concept guides the creative modification of the other. Thus conceptual combination is not simply additive, but is a case of emergence—concepts are combined in a complex system of higher-level concepts, and each of the component concepts is itself changed by its participation in the higher-level concept. Because the parts change when they're combined together, the new concept can't be understood by breaking it apart into its component concepts and studying them in isolation.

Before we can explain how the mind combines concepts, we need to start with a good theory of what a mental concept looks like. Since the 1970s, cognitive psychologists have proposed schema or frame models that represent a concept as a data structure with variables or "slots" that can be set to different values. For example, the schema for "vehicle" would include slots for:

- *number of wheels* (two for a motorcycle, four or more for a truck, but with a default value of four for a car)
- *number of seats* (again, a default value of four). Slots can themselves be filled with representationally complex concepts; the "seat" in the vehicle schema can be a motorcycle seat or a car seat, which have very little in common.

If we accept that concepts are schemas, then we can explain conceptual combination as a process of slot filling, with values of the slots of one schema filling in values of the other, as the two schemas merge to form a single new one.

However, it's a long way from "car boat" to the development of creative products that transform a domain (as noted by Simonton, 1997b; Ward, Smith, & Vaid, 1997a, p. 4), and one might reasonably wonder whether exceptional creativity really occurs in the same way. For the most part, cognitive psychologists haven't examined creativity directly; instead, they focus on everyday cognitive processes (Ward, Smith, & Vaid, 1997a, p. 1)—what many creativity researchers refer to as "small-c" creativity, in contrast with the "big-C" creativity of major historical breakthroughs.

The problem with studying underlying cognitive mechanisms like conceptual combination is that higher-level mental processes like creativity are built out of many mental mechanisms. After all, most big-C creative innovations are complex networks of many concepts, not a single concept; ramping up from conceptual combination to creative innovation is likely to be quite difficult. For example, Dunbar (1997) found that creative ideas in science emerge over the course of a collaborative meeting, from a series of small changes, each produced by a different cognitive mechanism—one by analogy, another by induction, yet another by causal reasoning (see chapter 14). Even though cognitive psychology can help us to understand each of these component mechanisms, it may not help us much with understanding the complex system that ultimately results in the emergence of creativity, because the creative insight might contain hundreds of concepts in complex combinatorial relations (cf. Ward, Smith, & Vaid, 1997a, p. 18). Again, it comes down to a question about emergence: although creative insights emerge from complex underlying cognitive processes, the emergence may be so complex that the creative insight could not have been predicted in advance (Finke, Ward, & Smith, 1992, p. 8). For these reasons, many prominent creativity researchers believe that cognitive psychology is fundamentally limited and can't provide the full explanation of exceptional creativity (Csikszentmihalyi, 1988a; Simonton, 1997b).

Stage 3: Insight

> The mind being prepared beforehand with the principles most
> likely for the purpose . . . incubates in patient thought over
> the problem, trying and rejecting, until at last the proper
> elements come together in the view, and fall into their places
> in a fitting combination.
> —*Alexander Bain, The Senses and the Intellect (1855/1977, p. 594)*

In incubation, existing ideas blend and combine to form complex mental structures. Some of these mental structures—no one knows exactly which ones or why—surface into consciousness, and the creator experiences an "aha" or "eureka" moment. The existing ideas that form the mental structure are not new; they are familiar ideas and conventions that are already in the domain. A creative insight is never 100% original. What makes an insight novel is the way that these existing ideas are put together.

Creativity science doesn't yet know very much about the psychological structure of creative insights. We don't know exactly how existing pieces of the domain mix together in the creator's mind. To explain creativity, we'll need to have a pretty good theory of how the parts of the domain are stored in the creator's mind, because without knowing what they look like, we won't be able to explain how they combine to form novel insights. One example is the schema theory that I just discussed. Other theories of these mental structures include Sternberg and Lubart's (1991) model of "selective encoding" and "selective comparison," and Wisniewski's (1997) theory of conceptual change.

There's one important alternative to the dominant associationist explanation of insight: Wertheimer's gestalt theory of productive thinking (1945). He started by observing that many creative people seem to experience a sudden burst of insight, when the entire way they think about the problem suddenly changes. Wertheimer didn't think you could explain this by talking about associating small, simple ideas to build a complex structure; instead, it seemed that the mind jumped all at once from one complete structure to a new one. So Wertheimer explained creativity by examining the structural properties of the problem. Every mental structure is incomplete; there are tensions, sometimes contradictions, built into the structure. The creator's mind has an ability to transform the structure into a more stable, better structure, and insights happen when a complex mental structure suddenly transforms into a more stable structure. But this holist gestaltist theory has several weaknesses. For example, by focusing on the structural characteristics of the problem, it almost seems that all problems would quickly solve themselves. And it's hard to explain why one person can do the transformation but another can't.

Boden's (1999) theory of transformational creativity is a modern variant of Wertheimer's gestaltist theory. Boden argued that although some forms of creativity are combinations of existing elements, the most important creativity involves a transformation of conceptual space. Using a linguistic analogy, Boden observed that generating a new sentence from the rules of grammar—a sentence that no one had ever said before—would be creative but it wouldn't be surprising, because everyone would realize how that sentence could have been said by anyone before even though it wasn't. But transforming a conceptual space is like someone who develops a modification to the rules of grammar themselves, so that completely new kinds of sentences can now be uttered, sentences that would not have been possible, or would have sounded nonsensical before. This kind of creativity couldn't be the result of associations between existing elements, because it would change the way associations themselves could be made.

Stage 4: Verification: Evaluation and Elaboration

After the insight emerges into consciousness, the creator has to evaluate the insight to determine if it's really a good idea. After all, many creative insights turn out to be bad ideas, even though they were appealing enough to jump from incubation to consciousness. Scientific insights may turn out to be wrong; business innovations may not work for some technical reason; new artistic ideas that sound good in theory might look stupid once executed. The evaluation stage is fully conscious, and the creator draws on his or her immense knowledge about the domain. Is the insight an idea that someone already had in the past? Is the insight kind of interesting, but trivial? How can this insight be integrated with the creator's existing body of work? Or does it require a complete rethinking of a career, perhaps something the creator isn't prepared to do at this time? How can this insight best be connected to other work that is going on in the domain?

Many creators say that the best way to have a good idea is to have a lot of ideas, and then just get rid of the bad ones. I call this the *productivity theory*. Poet W. H. Auden said that "the chances are that, in the course of his lifetime, the major poet will write more bad poems than the minor" because they "write a lot" (quoted in Bennett, 1980, p. 15). It's a creativity myth that geniuses are always right; geniuses are wrong in a similar proportion to everyone else, and may generate more wrong ideas simply by virtue of generating more ideas overall (Weisberg, 1986; see chapter 2). Galileo insisted that planets traveled in a circular orbit, even with the increasing evidence for comets' elliptical paths; Darwin undermined his evolutionary theory with the doctrine of pangenesis, now known to be false; and Einstein persisted in arguing for a unified theory, and rejected quantum mechanics.

In addition to such anecdotal evidence, quantitative research supports the productivity theory. Simonton (1988a, 1988b) measured the raw productivity of historical creators, and also identified the creations that had stood the test of time as truly significant works. He found a strong relationship between productivity and significant creations: when comparing individuals, the creators that had the highest overall lifetime output were the people most likely to have generated a significant work. Even when he measured year-to-year productivity within a single person's lifetime, he found that the most productive periods were the times when a creator was most likely to have generated a really significant work (pp. 88–91). A 1998 study of patented inventions (Huber, 1998) found that in a group of 408 full-time inventors, those with the most patents were those whose patents were judged the most significant.

At first glance, the productivity theory seems to defy common sense. It seems that the person who's really productive must be a little sloppy, cutting corners and generating second-rate work. It seems like the most important works would require a lot of time and energy to generate; the person who generates a really important work should be the one who dedicates all of his or her energies to that one project. We can all conjure up an image of a solitary creator, working alone for years in isolation, growing increasingly eccentric, until he finally comes out of the lab or studio to reveal the masterpiece that will change the world. But this image is a creativity myth; it doesn't happen very often. In fact, the productivity theory proves several of our creativity myths to be false or misleading—that geniuses are special people who are always right, or that creative works spring to mind fully formed (as the idealist theory would have it).

After evaluation comes elaboration, the conscious hard work where the creator takes the raw insight and molds it into a complete product. Most creative insights are not fully formed; the creator has to use his or her immense domain knowledge—in particular, how to work using the materials and techniques of the domain—to convert the idea into a finished work. Monet had the idea to paint a haystack in a field at different times of the day and the year; but his idea wouldn't have gone anywhere unless he also had the painting skills to mix the right colors, to hold and to move the brush to make the right strokes, and to compose the overall image to get the desired effect. A person might have a new idea about how to design a computer word processor, but that idea would be lost to history if the person didn't know how to write computer programs.

Elaboration always goes together with evaluation, because it's often hard to tell if an insight is a good one without elaborating it at least part way. You'll probably have to work with an idea at least a little bit before you can tell if it's a good one. And you always end up modifying the initial insight during elaboration. Raw insights are just sparks, nothing but rough outlines; the creator usually experiences a continued cycle of mini-insights and revisions while elaborating the insight into a finished product.

Problems With Stage Theories

> You have these ideas, and then you work on them. As you work on them, you get new ideas . . . one makes the other one come out.
>
> —*Sculptor Nina Holton, quoted in Csikszentmihalyi & Sawyer (1995, p. 353)*

Many influential studies have demonstrated the complexity of creativity by focusing on the ontogenesis of the creative product—biographical studies of the day-to-day development of creative products over months and years. The first influential study like this was Gruber's close reading of Darwin's journals (Gruber, 1974). Creativity researchers are still fleshing out theories about these long-term processes: how long creative periods are sustained, and how one multiyear period is succeeded by a shift to another research question, or another style of visual representation (cf. Gruber, 1988; Nakamura & Csikszentmihalyi, 2003).

The four-stage model I've just described is a little too linear; the creative process is more cyclical. These ontogenetic studies have found that creators work on many problems at the same time, and that in most creative careers, an insight often generates even more questions than it answers. A creative insight that generates good questions is more valuable than one that conclusively answers every known question but doesn't suggest any further research. The task of solving a good question leads to the reformulation of difficult problems and the generation of completely new questions.

Rather than coming in a single moment of insight, creativity involves a lot of hard work over an extended period of time. While doing the work, the creator experiences frequent but small mini-insights. Unlike the mysterious insight of our creativity myth, these mini-insights are usually easy to explain in terms of the hard conscious work that immediately preceded them.

Psychoanalytic theorists were some of the first to explore the cyclical nature of mini-insights. Arieti (1976) noted that "complex works that can be divided into parts" involve a series of insights, with incubation occurring throughout the creative process, and he concluded that the four stages aren't separated through time (p. 18). Rothenberg (1979) argued that creation is not found in a single moment of insight but is "a long series of circumstances . . . often interrupted, reconstructed, and repeated" (p. 131). He criticized stage theories, arguing that "the temporal distinction made between inspiration and elaboration in the creative process is an incorrect one; these phases or functions alternate—sometimes extremely rapidly—from start to finish" (p. 346). And Vinacke (1952) argued that in many creative fields, especially fine art, the final work results from a series of insights beginning with the first draft or sketch and continuing until the work is completed. Incubation does not occur in a particular stage but operates to varying degrees throughout the creative process. For example, poems and plays do not emerge suddenly or completely, but are gradually developed through a process of many incubations and insights (see chapter 11).

Every so often a creator will have a subjective experience of a moment of insight. But even though it may seem sudden to the creator at that moment, in retrospect it can always be traced to the prior work that the creator was engaged in. By analyzing the sketches and notebooks leading up to the insight, we see that each innovation resulted from a connected, directed, rational process (Weisberg, 1986, 1993). For example, Jackson Pollock's paintings are now known to have emerged from a long process of careful deliberation, and not from a sudden insight in the middle of the night followed by a binge of paint pouring. Darwin's groundbreaking innovation—the theory of natural selection—is now known to have emerged from a multitude of smaller, incremental insights (Gruber, 1974). This history is lost unless there are detailed notebooks (like those left by Charles Darwin) or video recordings (made by creativity researchers who happen to be present during the process). But in every case where researchers have access to this kind of detailed record, they can trace the final product from a complex series of small mini-insights that are closely tied to the work of the moment. In the chapters of part 4, I present the best of this process-analytic research, and show how it supports the action theory of creativity.

These new studies show that insight is overrated. Studies of the work processes of creative individuals have revealed that the typical creator experiences many small mini-insights every day, and that these mini-insights can be traced back to the material they were consciously working on. We only think we see leaps of insight because we didn't observe the many small, incremental steps that preceded the "insight." Creative activities require problem solving and decision making throughout the process, and each one of these decision points involves a small amount of creative inspiration; yet, when these mini-insights are viewed in the context of the ongoing creative work, they no longer seem so mysterious. Creativity researchers today agree "that creativity takes time . . . the creative process is not generally considered to be something that occurs in an instant with a single flash of insight, even though insights may occur" (Tardif & Sternberg, 1988, p. 430).

The mythical view of a moment of insight overly simplifies the complexity and hard work of most creativity. Instead of a single glorious moment, creators experience small insights throughout a day's work, with each small insight followed by a period of conscious elaboration; these mini-insights only gradually accumulate to result in a finished work, as a result of a process of hard work and intellectual labor of the creator. The continued fascination with a moment of insight is another example of the persistence of our culture's creativity myths—the Romantic era belief that the creator should be inspired while in a spiritual, mystical state.

Finding Problems

> We say that a question well put is half resolved. True invention thus consists in posing questions. There is something mechanical, as it were, in the art of finding solutions. The truly original mind is that which finds problems.
> —*Paul Souriau (1881, p. 17, translation in Wakefield, 1991, p. 185)*

> The formulation of a problem is often more essential than its solution. . . . To raise new questions, new possibilities, to regard old questions from a new angle, requires creative imagination and marks real advance in science.
> —*Albert Einstein & Leopold Infeld (1938, p. 92)*

At the beginning of a painting class in 1992, instructor Michell Cassou began by asking his students, "How many of you came here with your first painting already done in your head?" Half of the students raised their hands. Cassou continued, "If you paint that painting, you'll just be copying what you've already done." These students came to the class holding our idealist-theory myth, that creativity is when you have the idea. Instead, Cassou told his students to "open themselves to the moment," without predetermined plans (Cushman, 1992, pp. 54–55). Creativity researchers call this the problem-finding creative style.

Many cognitive psychologists compare the stages of creativity to the stages of problem solving (Flavell & Draguns, 1957, p. 201; Guilford, 1967; Kaufmann, 1988; Klahr, 2000; Klahr & Simon, 1999). But creativity researchers have discovered that some creative people work in areas where problems are not specified in advance, where a big part of success is being able to formulate a good question (Beittel & Burkhart, 1963; Csikszentmihalyi, 1965; Getzels, 1964; Mackworth, 1965). As a result, many creativity researchers now believe that creativity involves both problem solving and problem finding.[1]

Of course, in the real world—whether in the arts, science, or business— problems are rarely neatly presented. The only place where you're likely to be asked to solve problems is on a test—either an intelligence test, or a measure of creative ability. Problem solving, like IQ testing, is a convergent activity, and problem finding is a divergent activity. All real-world creativity involves some degree of problem finding; in fact, this is one of the common critiques of standardized testing—that it only measures problem-solving, but not problem-finding ability (Sternberg, 1985).[2]

American society in the 20th century valorized spontaneity, but this emphasis on problem-finding creativity is relatively recent (Belgrad, 1998; see chapter 2). Prior to the 19th-century Impressionists, who were influenced by the naturalism and spiritualism of the earlier Romantic writers, painters were definitely *not* supposed to paint without prior planning. The great academies of Europe, such as the École des Beaux-Arts in France, taught the importance of choosing an appropriate subject (ideally, a historical or mythological theme), of carefully composing its placement on the canvas, of experimenting with color mixes for each portion of the painting, and of sketching and painting preliminary drafts or "studies" before beginning the actual work. This was how painting had been done in Europe for centuries. Problem finding is a bigger part of our conception of creativity today than it's ever been.

Summary

Psychologists were the first scientists to seriously study creativity. The psychological study of creativity has gone on for so long that I've grouped it into two distinct periods: a first wave of personality psychology in chapter 3, and a second wave of cognitive psychology in chapter 4. After all of this research, we have some pretty solid knowledge about creativity.

- Creativity is not a special mental process, but involves everyday cognitive processes.
- Creativity is not a distinct personality trait; rather, it results from a complex combination of more basic mental capabilities.
- Creativity does not occur in a magical moment of insight; rather, creative products result from long periods of hard work that involve many small mini-insights, and these mini-insights are organized and combined by the conscious mind of the creator.
- Creativity is always specific to a domain. No one can be creative until they internalize the symbols, conventions, and languages of a creative domain.

Although these are all important scientific findings, we haven't yet explained creativity. Psychology only provides one piece of the complex explanation of creativity that modern science has developed. In the next two chapters, we'll explore two exciting new individualist approaches to the study of creativity: the biological and the computational. And after that, in part 3, we'll broaden our scope to examine contextualist approaches to creativity.

Thought Experiment

- Think of a time when you made something that you think was particularly creative—a school project, a written report, a mechanical device, a block tower, a painting, or musical performance.
- What mental process led to its creation?
- Did you have the idea all at once, fully formed, and then all you had to do was make it? If so, what preceded the insight—what preparation did you do, and was there an incubation period?
- Or did you begin with only the germ of an idea, having mini-insights throughout the process, so that the final product was not exactly what you started out to make?
- Would you call this a problem-finding or a problem-solving type of creativity?

Suggested Readings

Csikszentmihalyi, M., & Getzels, J. W. (1988). Creativity and problem finding in art. In F. H. Farley & R. W. Neperud (Eds.), *The foundations of aesthetics, art & art education* (pp. 91–116). New York: Praeger.

Csikszentmihalyi, M., & Sawyer, R. K. (1995). Creative insight: The social dimension of a solitary moment. In R. J. Sternberg & J. E. Davidson (Eds.), *The nature of insight* (pp. 329–363). Cambridge: MIT Press.

Feldman, D. H. (1974). Universal to unique. In S. Rosner & L. E. Abt (Eds.), *Essays in creativity* (pp. 45–85). Croton-on-Hudson, NY: North River Press.

Gruber, H. E. (1988). The evolving systems approach to creative work. *Creativity Research Journal, 1,* 27–51.

Ward, T. B., Smith, S. M., & Vaid, J. (1997a). Conceptual structures and processes in creative thought. In T. B. Ward, S. M. Smith, & J. Vaid (Eds.), *Creative thought: An investigation of conceptual structures and processes* (pp. 1–27). Washington, DC: American Psychological Association.

Weisberg, R. W. (1993). *Creativity: Beyond the myth of genius.* New York: Freeman.

Notes

1. These terms were first used by Mackworth (1965). There are some parallels with Kirton's (1988) ideas about creative styles; his *adaptors* are the problem-solving people and his *innovators* are the problem-finding people.

2. However, complicating the picture, psychologists haven't found any relationships between divergent thinking and problem-finding ability (Starko, 1999, p. 90).

CHAPTER 5

Biology

On April 18, 1955, the famous physicist Albert Einstein died in Princeton, New Jersey. He had requested that his body be cremated. However, he was such an exceptional genius that the Princeton pathologist Dr. Thomas S. Harvey removed his brain and quickly placed it in formaldehyde to preserve the nerve cells. Medical doctors and psychologists hoped that by close examination of Einstein's brain, they might gain insight into what made him so smart. But none of the studies of Einstein's brain were able to identify any significant biological differences between his brain and the average brain. In fact, his brain weighed only 1,230 grams, much less than the adult male average of 1,400 grams.

Einstein's brain became an almost religious icon in our secular age. Even during his lifetime, Einstein's brain was examined by the primitive brain science of the time: electrodes were attached to his head to record his brain waves while he thought about his theory of relativity. This would only happen in a culture that believed that differences between people are biologically based.[1] We believe that exceptional genius must be hardwired in the brain, and that the explanation for extreme creativity must be biological. We look at Einstein's brain rather than his education or family environment.

Since Einstein's death in 1955, contemporary U.S. culture has increasingly biologized human behavior. The biological approach is consistent with our individualist cultural beliefs about creativity. We tend to think that we can explain every aspect of the human personality by looking into the genetic code deep inside the individual's cells. This broad cultural attitude has many concrete manifestations: newspaper and television science reporting focuses on every new genetic discovery, and government agencies fund cognitive neuroscience and behavioral genetics at much higher dollar amounts than most other social and behavioral sciences. Because of this general cultural attitude, many readers of this book are likely to be receptive to the idea that there might be a creativity gene that makes the human species the most innovative one in creation, or that genetic differences between people might make one person more creative than another.

But in fact, most scientists believe that there is no creativity gene.[2] Of course, the psychological findings of the last two chapters already showed us that there couldn't be such a gene, because creativity is based in everyday cognitive processes—the same mental abilities that are used in noncreative activities (chapter 4). And in chapter 3, we learned from the failure of personality psychology that creativity is not a personality trait. Although there might be genes related to these general cognitive abilities, there can't be genes that are specific to creativity.

But biology can still help us to explain creativity. This chapter has three main themes. First, I discuss studies in neuroscience—the biology of the brain—including the famous left brain/right brain studies. Second, I discuss studies of mental illness and creativity, from Hans Prinzhorn in the 1920s through contemporary studies of schizophrenia and manic-depressive disorder. Third, I discuss theories of how creativity evolved along with the human species.

Right Brain or Left Brain?

Since the dawn of the new science of psychology in the early 19th century, scientists hoped to identify the specific functions of each region of the brain. The first nineteenth-century psychologists to map the brain were called *phrenologists*. Figure 5.1 is a reproduction of an image of the brain from 1826, showing where phrenologists believed that different personality traits were located. The first impression you get from looking at the list of "brain organs" is that many of these traits sound really old-fashioned—few psychologists today believe that benevolence or secretiveness are personality traits based in the brain. Studying the history of personality psychology is humbling, because the traits always change as the times change.

If you look a little closer at figure 5.1, you'll notice that there's no organ for creativity. The absence of an organ of creativity suggests that phrenologists did not believe that creativity was a brain-based personality trait. This absence in

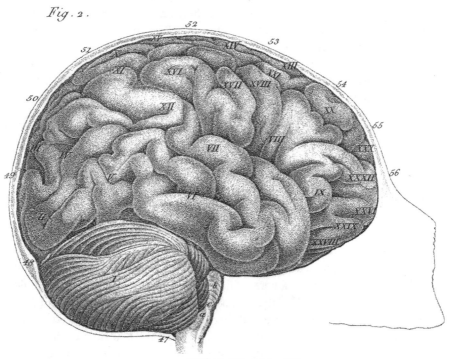

Fig. 2.

Published by D.ʳSpurzheim 1826

FIGURE 5.1. A phrenologist's view of brain organization and function. Reprinted from Johan Kaspar Spurzheim, 1826. Guide to the Principal Zones:

I. Organ of amativeness
II. Organ of philoprogenitiveness
III. Organ of inhabitiveness
IV. Organ of adhesiveness
V. Organ of combativeness
VI. Organ of destructiveness
VII. Organ of secretiveness
VIII. Organ of acquisitiveness
IX. Organ of constructiveness
X. Organ of self-esteem
XI. Organ of love of approbation
XII. Organ of cautiousness
XIII. Organ of benevolence
XIV. Organ of veneration
XV. Organ of firmness
XVI. Organ of conscientiousness
XVII. Organ of hope
XVIII. Organ of marvellousness
XIX. Organ of ideality
XX. Organ of mirthfulness
XXI. Organ of imitation
XXII. Organ of individuality
XXIII. Organ of configuration
XXIV. Organ of size
XXV. Organ of weight and resistance
XXVI. Organ of coloring
XXVII. Organ of locality
XXVIII. Organ of calculation
XXIX. Organ of order
XXX. Organ of eventuality
XXXI. Organ of time
XXXII. Organ of melody
XXXIII. Organ of language
XXXIV. Organ of comparison
XXXV. Organ of casuality

1826 is consistent with historical research showing that the modern creativity myths originated only in the mid 19th century, as Romantic conceptions spread through society (chapter 2).

By the 1960s, brain science had advanced significantly, with new tools that allowed more accurate mappings of brain functions onto brain regions. Beginning in the 1960s, neurobiologist Roger Sperry began to study split-brain patients—patients whose two brain hemispheres had been surgically separated in an attempt to control their severe epileptic seizures (Gazzaniga, 1970; Sperry, Gazzaniga, & Bogen, 1969). In 1972, Robert Ornstein's best-selling book *The Psychology of Consciousness* popularized the idea that the two hemispheres play different roles in our mental lives (1972; also see Ornstein, 1997). During the 1970s, this work began to receive media coverage, and one of the ideas that emerged was that creativity was based in the right brain. For example, Betty Edwards's 1979 book *Drawing on the Right Side of the Brain* told artists how to be more creative by releasing the power of their right brains. And today, decades later, many people think that creativity is a right-brain function.

The left and right hemispheres of the brain are highly connected—a bundle of 100 million neurons called the corpus callosum connects the two. Split-brain patients have had their corpus callosum surgically severed, a procedure reserved for very extreme cases of epilepsy. Because the two sides of the brain can no longer communicate with each other, Sperry was able to create experimental tasks that could be presented to only one hemisphere. For example, using a specially constructed laboratory, an image could be presented only to the right eye and then the subject asked to respond in some way using his or her right hand. Because both the right eye and right hand are connected only to the left brain, the behavior observed would be strictly a product of the left brain. The same task could then be presented to the left eye and left hand (which connect only to the right brain), and the results compared. Such studies revealed that although the two hemispheres are anatomically identical, the two sides of the brain have subtle differences in function. The best example of functional specialization is language; 70% to 95% of people have language specialization in the left hemisphere. Being left-handed doesn't mean that you're right-brain dominant for language; the same percentage of right- and left-handed people have language specialization in the left hemisphere.

Split-brain research has found that roughly speaking, the right brain is associated with rapid, complex, whole-pattern, spatial, and perceptual processes, and the left brain is associated with verbal, analytic, and linear processes. The right brain is dominant for recognizing and identifying natural and nonverbal sounds, whereas the left is dominant for recognizing and identifying language.

The right brain is better at depth perception, at maintaining a sense of body image, at producing dreams during REM sleep, at appreciating and expressing emotion aroused by music and the visual arts, and at perceiving emotional expression in others (Restak, 1993).

But these results are only very general; the story is actually much more complicated. For example, when people both with and without musical training were asked to recognize fragments of music, there were interesting differences in hemispheric specialization. Those who had no formal training carried out the task in their right hemispheres, whereas those with formal training used both hemispheres equally (Bever & Chiarello, 1974). In general, researchers have discovered that it's too simplistic to associate any particular domain of creative activity with either hemisphere; rather, the various components of skill required for performance in any creative domain are located throughout the entire brain—components like motivation, inspiration, performance, perception, and evaluation—and they move around as domain expertise increases. Because of these well-documented expertise-related shifts, hemispheric localization can't be completely genetic or innate.

In addition to split-brain patients, studies of brain localization have been done on patients with brain lesions resulting from strokes, and with head injuries sustained during wartime. Most of these studies are, of necessity, done on people without artistic training and without exceptional creativity in any given domain; after all, brain damage is rare, only a small percentage of people are highly talented in any creative domain, and the odds of finding a brain-damaged creative person are consequently very small.

For example, scientists have compared the drawings of people with left and right hemisphere damage (Gardner, 1975; Warrington, James, & Kinsbourne, 1966). In one study, subjects were asked to copy a picture of a house. Those with left-hemisphere damage drew simpler images with fewer details. Those with right-hemisphere damage drew confusing pictures in which the overall form is incorrect; but within this hodgepodge, specific segments of the house might be quite detailed—a chimney with each of the bricks carefully drawn, for example (see figure 5.2).

These studies show that both hemispheres play a role in drawing, with each hemisphere making a different but essential contribution. The left hemisphere seems to function to capture details and the right hemisphere captures the overall image. In general in such studies, the right hemisphere seems to be dominant for holistic perception, with the left dominant for analytic skills—the same results found in split-brain studies.

The story gets yet more complicated when we consider the very small population of artistically trained individuals with brain damage. In trained paint-

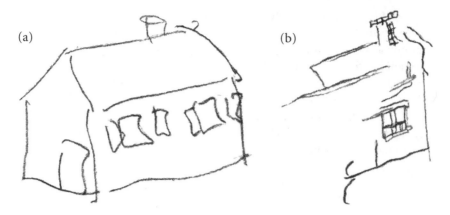

FIGURE 5.2. (a) Sketch of a house by a right-handed patient with left-hemisphere damage (drawn with the nonparalyzed hand); (b) Sketch of a house by a right-handed patient with right-hemisphere damage. Reprinted from Howard Gardner's *The Shattered Mind*, 1975, pp. 306, 307. With permission of Howard Gardner.

ers, there's some evidence that the left-hemisphere plays a less crucial role (Alajouanine, 1948). Other studies show that loss of linguistic skills, a left-hemisphere function, does not severely affect the ability to paint (Zaimov, Kitov, & Kolev, 1969). And right-hemisphere damage doesn't cause trained painters to lose the ability to capture the overall form of an image, as it does in untrained painters. One possible explanation is that training distributes skills more evenly throughout the brain. But this is only a hypothesis; it's impossible to explain these differences given the current state of scientific knowledge. We can't draw firm conclusions because among these subjects, the sites of their brain lesions were not identical.

Many art critics have observed that there seems to be a heightened emotionality and expressivity in the works of established artists after right-hemisphere strokes. In a famous example, painter Lovis Corinth suffered right-hemisphere damage, and began to draw in a bolder, more intense, and more emotionally expressive style than before his stroke (Kuhn, 1925, p. 107). Left-hemisphere damage doesn't have the same effect, suggesting some as-yet-unknown connection between the right hemisphere and emotionality in art.

The results of localized brain damage change depending on the creative domain. Because language, of all brain functions, is perhaps the most localized—usually in the left hemisphere—writers who suffer left-hemisphere lesions often never write again, whereas writers with right-brain damage can write, but none-theless suffer subtle difficulties—such as an impaired ability to understand metaphorical uses of language (Winner, 1982, p. 345). Music is the most complex case of all, made more complex because there are so many distinct musical abilities—composition, performance, perception, and technical skill with an instrument. Studies show that the many components of these skills are distributed throughout the brain, and that brain damage has different effects on trained and untrained musicians.

There's a popular conception that "left brain" and "right brain" represent personality traits and that some people are dominant in one or the other hemi-sphere. In the 1970s, the popular media took hold of these research findings, and soon it became widely believed that the left brain was the rational mind, while the right brain was the creative mind. But there's no scientific evidence for this widely held notion. No one has ever found a specific brain location for creativity. Some researchers have suggested that convergent thinking is a left-brain strength, with divergent thinking in the right brain (Springer & Deutsch, 1981). And because for decades creativity was associated with divergent think-ing (although we now know that's not accurate, see chapter 3), this may have contributed to the myth about right-brain creativity.

Brain research has found that brain damage usually reduces or completely terminates creative expression (Restak, 1993, p. 170). Split-brain patients show low creativity as measured by tests of language and thinking. This is probably because creativity requires a constant dialogue between the hemispheres; the imagery and symbols generated by the right hemisphere require the left hemi-sphere to translate them into creative verbalizations (Restak, 1993). In fact, re-searchers have hypothesized that creative people have enriched communication between their hemispheres (Hoppe, 1988).

The idea that creativity is in the right brain is false, a myth that's lasted long past its time. Scientific research shows that creativity is not a specific, identifi-able trait that can be localized to one region of the brain. Creativity is located in different parts of the brain depending on the domain; different subcomponents of ability in a single domain are located throughout the brain; and the location of these different subcomponents seems to differ in trained and untrained in-dividuals. Creative ability involves both hemispheres equally.

Brain science has not yet advanced to the point where it, alone, can ex-plain creativity. As cognitive neuroscientist Antonio R. Damasio (2001) re-cently concluded, creativity "cannot be reduced simply to the neural circuitry of an adult brain and even less to the genes behind our brains" (p. 59). These findings paint a complex picture of the relationship between brain science and creativity.

Mental Illness and Creativity

Everyone knows that madness is devastating and limits one's ability to function in everyday life, but we often think that the madness brings along with it a special wisdom, a ready access to the deep, unconscious sources of creative imagination. It's easy to think of famous examples of writers, artists, and scientists with mental diseases. Virginia Woolf was sexually abused as a girl, suffered severe mood swings as an adult, and committed suicide. Sylvia Plath experienced episodes of psychotic depression, and committed suicide. Ernest Hemingway was a notorious heavy drinker, suffered bouts of depression, and committed suicide.

Dr. Janos Maron, founder of the Living Museum—a gallery founded in 1983 at the Creedmoor Psychiatric Center in Queens Village—said that "the creative juices of the mentally ill flow more freely . . . if you're not mentally ill, you have to work much harder to get up to that level of creativity" (quoted in Budick, 2002). The idea that mental illness and creativity are linked has taken on the status of a cultural myth; any Hollywood movie that features a mentally ill character will portray that character as unusually creative. *A Beautiful Mind* (2001) implies that the Nobel Prize–winning economist John Nash derived his brilliance in part from his schizophrenia; other such films include *Rain Man* (1988) and *Shine* (1996).

The idea that madness and creativity are linked originated in the early 1800s, and became more sophisticated with Freud's psychoanalytic theories of primary process thought. But as we saw in chapter 2, this idea is not universal, and can be shown to be the product of our particular historical and cultural time. Rationalist conceptions of creativity emphasize conscious deliberation and reasoning; only during Romantic cultural periods do people think that emotionality and madness somehow contribute to creativity. In fact, the modernism and postmodernism of 20th-century art is more rationalist than Romantic (Becker, 2000–2001; Sass, 2000–2001).

Two mental disorders have been most closely associated with creativity: schizophrenia and manic-depressive disorder.

Schizophrenia

German psychiatrist and art historian Hans Prinzhorn managed a clinic for the mentally ill in Heidelberg, Germany. He believed in art therapy, and he gave many of his patients paints, brushes, and canvases, and encouraged them to paint, even though most of them had never painted before. In the 1920s, he published a collection of fascinating paintings created by hospitalized schizophrenics (Prinzhorn, 1972); these paintings made a big impact on the art world, and modern painters like Jean Dubuffet began to collect the paintings and to imitate aspects of them in their own works (see chapter 10, pp. 189–190). Schizophrenic paintings have several distinctive features: a compulsive working style and a focus on detailed ornamentation, so that every single square inch of the canvas is filled with intricate material; a focus on local detail, with little attention to composition or integration; and repetition of patterns (see figure 5.3).

The publicity surrounding Prinzhorn's clinic led many scientists to believe that creativity and schizophrenia are linked. Typical schizophrenic behaviors are found, in a less extreme form, in many artists. Schizophrenics have lost contact with reality; likewise, many artists live within their own inner world. Schizophrenics have hallucinations; likewise, artists see things in unusual and unconventional ways. Schizophrenics have all sorts of seemingly irrelevant ideas

FIGURE 5.3. *Medical Faculty*, by schizophrenic artist Adolf Wolfli, 1982. Reprinted with permission of Adolf Wolfli-Stiftung Kunstmuseum, Bern. Photograph from Adolf Wolfli Foundation, Museum of Fine Arts, Bern. Copyright 1982.

pop into their heads without conscious control, and at least on the surface, this seems similar to the moment of creative insight (Eysenck, 1995).

But rigorous scientific studies have not found associations between schizophrenia and creativity. Although some of the patients at Prinzhorn's clinic in Heidelberg generated some fascinating art, quantitative surveys suggest that less than two percent of mental hospital inmates began to engage in any form of creative activity (Kris, 1952; Winner, 1982, p. 362). Why did so many people, including psychologists, believe so long in a connection between schizophrenia and creativity, when there was so little evidence for it? It was because they were misled by our culture's creativity myths. Schizophrenia, particularly among psychoanalysts, was thought to involve a regression to a primitive Dionysian state, to infantile forms of irrationality (Sass, 1992). This conception of schizophrenia is almost identical to Romanticist ideas that creativity involves spontaneous, emotional expression, not constrained by rational judgment, and that the artist is similar to a child (see chapter 2).

Manic-depressive Illness

Writers and poets seem to be a depressed bunch of people. Several studies have found that almost half of all writers suffer from major depression (Andreasen, 1987; Jamison, 1993, 1995), and about 10% of writers and poets have committed suicide (Ludwig, 1992). But if a writer were severely depressed all the time, she'd never get any writing done. That's why some psychologists have proposed that writing creativity is related to manic-depressive illness, also known as bipolar disorder (Jamison, 1993). The manic phase exaggerates the incubation processes that lead to an original creative insight, and the normal and depressive phases allow the reflection necessary for evaluation and elaboration.

But there's a problem with these studies: many of the writers who are tagged as manic-depressive are already dead, and researchers can't actually interview them. Instead, they have to make the diagnosis from the historical record, and it's almost impossible to diagnose individuals who are long deceased. Louis Sass (2000–2001) has argued that Jamison's studies of manic-depression in writers resulted in a self-fulfilling prediction, because she adopted an exceedingly broad definition of affective psychoses (p. 66).[3] And in a further complication, many of Jamison's subjects are literary figures from the romantic tradition, and not many are creative people from other spheres of human activity (science, engineering, musical performance) and pre- or post-Romantic periods. One of her studies analyzes major British and Irish poets born between 1705 and 1805, a cohort whose creative productivity overlapped considerably with the Romantic period (1780 to 1830). But we've already learned that writers in the romantic period held to a cultural belief that creativity and madness were related. When creative people believe that creativity and madness are linked, they often invite madness and purposely volunteer evidence of madness, in lifestyle and in diagnostic examinations. Two hundred years later, this can make it almost impossible to tell real from fake mental illness.

The connections between creativity, schizophrenia, and manic-depressive illness are intriguing. But when you review all of the scientific research, the bottom line is that we haven't found convincing evidence of a connection between mental illness and creativity. Despite almost a century of work attempting to connect creativity and mental illness, evidence in support of a connection has been remarkably difficult to find. After all of these efforts, most psychologists believe that the link between creativity and madness is nothing more than a creativity myth, springing from the Romantic-era conceptions that I discussed in chapter 2.

For example, in the first attempt to systematically study the relation between mental illness and genius, Ellis (1904) selected 1,030 names from the *Dictionary of National Biography* and found that only 4.2% had suffered from mental illness, a figure only slightly higher than the whole population. More recent surveys confirm these findings; Juda (1953) studied 113 artists and 181 scientists, all identified by experts in their fields. Juda found that among the artists, 2.8% were schizophrenic, and 2% had some other form of psychosis; among the scientists, there was no schizophrenia, but 4% of them suffered from manic-depressive disorder. These percentages match the incidence of mental illness in the general population. Such studies show that geniuses are not any more likely to suffer from mental illness than the rest of us.

If anything, mental illness interferes with creativity. In real life, John Nash, the schizophrenic mathematician who was the subject of the 2001 movie *A Beautiful Mind*, accomplished his greatest mathematics before his illness took hold. Most creative people afflicted with mental illness believe that their disease interferes with their creativity. With Sylvia Plath, for example, there was no question that her severe depression negatively affected her work. As she herself said, "When you are insane, you are busy being insane—all the time. . . . When I was crazy, that was all I was" (quoted in Ludwig, 1995, p. 4). Most creative people who suffer from mental illness are relieved to get rid of their symptoms after treatment with therapy or prescription drugs (Friedman, 2002).

Freud thought that creativity was a regression to the primary process thought of the unconscious; if so, you'd predict a connection between mental illness and creativity, because regression usually causes mental problems. In the last 50 years, psychoanalytic psychologists have updated Freud in response to the failure to find evidence of a link between madness and creativity. They no longer believe that creativity involves a regression to a more primitive state; now they believe that creativity is "an advanced type of secondary process," even more rational and effective than ordinary conscious thought (Rothenberg, 1979, p. 42; also see Rothenberg, 1990). Since the 1950s, personality psychologist Hans Eysenck has proposed a major personality trait called *psychoticism* that is correlated with creativity in normal populations. People who score high on measures of psychoticism have an over-inclusive cognitive style, resulting from a reduction in cognitive inhibition. But these people are not clinically ill; in fact, Eysenck, like other creativity scholars, found that psychoses (including schizophrenia and manic-depressive disorder) were rarely found in creative people in any field (1995).

Given what we've learned about creativity in chapters 3 and 4, it's not so hard to explain why mental illness and creativity aren't connected. First, much of creativity involves working with existing conventions and languages; you can't just make up your own separate universe. Second, creative success requires networking and interacting with support networks (see chapter 7). Third, creativity is mostly conscious hard work, not a sudden moment of insight, and getting the work done takes a highly effective person. The mental illness myth focuses too narrowly on the moment of insight; and we saw in Chapter 4 that insight is overrated. The mental illness myth is based in cultural conceptions of creativity that date from the Romantic era, as a pure expression of inner inspiration, an isolated genius, unconstrained by reason and convention.

Savants

Some children with autism have amazing artistic skills; these individuals are known as *savants*. However, these artistic abilities are generally thought to be based on calculation and memory alone, rather than true creativity or originality (Selfe, 1977). For example, autistic artists are quite skilled at reproducing an image, sometimes even after only one quick glance, but they rarely create novel images that they have not seen. Oliver Sacks (1970) described at length José, a severely autistic individual who had always displayed a fascination with pictures in magazines, and frequently copied what he saw. José's concreteness of detail in representing nature, in particular, was always phenomenal, but as Sacks wrote, "His mind is not built for the abstract, the conceptual" (p. 228), rather "the concrete, the particular, the singular, is all" (p. 229).

Savants are found in very specific domains—especially in music, chess, and math. These are all domains with well-defined, well-articulated symbol systems—more problem-solving than problem-finding, if you like. There may be a biological basis for performance in these rule-driven creative domains. For example, when Howard Gardner developed his theory of multiple intelligences (1983), the idea that intelligence isn't a general trait but is actually seven distinct mental abilities, he believed that the existence of prodigies in a domain was evidence that the domain had a basis in the biological brain. Savants show us that you can't explain creativity without having a good theory of creative domains, and that creativity always has to be explained in the context of a specific domain.

The Evolution of Creativity

For the human species to survive for so many millennia, people must have been pretty conservative, good at imitating the behaviors of their parents. After all, the collective wisdom of the human species accumulated over time, and it wouldn't make sense for each generation to reinvent agriculture, language, and child-rearing practices. Evolution must have selected for children with the ability and desire to learn from the adults around them. At the same time, if our species always kept blindly repeating the same behaviors, we wouldn't have been able to adapt to changes in circumstances—the ice age or a drought, military attack, or a plague or infection.

Archaeologists associate the dawn of creativity with increasingly complex social organization, because most of the aesthetic objects found by archaeologists are designed to be worn—strings of beads and shells, brightly colored, and etched with repetitive patterns. Such objects probably communicated information about kinship or status. These decorative objects would only be necessary in a society so large that it would be impossible to personally know every other member. These larger societies also probably were characterized by increasing social competition, as distinct groups came into contact as they moved into new lands, and aesthetic objects could have served a function here as well (Henderson, 2003).

Most scientists agree that people who look like us had evolved by at least 130,000 years ago (Wilford, 2002). But it took much longer before these early ancestors first acted like us. Scientists disagree about when, where, and how these anatomically modern humans began to display creative and symbolic thinking. Some scientists believe that the anatomical brain was fully evolved as of 130,000 years ago, but the ability for creativity remained hidden until society evolved; others believe that some as yet undetected genetic advance resulted in a later change in brain wiring. This latter group argues for a *creativity explosion*, a sudden emergence of creative ability that occurred about 20,000 years ago (Pfeiffer, 1982) or perhaps 50,000 years ago (Klein & Edgar, 2002). These dates were originally proposed as a time of creative "explosion" because many of the cave paintings found in Europe date from then. These archaeologists hypothesize that some change suddenly occurred that led to the onset and rapid dissemination of painting—perhaps a biological change in the brain, perhaps a cultural innovation, disseminating through Europe like any other fashion.[4]

But most archaeologists reject the explosion theory altogether, and believe that art evolved along with the human species, in a gradual and progressive fashion. These scientists point to recent discoveries in Africa and the Middle East, arguing that they support an older, more gradual evolution of creative behavior, one that isn't centered in Europe. For example, Dr. Christopher Henshilwood (Henshilwood et al., 2002) found objects that were 77,000 years old in South Africa that were decorated with symbolic patterns, suggesting that their creators had the capability for symbolic thought and creativity. Lorblanchet (2002) examined hand-carved stones found in Africa dating back two million years, and noticed that many of these carvings were made using stones with particular aesthetic qualities—pleasing colors and textures. He concluded that these primitive people must have used aesthetic taste to pick out these stones rather than other, more ordinary ones.

The argument that creativity emerged suddenly due to a genetic change has been batted around in anthropological circles for several decades. But it's not widely accepted among neuroscientists; most scientists do not believe there is a single gene for creativity. Of course, the general cognitive functions of the brain are inherited; but proper operation of the complex brain involves a vast array of different processes and regions, and these emerge during the organism's development through a complex and long-term process of genetic expression that is heavily influenced by the environment (Pfenninger & Shubik, 2001; see also Elman et al., 1996).

Genetic Creativity

In *The Descent of Man*, Charles Darwin speculated on the evolution of art, suggesting that our sense of beauty is shared with other animals including birds and apes, and that music was the origin of human language. In contemporary times, the first scholar to focus on art and evolution was Ellen Dissanayake. Dissanayake argued that art must be adaptive in some way; otherwise, how could we explain its cross-cultural universality? Since all human societies make and enjoy art, it must contribute something important to our lives, and it's probably an inherited predisposition, selected for in Darwinian fashion. Dissanayake rooted the arts in two universal human activities: play and ritual. Many nonhuman animals also engage in play and ritual behaviors, providing additional evidence of their biological basis. She claimed that in primitive societies, the arts "are in most instances intimately connected to ceremonies or ritual practices" (1988, p. 74) and that even in modern European societies, an autonomous sphere of art for art's sake is a relatively recent innovation. The development of Western music was inseparable from the Christian liturgy; through the 16th century, visual art was connected with Christian practices as well; and drama had its origins in Greek rituals. Art, play, and ritual share many features; they're social, they involve make-believe and the use of metaphor, they're each fundamentally communicative, with their own special language in which otherwise incommunicable things can be said, and they each involve exaggeration and repetition.

What, then, is unique about human beings? After all, as Dissanayake noted, many animals—including birds and insects—engage in ritual behaviors, and chimpanzees have been taught to paint using brush and canvas (see figure 5.4). But in human art, specific information is communicated, and its content isn't predictable; it varies from one work to another. Another difference is that the human arts aren't instinctive; they're cultural activities that have to be learned.

Other evolutionary psychologists argue that art has no adaptive value and didn't evolve due to natural selection. Instead, they believe that art is a by-

FIGURE 5.4. A painting by Congo, a chimpanzee using a stiff-bristle paintbrush. Reprinted from *The Biology of Art*, by D. Morris Knopf, 1962, plate 19. With permission of Desmond Morris.

product of other adaptations; art products satisfy us because they push "pleasure buttons" that evolved for other purposes—the ability to perceive symmetry and color, for example. Evolutionary psychologist Steven Pinker argued that the arts take more time than other activities that could accomplish the same evolutionary functions; because they're inefficient, they couldn't have evolved solely for that function (Crain, 2001, p. 35).

These evolutionary perspectives have recently begun to filter into professional criticism in the arts. The new field of *biopoetics* uses Darwinian ideas to analyze literary works, for example, by analyzing the evolved cognitive structure of the brain to determine what makes us prefer one work over another (Carroll, 1995). For example, our preference for plot structures and narrative forms might be a result of natural selection.

You might expect artists to resist the idea that one of the deepest spiritual and personal elements of our being had its origin in our genes. After all, the evolutionary-psychological idea that human behaviors might be genetically based has been resisted by a broad range of both social scientists and humanists, because it seems to imply a deterministic view of human nature, the impossibility of development and change, and the undemocratic idea that individual differences may not result from the opportunities provided by one's environment, but might be hardwired in the genes. Herrnstein and Murray's 1994 book *The Bell Curve* was almost universally criticized for its claim that intelligence was genetically based and was passed on from parents to children.

But instead, Dissanayake's 1988 book *What Is Art For?* was welcomed by art educators, art therapists, and working artists because of her conclusion that the arts are a fundamental element of human nature and that the arts serve a basic human need. Through the 1990s, school districts with tight budgets frequently viewed the arts as an unnecessary frill, the first part of the school instructional budget to be cut, and Dissanayake's book seemed to provide an argument that the arts had value on par with the sciences. In 1991, the National Art Education Association invited her to give the keynote speech at its annual conference, and she received a standing ovation.

Is Creativity a Heritable Trait?

Inspired by the 1994 publication of Herrnstein and Murray's book *The Bell Curve*, there's been a lot of debate about whether intelligence is inherited. And with the recent growth of evolutionary psychology (Pinker, 2002), people have proposed that all sorts of human mental abilities have genetic bases. Given all of this genethink, it's only natural that some people might wonder whether creativity is one of these genetically based, evolutionarily selected human abilities.

One of the best ways to evaluate heritability is through twin studies. To conduct a twin study, you have to find equal numbers of both monozygotic and dizygotic twins. Monozygotic twins are genetically identical, while dizygotic twins are no more alike genetically than brothers and sisters born at different times. Both types of twins are presumably subject to the same environmental influences during their developmental years, because both pairs of twins are born at the same time and raised into the same family. On many traits, we'd expect both types of twins to be more similar than two random people, because of the environmental influences of being raised in the same family. But the critical factor in determining heritability is that traits that are genetic should show higher inter-twin correlations for monozygotic than for dizygotic twins. If both types of twins are equally similar on a trait, it is generally thought not to be heritable and thus not genetic.

Barron (1972) administered a range of tests associated with creativity to just over 100 pairs of twins. Two groups of adolescent twins were used: one group of Italian twins from Rome and Florence, and the other a group of American twins studied at the Institute of Personality Assessment and Research (IPAR) at the University of California, Berkeley. Of the five traits measured that were hypothesized to be connected to creativity, only two of them showed evidence of heritability: adaptive flexibility and aesthetic judgment of visual displays (pp. 176–177). However, on the two traits thought to be most closely connected to creativity—ideational fluency (divergent thinking) and originality—there was no evidence of heritability.

Other twin studies have also found no evidence that creativity is heritable. Vandenberg (1968) found no evidence of heritability in divergent thinking scores. In perhaps the most comprehensive study, Reznikoff, Domino, Bridges, and Honeyman (1973) studied 117 pairs of monozygotic and dizygotic twins found through the Connecticut Twin Registry, which maintains a list of all multiple births in Connecticut since 1897. They administered a battery of eleven tests of creativity, including Mednick's Remote Associates Test and five of Guilford's trait measures. Despite the thoroughness of the method, they could not find any convincing evidence of a genetic component to creativity; of all 11 tests, only on the Remote Associates Test were monozygotic twins more similar than the dizygotic twins. However, they found that twins overall had more similar scores on all of the measures than random pairs from the general population. Because there was no significant difference between the two types of twins, the best explanation is that twin similarity results from their similar environment.

Creativity is not a heritable trait, and there's no single gene for creativity. We can't look to genetics for the explanation of creativity.

Creativity As Evolution

Prior to Darwin, people thought that the amazing complexity and beauty of the natural world could only be explained by the presence of an intelligent creator. The complexity of the human eye or hand was taken as evidence of prior design. But Darwin's theory was, above all, a theory of the creative force of impersonal evolution—his book was titled *The Origin of Species*, and in it, Darwin explained novelty without appeal to any intelligent organizing force, by showing how random changes were selected by their consequences—the faceless, distributed, and random process of evolution. The three-stage evolutionary process of blind variation, selection, and retention could explain all life on planet earth.

Darwin's theory of natural selection isn't such a bad theory of the creative process. The creative ideas that emerge from incubation are the "variation"; the evaluation stage provides the "selection"; and the execution of the work into physical form is "retention." This evolutionary theory of creativity was first argued in an influential 1960 article by Donald Campbell; he called his theory *evolutionary epistemology.*

The behaviorist B. F. Skinner also proposed an evolutionary theory of creativity, and he used that theory to draw a pretty radical behaviorist conclusion: "It is not some prior purpose, intention, or act of will which accounts for novel behavior; it is the 'contingencies of reinforcement'" (1972, p. 353). After all, Skinner reasoned, new species are created even though there is no intentional, willful creator behind their origin. So why should we assume that new ideas require purpose and intention? Referring to this theory of creativity, Skinner wrote, "For the second time in a little more than a century a theory of selection by consequences is threatening a traditional belief in a creative mind" (1972, p. 354). Behaviorism was often criticized for being unable to explain creativity; Skinner's ingenious response was to claim that creativity was only a myth anyway.

The main problem with the evolutionary metaphor is that it implies that the variation stage is random and unguided by the conscious mind. But in chapter 4, we learned that most creativity researchers think that the incubation stage is guided in some way—by conceptual structures, by association networks, or by unconscious processes of evaluation. And if incubation is guided, the evolutionary metaphor of blind variation and selective retention doesn't really apply. But because the nature of the incubation stage is not well understood, some creativity researchers continue to argue for creativity as evolution.

Conclusion

> You could know every bit of neurocircuitry in somebody's head, and you still would not know whether or not that person was creative.
> —*Howard Gardner* (*2001, p. 130*)

Biology is the smallest level at which we could explain creativity. Biology's units of analysis are genes, DNA, and specific regions of the human brain. In general, scientists agree that explanations at such lower levels of analysis are more general, more universal, more powerful, and have fewer exceptions than explanations at higher levels of analysis—like the explanations of psychology or sociology. It always makes scientific sense to start your study by attempting to explain something at the lowest possible level.

However, at present the biological approach cannot explain creativity. All of the evidence suggests that creativity is not coded in our genes. And decades of study have found no evidence that creativity is localized to any specific brain region; in fact, all of the evidence suggests that creativity is a whole-brain function, drawing on many diverse areas of the brain in a complex systemic fashion. And there is no evidence of a link between mental illness and creativity. To explain creativity, we need to look to the higher levels of explanation offered by psychology, sociology, and history, and we'll do that in part 3.

Thought Experiments

- Is your personality similar to one or both of your parents?
- Is your level of creativity about the same as your parents?
- According to your parents, did you show a special creative talent very early in childhood? Do you think you were born with that talent?
- Did your parents do anything while you were growing up to encourage your creative abilities? If your parents hadn't done those things, would you still be just as creative now? Or, if they had done more, would you be more creative now?

- Think of one of the most creative people that you personally know. Does he or she have any signs of mental illness?
- If you have a pet—a dog or a cat—can you recall your pet doing anything that you would call creative?

Suggested Readings

Becker, G. (2000–2001). The association of creativity and psychopathology: Its cultural-historical origins. *Creativity Research Journal, 13*(1), 45–53.

Campbell, D. T. (1960). Blind variation and selective retention in scientific discovery. *Psychological Review, 67,* 380–400.

Ludwig, A. M. (1995). *The price of greatness: Resolving the creativity and madness controversy.* New York: The Guilford Press.

Prinzhorn, H. (1972). *Artistry of the mentally ill.* New York: Springer.

Reznikoff, M., Domino, G., Bridges, C., & Honeyman, M. (1973). Creative abilities in identical and fraternal twins. *Behavior Genetics, 3*(4), 365–377.

Sass, L. A. (2000–2001). Schizophrenia, modernism, and the "creative imagination": On creativity and psychopathology. *Creativity Research Journal, 13*(1), 55–74.

Notes

1. This is not only an American fixation; Lenin's brain was removed by Soviet scientists after his death in 1924 for examination.

2. A notable exception is Stanford anthropologist Richard Klein; see note 4.

3. Arnold (1992, 2002) hypothesized that some of these creators suffer from porphyria. Arnold (2002) said, "There is no cause and effect relationship between insanity and creativity" and called Jamison's hypothesis "complete nonsense" (Arnold, 2002). He argued that Vincent van Gogh—one of Jamison's favorite examples—suffered from an inherited disease, porphyria, which is exacerbated by malnutrition, infection (from gonorrhea), smoking, and absinthe drinking; because these traits were quite common among artists, those with an inherited tendency toward porphyria would have manifested its symptoms (Arnold, 1992).

4. Richard Klein has recently argued that the discovery of the FOXP2 gene—apparently linked to linguistic ability—demonstrates that creativity may have also suddenly evolved with the mutation or emergence of a new gene (Henderson, 2003). FOXP2 seems to have mutated less than 200,000 years ago, the right time frame to potentially be a cause of the creativity explosion that Klein argues happened about 50,000 years ago.

CHAPTER 6

Computational Approaches

In October 1997, an audience filed into the theater at the University of Oregon and sat down to hear a very unusual concert. A professional concert pianist, Winifred Kerner, was performing several pieces composed by Bach. Well, actually, not all of the pieces had been composed by Bach, although they all sounded like they were. This was a competition to determine who could best compose pieces in Bach's style, and the audience's task was to listen to three compositions, one by Bach and the others by two different composers, and then vote on which was the real thing. Yet this information age competition had a novel twist: the audience had been told that one of the composers was a computer program known as EMI (Experiments in Musical Intelligence) developed by David Cope, a composer and a professor of music at the University of California, Santa Cruz. The audience knew that of the three compositions, one would be an original Bach, one would be a composition by Steve Larson—a professor of music theory at the University of Oregon—and one would be by EMI. For each of the performances, the audience had to choose which of the three composers had generated it.

The audience first voted on Professor Larson's composition. He was a little upset when the audience vote was announced: they thought that the computer had composed his piece. But Professor Larson was shocked when the audience's vote on EMI's piece was announced: they thought it was an original Bach![1] After the concert, Professor Larson said "My admiration for [Bach's] music is deep and cosmic. That people could be duped by a computer program was very disconcerting" (quoted in Johnson, 1997, p. B9).

The first computer was conceived by Charles Babbage in the 19th century; he called it the Analytical Engine. His complicated contraption of gears, pulleys, and levers was never built, but it caused a lot of Victorian-age speculation. Babbage's friend Ada Augusta, the Countess of Lovelace, famously wrote that "the engine might compose elaborate and scientific pieces of music of any degree of complexity or extent . . . [but] the Analytical Engine has no pretensions whatever to *originate* anything. It can do whatever we *know how to order it to perform*" (Augusta, 1842, notes A and G).

Like Lady Lovelace long ago, most of us don't believe that computers can be creative. If EMI seems creative, then many of us would attribute that creativity to programmer David Cope; after all, the computer is only following the instructions that Cope provided in his line-by-line program. Computers don't fit into our conception of creativity, the Romantic and new age idea that creativity is the purest expression of a uniquely human spirit, an almost spiritual and mystical force that connects us to the universe. And in fact, very few books about the psychology of creativity contain anything about these programs, which I call *artificial creators*.[2] I find this surprising; although I have many criticisms of artificial creators, they're without doubt some of the most intriguing and exciting developments among the individual approaches to creativity. In this chapter, we'll examine some of the most successful artificial creators, and we'll be one step closer to our explanation of creativity.

The Artificial Painter: AARON

Harold Cohen was an English painter with an established reputation when he moved to the University of California, San Diego in 1968 for a one-year visiting professorship. He worked with his first computers there, and after the experience he chose to stay in the United States and explore the potential of the new technology. In 1973, while Cohen was a visiting scholar at Stanford University's Artificial Intelligence Laboratory, he developed a program that could draw simple sketches. He called it AARON (see figure 6.1). In the decades since, Cohen has continually revised and improved AARON. AARON and Cohen have exhibited at London's Tate Gallery, the Brooklyn Museum, the San Francisco Museum of Modern Art, and many other international galleries and museums, and also at science centers like the Computer Museum in Boston (McCorduck, 1991).

Harold Cohen's system is the best-known and most successful example of a computer program that draws by itself. An ever-growing number of artists are making electronic art; recent years have witnessed exhibits and criticism (see

FIGURE 6.1. A painting by Harold Cohen's computer program AARON. Reprinted with permission of Harold Cohen.

Candy & Edmonds, 2002). Cohen trained AARON to create drawings by using an iterative design process; at each stage, Cohen evaluated the output of the program, and then modified the program to reflect his own aesthetic judgment about the results. We can see the history of this process in his museum exhibits: AARON's earlier drawings are primarily abstract, its later drawings become more representational, and still later, Cohen added color to what had previously been black-and-white sketches.

Some would say that AARON isn't creative, for the same reason that Lady Lovelace gave: because the programmer provides the rules. In fact, Cohen says that AARON doesn't equal human creativity because it's not autonomous: an autonomous program could consider its own past, and rewrite its own rules (Cohen, 1999). AARON doesn't choose its own criteria for what counts as a good painting; Cohen decides which ones to print and display. In one night, AARON might generate over 50 images, but many of them are quite similar to one another; Cohen chooses to print the ones that are the most different from one another (personal communication, January 14, 2004). To be considered truly creative, the program would have to develop its own selection criteria; Cohen

(1999) was skeptical that this could ever happen. Cohen's process of creating AARON fits in well with the lessons of Chapter 4: his creativity was a continuous, iterative process, rather than a sudden moment of insight or the creation of a single brilliant work.

You might say that the drawings aren't by AARON, that they are really by Cohen—Cohen, along with a very efficient assistant. And in fact, Cohen gets the credit for whatever AARON generates; when AARON sells a drawing, Cohen deposits the money in his own bank account. But attributing ownership and authorship to Cohen is a little too simplistic; it doesn't help us to explain the creative process that generated these drawings. If we hope to explain how these drawings were created, we have to know a lot about the program, and about how AARON and Cohen interacted over the years. Explaining artificial creativity requires new approaches, and raises new questions.

The Artificial Mathematician

The Artificial Mathematician (AM) program was developed by computer scientist Doug Lenat (1977, 1983). Lenat taught AM a hundred simple mathematical concepts, and then gave it about 300 general rules for transforming these concepts. These transforming rules include generalizing, specializing, inverting, exemplifying, and combining concepts. As AM runs, it plays around with the 100 starting concepts, using the transforming rules to add new concepts to the pool. Each new concept is evaluated to determine if it's "interesting," and if it is, it's further transformed. To determine which new concepts are interesting, Lenat gave AM another set of rules. These rules include the conservation rule, which states that "if the union of two sets possesses a property that was possessed by each original set, that is interesting," and the emergence rule, which states that "if the union of two sets possesses a property that was lacking in each original set, that is interesting."

Starting from the 100 basic concepts, AM has generated many valuable arithmetic ideas, including addition, multiplication, prime numbers, and Goldbach's conjecture. As a result, Lenat claimed it is creative. Lenat later developed a more advanced version of AM called EURISKO. It adds to AM the ability to transform its own rules, and it does this with a second set of rules describing how the main rules can be transformed. For example, one of these "metarules" lowers the probability that a given rule will be used, if it has been used already a few times without ever resulting in anything interesting. Other metarules generalize the basic rules, or create new ones by analogy with old ones. EURISKO has had some surprising successes. It came up with an idea for a three-dimensional unit for a computer chip that could carry out two logical functions simultaneously, and this idea was awarded a U.S. patent for its innovation. It also was able to defeat human players in a national competition of a battleship war game (Boden, 1999, p. 366).

Like EMI and AARON, AM raises interesting questions about creativity. In some ways, it seems to satisfy the basic definition of creativity—it comes up with products that are both novel and appropriate. For example, when it started it did not know about addition or multiplication, so its discovery of both of these is novel; and we all know how useful addition and multiplication can be.

However, experts disagree about whether or not AM is creative (Rowe & Partridge, 1993). The first and biggest problem is that AM generates a huge number of ideas and most of them are boring or worthless; Lenat has to sift through all of the new ideas and select the ones that are good. But as we saw in chapter 4, evaluation is one of the most important stages of creativity. A second problem is that during development, Lenat was able to keep adding new rules if he noticed that AM wasn't coming up with anything interesting. We'll never know how much of this sort of massaging and revising took place during the development of the program. After all, AARON makes good art today because Cohen spent 30 years revising the program to suit his taste. A third factor reducing its creativity is that AM allows Lenat to guide its processing, pointing out a concept that he thinks AM should explore more fully.

Yet like EMI and AARON, even AM's weaknesses can help us to explain creativity. We can learn a lot about human creativity as we examine how these programs differ from it. Artificial creators can help us to clarify our own definitions and conceptions of creativity.

Artificial Writers

Several computer scientists have attempted to write programs that can write literature or poetry. Although these writings won't win any prizes, they can help us to explain creativity.

For example, how would you explain the fact that programs that write poetry have been more successful than programs that write prose? It isn't because poetry is easier to write; it's because human readers are used to reading meaning into ambiguous poems. In other words, when we read a poem, we expect to be doing a lot of interpretive work, providing much of the meaning ourselves. As a result, the program doesn't have to be so good at writing meaning into the poem (Boden, 1999, p. 360).

Story-writing programs can't yet write prose that's artfully constructed or that's pleasurable to read. Instead, they focus on creating interesting plots, with characters that have motivations, and actions that make sense in the context of those motivations. These programs—like the pioneering TALE-SPIN program (Meehan, 1976, 1981)—start with scripts that represent stereotypical behavior, and character motivations and their likely resulting actions, including help, friendship, competition, revenge, and betrayal.

TALE-SPIN represents character motivations, but it has no concept of an overall narrative structure, or how those goals can best fit together to make an interesting story. It generates stories, but it has no ability to evaluate the resulting stories, or to modify them to satisfy some aesthetic criteria. Thus, like AM, it's missing the evaluation stage. A more recent program known as MINSTREL (Turner, 1994) makes a distinction between the overall goal of a good story and the goals of the characters; a character's goals may be rejected if they don't fit into the overall structure of the narrative. MINSTREL relies on 25 transformative rules called TRAMS, for Transform, Recall, Adapt Methods. Some of the most common TRAMS are "ignore motivations" and "generalize actor"; one of the less common TRAMS is "thwart via death." MINSTREL's stories aren't great, but they're not horrible, either; when people are asked to judge the quality of the stories—without knowing that they're computer generated—they usually guess that the author is a junior-high-school student.

MINSTREL has an extra stage of evaluation that's not present in TALE-SPIN. TALE-SPIN uses the characters' different motivations to construct plots, but those motivations often don't fit together to make a coherent narrative. But MINSTREL fixes this problem with an extra stage of evaluation; motivations are created for each character, but then MINSTREL evaluates them all to see which ones will work best to make a coherent narrative. But MINSTREL still doesn't contain the ultimate evaluation stage—it doesn't have the ability to examine the stories that it generates to determine which ones are the best.

The Artificial Orchestra

Artificial intelligence programmers have begun to realize that intelligence is not always a property of solitary individuals; collaborating groups are sometimes more intelligent working together than individuals working alone. This is reflected in the cutting-edge field of distributed artificial intelligence, "DAI" for short, in which developers program many independent computational entities—called agents— and then let them loose in artificial societies to interact with one another. What emerges is a form of group intelligence called *distributed cognition.*

This field has only existed since the mid 1990s, and in the last couple of years, these techniques are being used to simulate the group dynamics of collaborative creative processes. At MIT's Artificial Intelligence Lab, James McLurkin (2002) developed a robotic orchestra with 40 robots, each with a sound synthesizer chip (see figure 6.2). The robots worked together to make collective decisions about how to split a song into parts, so that each robot would know which part to play on its sound chip. This simulated orchestra didn't need a conductor or an arranger to play together; that would have been centralized cognition, and McLurkin's orchestra was a classic example of distributed cognition.

In 2003 at Sony's Computer Science Lab in Paris, a second virtual orchestra performed. Eduardo Miranda had developed a virtual orchestra with 10 computerized performers. But rather than perform an existing score, Miranda used the theories of distributed cognition to have them collectively create their own original score. Each player was programmed to be able to generate a simple sequence of musical notes. But more important, each player was programmed to listen to the other players, to evaluate their novel sequences, and to imitate some of them with variations. Miranda then left his virtual orchestra to "rehearse" for a few days; when he came back, the orchestra had produced haunting melodic streams. This was

FIGURE 6.2. James McLurkin's Robotic Orchestra. Photo courtesy of iRobot. Reprinted with permission.

collaborative, distributed creativity; the melodies were created by a group of 10 virtual players, independent agents that worked together to create (Huang, 2003).

Creativity researchers have discovered that creative work often occurs in collaborative social settings. These collaborative orchestras are based on these new research findings; distributed creativity simulates creative collaboration. With these exciting new developments, the computational approach is shifting away from a purely individualist approach.

The Lessons of Artificial Creativity

Whether or not you think these programs are truly creative, they can help us explain creativity. First, they allow us to simulate and test different theories of the incubation stage. Does incubation occur by guided analogy or by random combination? Try simulating both in an artificial creator, and observe the differences in behavior. Second, they allow us to explore in detail how the mental elements of the domain are structured and stored in the mind—again, by simulating each theory in a computer program and then comparing the results.

These programs also teach us by virtue of what they leave out. None of these programs models emotion, expression and communication, motivation, or the separate generation and evaluation stages distinctive of human creativity.

Criticism 1. Cognition and Emotion

Artificial creativity simulations are part of the computer science subdiscipline known as artificial intelligence (AI). Artificial intelligence is based on the claim that the mind is a computational device. AI limits its study of the human mind to cognition—rational, analytic, linear, propositional thought. These programs are especially helpful in understanding the cognitive components of creativity: analogy, metaphor, concepts and conceptual spaces, sequential stages, and transformative rules (see chapter 4).

But artificial creators don't model emotion, motivation, or irrationality. As a result, the best artificial creators can hope to do is to simulate those elements of human creativity that rely on cognition.

Criticism 2. Problem Finding

> Computers are useless. They can only give you answers.
> —*Pablo Picasso* (*Byrne, 1996, 2:623*)

We saw in chapter 4 that perhaps the most important part of creativity is knowing how to ask a good question; creativity researchers call this problem finding. But artificial creators never have to come up with their own questions; their human creators decide what problems are important, and how to represent the problem in computer language. Artificial creators simulate problem solving rather than problem finding (Csikszentmihalyi, 1988a).

This doesn't bother some AI researchers, because they believe that creativity isn't much different from everyday problem solving (see Simon, 1988). They argue that most creativity really is problem solving; after all, most of us don't experience problem-finding insights on a regular basis, and in fact, even genius-level creators don't find problems every day. But most creativity researchers believe that problem finding can't be explained as a type of problem solving; coming up with good questions requires its own explanation.

Criticism 3. Creativity Can't Be Algorithmic

Teresa Amabile (1983, 1996) argued that to be creative, a task can't be algorithmic (p. 35). An algorithmic task is one where "the solution is clear and straightforward," and a creative task is one "not having a clear and readily identifiable path to solution" so that a new algorithm must be developed before the task can be accomplished. As an example, Amabile said that if a chemist applied a series of well-known synthesis chains for producing a new hydrocarbon complex, the synthesis would not be creative even if it led to a product that was novel and appropriate; only if the chemist had to develop an entirely new algorithm for synthesis could the result be called creative (p. 36). Amabile's (1983) definition of creativity, although it predates most of the work on computational creativity, excludes the possibility of computer creativity, because computer programs are algorithmic by definition.

AI researchers would respond that this definition is unfairly limited; after all, it seems that many creative products result from algorithmic processes. Why shouldn't we agree that the chemist's new hydrocarbon complex is creative? And it raises a critical definitional problem: How can we know which mental processes are algorithmic, and which ones are truly creative? After Picasso and Braque painted their first cubist paintings, were all of the cubist paintings they did afterward just algorithmic? After Bach composed his first minuet, were all of his later minuets just algorithmic? Most of us wouldn't be satisfied with such a restrictive definition of creativity. Still, it seems that Amabile is on to something. If an algorithm tells you what to do—if you follow a set of existing rules to create—most of us would agree that's less creative than if you come up with something without using existing rules, or if you invent a whole new algorithm.

Criticism 4. No Selection Ability

Although these programs generate many novel outputs, the evaluation and selection is usually done by the programmer. But in chapter 4, we learned that the evaluation stage is just as critical as the incubation and insight stages. For example, many creative people claim that they have a lot of ideas, and simply throw away the bad ones. And researchers have discovered that creators with high productivity are the ones who generate the most creative products.

Lenat's AM math theorem program generates a lot of ideas that mathematicians think are boring and worthless (Boden, 1999, p. 365). But AM doesn't have to select among its creations; Lenat himself painstakingly sifts through hundreds of program runs to identify those few ideas that turn out to be good ones.

David Cope, EMI's developer, carefully listens to all of the compositions generated by EMI, and selects the ones that he thinks sound most like the composer being imitated. EMI itself has no ability to judge which of its compositions are the best. When EMI is trying to imitate Bach, Cope said that one in four of the program runs generates a pretty good composition. However, Bach is easier for EMI to imitate well than some other composers; the ratio for Beethoven is one good composition out of every 60 or 70 (Johnson, 1997).

This limitation helps us to understand the importance of evaluation and selection in the creative process. Our creativity myths emphasize the unconscious incubation stage and the moment of insight; we tend to neglect the hard conscious work of evaluation and elaboration. Artificial creators show us how important evaluation and elaboration really are. Evaluation often goes hand-in-hand with the execution and elaboration of an insight; yet artificial creators never "execute" in the embodied way that a human creator does—hands-on work with paints and brushes, or trying out a melody on a piano to see how it works. Evaluation can't be done effectively without a deep understanding of the domain—the conventions and the language of a creative domain, and the history that resulted in the body of existing works that is known and is shared knowledge among creators in the area. In our creativity myths, the domain isn't that important; we tend to think that conventions are constraints that limit the individual's creativity.

Because artificial creators don't evaluate and elaborate their own creations, they represent an idealist theory of creativity instead of an action theory (chapter 4). Yet scientists believe that the idealist theory is wrong; evaluation and elaboration play central roles in human creativity. Artificial creators can simulate divergent thinking, insight, and novelty, but these are only half of human creativity; evaluation, selection, and execution are equally important.

Criticism 5. What About the Development Process?

These developers rarely analyze their own debugging and development process. But typically, early versions of a program produce many unacceptable or uncreative outputs, and the programmer has to revise the program so that these don't happen in later versions of the software. Only by becoming familiar with the development cycle of the program—with how the programmers sculpt and massage its behavior through successive and iterative revisions—could we really understand the role played by the human metacreator.

All of these artificial creators were developed by programmers who were also creatively talented in that particular domain. Donald Cope was a professional composer before he started EMI; Harold Cohen was a successful painter before beginning work on AARON. After all, only a talented musician would be able to "debug" the Bach-like compositions of EMI; a nonmusician wouldn't have the ability to judge which versions of the program were better. Only a talented visual artist like Harold Cohen could tell which paintings by AARON were better paintings; a non-artist wouldn't be able to select between different versions of the program, and choose a promising future path for development.

Because we never hear about the development process, we don't know how the programmer's creative choices are reflected in the program; it's easy to come to the incorrect conclusion that the programmer simply wrote a program one day, and out popped novel and interesting results. Programming an artificial creator is just like any other creative process—mostly hard work, with small mini-insights throughout, and with most of the creativity occurring during the evaluation and elaboration stages.

Artist-Technology Collaborations

> Imagine a scene: in a darkened room a moving image is projected onto a large screen. In front of it, several people are moving rapidly in different directions, waving their arms and simultaneously watching the screen. They might be laughing or chatting to one another or quietly observing the shapes, colours and sounds that are continually changing as if in reaction to the movements of those present. As a matter of fact that is exactly what is happening. In today's world of art and technology this is an interactive or "participatory" art experience. Together, artists and technologists have created spaces in which infra-red sensors detect people's movements

and by detecting the movements in the space, a computer generates visual images and sounds which are displayed so that everyone can see the artwork as it evolves.
—*Linda Candy and Ernest Edmonds* (2002, p. xi)

For over twenty years, visual artist Jack Ox has been using technology to translate music into visual images (Ox, 2002). Ox's GridJam system is Internet-based and supports collaborative musical improvisation among players at different geographic locations. Computer sound files and three-dimensional visualizations come together in a virtual performance space. Musicians can improvise together no matter where they are in the world; they can hear and see each other in the GridJam interactive environment. Building on such a virtual environment, it's a small additional step to add nonhuman musicians to the mix, or to write programs that transform each musician's riffs before they reach the other musicians. As with many of these new artistic uses of technology, the product that results is a hybrid creation, part human and part computer.

Computer technology is increasingly being used in creative ways by artists to create multimedia interactive works of art. In fact, sometimes these creations are called *art systems* rather than art works, because "system" emphasizes that the viewer participates in the creativity (Cornock & Edmonds, 1973). In art systems, the role of the artist is no longer to create a product; it's instead to create a set of rules that structure the relationship between the audience and the artwork (Candy, 2002, p. 263). This new form of visual art emphasizes interaction, participation, and collaboration.

The history of artists using computers in their work extends back at least to 1963, when the magazine *Computers and Animation* began its annual competition of computer art (Candy & Edmonds, 2002, p. 5). Many of these first computer artists were inspired by the writings of the Russian constructivists; in the 1920s, long before the invention of the digital computer, Russian artists like Malevich proposed that mathematical or geometric algorithms could be used to aid in the generation of visual art (Malevich, 1919/1968). In January 1965, perhaps the world's first gallery exhibit of computer art was displayed by Georg Nees at the Studio Galerie at the University of Stuttgart. These works were produced with a graph plotter, and generated by programs written by Nees. Later in that year, A. Michael Noll and Bela Julesz showed computer graphics at the Howard Wise gallery in New York. In 1968 in London, many of these works appeared in the Cybernetic Serendipity exhibition held at the Institute for Contemporary Art, curated by Jasia Reichardt, who later produced *The Computer in Art* (1971). The interdisciplinary science, art, and technology journal *Leonardo* was founded in 1968.

This was really cutting-edge work; in the 1960s, computers were big and expensive. There were no personal computers, and most computers were owned by big businesses and by the military. Few people predicted how much more sophisticated and inexpensive computers would become. By the 1990s, as powerful personal computers became widely available, artists' uses of technology increased dramatically. One of the main venues for this exciting new work has been the Creativity and Cognition conferences in England (conferences have been held in 1993, 1996, 1999, 2002, and 2005).

This type of creativity doesn't fit well with our creativity myths. Contrary to the classic image of the painter working alone in a studio, 62% of the artists who work with technology collaborate with others (Candy, 1999). Scientific studies of these artist-technology collaborations have found that they have a lot in common with the design processes of engineering teams. These collaborative teams use group creative processes; the creative process is a hierarchically organized, planned activity, an opportunistically driven mix of top-down and bottom-up strategies (see chapter 15).

To explain art systems like these, we have to analyze not only the mental processes and personality of the creator, but also the group dynamics and collaborations of systems of people. We need to combine individualist and contextualist approaches to explain computer creativity.

Conclusion

People seem to like computer art. Audiences at EMI concerts, and gallery viewers at shows of AARON's paintings react the same way that they do to human creations. When Dr. Cope sits at the piano and plays computer-composed Chopin for people, audiences respond just as they would to a human composer; they act as if a creative being is reaching out to them through the music. When people look at an AARON painting, they instinctively try to interpret what it means—what is the artist trying to say?

Computer art raises an interesting possibility: the viewer may contribute as much to a work as the artist does. After all, people also see images of Jesus in dirty windows and think their cars have quirky personality traits. Artistic meaning isn't only put into a work by the artist, but is often a creative interpretation by the viewer. In fact, many theories of art emphasize audience reaction rather than the creator's intention.[3]

Are these programs creative? They indeed generate novelty, even if they aren't aware that they've done so. But artificial creators are missing several important dimensions of the human creative process.

Evaluation. Artificial creators are never responsible for the evaluation stage of the creative process. The programmers decide when the program has discovered something interesting; many times when such a program runs, nothing interesting results. These computer runs are discarded and never reported. In contrast, human creators have lots of ideas, and an important part of the creative process is picking the most promising ones for further elaboration.

Elaboration. Artificial creators come up with an idea and that's the end of their creative process. Their creative process matches the idealist theory—the theory that the creative process is complete once the creative idea has been conceived in the head (chapter 4). But scientific studies of creativity have revealed that's not the way humans do it. People have most of their insights during the execution and elaboration of the work; to explain human creativity, we need an action theory. Computer artists don't need to act in the world to create; they don't work the same way that human artists do.

Communication. Artificial creators don't have to communicate and disseminate their novel work to a creative community. Yet as we'll see in our examination of contextualist approaches in part 3, the communication stage is complex and involves immense creativity. Attempting to communicate a creative work often feeds back to fundamentally transform the creative work itself.

Artificial creators are interesting both for their successes and also because they show us the limitations of the individual approach to creativity. Artificial creators are weakest when it comes to the social dimensions of creativity. Because they don't have to evaluate, elaborate, or communicate, they don't contain the important conventions and languages that allow communication between a creator and an audience. Because they create according to an idealist theory, there is no creativity during the elaboration stage. In human creativity, the elaboration stage is often deeply collaborative, as we'll see when we turn to contextualist approaches in part 3.

Thought Experiments

- When you use a word processor to write, does that influence the type of writing that you do? In other words, do you write differently than when you write with pencil and paper?
- Have you ever used a computer program to draw, paint, design a Web site, or compose or produce electronic music? Does the design of the program influence your creative process, or affect the final created product?
- Would you say that the computer is a collaborator in your creativity? Or is it just a very complicated tool, like a pencil on steroids?
- Has your personal computer ever done anything that you didn't expect? Would you say that this unexpected behavior was creative?

Suggested Readings

You can view artworks by AARON, and download a free screensaver program that paints a new picture every time you start your computer, at: http://www.kurzweilcyberart .com/ (accessed 7/29/05).

You can listen to songs composed by EMI at David Cope's Web site: http://arts.ucsc.edu/ faculty/cope/ (accessed 7/29/05).

Boden, M. A. (1999). Computer models of creativity. In R. J. Sternberg (Ed.), *The handbook of creativity* (pp. 351–72). New York: Cambridge.

Candy, L., & Edmonds, E. (Eds.). (2002). *Explorations in art and technology.* Berlin: Springer.

Csikszentmihalyi, M. (1988a). Motivation and creativity: Toward a synthesis of structural and energistic approaches to cognition. *New Ideas in Psychology, 6* (2), 159–76.

McCorduck, P. (1991). *Aaron's code: Meta-art, artificial intelligence, and the work of Harold Cohen.* New York: W. H. Freeman.

Notes

1. Compositions by EMI in the styles of composers from Bach and Beethoven to Stravinsky and Webern can be heard at: http://arts.ucsc.edu/faculty/cope/ (accessed 2/19/04).

2. A notable exception is Boden's 1991 book *The Creative Mind*, republished in 2003 in a second edition by Routledge.

3. For example, German literary theorist Wolfgang Iser (1978) argued that a literary text provides only a rough guideline to the reader; the reader's job is to create an aesthetic experience by interacting with the text. Reader-response theorists also include even more radical literary theorists; most famously, Stanley Fish (1980) has argued that there is *nothing* in the text that is not put there by the reader (see chapter 11, pp. 217–218).

INTERLUDE 2

From Individual to Context

Scientists have discovered that creativity is one of those complicated topics that requires the contributions of multiple scientific disciplines. That's why we need the sociocultural approach to explain creativity. In part 2, the unit of analysis was the individual, and our levels of analysis included biology and psychology, with computation an important and relatively recent approach.

Most books about creativity are written by psychologists, and as a result, they often stop after describing individual approaches to creativity. The sociocultural approach goes further, exploring research in anthropology, sociology, and history. For example, psychological theories of creativity are based on our cultural conception of creativity as an individual trait. This individualist conception of creativity is dominant in Western cultures, but anthropological research has discovered that it's not universal (cf. Purser & Montuori, 2003). And historical research has discovered that the individualist conception of creativity is relatively recent, and wasn't common 500 years ago. These disciplines show that to fully explain creativity, we need to move beyond individualist perspectives.

In part 3, we'll learn about exciting new research into the contexts of creativity: the societies, cultures, and historical periods where individual creativity takes place. Individual-level explanations are the most important component of the explanation of creativity, and that's why I started the book with them. But individuals always create in contexts, and a better understanding of those contexts is essential to a complete explanation of creativity.

Each individual is a member of many overlapping social groups. Each social group has its own network, with links among different members of the group. Each social group has its own structure, an overall organization that determines where each person fits in, and what role each person will play in the group. Sociologists are scientists who study these networks and organizations, and how human groups can accomplish tasks and perform at levels beyond the capability of the individual, and we'll explore the findings of their research in chapter 7.

Each individual is a member of a culture, with its own implicit, unspoken, and unwritten rules about how the world works, about what is important, about what categories are used to break up and understand the world. Creativity itself is culturally defined; some cultures don't even have a concept of creativity, and in many others, the concept doesn't look anything like our own. Anthropologists are scientists who are trained to delve inside a culture and capture its hidden, unspoken rules. Anthropologists have learned a lot about creativity in the last few decades, and we'll explore this research in chapter 8.

Finally, each individual creates as a representative of a certain historical period. This is harder to recognize with our own creativity, but it becomes obvious when we look back 100 or 200 years at the creative products that were generated in another era. You don't have to go back 100 years to see that creativity is always a product of its time; probably half of all U.S. college students, when presented with a pop song that they have never heard before, can identify the year when it was recorded simply based on its stylistic and formal features. We can't explain why all songs recorded in 1973 sound similar by studying musicians' motivations, cognitive processes, or personalities. We need another sort of explanation for the similarities in creative products within a given time period, a level of analysis above the individual, a way to explain the historical context of human creativity, and we'll explore the findings of historians in chapter 9.

We've prepared for this exploration by starting with the individual approaches. Although the chapters to come emphasize the contexts of human creativity, creativity doesn't exist without the individual. Each approach represents only one piece of the explanation of creativity; all of them have to be combined to explain creativity. Once we finish exploring the contextualist approaches, we'll move on to part 4 of the book, where we'll use the sociocultural approach to explain a wide range of creative activities.

Part III

Contextualist Approaches

CHAPTER 7

Sociology

No partial intelligence can so separate itself from the general mass as not to be essentially carried on with it. . . . The most profound thinker will therefore never forget that all men must be regarded as coadjutors in discovering truth.
—*Auguste Comte, Positivism (1842/1854, vol. 2, p. 522)*

Art is the social within us, and even if its action is performed by a single individual, it does not mean that its essence is individual.
—*Lev Vygotsky, The Psychology of Art (1971, p. 249)*

The great problems are handed on from generation to generation, the individual acting not primarily as an individual but as a member of the human group
—*Max Wertheimer (1945, p. 123n26)*

Another late night in another smoke-filled Chicago jazz club. It was 2 AM and pianist Howie Becker was having trouble staying awake during the chord changes. Part of the problem was that it was a Monday night, and as all jazz musicians know, Monday is the night for an open jam session, when musicians from many bands come together in a single club and take turns on the bandstand. An open jam starts with a house band—piano, bass, and drums—that provides the musical backdrop for a rotating series of visiting saxophone and trumpet players. And on this Monday night, Becker's band was the house band, and the club was filled with horn players—some of them professionals from other local bands, but others aspiring beginners who frankly didn't deserve to be sharing the same stage. Yet, the egalitarian ethos of an open jazz jam required that they be given the same opportunity as everyone else.

Becker was getting tired of Monday nights. Each horn player takes his turn on the stage, and then sits down with a drink to socialize. But the pianist has to play all night long, providing accompanying chords, or "comping," behind all of the solos. This can get pretty boring for a pianist, because there are only so many different ways you can arrange the chords while comping on a song. A typical soloist might play through the song eight times, followed by five or six other players. Add that up, and Becker was playing the same song almost 50 times. In fact, by 2 AM he had already dozed off *while playing*, and just like an interstate driver sometimes falls asleep at the wheel and nonetheless manages to stay on the road, when Becker briefly fell asleep, none of the other musicians noticed; he kept playing just fine.

Pianist Howie Becker is now a famous sociologist.[1] He played piano in Chicago in the 1950s to support himself while in the legendary sociology doctoral program at the University of Chicago. One of his earliest scientific studies was about the Chicago community of jazz musicians. And years later, in 1982, he published *Art Worlds*, an influential book on the sociology of art. In *Art Worlds*, Becker chose to focus not on the internal mental process of the artist; rather, he expanded the focus out to the contexts surrounding the artist. He examined the networks of support that are necessary for creative work to take place—the gallery owners, patrons, and educated viewers, the manufacturers of paints and canvasses, the educators at art schools. And perhaps most intriguing, he examined our society's conceptions of art and the artist, and why we call some activities art while calling other activities crafts or hobbies.

As a sociologist, Becker was also interested in the standards and conventions shared by an art world. Becker knew that the reason complete strangers could play together on a Monday night was because they all knew the same rules about how the music was supposed to work. For example, the first horn player to solo on a song might solo for five times through the song, or as long as eight or nine times through the song, depending how his inspiration moved him. But the musicians knew that the second musician, and every one after that, had to solo the same number of times as the first. Why? No one ever talked about it; this was an unwritten rule. Becker's insider interpretation was that if the second musician played fewer times, it would imply that he was a less creative musician, without as much inspiration as the first guy. On the other hand, if he took up more time, it might look like he was trying to show up the first guy, trying to prove that he had more ideas. This unwritten rule emerged from the deeply egalitarian ethos of the jazz community (Becker, 2000). Becker also realized that if he could keep playing even while he was asleep, the conventions of comping on piano had to be pretty structured. If jazz piano required true innovation and creativity every single moment, then certainly a person couldn't be asleep and do it.

Our conceptions of creativity are inspired by 19th-century Romantic images: the starving poet who can't afford to leave his barely furnished apartment; the genius composer with the stub of a chewed pencil, working out a symphony in his head while he lies in bed, sick and alone; or the visionary painter, out of step with convention and his peers, whose work never leaves his studio until long after his miserable death. But today more than ever, the most important forms of creativity in our culture—movies, television shows, big science experiments, music videos, compact discs, computer software, videogames—are joint cooperative activities of complex networks of skilled individuals. A jazz group is a perfect metaphor for these forms of collaborative creativity (Sawyer, 2003). With collaboratively created products, it is extremely difficult to apply our individualist conceptions of creativity (see figure 7.1).

It's ironic that the United States today has one of the most individualist conceptions of creativity in history, because perhaps more than in any other society, creativity in the United States is a collective, institutional activity (Garber, 2002). The creative products that U.S. society is best known for today, including movies, music videos, and videogames, are all made by organized groups of highly specialized individuals. To explain the creativity of complex collaborating groups, we need a scientific perspective that allows us to understand how groups of people work together, and how the collective actions of many people result in a final created product. The scientific discipline that studies complex cooperative networks of activity is sociology, and this chapter contributes to our explanation of creativity by drawing on sociological research and findings.

Group Creativity

> [Thomas] Edison is in reality a collective noun and means the work of many men.
> —*Francis Jehl, Edison's longtime assistant, referring to the fact that Edison's 400 patents were generated by a 14-man team, quoted in Kelley (2001, p. 70)*

In collaborative creativity, a product is created by a group, a work team, or an ensemble.[2] For example, the improvisations of a jazz ensemble are group creations. To explain jazz creativity, scientists focus on the musical interaction

FIGURE 7.1. A team of glass blowers completing a Venetian in the Dale Chihuly Studio. Chihuly stands at the back, overseeing the work. Reprinted from *The Origins of Creativity* by Pfenninger and Shubik, 2001. "Form From Fire," D. Chihuly, photograph by Russell Johnson. With permission of Oxford University Press Inc.

among members of the ensemble (Sawyer, 2003). Of course, each musician is individually creative during the performance, but the creativity of the group as a unit can only be explained by examining social and interactional processes among the musicians. No one can generate a performance alone; the performers have to rely on the group and on the audience to collectively generate the emergent performance. For example, in improv theater the actors always ask the audience members to shout out suggestions before they begin to improvise a scene, and many groups stop in the middle of a scene to ask the audience to tell them what should happen next (see chapter 13). As with all humor, the actors assume that the audience shares a large body of cultural knowledge and references, and in this way the audience indirectly guides their improvisation; it wouldn't work for the audience unless both actors and audience were from the same social group.

Like the great scholars who penned this chapter's three epigraphs—Comte, Vygotsky, and Wertheimer—many people have observed that groups are more creative than individuals. Advertising executive Alex Osborn (1953) coined the term *brainstorming* to describe his method of creative problem solving, and Gordon's *synectics* (1961) claimed that group thinking is always superior to individual thinking. Brainstorming continued to be a widely used technique right through the dot-com era of the late 1990s; Tom Kelley, founder of the famous Silicon Valley firm IDEO, proclaimed that "brainstorming is the idea engine of IDEO's culture" (Kelley, 2001, p. 56; also see chapter 16).

In the 1980s, sociocultural scientists began to examine how groups change over time.[3] Rather than focusing on specific individuals in the group, they treated the group itself as an entity that evolves. Group creativity involves distributed cognition—when each member of the team contributes an essential piece of the solution, and these individual components are all integrated together to form the collective product. Most of our culture's important creative products are too large and complex to be generated by a single individual; they require a team or an entire company, with a division of labor and a careful integration of many specialized creative workers.

Scientists have discovered that some groups are more creative than others (Larey & Paulus, 1999; Taylor, Berry, & Block, 1958). Groups are more creative than individuals when they have worked together for a while; when they share a common set of conventions and knowledge, and yet also have complementary sets of expertise; and when the organization rewards group collaboration. Groups are more creative than individuals when the amount of shared knowledge corresponds to how well the problem is understood. If the group has to find a new problem, it's better if they don't share the same background and expertise; if the group has to solve a known problem, it's better if they share more similar expertise (Sawyer, 2003).

Defining Creativity

In chapter 2, we learned that sociocultural definitions of creativity include two important properties: the product or process must be *novel*, and it must be *appropriate* to some domain of human activity. The sociocultural approach started with the 1983 appearance of Teresa M. Amabile's book *Creativity in Context* (also see Amabile, 1982; Hill & Amabile, 1993). Amabile examined the first-wave personality tests that measured an individual's originality, and she discovered that there was always an implicit subjective assessment built into these tests. Originality wasn't measured objectively; in these psychometric tests, originality was scored by a team of raters. Ultimately, these raters were applying their own criteria of appropriateness to make these judgments. Amabile concluded that social appropriateness could never be avoided in creativity research, not even by personality researchers who claimed to be focusing on individual traits and processes. She proposed a *consensual definition* of creativity: a product is creative when experts in the domain agree it is creative (Amabile, 1982, p. 1001; 1983, 1996, p. 33). If experts from a domain come to a consensus, it means the product is appropriate in that domain.

If creativity can't be defined without appropriateness, and appropriateness can only be defined by the people working in a domain, then the definition of creativity is fundamentally and unavoidably social. Appropriateness is defined by social groups, and it's culturally and historically determined (Amabile, 1982, p. 1010). This radical idea led to an almost complete break with personality trait conceptions of creativity, and a shift to the sociocultural approach to creativity.

The legendary creativity researcher Mihaly Csikszentmihalyi had always been interested in the great fine artists of the European tradition; he had a particularly strong interest in the Italian Renaissance of the 1400s. When he was a young child, he lived for a while in Venice, a few steps from St. Mark's Square. Later his family moved to Florence, where every morning he walked past Brunelleschi's elegant Foundling Hospital with its sculpted ceramic façade. As a teenager, he lived on the Gianicolo Hill in Rome, overlooking Michelangelo's great dome. Why did the city of Florence experience such a dramatic and sustained burst of creativity during the Renaissance? Csikszentmihalyi knew that the answer couldn't be strictly psychological; it would be highly unlikely that simply through genetic luck, a lot of creative people just happened to be born in Florence at the same time. He knew that explaining the Florentine Renaissance required a knowledge of historical, social, and economic factors. For example, the Italian nobles had a virtual monopoly on the lucrative trade with the Orient. They had a political structure—a multiplicity of sovereign states, principalities, and republics—that encouraged competition for the best artists and artworks. They had a high level of education among the middle classes, and this resulted in widespread support for the arts. They had the good fortune to be the second home of choice for expatriate intellectuals fleeing the crumbling Byzantine Empire to the east. Csikszentmihalyi's knowledge of this period kept him from reducing creativity to a purely psychological explanation. Like Amabile, Csikszentmihalyi realized that creativity is not only a property of individuals, but can also be considered to be a property of societies, cultures, and historical periods (Csikszentmihalyi, 1988b, 1990a, 1996, 1999).

During the 1980s and 1990s, creativity researchers refined the insights of Amabile and Csikszentmihalyi to develop the *sociocultural model* of creativity (figure 7.2).The sociocultural model contains three components: the person,

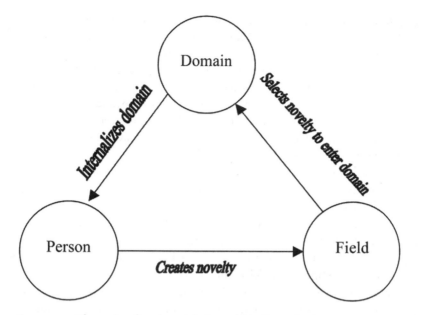

FIGURE 7.2. The sociocultural model of creativity (by author).

domain, and field. The person is the source of innovation; a person begins the process by developing a created product. But that alone cannot be called creative, because the product might not be novel, and it might not be appropriate. How can we judge a product's novelty and appropriateness? Like Amabile, creativity researchers today agree that researchers shouldn't decide that themselves; rather, they should look to the consensus of people that are experts in that creative domain: the field. The field determines whether a product is novel and appropriate. If the field decides that the product meets these criteria, the product enters the domain, where it's preserved and disseminated to other members of the field. Works that are rejected by the field do not enter the domain, and are often forgotten and destroyed.

The Field

Morris Stein was one of the most important first-wave creativity researchers. Stein had worked in business and was deeply familiar with marketing research on how new products are disseminated and adopted by consumers. In an early version of the sociocultural approach, he analyzed the intermediaries of the field that legitimize certain works as creative and deny that status to others—sometimes they're called *gatekeepers* (Stein, 1961/1963, 1967, 1974). Intermediaries include the patrons who provide emotional and financial support; experts like authorities and critics; and transmission agents who disseminate the work to the public, such as gallery owners, salesmen, advertising agencies, publishers, bookstores, and opinion leaders. Stein also studied how innovations are adopted by the public; he distinguished different categories within the audience—early adopters, early majority, late majority, and laggards—drawing on influential marketing research (Rogers, 1962).[4]

Csikszentmihalyi used the term *field* to refer to the group of intermediaries that determine what's accepted and disseminated. As Stein first pointed out, the field is a complex network of experts, with varying expertise, status, and power. After a person creates a product, it's submitted to the field for consideration, and the field judges whether or not it's novel, and whether or not it's appropriate. In science, the field would include the journal editors and peer reviewers of submitted articles, the heads of top departments at major universities, and the senior scientists that review grant proposals at government agencies. In painting, the field would include gallery owners, museum curators, editors of national art journals, reviewers at Washington funding agencies, and faculty at leading MFA programs. These influential gatekeepers determine not only which created products are published but also what types of creative work will receive funding. French sociologist Pierre Bourdieu's (1993) influential theory of cultural production emphasizes that the field is constituted by economic and power relations among subgroups, and analyzes creativity as a sort of market transaction between producers and consumers. Sociologists of science have argued that the field determines which creative events history will later judge to be significant discoveries, in a complex social and historical process of retrospective attribution (Brannigan, 1981; Schaffer, 1994; see chapter 14).

Members of a field tend to agree with one another in judgments of who and what is creative. In the IPAR study of architects (chapter 3), 40 top architects were selected and then rated by 11 editors of major architectural journals, and each of the 40 rated all of the others. The two groups' judgments correlated at .88, a remarkably high rate of agreement. As in architecture, in almost all creative domains the experts agree. Researchers have studied the effect of training on aesthetic judgment in many domains, and they've found that the more expert the pool of raters, the more in agreement their ratings will be. Naive, untrained evaluators of paintings provide ratings of quality that are all over the map. But when the same painting is evaluated by a group of art experts, it receives remarkably consistent ratings (Child, 1968). Trained experts agree because they have internalized the conventions of their domain, and these conventions include criteria for judgment.

The Domain

The domain consists of all of the created products that have been accepted by the field in the past, and all of the conventions that are shared by members of the field: the languages, symbols, and notations (also see Ward, Smith, & Vaid, 1997a). The domain of jazz is what allowed Becker's jam session to work. The domain of classical music consists of the best-known works composed by Bach, Beethoven, Wagner, Schoenberg, and perhaps a hundred others. The domain of Western music also includes the standard system of musical notation, the set of instruments that are manufactured and that musicians know how to play, and the conventions of performance practice for each genre and composer.

To become a member of the field, a person has to first learn everything about the domain. That's why every successful creative career starts with a long period of training and preparation. A composer won't create a brilliant symphony without first absorbing a huge amount of information about prior styles and genres—about standard song forms like sonatas and fugues; about the different capabilities and weaknesses of different instruments; about how to represent all of this on the page using musical notation. An aspiring jazz musician can't even sit in with a band without years of practice (Berliner, 1994), If you aren't prepared to play jazz, you'll be laughed off the stage and you won't be invited back.

Support for the Sociocultural Model

The sociocultural model bothers people who strongly believe in our creativity myths. They don't like the idea that creativity is socially defined. They point to examples of individuals whose brilliance was not recognized in their lifetimes, but who were later identified as creative, and they argue that provides evidence that the field is often wrong. They might point to the experiences of plant breeder Gregor Mendel or painter Vincent van Gogh,and say that neither of them was recognized until after his death. But in fact, quantitative measures across large numbers of artists and scientists reveal that it's rare for unrecognized creators to be reevaluated as brilliant after their deaths. Even commonly cited cases like Mendel and van Gogh include large portions of romantic myth (see chapter 14 on the Mendel myth, p. 271). Scientific and artistic reputation remains remarkably stable over time, even across centuries (Over, 1982; Simonton, 1984). For example, for any scientist, the number of citations to their publications stays the same from year to year (with correlations in the upper .90s); this consistency of reputation is found across generations as well. For example, in psychology, no one who was out of favor in 1903 was in favor in 1970, and no one in favor in 1903 had been rejected by 1970 (Over, 1982, p. 60). Reputation in the arts and humanities is also very consistent over time (Farnsworth, 1969, Rosengren, 1985, Simonton, 1984).

In all creative domains, a person's reputation is more stable over time than the reputation of any of the individual creative works that reputation is based on (Simonton, 1976). Creators with enduring reputations are those who've created a large body of diverse contributions, and their status doesn't rise or fall with the fate of any single creative work. If one work becomes dated or falls out of favor, another has high odds of being rediscovered. Often, the contributions for which historical scientists are best known today aren't those that earned them fame in their own lifetimes; for example, Einstein is now most famous as the father of relativity theory, but his 1921 Nobel Prize was granted for work he did in 1905 on the photoelectric effect.

The Audience

> All works of art or stylistic cycles are definable by their built-in idea of the spectator.
> —*Leo Steinberg (1972, p. 81)*

> The work of artistic creation is not a work performed in any exclusive or complete fashion in the mind of the person whom we call the artist. That idea is a delusion bred of individualistic psychology. . . . This activity is a corporate activity belonging not to any one human being but to a community.
> —*R. G. Collingwood (1938, p. 324)*

Every year, investors spend millions of dollars creating movies and Broadway plays that fail to connect with an audience, even though the gatekeepers in the field had selected them over hundreds of other ideas. Every year, scientific journals publish articles that will never be cited by other scientists and will have almost no impact on future research, even though those articles were selected by expert editors and reviewers. The intermediaries in the field play a critical role in evaluating creative works, but after they've made their choices,

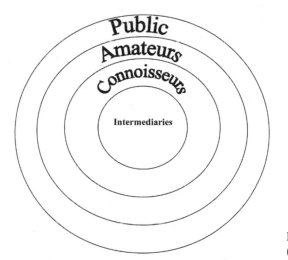

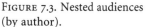

FIGURE 7.3. Nested audiences (by author).

the ultimate test for a creative work is whether or not it's accepted by a broad audience.

Sociologists have discovered that audience members are not all the same. They can be grouped depending on their level of expertise, and how connected they are to the creators who work in the field (see figure 7.3). We've already learned about the intermediaries at the center of the field. Works selected by these intermediaries then pass outward, to connoisseurs, amateurs, and the broad public.

Connoisseurs

The audience's inner circle is filled with the connoisseurs, those people who know the most about the domain. Connoisseurs have been socialized into the domain, almost as thoroughly as the intermediaries of the field. They play a disproportionately important role in the audience; they know more, they are more active, they are more opinionated, and less experienced people trust their opinions.

A large percentage of the audience at any dance performance have themselves had some training in dance; and as many as 15% of all theater tickets sold in New York are sold to students in drama programs (Becker, 1982, p. 53). Hans Haacke's surveys of art gallery visitors revealed that between 40 and 60% were either artists or art students (Haacke, 1975, pp. 17, 42).

Many successful artists and musicians have fans who closely follow their careers; these connoisseurs may remember more about the artist's past work than the artist himself. Fans expect similar work in the future, and they get angry when their favorite artist shifts styles. Popular bands know that the audiences at their next tours will want to hear the hits from their past albums; and if they dare to play new music, the fans will want those new songs to sound pretty much like the old ones. Bands ignore the fans at their peril; they know that their core fans are those most likely to buy their new CDs.

Stravinsky's comic opera *Mavra* was quite different from the ballets that made him famous, *Petrushka* and *Rite of Spring;* it was much simpler and based in folk music genres. The audience at the premiere of the work was disappointed not to hear the familiar Stravinsky sound (White, 1966, pp. 59–60). When American photographer Edward Weston, who was famous for still lifes and landscapes, started producing bitter and political images during World War II (like "Civilian Defense," a nude woman lying on a couch wearing nothing but a gas mask), his best fans became his most bitter critics (Becker, 1982, p. 291).

All artists are deeply aware of who their fans are and what they like. Most of them try to satisfy their fans; the fans have an influence on the creative process, even if the creator is alone in a room in the woods. Of course, an artist can choose to ignore the fans and do whatever he or she wants. But when artists choose to create works that their existing fans won't like, they know they'll have to struggle to connect with a new audience, and that's often a tough decision to make. In one way or another, fans play an indirect role in the creative process.

Fans of Unpopular Genres

If you like an art form that isn't widely popular—modern dance, polka, early silent films—you may very rarely get to see that art. A person who's interested in these marginal art forms has to be a little more active than a person who prefers mainstream fare (Becker, 1982, p. 67). If you like network sitcoms and Top 40 songs, you can be confident that you'll never lack for entertainment, because there are massive industries and large audiences that ensure such genres will always be easily available to you. But if your taste runs to obscure black-and-white sitcoms from the early 1950s era of television, or contemporary classical music, you may need to band together with like-minded people and actively organize to create opportunities to view these forms.

Fans of marginal art forms often form informal associations, because they realize that without their active support, the genre might die out altogether.

For example, the typical American city is lucky to have even one modern dance or contemporary classical music ensemble; in my home of St. Louis, we have one of each. But even in a midsized city like St. Louis, these groups get very small audiences, and never make enough money from ticket sales to be self-supporting. If serious fans want to be able to see a marginal art form, some of them have to donate significant money and become patrons, or else the group will fold. To take a different example, polka music is another marginally popular genre in St. Louis. Performances are not even advertised in the local weekly newspaper. Instead, all of the local fans subscribe to a newsletter and pay membership dues every year to ensure that they'll continue to have opportunities to hear polka. Other marginal genres include hypertext fiction, with groups organizing primarily over the Internet (see chapter 11), or obscure black-and-white movies, with film societies typically based at local universities.

Marginal art forms like polka and contemporary dance can only survive because fans of the genre have decided to provide financial support, free services, and their own social network. Such groups often engage in outreach efforts, trying to increase their membership by broadening their audience. You can't explain creativity in these marginal creative genres without understanding the important role played by the audience.

Amateurs

In the fine arts, amateurism is diffused through society. In France, 47% of all people over 15 years of age have practiced one of the fine arts—fiction writing or poetry, painting, musical performance, or dance; and 22% have done so within the last year (Donnat, 2002, p. 70). Amateur participation at museums, concerts, and theaters is highly correlated with educational level, much more so than with income. Amateur participation in the fine arts is also related to gender; among amateur dancers and writers, there are twice as many women as men, and even in music and painting, there are more women. Only with guitar and drums are there more men.

Most amateurs are exposed to their art while still in school; it's rare for an adult to take up a new creative activity. Some hard-core amateurs continue to paint or to play an instrument throughout life. Some of these amateurs are almost semiprofessional and may even continue to hope for some professional success with their hobby. A much larger group engages in the activity for relaxation; they don't stay in touch with what's going on in the field and they know it will always remain a hobby for them. And the biggest group of amateurs is exposed to the art while in school but give it up after college. Even though they don't actively engage in the art, because of their knowledge of the domain they're much more likely to attend performances or art events, and they're much more likely to enjoy and understand them.

A large pool of amateurs doesn't guarantee an audience for cutting-edge new works. Most amateurs are pretty conservative in their tastes. Among amateur painters in France, only 12% of them do any contemporary art; 76% of them do figurative art; 75% of them do landscapes and still lifes; and 16% of amateur painters say outright that they don't like contemporary art (Donnat, 2002, p. 73). The same numbers would probably result from an interview with amateur musicians about contemporary composers. Cutting-edge works tend to draw their support from the inner-audience circles: the connoisseurs.

The General Public

At the outermost circle of the audience is the general public. The public has very little power over what art gets recognized, distributed, and valued. Their only choice is whether or not they attend museums or concerts. Their interest can be measured only collectively, in mass numbers. But for many creative domains—like movies, TV shows, or music recordings—the size of the audience is a key measure of success. The intermediaries of the field often keep track of audience size and demographics, and this way the collective choices of the general public can have an indirect influence on future creative works.

Social Class and the Audience

> From information about an individual's age, sex, race, social
> background, and primary group membership, one could make
> a reasonable attempt at predicting his musical preferences.
> —W. Ray Crozier and Antony Chapman (1981, p. 268)

The kind of art you like tells people a lot about you. Since at least the 1960s, high school students have identified themselves by their musical preference. For example, part of adolescent self-identity in the 1990s was whether one was into rap or metal. These preferences become even more closely tied with identity in certain musical subcultures, such as the 1990s subcultures associated with goth, deadheads, ska, and rockabilly (Epstein, 1994). These choices aren't only a reflection of aesthetic preference; white suburban boys are drawn to rap because of its associations of tough, authentic, inner-city street culture, as much as for its formal musical properties.

There are huge class differences in consumption of art (Dimaggio & Useem, 1978). Cross-cultural studies have found that variability within societies is greater than variability across societies (Anderson, 1976; Berlyne, 1971; Ross, 1976). In other words, your social class is a better predictor of what you'll like than what country you grew up in. Working-class people often feel that certain forms of art are "not for us" and are directed at a higher strata of society. For example, a 1978 study found that blue-collar workers were underrepresented in art audiences; in a 12-month period, only 10% of a large sample had attended the theater, and only 4% a symphony concert. In general, the high arts—fine art, ballet, classical music—tend to draw interest from the upper-middle-class. Educational level is the best predictor of audience composition; occupation is the second best predictor; and income is the least effective predictor (Crozier & Chapman, 1981). People don't consume art simply because they can afford to; they consume art because they have been trained to do so, either by their families or by their schooling. French sociologist Pierre Bourdieu (1979/1984) argued that by consuming culturally valued creative products, individuals increase their store of cultural capital. Bourdieu's analyses of French society discovered correlations between a person's consumption patterns and the educational level of his or her parents, demonstrating that cultural capital is transmitted from parent to child through socialization practices.

Several studies found that higher socioeconomic status correlates with appreciation of classical music, the preference for complex paintings, and the preference for abstract paintings. There are three possible explanations for these differences: first, social-class differences might be related to personality differences, and it's actually the personality differences that account for the different preference; second, exposure to art and training in art increases the preference for it, and socioeconomic status increases the likelihood of exposure to high art; third, art preference is a social-class identifier, and during socialization, children learn what types of art people like them are supposed to like.

Some postwar researchers argued for the first explanation: these differences in attendance are due to differences in personality. Because different social classes raise their children differently, the children grow up with different personality traits characteristic of their social class. For example, middle- and upper-class families were once thought to raise children with a higher "preference for complexity," and several studies identified correlations between social class and the degree of complexity of the artworks preferred (Crozier & Chapman, 1981, pp. 259–262). Other researchers hypothesized that higher-income families raised children who would prefer abstract art, while working-class families would raise children who preferred simplicity and photographic realism (Kavolis, 1968).

The second explanation for social class differences in aesthetic preference is that different social classes provide their children with different opportunities to engage in art. Higher-income families are more likely to provide their children with painting or music lessons, and are more likely to take them to museums or concerts, and it's this familiarity that leads to social-class differences in adult preferences for art. The problem with this second explanation should be obvious to anyone who hated going to the museum as a child: in many cases, the activities that parents force on their children result in a decrease in preference for that activity. American children who grow up in regions that were heavily settled by German immigrants, like Milwaukee and St. Louis, are likely to hear a lot more polka music than children in other regions, but if anything this is likely to increase their dislike of polka. And staff workers at modern art museums, like gallery attendants, janitors, and security staff, don't gradually come to enjoy modern art any more than their working-class peers who don't have such exposure to art.

Both the first and the second explanations implicitly accept that high art really is better, and try to explain why it is that lower-class people don't get it. The personality-based explanations suggest that lower-class people score low in some important personality trait and this lack prevents them from appreciating high art; the exposure explanations assume that if you're exposed to high art, you'll realize its superior value and begin to appreciate it. And in fact, most of these studies were conducted in an earlier era, in a time when the reign of high art had not yet been challenged by the pop art of the 1960s, and by the increasing influence of popular culture and the media from the 1970s on. And most of these studies were conducted by researchers who themselves implicitly believed in the objective superiority of the high arts of the European canon. These explanations don't work if you don't think high art has any objective superiority, and they don't work to explain aesthetic preferences outside of high art, which in fact are the preferences that most of us have most of the time—a high school student's preference for jam bands, metal, or rap.

The third explanation is the one that most scientists now accept: children are socialized to learn that certain forms of art are associated with certain group identities, and expressing a preference for those forms is a way of expressing their identity as a member of that group. Since at least the 1950s, scientists have known that music plays a role in the identity construction of youth. Research connecting music preference and group identity in young people extends back to the 1970s and has confirmed the importance of group identity in musical preference (Chapman & Williams, 1976; Frith, 1978).

This third explanation actually has little to do with aesthetic preference per se, but rather with the desire to be seen to be consuming and enjoying a certain style of work. For example, think of the middle-aged executive who attends the symphony because all of his company's vice presidents also attend, or of the couple who attends the museum opening because "all of our friends" will be there. This third explanation also explains preferences for non-high art in a way that doesn't implicitly privilege high art. For example, think of the college student who attends the concert because everyone in her dormitory will be going, and who likewise would never consider attending the symphony because there will not be any other college students there.

Prestige Effects

When we like a work of art, we usually say it's because of something about the work itself. But it turns out that our judgments of artistic quality are often influenced by the prestige of the context—whether the painting is by a famous painter, or whether we see it hanging in the art museum. Scientists have tested the role of prestige effects by showing people relatively unknown paintings of similar quality, and then telling half of them that the painter is a great master and telling the other half that it's by a beginning art student. Or they might tell half of them that the painting is a masterpiece and the other half that it's a minor work. Or they might tell them different prices that the work sold for at auction.

Studies of prestige effects have a long history; in 1929, Farnsworth and Beaumont selected 10 paintings by unknown painters, and asked college students to rate them. For each painting, two alternative descriptions were prepared, one that reported that the painting was an important work by a great master that had fetched a high price at auction, and another that said that the painting was a relatively minor work by a student. The ratings of the pictures varied as predicted, according to the description. Similar effects have been experimentally reproduced in judgments of literature and music (see Crozier & Chapman, 1981).

There are individual differences in susceptibility to prestige effects; some people are more easily swayed by the consensus of expert opinion. Susceptibility seems to be inversely related to background knowledge; subjects without much knowledge of art are more sensitive to prestige cues (Michael, Rosenthal, & DeCamp, 1949; Mittler, 1976). Knowledgeable subjects are more likely to trust their own judgment and are more willing to be critical of the experts' consensus.

Prestige effects, however, have small effect sizes in these experiments, and they seem to emerge only when there aren't any other criteria that can be used to make aesthetic judgments (Mumford, 1995). For example, in these experiments the works to be compared are, by design, essentially of identical quality; people would be less likely to be swayed by prestige effects if the works were more obviously of different quality (Crozier & Chapman, 1981, p. 255).

The findings emerging from prestige effect studies can best be explained using a sociological approach. Sociology explains most of the difference in aesthetic preference by looking at factors like socialization practices and group identity. We don't need to know much about a person's individual psychology or personality traits to make predictions about what kind of art he or she will like; we can make pretty good predictions just by knowing the person's social situation.

Conclusion

In this first chapter of part 3, we've explored how sociologists and social psychologists explain creativity. It's a very different approach from the individualist approaches of part 2. Instead of assuming that all of the interesting things to explain are inside a person's head, sociologists assume that the most important things to explain are *outside* of people's heads—the social groups that we belong to; the networks of affiliations; the complex structures of modern creative work in large institutions; the complex and varied types of audiences that view, attend, purchase, and consume creative products; the nature of the market that governs the transactions between creators and consumers.

For a sociologist, there is no such thing as objective, timeless, true creativity; creativity can only be identified and judged within a social system. The social system includes complex systems of social networks (the field) and complex languages and systems of conventions (the domain). If you're committed to our individualist creativity myths, this approach to creativity might be hard for you to accept. But in fact, the sociocultural definition of creativity has been embraced by almost all of the scientists who study creativity. We can't explain creativity if we persist in thinking it's a trait of individuals.

Only a sociological approach can explain those creative products that are generated by large, complex groups of people—movies, videogames, computer applications—or by small, intimate ensembles like jazz groups or brainstorming work teams. Our creativity myths generally lead us to try to identify the creator who is responsible for such group products, but this is a fruitless and impossible search because there is no single creator for many of these modern creative products. Throughout the chapters of part 4, we'll see examples of creative products that are fundamentally collaborative, group creations.

Once we realize this fact, we can never go back to a purely individualist approach to creativity.

Thought Experiments

- A jazz performance, by definition, could not be created by a single solo performer. Think of some other creative activities that require a group.
- Have you ever worked on a creative project as part of a team? A high school or college play, a rock or jazz band, a dance ensemble? How did the creative process differ from when you work alone?
- Think of a close group of friends that you spend a lot of time with. Do you have any private jokes, or special slang words that no one else understands? Can you remember who created those inside jokes and terms, or how they were selected by the group for continued use?
- Have you ever been creative in a domain where you had no training or experience whatsoever? If so, how do you know you were creative—did someone in that domain's field tell you so?
- Think of the most creative thing you've ever done. How much training and experience had you had in that creative domain? How do you know it was creative? Were there any members of the field that examined your product and evaluated it?
- Have you ever had a supportive, collaborative relationship with a senior member of a field—an editor, a reviewer, a producer or director, a curator, a college professor? Or if not, do you think of those sorts of people as obstacles, and never as helpers?

Suggested Reading

Amabile, T. M. (1982). Social psychology of creativity: A consensual assessment technique. *Journal of Personality and Social Psychology, 43*(5), 997–1013.

Becker, H. (1982). *Art worlds.* Berkeley and Los Angeles: University of California Press.

Crozier, W. R., & Chapman, A. (1981). Aesthetic preferences: Prestige and social class. In D. O'Hare (Ed.), *Psychology and the arts* (pp. 242–78). Brighton, Sussex, England: Harvester Press.

Csikszentmihalyi, M. (1988b). Society, culture, and person: A systems view of creativity. In R. J. Sternberg (Ed.), *The nature of creativity* (pp. 325–39). New York: Cambridge University Press.

Sawyer, R. K. (2003). *Group creativity: Music, theater, collaboration.* Mahwah, NJ: Erlbaum.

Notes

1. He tells the story of falling asleep at the piano in Becker, 2000.

2. Some good reviews of creative collaboration include Abra, 1994; John-Steiner, 2000; Paulus & Nijstad, 2003; and Sawyer, 2003.

3. Such work includes the research of Kevin Dunbar, Rogers Hall, Ed Hutchins, and Barbara Rogoff.

4. Even prior to Stein, sociocultural theories of creativity had appeared in literary theory and aesthetics; for example, in the 1930s Walter Benjamin had argued that every historical situation alters and "translates" a work so that it can never again be what it originally was for the artist and his initial audience (as described by Marcuse, 1970).

CHAPTER 8

Culture

The light dove cleaving in free flight the thin air, whose
resistance it feels, might imagine that her movements would
be far more free and rapid in empty space.
—*Immanuel Kant, Critique of Pure Reason (1781/1900, p. 6)*

In the last chapter, we learned about the important role played by the domain
and the field. In our culture's creativity myths, the domain—the set of conventions, past works, and standard ways of working—just gets in the way of creativity. It's too constraining; the true creator ignores the domain and breaks all
of the conventions. But that's the wrong way to think about it. Instead, creativity researchers think of the domain as a kind of creativity language. Of course,
you have to learn a language before you can talk; it's impossible to communicate without sharing a language. In the same way, it's impossible to create anything without the shared conventions of a domain. Just because you use the same
words and grammatical rules as everyone else, you still manage to create a novel
utterance almost every time you speak. And just because the creator accepts the
conventions of a domain doesn't mean they aren't creative.[1]

Kant's dove can only fly because of the invisible support of tiny air mol-
ecules. There could be no flight without air. The dove might feel the air only
as resistance, and wish for the air to go away; but of course, in a vacuum the
dove would fall to the ground. The air is a metaphor for the creative domain;
many creators are frustrated by the constraints of the domain, but in fact,
without the domain they wouldn't be able to create at all. If you have trouble

expressing yourself to a friend, do you blame the constraints of your native language? Of course not; without that language, you couldn't even begin to express yourself.

Kant's air is a metaphor for culture, the subject of anthropology. When you think of "anthropology" your first image is likely to be of the archaeologist, digging for ancient bones or pottery in a remote desert environment. But archaeology is only one branch of the discipline of anthropology. In this chapter, we'll be concerned with another branch known as *cultural anthropology*: the study of living, active cultures. Cultural anthropologists often say that their job is to "make the familiar strange, and the strange familiar." Most anthropologists choose to study a culture that's as different from their own home culture as possible. They then use a research method called *ethnography* or *participant observation*, living as a member of the culture for at least one or two years. The goal of this experience isn't just to learn about the other culture; unavoidably, while learning about a radically different culture, they learn a lot about the implicit and unwritten assumptions guiding their own culture, thus "making the familiar strange."

Anthropologists use the word *culture* in a way that's related to common contemporary phrases like "popular culture," "mass culture," and "subculture." But it's a little more complex than that, and anthropologists have debated the definition of culture ever since Edward Tylor (1871/1889) proposed one of the first definitions in the late 19th century:

> Culture . . . is that complex whole which includes knowledge, belief, art, law, morals, custom, and any other capabilities and habits acquired by man as a member of society. (p. 1)

In the 1960s, a school of American anthropology known as *symbolic anthropology* developed a slightly modified definition of culture. Clifford Geertz (1966/ 1973) defined culture as:

> An historically transmitted pattern of meanings embodied in symbols, a system of inherited conceptions expressed in symbolic forms by means of which men communicate, perpetuate, and develop their knowledge about and attitudes toward life. (p. 89)

When you define culture in terms of symbols, culture becomes something like a language—and that's where anthropology connects to the sociocultural approach. A creative domain is like a small cultural sphere. And a domain is like language, in that you can't create anything without a domain even though most of the time, you're unaware of its importance. Cultures are systems of interrelated domains, and culture influences creativity primarily through influences on domains (Csikszentmihalyi, 1999, p. 317).

Beginning in the early 1980s, anthropologists began to examine how cultures transform and reinvent themselves. Cultural change always involves creativity. But this kind of creativity is very different from fine art painting or musical performance because it's a creativity of everyday life. In cultural creativity, novelty is a transformation of cultural practices and appropriateness is the value to a community. This approach is different from psychological conceptions of creativity because it emphasizes the creation of *practices*, not the creation of *products* (Rosaldo, Lavie, & Narayan, 1993).

Imagine an unschooled folk musician in a time long before the invention of sound recording. She gives repeated performances of the same song, a song that's never been written down. In each performance, she embellishes the melody a little differently; she might add a few words or modify a phrase to signify the context of the performance—the holiday, the audience members, or the time of year. And every other performer who sings the song adds his personal style to the performance. After a hundred years pass, the song will be different, even though no one person is responsible. Think of the variations in performances of the national anthem that precede high-profile sporting events; they're all different but we still recognize it as the same song.

An older generation of anthropologists and folklorists argued that these performance variations weren't significant. They argued that they were more like personal quirks than really different performances—like differences in handwriting or in a person's accent. But today anthropologists believe that the creation of novelty through these subtle variations is an essential part of many creative domains, particularly in performance (see chapters 12 and 13). After all, the difference between creating a completely new work and simply varying an existing one is a matter of degree.

Members of a younger generation select from the traditions they inherit, but then they elaborate and transform those traditions. In the normal, everyday process of cultural transmission, there's always both invention and imitation. Even when members of a culture believe they're not changing the traditions, they can't help changing, due to universal cultural processes that have been well documented by anthropologists. Once anthropologists realized that cultural transmission was not a mechanical replication of the past, they realized that creativity is always a part of culture (Bruner, 1993). Everybody in a culture participates in its reproduction and its evolution—not only special figures like musicians or storytellers, but everyone. Cultural creativity is found in the practices of everyday life—eating, sleeping, everyday conversation—not only in ritual or shamanic performance. Creativity is a common part of everyday life; culture can't survive without continued improvisation and embellishment.

Individualism Versus Collectivism

Anthropologists have documented an amazing variety of cultural practices and beliefs around the world. Of all of the ways to compare cultures, perhaps the most widespread is the individualism-collectivism contrast (Markus & Kitayama, 1991, Triandis, 1995). Collectivist cultures are those in which people are integrated into strong, loyal groups. These cultures value group goals and outcomes over the individual. The self is defined by reference to the group, and to one's position in it; there is not a firm separation between individual and group. In individualist cultures, in contrast, the ties between individuals are looser. Individualist cultures value individual needs and interests over those of the group, and they value personal outcomes and goals more than social relationships. The self is defined as an inner property of the individual, without any necessary reference to the group. Of course, these are differences in degree; even individualist cultures may have some collectivist elements, and vice versa.

Cross-cultural research has found that the U.S. culture is extremely individualist. For example, studies of family sleeping arrangements have found that over 90% of the world's cultures practice co-sleeping, in which the newborn child sleeps in bed with the parents until at least the age of two (Morelli, Rogoff, Oppenheim, & Goldsmith, 1992). When members of such cultures are told about the U.S. practice of providing newborn infants with their own cribs—and even their own rooms—they are horrified, and consider it to be tantamount to child abuse. When Americans are asked to justify the practice, they provide medical explanations, to be sure, but they also provide explanations that are telling in their implicit valuing of individualism: "He was old enough to be by himself" or "She was ready" (Morelli et al., 1992, p. 609). Many parents explicitly say that separate sleeping arrangements will foster independence in the child; in one interview study, 69% of parents emphasized that sleeping alone would foster independence and self-reliance (Morelli et al., 1992). A contrasting example is Japanese culture, which practices co-sleeping, and which is usually considered to be a highly collectivist culture. Japanese parents believe that their infants are born as separate beings; they must be encouraged to develop interdependent relationships with community members to survive, and co-sleeping is thought to be essential to that process.

In individualist cultures—like the United States—individuals emphasize how they are unique, different, and better than others. They tend to see themselves as separate from others. In such cultures, people believe that artists embody these traits to an extreme—artists are unique, more different, and more separate than the average person. In collectivist cultures, in contrast, people emphasize that they are ordinary, similar to, and no different from others; and rather than separateness, they emphasize their connectedness (Fiske, Kitayama, Markus, & Nisbett, 1998, Markus & Kitayama, 1991). And as we'll see below, in collectivist cultures, artists are perceived—and perceive themselves—very differently.

Works of art serve different cultural functions in individualist and collectivist cultures. In individualist societies, like the United States, some functions of art include:

- *Expression*: allowing the individual to express his or her inner experience;
- *Therapy*: providing an outlet; it's therapeutic to express through art;
- *Communication*: allowing the creator to communicate his or her unique vision or message to an audience;
- *Entertainment*: entertaining an audience during leisure time;
- *Enlightenment*: educating an audience, or raising spiritual awareness.

All of these functions derive from the individualism of U.S. culture. The functions of art are largely to support the individual, and to reward and acknowledge individuality.

In many small-scale cultures, art serves a more collectivist function: ritual effectiveness. If a shaman's carved mask doesn't fit in with the conventions of the domain, it's not perceived to be bad art, but rather it's perceived to be ineffective at accomplishing its function of controlling spirits. The Hawaiian ritual poetry known as *kaona* can only be composed by specialists because it uses veiled and hidden meanings that can only be obtained through special linguistic constructions. If the words are changed by a non-expert, it could make the poem ineffective, and perhaps even harmful (Kaeppler, 1987). The same is true of Hawaiian ritual dance; the dance has to be performed in exactly the right way, or else it won't accomplish its ritual function. In fact, if the desired outcome doesn't come to pass, members of such a culture typically attribute the failure to errors in performance.

The Lega are an African people who live in a dense tropical rainforest in Zaire (Biebuyck, 1973). At the center of their culture is the *Bwami* association, a cult that controls sorcery and initiation rites. During *Bwami* ceremonies, carved wooden animals are used by performers to communicate critical educational messages, but they aren't valued for their aesthetic form. What's most important is that the carving is exactly like the previous carving that served the same function, a "true equivalent or substitute of what existed before" (Biebuyck, 1973,

141

p. 178). The owner of a particular carving will trace its history by referring not only to the current object, but to all prior objects that it was designed to replace. Again, because ritual effectiveness is the key criterion, imitation and replication are emphasized more than the unique qualities of any given object, even though there's variation even among objects that are claimed to be exact replicas.

Different Artists

Up to the middle of the 20th century, many anthropologists held to theories of creativity that were derived from our culture's conceptions of the artist as a marginal outsider, a uniquely creative visionary. Anthropologist Victor Turner believed that artists were marginal people who attempt to avoid the stereotypical roles provided by their culture; he compared the artist to the prophet (1969). The cultural psychologist George Devereux likewise associated art with the outsider, arguing that art was a way for a society to stay healthy by channeling the least socializable impulses productively (1961). Economist Thorstein Veblin, in a famous 1919 paper, attributed the intellectual prominence of Jews in Europe to their marginal outsider status.

These scholars gave voice to one of our dearest myths about creativity: that the artist is a misunderstood outsider, ahead of his or her time, breaking the conventions that bind the rest of us, and remaining unconcerned about the social sanction that might follow. But new anthropological research has found that such beliefs, while common in individualist cultures, are not found in collectivist cultures. In our individualist society, the creator is considered to be the apotheosis of the individual, but in collectivist societies, the creator is considered to be the apotheosis of the group. In collectivist cultures, the artist is rarely marginal.

Between 1969 and 1971, anthropologist Marjorie Shostak lived with the !Kung San, a group living on the northern fringe of the Kalahari Desert in Botswana and Namibia (Shostak, 1993). While studying creativity in this culture, she discovered that art was central to !Kung San life; there were many musicians, healers, bead-weavers, and storytellers. To explore creativity in this culture, she began by asking members of the culture to direct her to their most creative members. But she found that this didn't work; when she asked them who the best bead-weavers or musicians were, her question was greeted by an embarrassed silence. When pressed, a person would simply list the names of every bead-weaver or every musician, claiming they were all equally "the best" (p. 56). She later found that the reason for their reticence was their egalitarian and collectivist culture. No one was supposed to be higher status or superior to anyone else.

On her second trip to the !Kung in 1975, Shostak asked people to judge photographs of bead-weavings that she had collected during her first field trip from 1969 to 1971. These weavings had already been judged and ranked by curators at the Museum of Primitive Art (now part of the Metropolitan Museum of Art) in New York City. Again, she found that people weren't willing to rank the weavings, even when they'd been done in another village and they didn't know the artist. Eventually she found one artist who was willing to evaluate the weavings in private with her, but that artist would not do this in public if members of her own culture were present.

!Kung San artists have to manage a difficult balancing act: expressing a unique individual voice, while avoiding any aura of superiority. Talented artists, just like talented hunters, are expected not to brag about it, and generally don't receive any reward or status for their skill. Shostak found that this created problems for powerful, idiosyncratic artists, because their persona didn't fit with the !Kung conception of the creative individual. She wrote about Jimmy, a !Kung musician whom she believed generated the most creative compositions. Many other musicians played his compositions, so they had clearly been judged as creative by other musicians in the culture. Surprisingly—given their egalitarian ways—everyone was willing to say that Jimmy was unusually gifted. Shostak explained that they were only able to acknowledge this status difference because he was so clearly an outsider. He had trouble finding a wife, he lived miles apart from any village, and by his own admission no one liked him; the name "Jimmy" itself testified to his outsider status, because almost no !Kung have Western names. But although he was recognized as a gifted musician, no one respected him, valued him, or considered him a real member of their group.

Jimmy had no acknowledged role in the !Kung culture because artists aren't expected to be the isolated, inspired, unique, convention-breaking individuals that we imagine them to be in the United States. To an American, Jimmy conforms well to our cultural conceptions of the artist. But among the !Kung San, there's no way to remain a member of the group while playing a role as the unique, idiosyncratic, gifted artist.

Shamans: The Original Performance Artists

Modern theater is often thought to have originated in shamanic ritual performance (see chapter 13). In all cultures, shamans face the tension between the uniqueness of their individual experience, and the need to publicly express their experience to the community. A shamanic vision of the otherworld is extremely personal, by definition; otherwise, any member of the culture could have had the same experience. However, the shaman must then communicate that experience through the conventional role of the shaman in that culture.

In many cultures, shamans wear masks during their performances, and it takes a lot of skill to carve an effective mask. The masks are designed to represent the spirits that the shaman encountered during his or her possession state, and help to translate his or her experience into something that the community can share. Although the vision is personal to the shaman, he or she must dramatize the experience and give it public expression (Layton, 1991, p. 195). Each culture recognizes a certain set of conventions for depicting spirits on masks, and a different set of conventions is often followed for ritual performance and for more popular, everyday celebrations.

These carved masks are obvious candidates for works of art, and they're collected and displayed by most major museums in the West. But taken out of their cultural context and displayed on the wall, it's easy to mistake them for the same kind of aesthetic object as the sculptures and paintings that artists in our own cultures generate. However, the motivations and processes whereby they are generated are different; the creative process is different; the conception of creativity is different; and the conception of the role of the creator is different.

Sometimes shamans carve their own masks, but more often they hire an expert carver to do it for them. The shaman describes his personal vision to the carver, and integrates established traditional conventions for depicting certain types of spirit. Sometimes the shaman carves the face of the spirit, and then lets another carver do the rest of the mask; sometimes the shaman sketches a quick outline on the surface of the wood, and the carver executes the design. But each carver then provides his own creative touch. The fact that certain carvers are commissioned is evidence that members of the culture think that some carvers are better than others. But the masks aren't chosen simply because they're beautiful; they're chosen because they're thought to be more effective at accomplishing their ritual function of controlling spiritual powers (Ray & Blaker, 1967).

Changing Conceptions of Primitive Art

So-called "primitive" or "ethnographic" art first came to prominence in Europe at the very beginning of the 20th century, and contributed a great deal to the foundation of modern art (Goldwater, 1938/1967; see figures 8.1 and 8.2). Painter Paul Gauguin personified the primitivism of modern art, writing that "you will always find nourishing milk in the primitive arts" and that "barbarianism has been a rejuvenation for me" (quoted in Goldwater, 1938/1967, pp. 66–67). These

FIGURE 8.1. (a) Pablo Picasso, *Nude*, 1907. With permission of Estate of Pablo Picasso/Artists Rights Society (ARS), New York. Copyright © 2004.

conceptions of primitive art were based on false ideas about primitive cultures that were widely held by Europeans at that time. They falsely thought that primitive societies were static and unchanging, and that they displayed no creativity because they emphasized tradition and convention. Their art was thought to be limited in its forms and unchanging in its patterns. Many European anthropologists and artists alike thought of this art as the collective expression of a

FIGURE 8.1. (b) A Senufo figure of the Ivory Coast, Africa. New York University, Institute of Fine Arts, Visual Resources Collection. Copyright © Walker Evans Archive, The Metropolitan Musuem of Art.

culture, and thought that individual creativity played almost no role in such art (see Goldwater, 1938/1967, Layton, 1991).

When Picasso and Gauguin first discovered the art of non-Western societies, they called it primitive art because they thought this art came from an ancient time in the past, because they thought these cultures hadn't changed in thousands of years. The term *primitive* implies a historical trajectory in which the origins and early development of our own Western art can be seen in these modern yet nonindustrialized small-scale societies. However, anthropologists have since learned that these contemporary societies have also undergone centuries of artistic evolution and are likely to be far removed from their own origins (Layton, 1991, pp. 1–3). Because culture is fundamentally creative, culture is always changing, even primitive culture. The term *primitive* is based on a false idea of the static, unchanging nature of these societies (Kuper, 1988). Based on decades of research, anthropologists of art now realize that the world is filled with diverse and independent artistic traditions, each of which has undergone the same centuries of independent evolution as our own. The paintings of the aboriginal Australians or the carvings of the Amazonian highland Indians don't come from some distant forgotten past time of the human species.

Scholars no longer use the term *primitive art* for two reasons. First, it's difficult to know what constitutes a significant innovation in the art form of another society. Even in Western cultures, creativity isn't opposed to convention and shared themes, but rather is always embedded in complex symbolic domains of creative conventions. A person who knows very little about baroque music may have difficulty distinguishing compositions by Bach, Vivaldi, and Mozart; and most Americans think that all polka sounds alike. Second—as we'll learn later in this chapter—it's common to exaggerate the degree of innovation of our own art forms, simply because we're intimately familiar with the domain and can detect even minor variations.

Innovation and tradition are not opposed, as in our creativity myth; they're always intimately and dialectically related. Some domains are more receptive to innovation, while others encourage consistency with conventions, and we can begin to look for broader cultural factors that might help us to explain these differences. We can then take these insights and use them to better understand these differences among domains in our own societies.

Conceptions of Creativity

In our individualist culture, we think that creativity is the expression of a unique individual. We believe that there are individual differences in talent that are probably innate. We believe that a created work is invested with the unique emotional and personal experience of the creator. And above all, we value innovation and breaking conventions. As a result, creators in our culture are likely to emphasize these aspects of their works—exaggerating the novel features of their work and talking about how they struggled with the limitations of the conventions of their domain. In part because they're expected to, creators talk about what they're trying to communicate with their work, and what personal experience led them to create this particular work. The now-required "artist statement" encodes this cultural belief; an artist can't get a gallery show without composing a statement specifying what inner state led to this work, and how he intends to communicate and express that state in this work (see chapter 10). And the legal system of copyright requires that a new work be original or else the artist is said to be plagiarizing or is required to pay royalties. Our system of copyright is another societal and cultural force causing artists to exaggerate the novelty of their work.

In collectivist cultures, conceptions of creativity are radically different. In these cultures, it's important for the work *not* to be different. In large part, that's because individuals in collectivist cultures emphasize that they are ordinary, similar to, and no different from others. And in small-scale cultures, artworks are supposed to be the same so that they'll be ritually effective. As a result, creators tend to emphasize exactly the opposite qualities of their work; they deny that the work contains any innovation, and they claim that it accurately represents tradition, even when Western outsiders perceive a uniquely creative talent.

The anthropologist Anthony Forge (1967) described the Abelam, a New Guinea culture in the southern foothills of the Prince Alexander Mountains, to the north of the Sepik River. They have an elaborate wood-carving tradition associated with the cult of the clan spirits, and Forge noted that the artist must work "within fairly narrow stylistic limits" (1967, p. 81). The carvings were designed to represent the clan spirits, and the artists insisted that their works were in the ancestral style. Yet Forge also found carvings being used that he was able to determine were almost 100 years old, and these were visibly different from the new ones. When Forge confronted members of the culture with these apparent differences, they ignored the differences or claimed that they weren't significant.

A similar pattern was found by folklorist Albert B. Lord (1960) in his study of South-Slavic epic poetry. Performers had always insisted that each story was performed identically on each occasion, and that the stories were told the same way that they'd been told by their ancestors. However, by using tape recorders, Lord discovered that these Serbo-Croatian epics were performed differently each time. The same song, sung by the same singer on multiple occasions, could vary in length by as much as several thousand lines. Even when the storytellers swore they were repeating verbatim the same story they had told a week ago, a close analysis of the audiotapes showed that the words used were actually very different, although the structure of the story—the meter and the rhyme—remained the same. When performers were confronted with these differences, they refused to acknowledge that they represented significant differences, and they insisted that the song was indeed the same on each occasion.

In individualist cultures, creators emphasize the innovation in their work, and in collectivist cultures, creators emphasize that their work is *not* innovative. But close scientific study has found that both of these views are partially wrong. Creators in individualist cultures draw heavily on conventions and tradition; creators in collectivist cultures display individual style and novelty in their works. Whether you live in an individualist or a collectivist culture, your culture's conceptions of creativity influence how you see creative works.

Continuity and Change

> Originality is the art of concealing your sources.
> —*Unknown quoted in Byrne (1996, 3:489)*

Some creators are more likely to use the conventions of a traditional domain, to make works that are recognizably similar to what has come before. Other creators are more likely to innovate, to emphasize novelty, to make works that contain elements not found in any prior works. In the United States, we value the innovator and disparage the traditionalist as derivative or imitative. Our individualist conception of creativity leads us to believe that whether a person's creations emphasize continuity or change, it must be because of some inner personality trait or mental processes unique to the creator.

But because collectivist cultures don't define creativity in terms of the novelty of the work, we can't explain why an artist emphasizes continuity or change by analyzing his or her psychological makeup; to explain such differences, we have to examine the culture of the artist. In the following sections, I'll discuss several different cultures and show how they provide incentives to continuity or incentives to change. We'll see that sometimes we can't explain creativity without appealing to culture.

Cultural Incentives to Continuity

In the traditional Asmat culture of New Guinea, men achieved status through headhunting (Gerbrands, 1967). Wood carving provides a vehicle to express the symbolism important to the culture in which men are thought to be spiritually related to trees, in part due to their creation myth that people emerged from carvings done by an ancient culture hero. Aesthetic carvings are of two types: ritual objects that are used once and then left to rot in the forest, and everyday goods that are frequently used, like the handles of spears and paddles, or musical horns used to warn of an impending attack.

Most men in this culture occasionally carve everyday objects, but certain men are recognized for the better quality of their objects. There's no formal training; some men are just drawn to it or have a talent for it, and teach themselves by observation and practice. Those recognized as better carvers are occasionally approached and asked to produce a carving for use on a ritual occasion—a drum, shield, or ancestor pole. These talented carvers don't occupy a distinct social role; they engage in the same daily activities as any other man. However, while they're creating a carving for a client, the client takes over the daily tasks that the artist would otherwise have performed, and also provides meals for the carver.

Although members of this culture have opinions about which artists are better, their decision of which artists are the best is not based solely on aesthetic criteria. Older artists are considered to be better, because older men are thought to be closer to the spiritual world portrayed in the carvings. Prestige at headhunting contributes to the status of an artist, because the rituals use the carvings as a way of increasing the effectiveness and power of the headhunters (Layton, 1991, p. 16).

The importance of ritual effectiveness is an incentive to continuity. Continuity is encouraged by several other factors: carvers don't occupy a distinct social role; everyone does some carving; and the carvers' reputations depend partly on non-aesthetic qualities such as age and prowess at headhunting.

The Asmat are perhaps closest to the older stereotype of primitive art as traditional, an expression of the spirit of the community, and unchanging. However, even in this culture there are individual differences in style and talent, and these differences are recognized and acknowledged by the Asmat.

Cultural Incentives to Innovation

Now let's examine a creative domain in a non-Western culture that provides incentives to innovation rather than incentives to continuity. During the 1960s, Marion Wenzel studied house decorations in a part of Africa known as Nubia, along the Nile River straddling the border between Egypt and the Sudan (Wenzel, 1972). The area was about to be flooded by the construction of the Aswan Dam, and the houses would be submerged forever. These decorative facades had only existing since the 1920s, and they'd first been designed by Ahmad Batoul, in the area north of Wadi Halfa. Other men had copied him; they competed with him by developing their own recognizable personal styles, and soon some of them were even better known than Batoul, even though he'd created the domain. In 1972, Wenzel was able to study cultural change by examining a range of villages along the Nile, because she knew that the genre had originated in the north, where Batoul had worked, and then slowly disseminated south along the river. Therefore, she assumed that the situation 75 miles to the south was similar to what the north must have been like 40 years earlier.

In the south, if a builder decorated a house after completion, he expected nothing more than a tip. It was rare to find an individual who was a full-time decorator; builders could make more money by building a house, and the women of the house could do the plaster decoration themselves. But by 1925 in the north, the occupation of plasterer had already become prestigious, a distinct profession. By 1940, the best-known decorators were successful enough to hire subcontractors to apply the plaster, so that they could focus on the decoration. These artists had no pressure to conform to any traditional role conception, because the status was completely new, and market competition drove both an increasing division of labor, and an increasing differentiation of style.

Market competition was an incentive to innovation. When the originator, Batoul, began to face competition from imitators, he developed several distinctive new motifs that set his work apart. This, in turn, inspired his competitors to introduce distinct motifs of their own (Wenzel, 1972, pp. 109–111). The competition for business encouraged artists to innovate and to explore the potential of traditional designs for creative variation. At the same time, the decorators had to conform to local expectations of how a house should look. For example, customers often wanted shining plates on the facade because they would "divert the evil eye" (Wenzel, 1972, p. 123).

In contrast to the Asmat culture—where cultural forces required continuity—in Nubia, cultural forces provided incentives to novelty and innovation. We can't explain creativity in these cultures by analyzing the personality traits of the Asmat and Nubian artists. To explain these forms of creativity, we have to look to the unique nature of the two cultures, using an anthropological approach.

Economic Status and Innovation

In many cultures, the degree of novelty in an artwork is related to the artist's position in a complex web of social and economic relationships. Forge (1967) described a painting of a ceremonial Abelam house that introduced a design variation: a narrow band of stylized leaves that were similar to the traditional pattern, but had some obvious differences. He wrote that "some of the older men were against it; [but] the two artists and their helpers were adamant—they were both of high reputation and no alternative artists were available . . . [and]

this innovation was much admired in the surrounding villages" (p. 81). Because the artists were highly respected and well established in the community, the elders eventually accepted the innovation. But if the artists had been beginners of lower status, they would have been forced to paint the house again and do it the way the elders wanted.

Silver (1981) studied modern Asante wood carvers, and found that the innovativeness of a person's style was almost completely explained by his status in the community. The village that Silver studied was established during the 19th century by the king as residence for a craft guild that supplied royal regalia, and to whom the king granted a monopoly on wood carving. But after conquest and colonialism, an open market emerged, and several different statuses of carver emerged. The highest status carvers were prosperous and well known. These established carvers often produced innovative work; although it reproduced traditional Asante proverbs, it used a nontraditional "naturalistic" style. The success of an innovation was unpredictable; because there was a greater market for conventional carvings, innovation was economically risky. Because of the risk, middle-ranking carvers didn't innovate; they had to create dozens of carvings every week simply to support themselves. However, the middle-ranking carvers adopted the successful innovations of the higher-ranking carvers, and their works kept evolving. The lowest rank of carvers were desperate to earn income, and had no prestige to fear losing. They typically created carvings for export to Europe, and this work imitated carving styles that were well known in Europe as "African" styles but were not authentic Asante styles; these carvers were never taken seriously locally.

Like the Asante wood carvings, many traditional crafts are no longer purchased by members of the culture—either because Western collectors have priced them out of the market, or because the traditional cultural practices that used them have been lost to modernity and colonialization (Graburn, 1976). Artists in many third-world cultures no longer produce art for local consumption, but instead for affluent Western collectors. These artists are under extreme pressure to create works that conform to Western expectations of primitive art: handcrafted objects that communicate to the Westerner's friends that the owner has traveled to an exotic place. Innovation is not rewarded by the international tourist market.

In all three of the cultures I just described—the Asmat, the Nubian, and the Asante—individual artists have different talents and styles, and an individualist approach could help us understand these differences. But in each of these cases, the cultural approach is also necessary to fully explain creativity. We need to understand a lot about the culture to explain the degree and the nature of the innovation that is generated by each artist.

Conclusion

Individualist approaches explain creativity by looking inside the person. In contrast, anthropology explains creativity by looking to the culture within which the creativity occurs. In this chapter, we've seen that anthropologists can explain a lot about creativity without knowing anything about the personalities or the mental processes of the creators. They can explain the degree of innovation or imitation in a given artwork—both how that varies between cultures, and how that varies among artists in the same culture. They can explain why a given culture has a distinctive conception of what an artist is, and how an artist works—by exploring whether that culture is individualist or collectivist. For example, the United States is extremely individualist, and anthropologists explain our creativity myths by showing how they emerge from our culture's extreme individualism.

Without anthropological research, we would never know how many different conceptions of art and styles of creative activity exist in the world. We might never know that our culture's conceptions of creativity are unique. We might never learn that the creativity myths of our individualist culture interfere with our ability to explain creativity scientifically.

Of course, even in collectivist traditional cultures, there are individual differences, and the psychological approach can help us to explain those differences. But individualist approaches can't explain creativity alone. They have to be contextualized within an explanation of society and culture. In many cultures, an artist's creative style is determined by his or her status or family connections. And in many cases, artworks can be explained by the economic system. These explanations limit the scope of individualist explanation, because we know that individuals can only vary within these broader constraints. To explain creativity, we must not only *include* these contextualist approaches; in many cases, we must *begin* with them.

Thought Experiments

- Have you ever traveled or lived overseas? If so, you probably realized for the first time how much living in the United States influenced your attitudes and approaches to life. Can you think of any of these differences that might relate to creativity?
- Think of a domain that you are particularly creative in. When you meet other people who create in that domain, would you say that your backgrounds are similar? Or does your background stand out somehow?

- Most people who read this book start out with the typical creativity myths of the isolated lone genius, ignoring convention, perhaps on the verge of mental illness. Did you? Where do you think you learned this conception of creativity? Do you still believe that it's basically correct? After all, deep-seated cultural conceptions are very resistant to change.
- If you still think your view is right, how do you explain the different conceptions of creativity held by other cultures? Are they just wrong?

Suggested Readings

Bruner, E. M. (1993). Epilogue: Creative persona and the problem of authenticity. In S. Lavie, K. Narayan, & R. Rosaldo (Eds.), *Creativity/anthropology* (pp. 321–334). Ithaca, NY: Cornell University Press.

Layton, R. (1991). *The anthropology of art.* (2nd ed.). New York: Cambridge. Especially recommended: Chapter 5.

Raina, M. K. (1999). Cross-cultural differences. In M. A. Runco & S. R. Pritzker (Eds.), *Encyclopedia of creativity, Volume 1* (pp. 453–464). San Diego, CA: Academic Press.

Rosaldo, R., Lavie, S., & Narayan, K. (1993). Introduction: Creativity in anthropology. In S. Lavie, K. Narayan, and R. Rosaldo (eds.), *Creativity/anthropology* (pp. 1–8). Ithaca, NY: Cornell University Press.

Shostak, M. (1993). The creative individual in the world of the !Kung San. In S. Lavie, K. Narayan, & R. Rosaldo (eds.), *Creativity/anthropology* (pp. 54–69). Ithaca, NY: Cornell University Press.

Note

1. Theories that compare creativity to language and communication have a long history, beginning with R. G. Collingwood (1938) and John Dewey (1934); see Sawyer, 2003 for a comparison. For an influential sociocultural elaboration of these ideas, see John-Steiner, 1985.

CHAPTER 9

History

Time is the greatest innovator.
—*Francis Bacon (1561–1626)* (*1868*, Essays,
in Works *Volume 12, p. 160*)

Paul Cezanne was one of the most important painters of the 19th century. Born in 1838, Cezanne had a long and productive career. Cezanne's paintings became more and more valuable throughout his life; his most valuable works were painted just before his death in 1906. The later paintings sell for more, and art professionals judge them to be more important (Galenson, 2001). This makes sense; after all, painters should become increasingly skilled with age, and their works should become increasingly more influential in the art world, and more valuable on the art market.

However, Cezanne's career pattern is not universal among artists. Pablo Picasso, born in Spain in 1881, also worked primarily in Paris. Picasso also had a long productive career, working right up to his death in 1973. However, while Cezanne painted his most important works late in life, Picasso painted his most valuable and most important works early in his career—while he was still in his twenties—and his output became increasingly less important over the rest of his life (see figure 9.1).

Explaining such differences is the job of the art historian. Art historians are trained to consider individual works and individual artists, often paying close attention to their financial and personal circumstances, the social and political context of their time, and the inner psychology of the artist that resulted in the

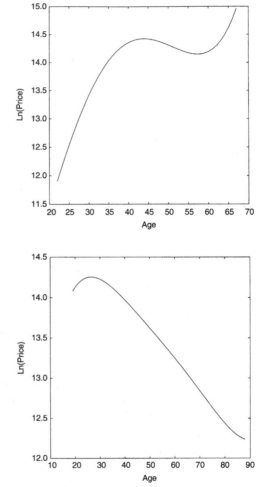

FIGURE 9.1. (a, top) Estimated age-price profile for Paul Cézanne (1839–1906); (b, bottom) estimated age-price profile for Pablo Picasso (1881–1973). Reprinted by permission of the publisher from *Painting Outside the Lines: Patterns of Creativity in Modern Art* by David W. Galenson, p. 15, Cambridge, Mass: Harvard University Press. Copyright © 2001, by the president and Fellows of Harvard College.

unique message and style of his or her works. Art historians generally focus closely on one artist or one period, and they explore how overall styles and genres develop over time.

When trying to explain the very different careers of Cezanne and Picasso, an art historian would typically proceed by closely studying the changes in style and technique across the two painters' careers, attempting to identify what led Cezanne's work to improve in quality while Picasso's declined. Art historians are also centrally concerned with the influence of one painter on another; paintings that have more impact on other artists tend to be considered more valuable, so the art historian might want to explore why Picasso's early works were more influential, whereas Cezanne's later works seemed to be. This explanation would typically be in terms of the formal properties of those works and how they could be shown to have influenced the formal properties of later works.

This is an *idiographic* approach, meaning that it focuses on the close analysis of single cases—individual artists and individual works. An idiographic explanation of the differences between Cezanne and Picasso can teach us much about the two artists and their careers. However, it turns out that the career-long patterns that distinguish Cezanne and Picasso are not unique to those two men; there is a deeper pattern at work that we can only see when we look at many artists at once.

Figure 9.2 contains data for 42 French painters, indicating their birthdate and the age at which they painted their most important painting—again, as valued by the market and by the experts. Figure 9.3 contains similar data for 57 American painters (both figures are based on data in Galenson [2001]). These tables show that the age at which artists paint their most important works varies depending on when they were born; for those born early in the 19th century, the most important works were painted late in life, but for those born nearer to 1890, the most important works were painted early in life. Cezanne, born 40 years before Picasso, is typical of his generation's painters, as Picasso is of his. The idiographic approach of the art historian is not equipped to explain these broader patterns. Although it's good for the in-depth analysis of individual painters and individual works, it's not well suited to the explanation of broader patterns that apply across many artists or across many historical periods.[1]

In recent decades, a few scholars of creativity have begun to use *historiometric* methods to analyze these broad patterns. Historiometry—also known as cliometry, after Clio, the ancient Greek Muse of history—is the numerical study of historical patterns. When you attach numbers to historical events, you can spot lawful numeric relationships across historical periods; historiometricians hope to identify universal historical laws, laws with explanatory, predictive, and perhaps even deterministic power (Martindale, 1990). All human inquiry, from art history to

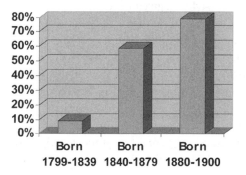

FIGURE 9.2. French painters, grouped by birth year, and the percentage of each whose peak career age was under 40 years, using data from Galenson, 2001, (by author).

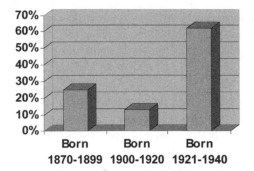

FIGURE 9.3. American painters, grouped by birth year, and the percentage of each whose peak career age was under 40 years, using data from Galenson, 2001 (by author).

particle physics, is divided between this sort of nomothetic study of lawful, generalizable patterns, and the idiographic study of unique events that don't repeat (Nagel, 1961, p 547). Because creativity research is a borderline, interdisciplinary study, it combines the approaches of both the sciences and the humanities, the nomothetic and the idiographic (Gardner, in Sawyer et al., 2003, p. 233).

In this chapter, we'll learn about historiometric explanations of creativity. Idiographic explanations of creativity are only relevant, by definition, to single cases; nomothetic explanations, because they apply across multiple cases, can explain broader patterns. If I used the idiographic approach in this chapter, I'd have to choose a few specific artists or scientists and delve deeply into their creative process and their productive output. But we'd have trouble generalizing from these few artists to develop a scientific explanation of all creativity.

Most art historians deny that there are universal laws of art history. They argue that historical events are not repetitive, but are individual and unique. Yet even those historians who prefer to pursue an idiographic approach agree that each individual creates as a representative of a certain historical period. This is harder to recognize with our own creativity, but it becomes obvious when we look back 100 or 200 years at the creative products that were generated in another era. After taking a couple of college courses in English literature, most people can identify, within 50 years or so, when a given paragraph was written, even without knowing its author. All of the music that was composed in the early 1800s can be recognized as being from that period, almost to the decade, by many people with expertise in classical music. A basic course in art appreciation equips one to identify the historical period and perhaps even the painter of paintings that one has never seen before. And over half of all U.S. college students, when presented with a pop song recorded since 1970 that they have never heard before, can identify when it was recorded within a couple of years (I've confirmed this in my own classes). Of course, none of the creators of these products were intentionally trying to sound like their historical period. Just the opposite; bands in the 1970s and 1980s were trying to sound unique and different, and at the time no doubt believed that they were doing something distinct from everyone else.

If you've ever attended an MFA show—which every art school requires its students to participate in before graduation—you're likely to get the impression of an incredibly diverse range of styles. But the creations of our own time always seem more diverse than they are. James Elkins, an art school professor, wrote about his reaction after he looked at graduation exhibition catalogs from decades ago.

> Art school catalogs from the turn of the century are filled with reproductions of student paintings that look like slavish copies of John Singer Sargent or Henri Toulouse-Lautrec, and exhibition catalogs from the 1950s show hundreds of students' works that emulate abstract expressionism. The lesson I draw…is that fifty years from now even the most diverse-looking work will begin to seem quite homogeneous. Works that seemed new or promising will fade into what they really are: average works, mediocre attempts to imitate the styles of the day. . . . In the oldest catalogs the students' work seems to be all done by one person, and in the newest, each student seems to be a lone innovator. (2001, p. 68)

How can we explain the similarities in creative products within a given time period? The explanation can't be found in the motivations of the creators, in their cognitive processes, or in their personalities. The individualist approach is the wrong level of explanation. We need to look above the individual, to the historical context of human creativity.

Creativity Over the Lifespan

The historiometric method has grown in use since the 1970s, largely under the influence of Professor Dean Keith Simonton of the University of California, Davis. Historiometry was, in fact, the first method applied to the study of creativity; the first historiometric analysis of creativity was published by the French mathematician and sociologist Adolphe Quetelet (1835/1969; also see Simonton, 1999a). Quetelet was one of the first scientists to use statistical methods in the social sciences. For example, he counted the number of plays produced by English and French playwrights over the course of their careers. When he plotted their year-by-year productivity on a graph, he saw an inverted-U shape. Their output increased up to a peak age, and then declined gradually. Quetelet also found that the quality of the plays that a playwright wrote in any given year was related to the total amount of creative output generated in that year.

The recent rebirth of historiometric method championed by Simonton has confirmed that these 19th-century patterns still hold for today's creators. Creative output tends to be an inverted-U function of career age, the length of time the individual has been working in the domain. Productivity in any given year increases as the individual continues to work in a creative domain, until it reaches a peak level; then, after some number of years, the productivity level begins to decline, and declines gradually through the remainder of the lifespan. Simonton (1988b) explained this with a formula based on the cognitive theories of chapter 4: he hypothesized an ideation rate that indicates the rate at which the incubation process will generate new configurations of mental elements, and an elaboration rate that indicates the rate at which these new ideas are elaborated into communicable form. The ideation rate is higher at the beginning of a career, when there are more free, unorganized mental elements. The elaboration rate is proportional to the backlog of new configurations that await elaboration. Simonton used these two rates to generate an equation for creative productivity at any given point in the lifespan:

$$p(t) = c(e^{-at} - e^{-bt})$$

Figure 9.4 shows a typical productivity curve generated by Simonton's equation, assuming that $a = .04$, $b = .05$, and $c = 61$, with t starting at the chronological age of 20. The equation generates the widely observed inverted "U" for career productivity, in this case with a peak in the early 40s. Figure 9.5 shows the actual productivity curves taken from the lives of creative individuals in different domains; they match the equation pretty well (data from Dennis, 1966).

These patterns are fascinating. After all, it's not obvious that there would be a late-career decline; individuals tend to become increasingly famous and to earn increasingly larger salaries throughout their careers. It might have been the case that individuals would experience multiple creative peaks, perhaps every five or 10 years.[2] Without the historiometric method, it might be hard to convince someone that career productivity was an inverted "U."

It's also not obvious that quality of output would be related to quantity, nor that an individual's best work would come in the year when he or she generates the most overall output; we usually think that quantity and quality are opposed, and that if a person is generating a lot of work then it must be slipshod or not fully thought through. An individual who works long and hard for years on a single project, investing a lot of energy and making sure everything is exactly right, might be expected to generate a more important work than his or her colleague who is churning out works every month. Yet historiometric data tell us that in the years

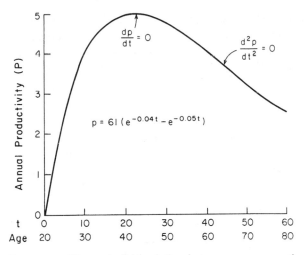

FIGURE 9.4. The periodical relation between career age, time, and annual production of creative ideas, *p(t)*, according to Simonton's (1984) model. In this figure, *e* is the exponential constant, the ideation rate *a* = .04, the elaboration rate *b* = .05, and the initial creative potential *m* = 305. Reprinted from *Developmental Review*, 4(1), pp. 86; Simonton, 1984, "Creative Productivity." With permission of Elsevier. Copyright © 1984.

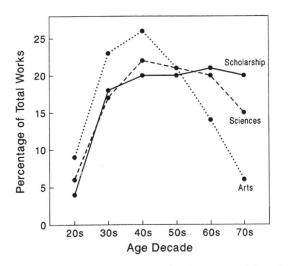

FIGURE 9.5. Typical age curves for three general domains of creativity, based on data from Dennis, 1966. Reprinted from *Psychology, Science, and History*, Simonton, 1990. With permission of Yale University Press. Copyright © 1990.

when an individual is generating the most products, he or she is most likely to generate his or her most important work. For example, the single best predictor of scientific fame is the number of times other scientists refer to the author's publications; and the primary predictor of this citation count is the scientist's total output. The correlation between overall career productivity and citation count ranges from .47 to .76 depending on the individual (Simonton, 1988b, p. 84).

In all of these studies, there are exceptions that prove the rule. For example, we can find perfectionists who devote all of their efforts to a small number of publications that are of high quality, and also scientists who publish a lot of worthless items (Cole & Cole, 1973). That's why we could never discover the underlying pattern without the use of a historiometric method that averages across many creators.

Every creative domain has its own characteristic inverted-U shape that tends to apply to all individuals working in that domain. Each domain has a typical peak age of productivity, the age at which the most significant innovation of a career is typically generated; and each domain has a distinctive shape to its "U" curve, with different slopes to the rise and decline. Physicists often joke to one another that if they haven't done Nobel Prize–winning work by the age of 30, they should hang up their hats, and in fact, historiometric analysis has confirmed that the inverted "U" for physics has a peak around the age of 30. Most other disciplines peak later in life; social scientists tend to reach peak productivity in their 40s or 50s, and humanities scholars in their 50s and 60s.[3]

These typical career trajectories can be explained with the sociocultural model of chapter 7. Remember that sociocultural theory argues that before becoming creative, individuals must become socialized into the field and internalize the domain. In this approach, individuals would not be expected to be productive or to generate important works until they'd fully internalized the domain. This explanation can account for the early rising part of the typical inverted-U career trajectory; output and importance increase as the domain is increasingly mastered.

Sociocultural theory can also explain why different domains have different peak ages. Csikszentmihalyi (1996, p. 39) observed that those domains that have a young peak age tend to be those with an intricate, highly articulated body of domain knowledge that is clear and logically consistent; in contrast, domains with an older peak age tend to be those in which the domain is more loosely defined, with greater ambiguity in its basic terms and concepts. This corresponds to the findings that mathematics, physics, and chess have many young masters, whereas history and philosophy have many older creators generating important works.

Simonton used his equation to explain these variations in the productivity curve across creative domains. The information-processing requirements for each domain are unique; each domain has a characteristic ideation rate, the rate at which new configurations are generated by the incubation stage, and each domain has a characteristic elaboration rate, the rate at which those new ideas can be elaborated into communicable form. For example, in theoretical physics and pure mathematics, both the ideation rate and the elaboration rates may be high, resulting in a career peak at a relatively young age followed by a quick drop (1988b, p. 72). Simonton (1988b) took the data generated by Dennis (1966) for productivity rates across the lifespans of hundreds of creators, and using different values of a and b in his equation, was able to replicate the documented career peaks in different disciplines: poets peak at a career age of 19 years, mathematicians at 26, and historians at 40 (note that because most careers don't start until around the age of 20, you can expect to add about 20 to these numbers to get the person's actual age at career peak). In some creative domains, productivity doesn't decline as much later in the career; those domains are characterized by a low elaboration rate, such that the new ideas "back up" and can never all be communicated (Simonton, 1988b, pp. 72–73).

Historians have observed that the peak age for scientific productivity was about 25 years of age in the year 1500, but by 1960 it was 37 (Zhao & Jiang, 1986). The increasing complexity of scientific domains seems to have caused this increase; this complexity would make the ideation and elaboration rates decline, and this results in a later career peak. As with our comparison of Cezanne and Picasso, only a historiometric approach could discover these broad historical shifts.

Creativity Across Time Periods

Historiometry reveals hidden patterns in creative output that are difficult to explain with an individualist approach. Of course, individualist approaches are an important part of the explanation of creativity, and they've been an important element in historiometry. But at the same time, the patterns that Simonton found make it clear that the individualist approaches cannot explain all of the data.

Perhaps even more intriguing than lifespan studies are historiometric analyses across many time periods; these analyses often reveal broad, long-term trends in creativity that hold true across individuals, across creative periods and domains, and even across many societies. Galenson's comparison of Cezanne and Picasso is a good example of the potential of such an approach.

Martindale began his historiometric study (1990) by outlining a sociological theory of creativity, a set of fundamental social laws.[4] He began by noting that society can tolerate only a small amount of novelty on a regular basis. However, creativity requires novelty. So what allows society to tolerate or even to encourage novelty, in spite of its general preference for rules and routines? Martindale proposed that it is societal habituation, a social version of a long-established psychological phenomenon—the gradual loss of interest in repeated stimuli. Habituation results in a pressure for novelty, and this demand is generally met by people who can supply the demand: artists. Novelty increases the arousal potential of an artwork, thus countering the society's habituation.

Just after a new style of art is created, the works in that style are relatively simple because the style itself is so novel that habituation is not a problem. Yet the longer the style stays around, the more the society will habituate to works in that style, and novelty and arousal potential will continue to increase. Eventually, the potential for that style to incorporate novelty is used up, and the only way to keep avoiding habituation is for the society to jettison that style, and to generate a new style.

Martindale associated arousal potential with the primordial content of a work, and with the primordial thought of the creator—based on the psychoanalytic concept of regression in the service of the conscious mind (chapter 3). Primordial thought is free-associative and undirected, and thus increases the probability of novel combinations of mental elements (1990, p. 57). Martindale associated primordial thought with the incubation and insight stages of psychological process theories of creativity, and contrasted it with conceptual thought associated with the preparation and elaboration stages (p. 58). Increased regression and primordial cognition should increase the arousal potential of a work. The works that are selected and valued at any given moment in history will be those that balance habituation and arousal potential in exactly the way that society requires at that historical moment.

Martindale tested his theory's predictions by coding the primordial content and arousal potential of works that were not only created in but also selected by society at each historical moment.[5] His theory predicted that (1) arousal potential will increase over time, (2) styles will change periodically, (3) primordial content will increase within each style, and (4) primordial content will decline when a new style is introduced. He tested the four predictions by examining French, British, and American poetry, European and American painting, Japanese prints, and other genres.

In his most ambitious analysis, Martindale evaluated these predictions by coding and analyzing over six centuries of British poetry, from 1290 to 1949. He began by dividing the 650 years into 33 successive 20-year periods, and selecting the top seven poets in each period by ranking their quality and influence on the basis of the number of pages devoted to them in the Oxford anthology of English verse (1990, p. 118). Martindale then randomly sampled poetry segments from poems written by each poet. To evaluate his first prediction, Martindale coded the arousal potential of each segment by using a formula based on the uniqueness and difficulty of the words found in the texts. Although this measure doesn't represent syntax, overall composition, or the meanings of the words—all of which could reasonably be expected to have an impact on a poem's arousal potential—Martindale's data nonetheless showed the predicted increase of the 650–year period (see figure 9.6).

Martindale's second, third, and fourth predictions were tested by using quantified measures of the primordial content of each poem. As with arousal potential, he defined primordial content by first developing a list of 3,000 words that were associated with primordial content in psychoanalytic theory (p. 92), and then he counted the number of those words that appeared in the writing of each poet. As with arousal potential, primordial content rose over time, but this time with periodic oscillations superimposed (see figure 9.7). By eyeballing the graph, Martindale discovered that the drops in primordial content corresponded to commonly agreed upon stylistic changes in poetry.

These are ambitious and fascinating studies. Any time all four predictions of a theory are supported across six centuries of data, you have to pay attention. The historiometric approach will never replace traditional idiographic art

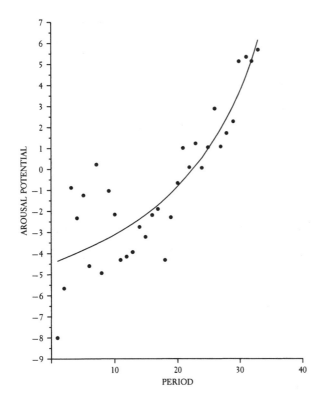

FIGURE 9.6. Martindale's measure of the arousal potential of a poem increases through 650 years of British poetry, from 1290 through 1949. Reprinted from *The Clockwork Muse* by Colin Martindale. Copyright © 1990 by Colin Marindale. Reprinted with permission of Basic Books, a member of Perseus Books, L.L.C.

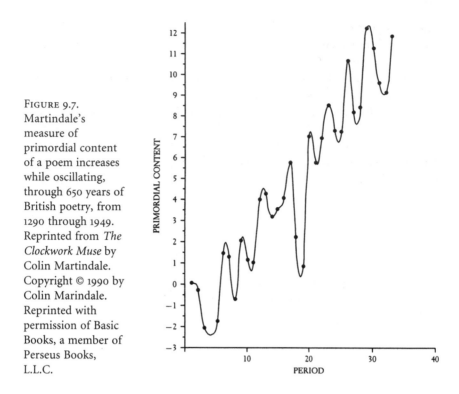

FIGURE 9.7. Martindale's measure of primordial content of a poem increases while oscillating, through 650 years of British poetry, from 1290 through 1949. Reprinted from *The Clockwork Muse* by Colin Martindale. Copyright © 1990 by Colin Marindale. Reprinted with permission of Basic Books, a member of Perseus Books, L.L.C.

history, but it can obviously be a useful partner in historical explanations of creativity.

Like Martindale, many historiometric researchers have examined the fluctuations in creativity across nations, cultures, and civilizations. They've found that historically creative individuals don't appear randomly in every year or decade; rather, they're clustered into periods of high creativity that are separated by much longer periods of creative stagnation. For example, Yuasa (1974) used archival data to determine the relative scientific "prosperity" of each nation from 1500 to the present. He defined a country as the world's creative center if the proportion of scientific output from a country was at least 25% of the entire world (p. 81), and he documented the following shifts in the center of scientific creativity:

1540–1610	Italy (Florence, Venice, Padua)
1660–1730	England (London)
1770–1830	France (Paris)
1810–1920	Germany (Berlin)
1920–	United States

The data within each of these golden ages form a productivity curve similar to that for the individual lifespan: an inverted-U shape with a single peak of maximum creativity. Political upheaval has often been suggested to result in a collapse of central control that then later leads to increased creativity, with a one-generation lag (Barnett, 1953). Yuasa likewise hypothesized that political revolution played an important role. For example, the French Revolution in 1789 and the preceding ferment led to France's period of dominance. But once a nation becomes a hub of scientific activity, a decline begins. Eventually, the potential of the scientific revolution loses its ability to generate new ideas. Just as with individual productivity, eventually the number of potential new configurations that can be derived from this initial set of cultural elements will decline.

For this pattern to be realized in individual productivity curves, the age of scientists should increase as the golden age progresses—because on average, older scientists are less productive. And in fact, several historiometric researchers have provided evidence that a country's science declines as the average age of its scientists passes 50 (Simonton, 1988b, pp. 100–101). As a result of these suggestive studies, some scholars have hypothesized that older scientists are less receptive to innovative ideas. This has been called *Planck's principle*, after the theoretical physicist who believed that the 20th-century developments in relativity theory and in quantum mechanics would only take hold after the older scientists, trained in Newtonian physics, died off: "a new scientific truth does not triumph by convincing its opponents and making them see the light, but rather because its opponents eventually die, and a new generation grows up that is familiar with it" (1949, pp. 33–34). But there's no empirical evidence for Planck's principle. Simonton reported that 94% of the variance in receptivity to a novel idea is due to factors other than a person's age (1988b, p. 103). There are many examples of very old scientists who immediately grasped the genius and truth of the latest innovations. Just because productivity drops doesn't mean that receptivity to the new ideas of others also drops.

The History of Domains

Are creative domains driven by a few genius creators, or does everyone in the field make a small but important contribution? In science, two very different answers have been proposed: the Ortega hypothesis and the great man hypothesis. The Ortega hypothesis (Cole & Cole, 1972) takes its name from a passage in *The Revolt of the Masses* by Spanish philosopher Ortega y Gasset: "Experimental science has in large part developed because of the work of men who were incredibly mediocre, and even less than mediocre" (1932, p. 97). Practicing scientists sometimes say that science is like building a wall, with each member of the discipline contributing a brick; in Ortega's view, those who are acknowledged with fame and Nobel Prizes just happened to be the ones who placed the last brick at the top of the wall. Newton famously said that he saw farther than other scientists because he stood on the shoulders of giants. This view has become newly popular among academics who reject great-man accounts of history in favor of more democratic and sociological accounts of scientific progress: "It is the aggregated contributions of thousands upon thousands of scientific foot-soldiers, junior officers, and men and women of middle rank that account for the great majority of scientific advances" (Waller, 2002, p. 158).

But there's some quantitative historical study that seems to support the great man theory. For example, in physics, the most frequently cited papers don't cite lesser known figures in the field; rather, often cited papers tend to cite publications by often cited predecessors, and similar results have been found for other scientific fields (Cole & Cole, 1972; Green, 1981; Oromaner, 1985). In any given year, around 35% of all existing papers are not cited at all; another 49% are cited just once, 9% twice, 3% three times, 2% four times, 1% five times, and the remaining 1% six times or more (Price, 1965). An extremely small percentage of all published papers has any impact on the field; based on citation counts, science seems more elitist than democratic.

However, this doesn't mean that only the top geniuses have any impact; many articles are written by mediocre scientists, simply because there are so many more of them, and by chance alone the odds favor that one out of this mass of articles will strike it big occasionally. Ultimately, citation studies can't definitively prove that the great man hypothesis is right; they don't capture the role of scientists who informally interact with the author at conferences or in lab meetings, although their names never appear on an important publication (see chapter 14).

Strengths and Weaknesses of Historiometry

Historiometry studies historical individuals whose work has passed the test of time (Simonton, 1999a, pp. 116–117). Because the work has passed the test of time, it's easier to resolve the basic question of who is creative; creative individuals and works are those that have made it into the history books, those that have been judged and selected by the field to have had a lasting influence after their creation. With contemporary works by living creators, it's harder to determine the creative value of the work. The downside of historiometric study of deceased creators is that we have limited information available; with living individuals, we can run experiments, or conduct extensive interviews, whereas with historical individuals we're limited by the historical record.

A problem facing all quantitative approaches in the social sciences is that the raw data of social life are not quantitative; social life is rich and complex. Nomothetic approaches have to somehow transform qualitative data into quantitative data, and this can sometimes be nearly impossible. Even in the best of circumstances, turning life into numbers means that some of the richness and complexity is lost, and we end up emphasizing certain aspects of the phenomenon and neglecting certain others. Critics can always argue that the researcher has chosen badly, transforming the wrong things into numbers and neglecting other important aspects of reality.

The benefit is that once the transformation has been accomplished, a wide array of statistical techniques are available that are fairly easy to apply. Inexpensive statistical software can be installed on any personal computer. These analyses don't require special expertise in art history or the history of science, and don't require the dedication of extensive and time-consuming research on specific creators. Once the numbers are in the computer, "one could study the history of any artistic tradition…without even knowing what the art form is, without knowing whether it is Chinese music or Greek vases" (Martindale, 1990, p. 14). Of course, whether or not this is truly a benefit is debatable; idiographic art historians may wonder how valuable an explanatory approach is, if you don't even have to know whether you're examining Chinese music or Greek vases.

The historical approach has the potential to identify broad, contextual findings that none of our other approaches would be able to explain. Whether or not you like the quantitative, number-crunching methodology, it changes the way you think about creativity. You can no longer think that Cezanne and Picasso are different just because they were born with genetically different styles of creativity, or because they had certain personality types. Now we know that Cezanne and Picasso are representative of entire generations; and to explain their differences, we have to explain why the generations are different, not only why two specific individuals are different. Knowing these patterns, you can't go back to a purely individualist approach.

Thought Experiments

- If I played for you a pop song recorded between 1970 and 2000, one that you had never heard before, do you think you could guess the year it was recorded? If so, why is that?

- When you hear a pop song from the 1920s, does it sound old-fashioned? Do you think it sounded old-fashioned back then?
- Think about something you've created—a song, a painting or drawing, a poem or short story. Think ahead to 30 years from now. In what ways will your creation seem dated?
- We generally think that we can be more creative when our lives are less pressured. But historiometric studies show that people tend to do their most creative, most important work in the years when they're busiest, when they're generating the most output. Has this happened to you? What does this finding tell you about the role of incubation and insight in creativity?

Suggested Readings

Galenson, D. W. (2001). *Painting outside the lines: Patterns of creativity in modern art.* Cambridge, Mass.: Harvard University Press, especially chapters 1 and 2.

Martindale, C. (1990). *The clockwork muse: The predictability of artistic change.* New York: Basic Books, especially chapter 4.

Simonton, D. K. (1997a). Creative productivity: A predictive and explanatory model of career trajectories and landmarks. *Psychological Review, 104*(1), 66–89.

Simonton, D. K. (1999a). Creativity from a historiometric perspective. In R. J. Sternberg (Ed.), *The handbook of creativity* (pp. 116–133). New York: Cambridge University Press.

Notes

1. Galenson explained these patterns by hypothesizing that the art world changed to increasingly value problem-finding creativity (which he called "experimental painting"); the 19th century, in contrast, valued "conceptual execution," the increasingly skillful implementation of a well-studied and well-worked idea, and these market forces encouraged problem-solving creativity. See chapters 4 and 10, where Getzels and Csikszentmihalyi (1976) found that problem-finding artists were more successful; their conclusion is that problem-finding artists are better artists. But Galenson's work suggests another interpretation: although our contemporary art market values problem-finding artists, this has not always been the case. Consequently, it's too simplistic to claim that problem-finding artists are more creative, as Getzels and Csikszentmihalyi do; rather, the picture is more complicated, and it seems that problem-finding artists

are only more valued in certain historical periods (and in certain cultures and societies, as chapters 7 and 8 suggest).

2. In fact, using more idiographic methods, Gardner has proposed a 10-year rule, which states that creators' significant innovations tend to be separated by 10-year gaps.

3. Note that the actual curves are in terms of career age rather than biological age, so that these numbers in terms of biological age are only approximations, because not everyone starts one's career at the same age.

4. His sociological concepts were named after psychological concepts but they are not psychological as he used them; rather, he applied concepts from the psychological domain to social groups (see Sawyer, 1993).

5. The necessarily sociocultural dimension of this selection process is implicit in Martindale's account; he didn't examine the sociological and historical processes that would explain why the works from a given historical period were selected and preserved for so many centuries.

Applying Individualist and Contextualist Approaches to Creativity

In parts 2 and 3, I've presented a wide range of approaches that scientists have used to explain different facets of creativity. Each of these seven chapters has reviewed explanations that are provided by a single scientific discipline, each with its characteristic methods and theories. These have been the most abstract chapters of the book. They've provided the scientific findings and the theoretical frameworks that we'll use as we move forward to explain creativity in specific domains. In part 4, we'll explore types of artistic creativity, ranging from painting to music and theater performance, and in part 5, we'll explore everyday forms of creativity, including science and business.

Throughout parts 4 and 5, I'll be considering not only the psychological processes that lead individuals to be creative but also the social and cultural properties of groups that lead the group to be collectively creative. Each chapter will be an interdisciplinary combination of individualist and contextualist approaches. That's why the modern science of creativity is the sociocultural study of creativity—these scientists move beyond psychology to incorporate sociology, anthropology, and history.

Part IV

Artistic Creativity

CHAPTER 10

Visual Creativity

When I teach the psychology of creativity at my university, painting is always the first example that comes up in class discussion—and it comes up more than music, theater, advertising, architecture, videogame design, Web site design, movie directing, or any of the many other creative domains of modern society. Painting dominates our discussions not because it's the most common or the most influential art form of today; my students are surrounded by music, movies, videogames, and Web sites, and they only occasionally go to art museums. The reason that painting always comes up is that it seems to fit better into our culture's individualist myths about creativity. More than any other creative domain, we imagine the painter working in isolation, without influence from the external environment and without concern for convention.

It turns out that these stereotypes about painters are wrong. In this chapter I'll show that explaining painting requires both individualist approaches and contextualist approaches. And of course fine art painting is only one of the many visual arts, so I'll move beyond fine art painting and discuss installation art, comics, videos, and movies. With these genres of visual creativity, our creativity myths begin to fail in very dramatic ways.

By expanding the discussion beyond painting, I'm simply acknowledging a shift in the art world that's been under way since at least the 1960s. It was in the 1960s that Roy Lichtenstein began painting comic strip panels and Andy Warhol began silk-screening publicity photos of movie stars. By 1970, artists everywhere were talking about the crisis in painting, and even worrying about the end of painting (Fry, 1970). By 1990 the boundaries between fine art painting and other forms of visual creativity were so fuzzy that the Museum of Modern Art in New York City mounted a show titled "High & Low: Modern Art, Popular Culture" (Varnedoe & Gopnik, 1990). If we limited our focus to fine art painting, our explanation would leave out most of today's visual creativity.

Who Is the Artist?

The village of Nathdwara, in the southern part of the Rajasthan province of India, contains the Shri Nathji temple. It's an important temple, founded in 1671, and most of the town's economy is centered on services for visiting pilgrims. For example, many of the visitors buy religious paintings, known as *Mewari* paintings, painted by a local community of about 150 traditional painters (Maduro, 1976). To a Westerner, the paintings might all look similar, but the Mewari painters can identify at least 18 different genres of paintings, each with its own target market and contextual use. For example, miniatures based on scriptures are sold to visiting businessmen, often for resale to Western tourists; *pichwais* depict Shri Nathji and are used in ritual contexts. Each painter is known for being good at a few specific genres, and some specialize exclusively in just one of the 18 genres.

During his 18-month stay there from 1968 to 1970, anthropologist Renaldo Maduro discovered that the painters of Nathdwara are a distinct caste; there's very little interaction between them and the other people in the village. And like all castes in India, membership is determined by birth. Not just anyone can be a painter; you have to inherit the profession from your father. One painter said, "Painting is what I have to do for a living. My forefathers did it, and so we do it. It is our tradition, that's all" (quoted in Maduro, 1976, p. 4). Only a small percentage of the artists report experiencing a sense of individual psychological growth or personal struggle in their artistic work—almost the defining feature of a painter in the United States.

To show how culturally specific our own conceptions of visual creativity are, it's always instructive to consider the conceptions of art found in other cultures, an anthropological approach that we first explored in chapter 8. There are individuals in the big cities of India that a Westerner would recognize as modern, Westernized painters. But in the smaller cities like Nathdwara in the more rural areas, you can still find traditional communities of painters, working in uniquely Indian ways.

Mewari painting is a home-based industry; everybody in the family helps out. The women and younger children mix the paints in the morning, and cut the paper to its proper size. Paints are still made in the traditional way, from local stone and vegetable pigments, even though chemical powdered paint is now available. Older children and men make the brushes from squirrel hair or horse hair, and they do the painting and the marketing.

Maduro identified three different levels of ability. At the lowest ability level, the *laborers* paint stereotyped portraits that imitate traditional religious paintings. Because there are so many pilgrims, even these relatively untalented painters find a market for their works. The *master craftsmen* are technically competent and are respected, but they don't create anything original. At the highest level of ability are the *creative artists*. They don't always attempt to be original, but they occasionally create original works. Their best innovations are copied by the lesser painters in the village. And when they're copied, these creative artists don't get upset, as a Western painter might; copying is standard practice among these artists, and being copied is a sign of respect and prestige.[1] After all, Mewari painters are generally anonymous; they don't sign their works. When they were interviewed, the painters said that the most important qualities of a painter were humility, self-effacement, and lack of self-assertion—nothing like the stereotypical New York art-world painter.

In Hindu tradition, all the arts and crafts were handed down to certain individuals by Lord Vishvakarma, and artistic work is considered a sacred ritual. Most artists talk about the significance of Vishvakarma in their work (Maduro, 1976, p. 75). The painters think that their own creative energy comes from a range of sources that is quite different from what Western painters would say: *prana* life-force from the subtle body, one of the three bodies that Hindus believe we all have; a special hereditary birthright; and an internal store of creative power, or *maya rupa* (p. 129). These Hindu beliefs—too complex for me to fully explain here—profoundly affect the way that painters think about their own creativity. The most creative painters often speak in spiritual terms; one painter said "Creativity? Oh, it's all *maya rupa*. . . everything. This *maya* that I have inside me is thrown out into my art. This is a sacred truth. . . . It is the dream of Brahman, and we painters contain a part of that force in us too because we are all part of Brahman" (quoted in Maduro, 1976, p. 141).

In chapter 8, we learned to be careful not to assume that traditional painting has been the same since the beginning of time. And indeed, Mewari painting has changed over the centuries. As recently as 100 or 200 years ago, the best paintings were sold to royalty, and most of the remaining paintings were sold to rural Indian poor and middle classes. But with the introduction of printing presses and lithographs, the general population stopped buying paintings; they could buy the mass-produced versions for much less. Today, most Mewari paintings are sold to Indian and foreign tourists, and the market demands are completely different. There's less value placed on originality and on traditional standards of craftsmanship. The mass tourism market has encouraged standardization; paintings have become smaller so that they can fit into suitcases; and painters increasingly purchase brushes and paints to free up more time for painting, even though the colors of the manufactured paints don't look exactly like the homemade ones.

Painting in Europe was once not so different from Nathdwara. First of all, paintings by old masters were rarely painted entirely by them; the master was the leader of a workshop or studio, with a group of apprentices working with him. Like the Mewari painter's family, the master's studio worked as a team. Before the industrial revolution allowed the manufacture of tubes of pre-mixed paint, European painters had to make their own paints and brushes. The master designed the composition, sketched in the rough outlines, and painted the parts of the painting requiring the most skill, like the faces of the central figures. Then the rest of the work was left to the apprentices, who painted the details of the clothing, the sky and the clouds, the buildings and furniture. We consider such a painting to be an authentic work of the master; but the creation of such a work is nothing like a contemporary painting. Today we expect a painting to be completely painted—every last brushstroke—by the artist whose name is signed at the bottom.

Because of the collaborative nature of the studio system, it's often difficult to attribute old-master paintings properly. Some apprentices started their own studios, and the hand of that apprentice is seen in the work of both his studio and his former master's studio. The concern with attribution reflects a contemporary conception of authenticity, the very modern idea that a painting has to be the work of a single isolated individual. We're more interested in attribution than the old masters were; back then, everyone knew that the master didn't paint every last brushstroke, and no one worried about it. Our fixation on attribution is an example of how a creativity myth—that paintings are the unique inspiration of a solitary individual—leads us to neglect the social networks and the systems of collaboration that result in many created works, including paintings.

In chapter 2, we learned that our contemporary conceptions of creativity are culturally and historically formed. For example, Western conceptions of visual art have changed dramatically over the centuries. Renaissance-era contracts made it clear that painters were thought of as technicians, not artists; for example, the contract often specified the percentage of blue and gold in the painting (see chapter 2, p. 13). And the idea that a painter should work alone is a recent one; in most cultures and most time periods, paintings were made by collaborative teams. In both the studio system of Europe and in Mewari painting of India, artists worked collaboratively.

Individualist Approaches

Mewari paintings are very different from today's Western paintings. They're collaboratively created and aren't expected to break with convention. In fact, European painting was quite similar until the last century or two; our contemporary Western conception of the artist as an inspired, solitary genius originated only in the early 1800s. Still, many of my readers will want to know how contemporary Western painters work. Because the first wave of creativity research was heavily influenced by our creativity myths, psychologists in the 1960s spent a lot of time studying the personality traits of painters, and I'll begin by reviewing these studies. Then, I'll move beyond the stereotype of the lone genius painting at a canvas, and I'll draw on contextual approaches to explain other genres of visual creativity.

The Personality of the Painter

During the 1960s, Dr. Frank Barron was one of the top researchers studying creativity, and he worked with Donald MacKinnon at the Institute for Personality Assessment and Research (IPAR) at the University of California, Berkeley. These were heady times to be studying creativity in the countercultural environment of Berkeley, just across the bay from San Francisco. Dr. Barron was friends with famous figures like Dr. Timothy Leary and poet Allen Ginsberg. Dr. Barron chose to focus his studies on artists and art students (Barron, 1972), and his team gave classic personality tests to art students at the San Francisco Art Institute (SFAI) and at the Rhode Island School of Design (RISD). The RISD students were given the Minnesota Multiphasic Personality Inventory, known as the MMPI, and the SFAI students were given the California Psychological Inventory, or CPI.

RISD students scored higher than the general population on the traits of flexibility and psychological-mindedness; they were less well socialized, more impulsive, and less interested in making a good impression. They were poised, confident, and self-accepting. They reported a lower sense of well-being than average. Females and males had comparable personality profiles, except for the expected difference in measures of femininity.

SFAI students had higher than average scores on schizophrenia and hypomania. But these students weren't actually mentally ill; Barron interpreted these scores as indications of openness, unconventionality, and originality. Again, males and females were comparable. The overall personality profile was not so different from the RISD students: both groups were flexible, energetic, and open to experience.

One problem with personality trait research is that after a while, the personality traits measured by the tests seem historically dated. Remember the 1826 map of the brain in chapter 5, with the traits of "amativeness" and "veneration"? Tests of creative people in the 1930s measured "sublimation and compensation," "coalescence of the instincts," and "constitutional delicacy" (Raskin, 1936). These traits seem so foreign to us now, it's hard to even figure out what they might have looked like. And even though it's only been a few decades, the narrative descriptions provided by Barron sound as much like an astrologist's reading or a personal ad as they do a scientific study: "The female student of design, like the male, is independent in thought, unconventional, flexible, creative, open. She approaches life with the same vigor, tempering spontaneity with an awareness of social necessities and a sensitivity to nuance. She also is complex, open to experience, and capable of dealing with the feelings of doubt such openness may bring" (1972, p. 45).

At many art schools, I've noticed that for some students, the idea of being an artist is just as important as actually doing art. Being thought of as creative is a central part of their identity. And particularly in the 1960s, art students probably wanted to be more unconventional and revolutionary than in any prior decade. That's why these tests, rather than measuring true creativity, may instead measure the traits of people who like to think of themselves as creative. Our cultural conceptions tell us that creative people should be unconventional, flexible, and open to experience; therefore people who want to be creative, or who want to be perceived as creative, often behave this way, or convince themselves they are this way (Kasof, 1995). This is basic human nature and it predates the 1960s. Romantic-era poets like Coleridge knew that they were supposed to conceive their poems in bursts of spontaneity, and that they were supposed to experience mental anguish and bouts of madness, and Coleridge made up stories about his creative process that fit this profile (see chapter 11).

Problem Finding in Art

I sometimes begin a drawing with no preconceived problem to solve . . . but as my mind takes in what is so produced a point arrives where some idea becomes conscious and crystallizes, and then a control and ordering begins to take place.
—*Sculptor Henry Moore (1952/1985, p. 72)*

I do not seek, I find.
—*Pablo Picasso (quoted in Byrne, 1996, 4:484)*

The 20th-century painter Francis Bacon said that his work emerged from "the transforming effect of cultivated accidents of paint" (quoted in Ades, Forge, & Durham, 1985, p. 231). In this improvisational problem-finding painting style,

Bacon said, "the creative and the critical become a single act" (p. 233). This modern style is very different from the carefully planned, composed, and executed works generated by European painters prior to the 20th century.

The 1950s New York action painters were perhaps the first to emphasize the process of painting rather than the end product. By the 1960s, the entire New York art scene—including filmmakers, performance artists, and musicians, as well as painters and sculptors (Tomkins, 2002b, p. 57)—was fascinated with process. In the 1960s, Robert Rauschenberg and other painters began to invite audiences into their studios as they painted, so that they could witness a "performance" of a work of art.

Creativity is often associated with the ability to solve problems. But as we learned in chapter 4, many significant creative advances result from problem finding, when the problem is not known in advance, but emerges from the process of the work itself. Some of the first studies of problem finding were done with artists during the 1960s (Beittel, 1972; Beittel & Burkhart, 1963; Csikszentmihalyi, 1965). In a classic study of problem finding in art, Getzels and Csikszentmihalyi (1976) identified 35 senior art students at the Art Institute of Chicago, and brought them each into a room with a table on which 27 objects had been placed. The artist was then asked to choose some of the objects and generate a pastel drawing based on them. The researchers found that the students tended to work in one of two styles (see figures 10.1 and 10.2). Before beginning their drawing, the problem-solving artists examined and manipulated fewer objects, and the problem-finding artists examined more objects. Problem-finding artists chose more complex objects; chose objects that were more unusual, in that they were selected by fewer artists overall; and spent more time examining and manipulating the objects that they had selected. During the drawing itself, problem-solving artists composed the essential outlines of the final composition very quickly—in one extreme case, six minutes into a 55-minute session. Problem-finding artists took much longer—in an extreme case, the form of the final painting was not visible until 36 minutes into a 49-minute session, 73% of the total drawing time (Csikszentmihalyi, 1965, p. 32).[2]

The problem-finding artists generated drawings that were judged to be more original by five independent professional art experts (Csikszentmihalyi, 1965, p. 66). The problem-solving artists generated drawings that were judged to be more craftsmanlike.

Getzels and Csikszentmihalyi stayed in touch with these art students after they received their BFA degrees in 1963 and 1964. They measured their success in 1970 (Getzels & Csikszentmihalyi, 1976), and again in 1981 (Csikszentmihalyi & Getzels, 1988). They measured success by asking art critics, gallery owners, and peer artists to rate each former student's current reputation in the field. By 1970, 24% of the original group of 31 students had disappeared and none of the judges had heard

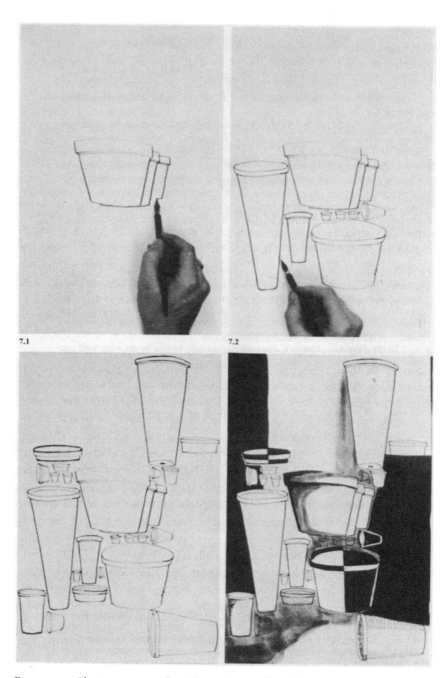

7.1

7.2

FIGURE 10.1. Photo sequence of problem-solving style of drawing. Reprinted from *Mind and Context in the Art of Drawing,* 1972, K. Beittel. With permission of Joan Beittel, www.healingartssanctuary.com.

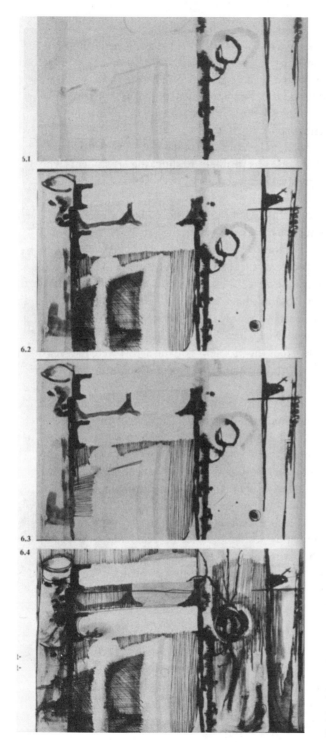

FIGURE 10.2. Photo
sequence of problem-
finding style of drawing.
Reprinted from *Mind
and Context in the Art of
Drawing*, 1972, K. Beittel.
With permission of Joan
Beittel, www.healingarts
sanctuary.com.

of them; another 24% were known to have left the field of art. Twenty-three percent were doing art with some success, and 29% were well known with substantial reputations. By 1981, five of the 31 could not be found; an additional 13 were doing work completely unrelated to art—a combined total of 58%. The remaining 13 students (42%) were working in the field of art—a few as full-time fine artists, but most as teachers and graphic illustrators.

What personality traits back in their art school days best predicted artistic success later in life? The main one was problem finding: the art students who worked in a problem-finding style in art school were those most successful in both 1970 and in 1981.

Both individualist and contextualist approaches are required to explain these results. We learned in chapter 9 that the problem-finding style of art only began to be valued around the turn of the 20th century. Before this time, artists like Cezanne explored a single "problem" for their entire career, and they gradually got better at it; that's why Cezanne's later paintings are worth more. The Getzels and Csikszentmihalyi study wouldn't have gotten the same results 200 years ago—the problem-finding artists would not have been as likely to have had successful careers, and their work would have been less likely to have been judged creative. After all, even in the 1960s the problem-solving artists were judged to generate more craftsmanlike work, and 200 years ago, craftsmanship was more highly valued than originality.

The 20th-century art world valorized process and spontaneity, and these values have affected our conceptions of creativity. The stereotype of Jackson Pollock, mindlessly pouring and dripping paint on a canvas while in a near-psychotic state, fits into our culture's conceptions of how the painter is supposed to work—in a burst of pure inspiration and without conscious restraint. But even Pollock painted with forethought and planning, realizing that art was impossible without norms and conventions. In fact, "Pollock learned to control flung and dribbled paint almost as well as he could a brush; if accidents played any part, they were happy accidents, selected accidents, as with any painter who sets store by the effects of rapid execution" (Greenberg, 1961/1996, p. 116). The painting process is conscious, intentional, planned hard work, sprinkled with frequent mini-insights, just like the creative process in any other domain (see chapter 4, pp. 71–72).

Can Art Be Taught?

> Out of a thousand art students, maybe five will make a living
> off their art, and perhaps one will be known outside her
> city. . . . It's the nature of fame, real quality, and genuine

influence to be rare. In addition the mechanisms of fame are strongly random. Many interesting artists don't make their work at the right moment or show it to the right people. A bad critique, or bad weather on opening night, can be enough to topple a career. . . . Most artists do not make interesting art.

—*James Elkins* (2001, p. 67)

In the early 1940s, there were 11 institutions offering the MFA, the Master of Fine Arts degree; today there are more than 180. In the 1940s, those attending the programs mostly had ambitions to become art teachers; today, many of them want to become professional artists. Today's art school is a historically and culturally unique institution, with its critiques and its MFA shows; and some professors have argued that art school doesn't teach how to make art at all (Elkins, 2001). And there are several types of art that are very difficult to make or even to learn about in art schools: art that takes more than one semester to complete (because students are graded each semester); art that requires the painter to work in a single style for a long period (because instructors encourage variety); art that varies across many different styles (because art schools want students to develop a recognizable "voice"); art that requires naïveté—about perspective, composition, color, or art history (because students are expected to know all of these things); art that requires years of mechanical preparation and practice (because art school is only two years long) (see Elkins, 2001, pp. 72–82). Art schools today focus on teaching the problem-finding style of creativity, and that's what the art world wants, as well. If you want to be a problem-solving type of artist, you were born 200 years too late.

Most art schools today don't focus on the technical skills of painting, drawing, and sculpting; rather, they emphasize the more intellectual and academic aspects of painting. Many art schools now use both grades and samples of paintings in their admissions decisions. Theresa Lynch Bedoya, vice-president and dean of admissions at the Maryland Institute College of Art, said that students with strong academic backgrounds produce more thoughtful art (Geraghty, 1997). By 1970, critic Harold Rosenberg had suspected a relationship: the expansion of university MFA programs after World War II had resulted in the "cool, impersonal wave in the art of the sixties" (Tomkins, 2002a).

Higher academic ability generally results in more articulate students, students who can connect their work to art historical themes or to material they've learned in science or literature classes. Throughout the 20th century, it became increasingly important for artists to be able to tell a good story about their motivations for doing art, how the themes and images emerged from their personal life experience, and what message they hoped to communicate to the audience with their art: "as an artist, you have to be able to keep up a steady,

FIGURE 10.3. This cartoon makes fun of an art student talking artspeak. Reprinted with permission of Eric Reynolds. Copyright © 1991, 2004 Daniel Clowes.

intriguing patter while the potential customer wonders whether or not you're worth as much as you say you are" (Elkins, 2001, p. 53). Both MFA programs and galleries alike enforce this expectation; art school classes teach students to talk artspeak (see figure 10.3), and they teach their artists how to write an effective "artist's statement." Artists have been making fun of artspeak and of the artist's statement since at least the irreverent 1960s. In a classic parody, Roger Lang explained his sculpture of a piece of pie on a plate:

> Pie was interesting to me first of all as food—then I found some triangular associations, geodesic, mathematical, sexual, using a pie wedge as a basis for plate decorations. Later, high in the sky, chicken pot pie, apple pie, cherry pie, and pie-eye thoughts pushed me into 3–dimensional usages. Fruit Pie is, after all, a very American food. Gradually, things accumulated and I came to think of pie as a vehicle for associations, things that come along for nothing, free. In addition, there are the visual changes which I impose, and I haven't even begun explorations of one-crust pies yet. Taking everything into account, pie is very rich. (quoted in Slivka, 1971, p. 43)

The jury is out on whether art can be taught. But even if art schools don't teach one how to make art, we know that they can teach one how to talk like an artist, how to write like an artist, and how to participate in the art world. In their teaching practices, art schools implicitly accept a sociocultural approach.

Beyond Painting: Contextual Explanations of Visual Creativity

In the second half of this chapter, we'll extend our explanation of visual creativity beyond painting. We'll see that outsider art—which is popular largely because it seems to confirm our individualist creativity myths—in fact can only be explained using a sociocultural approach. Then we'll finish the chapter by examining the most important visual art forms of our contemporary culture—photographs, cartoons, and movies.

Outsider Art

> Everything changes but the avant garde.
> —*Paul Valéry (1871–1945) (quoted in Byrne, 1996, 3:528)*

In January 1996 in New York City, artists, gallery owners, and wealthy patrons mingled in front of paintings, holding the always-present glasses of white wine. Thirty-five dealers displayed the works of hundreds of artists; 300 people attended the opening dinner. A very New York art scene, but with one difference: this show was the 4th annual New York Outsider Art Fair, and none of the hundreds of artists displayed was part of the New York art scene; many of them were visiting New York for the first time. Just a few months earlier, in November 1995, the American Visionary Art Museum had opened in Baltimore; it was designated in a Congressional resolution as "the official national museum, repository, and educational center for American visionary and outsider art," which was defined as "art produced by self-taught individuals who are driven by their own internal impulses to create" (quoted in Steiner, 1996). At the museum's opening exhibition, visitors could dine in the top-floor Joy America Café, directed by a self-taught chef whose outsider dishes included "Chinese dim sum with charred pineapple and coconut aioli." Two years later, in the spring of 1998, the first major retrospective show of outsider art was curated by the Museum of American Folk Art in New York City, and toured the country.

The term "outsider art" dates back to an influential 1972 book by that title by British art historian Roger Cardinal. Cardinal's vision of alternative art was derived from French artist Jean Dubuffet's writings on the art of European mental patients (Peiry, 2001; also see chapter 5, pp. 84–86). Dubuffet was interested in the paintings of children, primitives, and the mentally ill, grouping them all together because of his belief that these works were generated without the constraining influence of culture and convention. He was inspired by the legendary collection of paintings by mental patients of Hans Prinzhorn (1972).

Dubuffet's term for this art was *art brut*, literally "raw art," and today Dubuffet is generally acknowledged as the grandfather of the outsider art movement. Like Dubuffet, Cardinal believed that such art was directly connected with the primordial source of all creativity, because it was unconstrained by conscious attempts or subconscious influence to conform to art world conventions.

Today's outsider art is mostly produced not by the mentally ill, but by rural, poor, uneducated people; if you saw one of these works you might call it folk art. In the 1970s, people began to drive the backroads of rural America, collecting craft objects and Americana, but they didn't think it was on the same level as fine art. It wasn't until 1981 that an exhibition, curated by Elsa Longhauser, presented folk art objects as fine art. Her exhibit followed the conventions of the art world, emphasizing individual authorship and objects that could be classified as paintings or sculpture, not only as utilitarian craft objects.

To explain what's unique about outsider art, we need to utilize the sociocultural approach. Outsider art isn't defined by any formal properties of the works themselves, but by their field and domain. Although the works may have been generated on the "outside," outsider art has its own field (curators, galleries that specialize in it, and patrons who collect it) and its own domain (the American Visionary Art Museum, the Museum of American Folk Art in New York City, the quarterly magazine *Raw Vision* with the masthead "Outsider Art—Art Brut—Contemporary Folk Art—Marginal Arts").

The recent history of outsider art, documented in books like Julia Ardery's 1998 book *The Temptation: Edgar Tolson and the Genesis of Twentieth Century Folk Art* and Lucienne Peiry's 2001 book *Art Brut: The Origins of Outsider Art*, is like a natural laboratory to test the predictions made by the sociocultural approach. Score one for the sociocultural approach: the outsider art world has developed just as predicted. The new art world of outsider art has all of the same roles and relations as any other art world, and the field and the domain play the same roles. It *wasn't* "art" until this social system emerged to define it as such. Before these developments in the 1990s, more of us would have considered these works to be mere curiosities, or simple "folk art," an older term that's disliked by the outsider arts community because of its pejorative connotations. The contemporary interest in outsider art has brought it "inside"; paradoxically, just as it becomes recognized as "art," it loses its outsider status (Peiry, 2001).

The Original Outsider Art

Some art historians date the beginning of modern art to the sunny afternoon when Picasso, taking a walk through the streets of Paris, happened to pass a shop specializing in African tribal sculptures and noticed a particularly interesting sculpted head in the window.[3] Soon after, Picasso's paintings were replicating these designs (Goldwater, 1938/1967; see figure 10.4). Paul Gauguin decided that he couldn't paint true art while he was surrounded by the corrupting influence of Europe, and he left for the remote French island of Tahiti to find a natural, uncorrupted paradise. Gauguin's paintings while he lived in the South Pacific (between 1891 and 1893, and then from 1895 to his death in the Marquesas Islands of French Polynesia in 1903) are generally considered to

FIGURE 10.4. (a) Pablo Picasso, *Nude*, 1907. With permission of Estate of Pablo Picasso/Artists Rights Society (ARS), New York. Copyright © 2004.

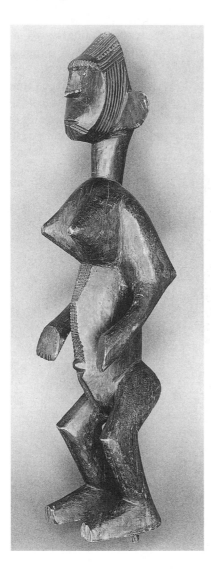

FIGURE 10.4. (b) A Senufo figure from the Ivory Coast, Africa. New York University, Institute of Fine Arts, Visual Resources Collection. Copyright © Walker Evans Archive, The Metropolitan Museum of Art.

be the source of modern painting's use of color; they influenced the movement known as Fauvism, which included influential painters like Matisse and Kandinsky.

Interest in primitive art spread quickly through Europe. African art was "discovered" almost simultaneously in both Germany (the *Die Brücke* Expressionist movement) and France (the Fauvists and Picasso, Matisse, and Derain) between 1904 and 1908. These European artists were attracted to the simplicity and intensity of expression in African art, which was thought to express pure emotion.

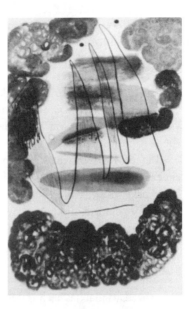

FIGURE 10.5. (a) Joan Miró, *Mediterranean Landscape*, 1930.

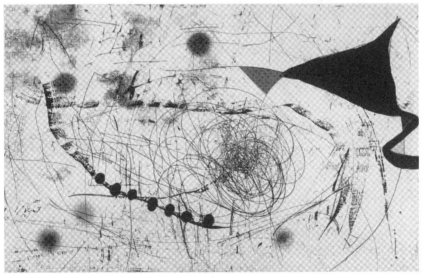

FIGURE 10.5 (b) Joan Miró, La Manucure Évaporée, 1975. Copyright © 2004. Artists Rights Society (ARS), New York/ADAGP, Paris.

In addition to primitive art, many of the greatest modern artists—Kandinsky, Klee, Picasso, Miro, Dubuffet—collected children's art and used it as source material for some of the most significant breakthroughs of their careers (Fineberg, 1997, 1998; Goldwater, 1938/1967; Golomb, 2002). These artists were influenced by the Romantic-era cult of childhood. They believed, as French poet Charles Baudelaire (1821–1867) famously wrote, that "genius is nothing more nor less than *childhood recovered* at will" (1863/1964, p. 8). They believed that children's art held the key to the internal world, spontaneous and free from conventions.

In 1902, Klee rediscovered his own childhood drawings in his parents' storage shed, and used material from them in many of his later paintings (see figure 10.5). Kandinsky studied children's paintings in order to find a universal visual language, one before culture imposed its own images. He believed that "the talented child has the power to clothe the abiding truth in the form in which this inner truth appears as the most effective" (Kandinsky in 1912, quoted in Goldwater, 1938/1967, p. 128).

These so-called "outsiders"—children, primitives, and the mentally ill—have influenced art that has been at the core of the art establishment for over 100 years. Outsider art is not new; what's new is that a domain and a field have emerged to redefine how we relate to the works.

Installation Art

> The thesis of the end of Art has become a familiar slogan.
> —*Herbert Marcuse (1970, p. 123)*

> Being an artist now means to question the nature of art.
> —*Joseph Kosuth (quoted in Rose, 1969, p. 23)*

In the 1960s, painters got nervous. It was beginning to seem like all of the action was happening somewhere else. Art critics were talking about artworks like Robert Smithson's *Spiral Jetty*, 6,650 tons of black basalt and earth in the shape of a giant coil, 1,500 feet long, jutting out into the Great Salt Lake in Utah. Bruce Nauman made movies of himself anxiously pacing in circles. Donald Judd's work is so large and imposing that it's displayed in a private museum in Marfa, Texas, on 340 acres of a former Army base; one of the pieces displayed consists of 100 milled aluminum boxes installed in two converted artillery sheds. In 1977, Heiner Friedrich's SoHo gallery in New York became the permanent home of Walter De Maria's work *The New York Earth Room*, which is 280,000 pounds of dirt, spread 22 inches deep, across a 3,600-square-foot room. The room requires constant maintenance to maintain moisture levels and to clear away the mushrooms that keep popping up.

These works challenge the dominance of painting. They're known as *installation art*, a broad term for art that seeks to shape the environment for its reception, changing how people view and relate to the artwork. Installation artists don't just create art, they also create the contexts in which their work will be seen. It's as if they are creating a new kind of museum, a new kind of relationship with the audience.

Installation art reflexively comments on the experience of interacting with art. Like modern theater, which breaks the fourth wall and draws attention to its own conventions (see chapter 13), installation art questions the boundary between artwork and audience, and questions the nature of art itself. But because such art breaks the most fundamental conventions of the art world, most people have never seen it. The art world's system of conventions—museums, galleries, traveling exhibitions, opening-night parties, mass mailings to museum donors—help to disseminate a new work, and make it possible for the field to judge the work. Installation art can't be sold because it can't be displayed in any collector's home, and it can't be carried from one place to another. It's hard to have an opening-night party, because most of the dealers and collectors are in Manhattan, not in Utah or Texas. To view the art you have to make a pilgrimage to its remote unconventional location. It's hard to imagine a market in such art.

At first glance, installation art seems to reinforce our creativity myths. These artists work in solitude and break all of the art world's conventions. But even installation artists have to pay rent and buy food. In the early years, many of the best-known installation artists were supported by independently wealthy private donors, resulting in a patronage system reminiscent of medieval Europe. How did these rich patrons know which artists to support? By seeking the advice of dealers and museum curators, creating a new mini-art world that operated much like the old traditional one.

By breaking the conventions of the art world, installation art calls attention to them. And at the same time, installation art teaches us why we have such conventions, and why they'll never disappear. Conventions, domains, and fields are required for art to exist as a social system, as a shared cultural activity that many people can jointly participate in. Installation art indeed breaks conventions. But the fact that most of my readers have never seen it reinforces the importance of those conventions.

Photography

Eugene Atget is today a famous French photographer known for his documentary-style photographs of everyday street life in Paris in the early 20th century. But he wasn't known as a photographer during his lifetime. Although he took thousands of photographs, few people knew his work. Just before his death in 1927, the young American photographer Berenice Abbott met him and thought his work was brilliant; when he died, she gained control of his negatives, examined thousands of them, and eventually chose to print the small set of photographs by which Atget is now known (Abbott, 1964). We usually expect the photographer himself to use his own creativity in this selection process. After all, Abbott selected only about 100 prints out of many thousands; how do we know Atget himself would have picked the same ones? So in this case, Atget and Abbott collaborated in the work that we today know as "Atget." After Abbott made Atget famous, other photographers went back to the same negatives and selected different photographs than she did.

The photographs in legendary Western photographer Ansel Adams's first book were selected from his negatives by Nancy Newhall; Adams was very much alive, but too busy to make the selections. Shouldn't we attribute Newhall as a collaborator in the creation of this first book? Both Atget and Adams became known from a body of work that reflected someone else's sensibilities and standards.

An art photograph, displayed on a gallery wall, is the result of a long sequence of small decisions. First, the photographer has to decide when to pick up the camera and point, and then when to press the shutter. Most photographers take far more photographs than they will ever be able to print, knowing that they'll be able to review their contact sheets in the studio. Becker (1982) described taking 20,000 photos in preparation for an exhibit containing no more than 100 prints (p. 195). The most critical decisions are made in the studio: which of the 20,000 photos is good enough to potentially result in a good print?

After the individual photographer has made her choices, the curators and gallery owners have to evaluate and select the photos of many different photographers. Only a minority of photographers ever receive a gallery show. And getting one gallery show doesn't result in fame or lasting reputation. For that to happen, many different galleries, curators, and patrons have to each individually decide to select that work. It is in this sense that "art worlds, rather than artists, make works of art" (Becker, 1982, p. 198).

Every artist becomes known from works that reflect the standards of the gatekeepers in the field. Especially with mass-produced works like books, movies, and music CDs, only works that are selected by the field for distribution ever reach a wide audience. The general public comes to know a creator "as selected by" multiple layers of intermediaries. Because evaluation and selection are critical parts of the creative process, these intermediaries become collaborators in the work.

Movies

> Movies reach almost everywhere. No other art form mobilizes
> a national discussion in such a big way.
>> —*Roger Ebert (1997, p. A23), in an editorial arguing that
>> there should be a Pulitzer Prize for movies as an art form*

It's a little strange that so much psychological research on visual creativity focuses on fine art painting when the most widespread and influential creative
visual products of our time are, without doubt, Hollywood movies. When the
Pulitzer Prizes were first created in 1917, movies were not yet a respectable art
form. And still today, there's no Pulitzer Prize for film, although there are prizes
for fiction, drama, history, biography, poetry, and music. In the first half of the
20th century—when movies were new—people could still get away with arguing that movies really didn't deserve the same status as fine art, and in fact, some
scholars were viciously dismissive of American movies (German Marxist
Theodor W. Adorno is perhaps the best known). But during the second half of
the 20th century, almost everyone came to agree that film had attained a status
as a creative art form, the equal of any other.

Movies don't fit in with our cultural conceptions of creativity for several
reasons. First, they're created by large teams of people, each with specialized
skills, who have to work together collaboratively to generate the final product. Film scholars have occasionally attempted to impose the lone-genius myth
onto movie creation, attributing the creativity to the director. But although
the director has a unique creative position, unlike the painter, he or she cannot create a movie without a large support staff (Simonton, 2004). The collaborative nature of movie production can't be explained with individualist
approaches.

One of the most widely known recent examples of movie creativity is
George Lucas's original *Star Wars* film of 1977. At first glance, the story of how
Star Wars came to be made seems to fit into our lone-genius myth. In the mid
1970s, Lucas's original 13-page treatment of *The Star Wars* (as he originally
called it) was rejected by Universal and by United Artists, even though Lucas
had already had a big success with *American Graffiti*. Only Alan Ladd, then at
Fox, considered it, and even then he had to work against the objections of the
Fox board. But even this first script for *The Star Wars* was not a burst of lone
genius; Lucas spent over a year writing the 13-page plot summary and another
year writing the first draft of the script. Even after all this work, his dialogue
wasn't very good, and he got several other writers to help rewrite the script.
After realizing the script was too long for one movie, he then broke it up into

six separate movies (the first movie was called *Star Wars, Episode IV: A New Hope*). At a private screening of an early cut of the film for his friends and Fox executives, everyone hated it, thought it was a bad movie, was convinced it would tank, and was embarrassed for Lucas (Seabrook, 1997).

They were all wrong. The success is legendary. The first movie alone earned 323 million dollars, more than any prior movie. It was the first movie to spawn a lucrative line of toys. And it fundamentally changed how movies are made. Before *Star Wars*, cinematic elements were secondary to the narrative and the literary elements of the movie. Now, the visual and cinematic elements are primary. Interestingly, none of the visual elements that Lucas used were themselves original. Film historians point out that many of Lucas's visuals were taken from past movies: the lightsabers and Jedi Knights were inspired by Kurosawa's *Hidden Fortress*; the robot C-3PO was a character straight out of Fritz Lang's *Metropolis*; Harrison Ford's portrayal of Han Solo resembles *Butch Cassidy*. It's often said of Lucas that "he didn't actually invent anything" (Seabrook, 1997, p. 48).

So was Lucas truly creative, or did he just get lucky? In one sense *Star Wars* fits the traditional genius myth narrative; he pushed through a creative vision in the face of opposition from the field, and he succeeded. But ultimately, the lone genius myth doesn't fit unless we ignore big chunks of the story. The idea wasn't a burst of inspiration, but evolved over a five-year period. The script was collaboratively written by several people. Most of the visual elements were borrowed from prior movies, and the story, as is widely known, is based on common mythical elements analyzed by Joseph Campbell. Many movie experts thought that it was a bad movie—famously, Pauline Kael of *The New Yorker*.

From the sociocultural perspective, *Star Wars* has to be considered creative because it's been judged creative by the field. It made it through all of the usual filters by first getting funded and distributed by a major studio, and then it facing the test of the movie-going audience and the expert film critics. Although some influential critics hated the movie, on balance the field has determined that it was creative. And since 1977, the ways that it changed the domain are increasingly clear.

Of all movies ever made, George Lucas's *Star Wars* is about as close as you can get to the cultural myth that we have about the creative artist, and even this story doesn't fit the myth all that well. But the great majority of movies aren't nearly as innovative or influential; most of them replicate what has come before, with only minor variations. According to Hollywood legend, there are only seven story lines underlying all movies and TV shows (Friend, 1998). Professional writers consciously stick with proven formulas, knowing that TV executives, advertisers, and viewers have grown to expect them. Many writers today use computer software that helps them to follow these rules (see chapter 11). Explaining movie creativity requires a focus on collaboration, networks, divisions of labor, and markets.

Cartoons

Like movies, cartoons are created by large organized teams of specialized individuals. They require a significant up-front investment of cash and expensive distribution through broadcast or cable television, and as a result, cartoons go through multiple layers of evaluation and modification long after the originating idea. Like sitcoms and movies, cartoons are often created by collaborative teams of writers (see chapter 11).

Here's a transcript of a story meeting of the artists working on the Cartoon Network's *Samurai Jack*, with the meeting led by creator Genndy Tartakovsky (the creator of *Dexter's Laboratory*). Andy (one of the artists) has come up with a new story idea. There are about 10 people in the room. Other than Andy and Tartakovsky, whenever one of the others speaks up I've simply indicated "artist" (from Wilkinson, 2002):

Andy:	We're looking to do the story we talked about, where Jack gets infected with a virus and it takes over his arm. Then it would slowly take over his whole body. Then half of him becomes evil, and he's going to fight himself.
Tartakovsky:	How do we set it up?
Artist:	Could he have battled Aku, and Aku has a cold, and he sneezes on him?
Tartakovsky:	(nods) It's almost like we're at the end of another show with a great fight. Except this one starts with a battle. And he's fighting these robots, and Aku's commanding them. It's cold and drafty, and Aku starts sneezing, and says, "Oy, I've got to get some chicken soup."
Artist:	Oy?
Artist:	How do we get it out that he's infected?
Artist:	We had talked about him showing a guy his face. And it's half in shadow.
Artist:	He becomes Aku.
Artist:	He becomes *Jaku.*
Artist:	The more evil he becomes, the more erratic his body is.
Artist:	Maybe somebody's getting robbed, he saves him, and the guy thanks him, and he's walking away, and in Jack's other hand is the guy's watch.
Artist:	Do we need to find somebody to summon him? Is there a psychic battle with himself?
Artist:	Or a fight in his head? I was thinking, he knows a place to cleanse himself—a monastery. And the monks help him.

Artist:	The B story is no one's trusting Jack—they see him and they run.
Tartakovsky:	It's always stronger if Jack can help himself. I like the image of Jack as Aku with one eye. I like it half and half. The more I think about it, the body of the show is him fighting himself.
Artist:	He realizes he'd better get out of the city before he hurts someone, so he travels to a village.
Tartakovsky:	I still want to keep it real simple, though.
Artist:	At the monastery, they tie him up so he can't do any harm.
Tartakovsky:	Does Aku know that Jack has what he has?
Artist:	No, he's too sick.

It's clear from this brief excerpt of the brainstorming session that no single person is in charge. No one creates any more than anyone else. Even though the discussion started with Andy's story idea, Andy says nothing after getting it started. Tartakovsky doesn't dominate the group. The cartoon emerges from the discussion, and ends up being a collective creation of 10 people.

Could We Make the Art World More Democratic?

What kind of art do Americans really want? If you took a poll of a random group of Americans, what art would they choose? Two recent conceptual artists from Russia decided to find out what kind of art Americans like by conducting a poll of their own. They asked 1,001 Americans about their favorite colors, forms, styles, and content; when they put Americans' top choices all together, they got a bluish landscape painting containing George Washington, a family of tourists, and a pair of deer, all in a painting about the size of a dishwasher (see figure 10.6). Vitaly Komar and Alexander Melamid did similar polls in countries from China to Iceland (Wypijewski, 1997). They found a lot of overlap, and also some amusing national differences.[4] Based on the poll results, they painted each country's "most wanted" painting, and also its opposite, a painting that contained everything the culture most disliked (all paintings can be viewed on the Web, at http://www.diacenter.org/km/ [accessed January 13, 2004]). These least wanted paintings look a lot like abstract modern art. Later, they showed the paintings to focus groups, and they found that most Americans really did like the "painting by numbers."

This art—created by audience consensus—is clearly tongue in cheek, but it raises some interesting issues for creativity. Why shouldn't art reflect what the

FIGURE 10.6. *America's Most Wanted Painting* (http://www.diacenter.org/km), a painting generated by the artists Komar and Melamid, based on a survey of 1001 adults that asked them what they most liked to see in a painting. Reprinted with permission of Komar. Copyright © Komar & Melamid.

people want? In fact, much of what we hear on our radio stations is directly influenced by polls of listeners conducted by the Arbitron market-research corporation (see chapter 12, pp. 230–231). Best-selling novelist James Patterson distributed drafts of his books to "test readers" for feedback before releasing the books for publication. He changed the ending of his thriller *Cat & Mouse* in response to reader feedback; the novel reached number 2 on *The New York Times* best-seller list. The producers of the Broadway musical *Ragtime* hired a polling firm to help them revise the script in response to audience reactions; the show went through 20 drafts before opening night (Kakutani, 1998). And "super fans" who maintain popular Web sites have started to influence Hollywood decision making. While *The Hulk* (2003) was being produced, studio executives surfed the Web to see what aspects of the original comic strip were most important to the most serious fans. Internet fan sites have influenced the creation of many movies, including *The Lord of the Rings* trilogy (2001, 2002, 2003) and *Spider-Man* (2002) (Bowles, 2003).

Is this so wrong? Or would we rather side with the art world attitude that it doesn't matter what people think? When the art world of New York gathered at the Whitney Museum to discuss Komar and Melamid's project, many of them agreed that "talking about what *the people* want is absurd" (art historian Dore Ashton, quoted in Sante, 1998). It's only absurd given our cultural conceptions of art—as the inspired outburst of the inner spirit of the artist, isolated, misunderstood, rejecting convention.

To explain today's most important forms of visual creativity, we need to move beyond painting. And when we move beyond painting, we need a sociocultural approach. Movies and cartoons are created collaboratively, and the intermediaries of the field play an increasingly important role. The example of photography shows us that evaluation and selection is often more important than incubation and insight, and this lesson extends far beyond photography. Even our contemporary conceptions of painting are historically unique, and can be traced back to our creativity myths and their origins in the 19th-century Romantic movement.

Thought Experiments

- Have you used a digital camera? Do you take pictures differently now that you know you can immediately delete a photo that doesn't look good?
- If you ever used a Polaroid camera, were you more careful about when you took pictures because you knew that each picture cost more than those taken with an ordinary camera?
- If you don't like abstract modern art, then how do you explain why it's dominated the art world for most of the 20th century? Have you ever said, "I may not know art, but I know what I like"?
- Would you agree with the following statement: "It doesn't matter what those gatekeepers in the field think, those snobby New York 'experts.' They don't get to say what counts as art." If so, then what alternative would you propose for how to select the best art works? Would it be a democratic system, like that of Komar and Melamid?
- Do you think we should do away with all criteria and selection? But if so, then we can no longer have galleries, art markets, and museums because those institutions all require that criteria be applied and choices be made. How do you think such institutions should function?
- Are movies art? Are they just as important as fine art painting? Or do you believe that there is something uniquely special about fine art painting?

Suggested Readings

Csikszentmihalyi, M., & Getzels, J. W. (1988). Creativity and problem finding in art. In F. H. Farley & R. W. Neperud (Eds.), *The foundations of aesthetics, art & art education* (pp. 91–116). New York: Praeger.

Elkins, J. (2001). *Why art cannot be taught: A handbook for art students.* Urbana, IL: University of Illinois Press, especially chapters 2 and 3.

Fineberg, J. D. (1997). *The innocent eye: Children's art and the modern artist.* Princeton, NJ: Princeton University Press.

Kimmelman, M. (2003, April 6). The Dia generation. *The New York Times Magazine*, 30–37, 58, 61, 72, 76–77.

Prinzhorn, H. (1972). *Artistry of the mentally ill.* New York: Springer.

Schuessler, J. (1999, December/January). The visionary company: Call it what you will, outsider art is making its mark. *Lingua Franca*, 48–58.

Seabrook, J. (1997, January 6). Why is the force still with us? *The New Yorker*, 40–53.

Steiner, W. (1996, March 10). In love with the myth of the "outsider." *New York Times*, pp. H45, H48.

Notes

1. Note the similarities with the three levels of Asante wood carvers, described in chapter 8, p. 152.

2. These may not be fixed personality traits. Beittel (1972, chapter 5) developed an instructional method to teach artists how to use the opposite style, and he found that it was fairly easy to teach artists to use both styles. In his theory, that's because both styles involve improvisational interactions with the act of painting, which he called "problem controlling" to contrast it with problem solving.

3. This story is apocryphal; there are conflicting accounts of when and where Picasso first encountered African sculpture. Picasso said he happened on it on a chance visit in 1907 to the Paris anthropological museum. However, Matisse said that he had shown Picasso an African sculpture from his collection in 1906, in Gertrude Stein's apartment. Vlaminck said that Picasso first saw African sculpture in Derain's studio (Goldwater, 1938/1967, pp. 144–145).

4. Similar findings were reported by Kaplan and Kaplan (1989). Their work focused on aesthetic preferences for different images of nature, in a wide range of cultures and subgroups.

CHAPTER 11

Writing

> It is tremendously important that great poetry be written, it
> makes no jot of difference who writes it.
>
> —*Ezra Pound* (*1954, p. 10*)

When the young American poet T. S. Eliot published *The Waste Land* in 1922—while still only 24 years old—it won him an international reputation. *The Waste Land* has no plot, but is instead a loosely connected series of images that capture the disillusionment and disgust at the death and destruction caused by World War I. The disconnected organization of the poem reflects the fragmented and confused nature of modern urban life. Eliot later proved that he was no one-shot wonder; he had a long, productive, and influential career in the decades after this first great success, capped with a Nobel Prize in Literature in 1948.

Most of us assume that Eliot created *The Waste Land*. After all, his name is on the title page, and he was the one who cashed the check for the royalties. And after all, isn't poetry one of the most solitary, private forms of creativity?

Not in this case. *The Waste Land* was a collaborative creation; two other poets significantly modified Eliot's first typed manuscript: his friend and colleague Ezra Pound, and his wife, Vivien Eliot.

Pound was older and more experienced than Eliot, and his support was critical in Eliot's early career. Eliot had great respect for Pound, and gave him the initial typewritten manuscript of his 800-line poem, asking for suggestions. Pound didn't hold back. Pound deleted entire pages from Eliot's first draft, moved stanzas around, and liberally reworded many lines. For example, the famous first

line "April is the cruellest month" is line 55 of Eliot's first typewritten manuscript. Pound shortened Eliot's initial typed manuscript by half; the published
poem came out at only 433 lines. Eliot's original manuscript had elements of
parody and dry humor—its original title had been "He Do the Police in Different Voices"—and Pound removed all of it to focus on the bleak imagery. Eliot
acknowledged his debt to Pound in his book's dedication: "For Ezra Pound, *il
miglior fabbro*" (the greater craftsman).

Eliot's wife Vivien was a second important editor. After Eliot sought out
Vivien's advice, she also deleted lines from the original manuscript and suggested
alternative wordings; she wrote one of the poem's memorable lines, near the
end of part 2, "What you get married for if you don't want children?" (Eliot's
original draft had "You want to keep him at home, I suppose.")

The original manuscript was lost for many decades, and no one realized that
The Waste Land was collaboratively created until scholars rediscovered the
manuscript in 1968 (Eliot, 1971). However, Eliot's reputation didn't suffer even
though it now seemed that Pound had written more than half of the poem. Eliot
is still considered to be the author of *The Waste Land*, even though the story of
the poem's creation makes us question whether any one person should actually
get all the credit.

At first glance, writing seems to be far removed from social and contextual influences. You don't need anyone's help to write poetry; you don't need
to use complex tools; and you don't have to collaborate in a system of cooperative work. If you think of poetry as the private, personal expression of a
person's inner vision, you might think that this story is abnormal. You might
even feel that Eliot was cheating by drawing on the help of others, or that
Pound interfered with Eliot's original vision. But these reactions stem from
our individualist myths about how creativity works. In fact, many successful
writers seek out good editing, listen very closely to such comments, and are
grateful for them. Eliot's story shows us that creative writing is often the result of collaboration. The story of *The Waste Land* has three important lessons to teach us about writing creativity.

Lesson 1: Writing Is Hard Work

Our creativity myth tells us that the inner voice of the creator is the unconscious,
yearning to find expression. Many successful writers speak of the important role
played by unconscious inspiration. Madeleine L'Engle, author of the classic *A
Wrinkle in Time*, said that "a lot of ideas come subconsciously. You don't even
realize where they're coming from" (quoted in Csikszentmihalyi, 1996, p. 256),
and poet Mark Strand, chosen in 1991 to be poet laureate of the United States,

said that "you don't know when you're going to be hit with an idea, you don't know where it comes from" (quoted in Csikszentmihalyi, 1996, p. 241).

In our romantic conception of creativity, the words pour onto the page in a burst of inspiration. But that's Hollywood, not real life. English novelist Anthony Trollope described a very businesslike writing method:

> [A writer] should have so trained himself that he shall be able to work continuously during those three hours—so have tutored his mind that it shall not be necessary for him to sit nibbling his pen, and gazing at the wall before him, till he shall have found the words with which he wants to express his ideas. It had at this time become my custom . . . to write with my watch before me, and to require from myself 250 words every quarter of an hour. I have found that the 250 words have been forthcoming as regularly as my watch went. (Trollope, 1883/1989, p. 197)

Can someone who works in such a businesslike way really be creative? Because our myth tells us that creativity emerges in a burst of inspiration from the unconscious, we naturally think that the inspired first draft is the best. If a poem is really good, then it won't need much revision after this moment of insight. But this is a false creativity myth; professional writers know that the first draft often needs heavy editing. Very few writers can attain their best without subjecting this spontaneous work to careful, tedious, time-consuming review and editing. Lyric poet Anthony Hecht, winner of a Pulitzer Prize in 1968, said that "there's an awful lot of fussing and fiddling; I feel that the writing of a poem is a very conscious act" (quoted in Csikszentmihalyi, 1996, p. 251). After his initial inspiration, Strand critically examines everything, consciously drawing on all of his knowledge of past poets and conventions to rework the raw material. German poet Hilde Domin said that a very experienced poet will be able to apply the critical eye almost simultaneously along with the unconscious inspiration: "Like, for example, when you eliminate a word. In the beginning you eliminate it *after* you have written it. And when you are more skilled you eliminate it while you are writing" (quoted in Csikszentmihalyi, 1996, p. 248).

Many aspiring writers believe that their unconscious should do all of the good creative work for them. Writing teachers believe that this creativity myth keeps these novices from getting started. Novelist Anne Lamott, in her writing advice book *Bird by Bird*, emphasized the importance of generating "shitty first drafts" (1994, p. 21), and Natalie Goldberg, in *Writing Down the Bones*, communicated much the same message, with rules like "keep your hand moving," "don't cross out," and "lose control" (Goldberg, 1986, p. 8). The first draft provides necessary raw material, but it's not anywhere near a finished product; it still requires the hard work of evaluation and elaboration.

Lesson 2: Writing Is Conscious and Directed

> Some editors are failed writers, but so are most writers.
> —*T. S. Eliot (in Charlton, 1980, p. 121)*

The late Raymond Carver's story *Cathedral* is the last of 33 drafts of the work. Carver said that he only knew when he was done with a story when he got to the point that he went over it, adding only occasional commas, and then in the next revision, he began removing some of those same commas (Dutton, 2001, p. 189). You probably never realized that professional writers sweat over every comma; such tedious work doesn't match our creativity myth.

The myth that a poem springs to mind fully formed by the unconscious genius originated in the Romantic era. In fact, the Romantic poets actively encouraged the public to believe in this myth, even when it wasn't true. You may have heard Coleridge's story about how he created the poem "Kubla Khan" all at once in an opium-inspired daze. But Coleridge's story is known to be false. For example, scholars have discovered an earlier version of the poem, and they know of many other examples where Coleridge lied about his work process (Schneider, 1953; also see Weisberg, 1988, pp. 170–171). Coleridge probably realized that the story about the opium would make the poem more interesting to a reading public suffused with Romantic myths about creativity. Coleridge's story tells us more about the Romantic-era conception of creativity than about his actual creative process, because we know that during his era, a poet who admitted to long periods of frequent revision would not have been consistent with Romantic-era conceptions of how true creativity worked.

Lesson 3: Writing Is a Collaborative and Socially Embedded Activity

Although both Pound and Vivien Eliot heavily edited Eliot's original manuscripts, we still credit the poems to Eliot alone. But editing can cross a line where we think it's too much, where we begin to wonder whether the "author" really should get the credit. Novelist Thomas Wolfe, author of *Look Homeward, Angel*, died in 1938, leaving about a million words behind, all unorganized and unfinished. Edward Aswell, an editor at Harper & Brothers, created two more books out of these scattered writings; he did it by creating composite characters drawn from separate bits of writing, and he sometimes added his own words. Aswell's efforts remained secret until the late 1970s, and when they became public, it diminished Wolfe's reputation.

When Raymond Carver died at age 50 from lung cancer, he was considered by many critics to be America's most significant short-story author. If there could be such a thing as an "outsider writer," Carver might qualify; he grew up in the rural northwestern part of the country and taught himself to write by taking a correspondence course. He lived in poverty and suffered from serious alcoholism. He seemed to represent a pure form of writing as the necessary expression of inner demons, and editorial collaboration doesn't fit well with such an image.

Gordon Lish was Carver's first editor, and he often claimed that he had so heavily edited Carver's early stories that they were as much his as they were Carver's. But his claim was never taken seriously; after all, stories authored by Lish himself had never been successful, and all authors rely on editorial advice to some extent. Yet when Carver's manuscripts were first examined in the late 1990s—and they are covered with editorial marks in Lish's hand—Lish's claim didn't seem so ludicrous. The scratched-out text is often more than half of each page; Lish added entire paragraphs to some pages, and shortened many stories by deleting the last few paragraphs of Carver's original draft. In some stories, Lish cut 70% of the original words and replaced many of them with his own text; in others, stories ended up 40% shorter than Carver's initial draft (Max, 1998).

In fact, critics had often noted that Carver's writing style seemed to change later in his career, after Lish was no longer his editor. The early stories, edited by Lish, are more minimalist and abstract in style, and the later ones are more sentimental and more elaborate in style. Literary critics had attributed this change to the fact that Carver seemed to become happier later in life, as he conquered his alcoholism and settled into a stable relationship with Tess Gallagher. But now that we have the original manuscripts, we know that we need a sociocultural explanation for this shift in style. It wasn't Carver who changed; it was the system of Carver's collaboration that changed.

These stories challenge our cultural myth about the authenticity of a writer's output. We want to believe that we're reading the author's deeply personal and emotional experience, that the author finds catharsis by getting it out onto the page. But most writers receive help, and editors have always modified the writer's original text. Dr. Carol Polsgrove, a professor at Indiana University, said, "If you exalt the individual writer as the romantic figure who brings out these things from the depths of his soul, then yes, the awareness of Lish's role diminishes Carver's work somewhat. But if you look at writing and publishing as a social act, which I think it is, the stories are the stories that they are" (quoted in Max, 1998, p. 51). A new form of literary criticism known as *genetic criticism* has begun to focus on the evolution of manuscripts from drafts to published form, examining the collaborative process that involves editors, colleagues, and publishers

(Deppman, Ferrer, & Groden, 2004). After all, why should we place such a high value on authenticity and purity with novels and short stories when we don't expect it of television sitcoms or Hollywood movies?

The Psychology of Creative Writing

> A writer is somebody for whom writing is more difficult than
> it is for other people.
> —*Thomas Mann* (*quoted in Charlton, 1980, p. 57*)

Writing is hard work. It takes dedication to craft and intense motivation. It's not pretty. Thomas Mann doesn't mean that nonwriters have an easier time with writing. What he really means is that writers are the only people who realize how hard writing actually is; people who think it's easy are naive and are deluding themselves. They're amateurs who generate a first draft and then never go through the hard work of editing and revising it.

In the 1960s at the Berkeley IPAR, Barron (1972) conducted a series of intensive interviews and observations with 26 professional creative writers. He found that the writers scored higher than the general public on several personality trait measures:

- Intellectual capacity;
- Value placed on intellectual and cognitive matters;
- Value placed on independence and autonomy;
- Verbal fluency;
- Conceptual thinking;
- Flexibility.

Csikszentmihalyi's extended interviews of five creative writers (1996) identified several important common threads. First, the writers could only be significantly creative by first immersing themselves in the domain of literature. None of them were "outsider" writers; they all read a lot, they had strong opinions about other writers, and they memorized their favorite works. In other words, they internalized more of the domain than nonwriters. All five of them eventually became part of the field of literature—they became friends with other writers, contributed to insider journals, and gossiped about each other. They became intermediaries, teachers, and editors.

Second, the writers all emphasized the constant dialogue between unconscious inspiration and conscious editing, between passionate inspiration and disciplined craft. They all agreed that it's important to listen to their unconscious. They kept notebooks nearby at all times so that sudden snippets of text or dialogue could be quickly scribbled down for later evaluation. They worked in a problem-finding style, starting a work with only a phrase or an image, rather than a fully composed plot, and the work emerged from the improvisational act of writing and revising. There was never a single big insight; instead, there were hundreds and thousands of small mini-insights. The real work started when many mini-insights were analyzed, reworked, and connected to each other; and as with every other type of creativity, many ideas that sounded good at first ended up in the trash.

Many creative writers talk about these mini-insights. Writers are constantly thinking, coming up with small bits of text that they write down in their notebooks. These are little snippets of a scene or a character, and the writer has no idea whether they'll ever be used in a finished published text. Poet Mark Strand starts writing this way: "I'll jot a few words down, and that's a beginning" (quoted in Csikszentmihalyi, 1996, p. 241). These pages are then stored in a folder or a notebook, frequently perused, and much later can be slipped into an ongoing story, one that was not even conceived when the original snippet was written. This is the hard work of writing, and it's why fiction is never only autobiographical reporting—characters in a novel are rarely exactly like any living individual, but are rather composites of observations of many people, strangers and intimates, built up over a long and hard day-to-day process of observation and writing.

Most creative writers use a problem-finding style; they don't know what they're doing until they've done it (Lamott, 1994, p. 22). Moore (1952/1985) replicated the famous Getzels and Csikszentmihalyi study of artists (chapter 10) with student writers. He found that student writers resembled art students in their problem-finding behavior; the writers whose stories were rated the most original by experts were the ones who used a problem-finding style.

Poetry As an Oral Art

In fall of 2002, rap recording mogul Russell Simmons produced the Tony Award–winning *Def Poetry Jam* on Broadway, bringing oral poetry into the heart of America's central entertainment district. Nine different poets reciting on stage in front of an audience—it might sound boring at first. However, this is poetry composed for the stage, not the page, and like other performance genres, the process is the product—it exists only in performance. Each poet was selected from the burgeoning small-club scene of poetry jams, a circuit that has resulted in a renaissance of what is often called "spoken word." The oral nature of the genre results in a return to certain core elements of poetry: the performative element, first of all, but also formal features like rhythm and rhyme that fell out of fashion in literary free verse. Literary values are secondary; these compositions often work better on stage than they do in private contemplation in the library. Only in performance would an audience see the hypnotic qualities of Staceyann Chin's description of lovemaking, or the posed militancy in the kung fu dandy poses of Beau Sia, the self-described "Chinese tornado."

Some people might argue that the theatrics of performance keep us from appreciating the underlying poetry. If it doesn't seem as creative when we study it in the library, then haven't we, in a sense, been fooled by the tricks of the performer? But this attitude is simply a manifestation of our culture's general distrust of performance creativity, and the higher value we tend to place on compositional creativity. This distrust of performance is pretty recent; historians agree that for thousands of years, poetry was primarily an oral, spoken genre.

Several scholars have studied how poetry is influenced by its oral roots. For example, because poetry was transmitted orally in cultures that were not literate, the structure of the poem had to be easy to remember. Cognitive psychologists have discovered that techniques associated with poetry, like alliteration, meter, and rhyme, increase the memorability of a text (Rubin, 1995). In other words, poetry doesn't have the distinctive features it does just because they look pretty on the page, or because they're fun to read; rather, they serve a very practical function of aiding in memory, a function that was, strictly speaking, no longer necessary after the introduction of literacy and written composition. Through most of human history, verbal creations had to be easy to remember; in oral cultures, all composed texts had features that we today associate with poetry, because otherwise they would not be remembered and would disappear from history.

In preliterate medieval Europe, a small cadre of trained scribes began to record traditional oral texts, fixing them on the page. This was time-consuming and expensive, and could only be done for highly valued ritual texts like the Bible. When the printing press was invented, it became economically possible to print a much wider range of texts. And until the growth of the novel as a prose genre in the 19th century, poetry continued to have the highest status of all written genres. The high value placed on poetry derived from its ancient pedigree, its historical association with religious texts, and the additional skill required to craft such texts.

Romance Novels

We don't have to return to Trollope's day to find examples of prolific, hardworking writers with rigid schedules. Romance novel authors are quite prolific; many of the most popular writers publish several books every year. Authors in several other genres—westerns, detective stories, children's books—are equally prolific. Ian Fleming wrote the first James Bond novel, *Casino Royale*, in under 10 weeks (Storr, 1972, p. 40).

Romance novels are written by women for women. A sociological survey conducted in Britain in the 1960s found that over half of readers were full-time housewives, that they read the books to relax and to escape from everyday problems, and that many women read these books in secret, suggesting that there was something of a stigma attached to them (Mann, 1969). It's interesting that although these findings come from over 30 years ago from Britain, they're still true of the readers of today's romance novel in the United States; they are still read with a bit of guilt, and primarily by married mothers between the ages of 25 and 50, with about half not employed outside the home (Radway, 1991).

Are these novels "art"? Are they as creative as so-called "literary" novels? Even if the genres can be distinguished, is there a difference in the creative process whereby writers generate them? With this high level of productivity, you can't create everything from scratch each time. Higher productivity seems to require a higher amount of convention and structure, and a lower amount of originality. In fact, the plots of romance novels are more formulaic than many other types of fiction. Many publishers of romance fiction have multiple series of novels, each designed to appeal to a different group of readers. These publishers have strict editorial guidelines for each series, "tip sheets" for writers that specify appropriate plot elements and character types, so that readers will get what they're expecting.

Group Writing

It is woefully difficult to write a play. A playwright is required
by the very nature of drama to enter into the spirit of oppos-
ing characters. . . . The job of shifting oneself totally from one
character to another . . . is a super-human task at any time.
—*Stage director Peter Brook (1968, p. 33)*

The 1970s TV show *M*A*S*H* is typical of how most sitcom episodes are written: not by a single solitary individual, but by a collaborative team of writers. Larry Gelbart was the head writer, but actor Alan Alda frequently collaborated with Gelbart on scripts, and in fact, he himself received writing credit for many of the episodes. The actors would go through the first finished draft of the script line by line and make comments, resulting in revisions before filming. In some cases, script ideas emerged from these discussions. In one episode, Alda's character, Dr. "Hawkeye" Pierce, decides to remove a man's appendix, even though the operation is unnecessary, so that the man won't have to return to the battle front. One writer rejected this element of the plot, arguing that no good doctor would do such a thing. Mr. Alda argued in response that war sometimes overrode the normal ethics of everyday practice. As the argument continued, the cast collectively realized that the argument itself could be the core of a good script, so they rewrote the script to incorporate the debate into the story (Bennetts, 1986).

A situation comedy is a weekly television episode with approximately 22 minutes of performance time, with advertisements filling out a 30-minute schedule slot. The 22 minutes are broken into two acts, and usually the episode has a story that is resolved by the end of the episode. The scripts are developed by a staff of writers, with the executive producer or "show runner" the head of the team. Some teams have two or three executive producers. Other team members include writers with titles such as supervising producer, producer, executive story editor, and creative consultant. The conceptual outline of an episode is conceived by the entire group, in a meeting where stories are worked out scene by scene. Then each scene is assigned to one or two people who write the dialogue. After these scenes are written, two or more rounds of comments and revisions by the team and writers follow. After multiple revisions, each resulting from a collaborative discussion among the writing team, the script is presented to the cast for a *table reading*. The table reading takes place on the stage, with network and studio personnel present, and it often results in suggestions for further revisions to the script. The last revision, called the final polish, is often done by the executive producer, perhaps with help from a few key staff members. Additional rewrites take place through the five days of rehearsal leading up to the final taping of the show, inspired by suggestions from actors or producers. Sometimes these suggestions are experimentally improvised by the cast, as they try out potential changes before sending the script back to the writing team.

In their interviews with comedy writers, Pritzker and Runco (1997) found that some teams were more collaborative than others, and in those teams "a sense of excitement and participation is experienced by everyone" (p. 123), and more creative scripts resulted. The writer Lynn commented on one such group: "It was more of a group thing—somebody having an idea and somebody else in the room adding to the idea and 'How about this?' 'How about that?'" (p. 124).

The collaborative writing style of *M*A*S*H* is typical of television. One reason that collaboration is essential is that each episode is only one in a whole season; the characters' personalities must be consistent, and their dialogue has to make sense within the overall trajectory of the season and the series (Pritzker & Runco, 1997, p. 128). A second reason for collaboration is that different writers contribute different skills; some are better at constructing stories, others write good characters, and still others are the best joke writers. In fact, in many sitcoms a joke specialist joins the group on the last major rewrite to punch up the show's dialogue.

With movie scripts, the process is often even more involved than with sitcoms, and extends over historical time as the script passes through the hands of multiple creative teams (Wolf, 1998). Hollywood types refer to this process as "script development." The script for the Dreamworks 1998 animated film *Small Soldiers* was originally written by Gavin Scott, purchased by Steven Spielberg in 1992, and revised four successive times by Anne Spielberg, Danny Rubin, Frank Deese, and Lewis Colick. Finally, yet another version by Danny Rifkin—this time incorporating Spielberg's suggestion that the soldiers be divided into two opposed factions—was approved for production in 1997. After this long creative process, the final product wasn't even that original. In 2000 Spielberg was sued by Gregory Grant, a short-film maker who alleged that Spielberg stole the plot from his 1991 short animation *Ode to G.I. Joe*; the short film contained similar plot elements of toy soldiers coming to life. Spielberg's production company defended itself by saying that neither of them had been creative; their defense was that the idea of "toy soldiers coming to life" was too generic to copyright.

When filming starts, the script isn't done—in fact, editing and rewriting accelerate. As Wolf (1998) reported, the first writers "merely stand at the head of a conveyor belt designed by producers and studios to precision-tool hits, sending their scripts along for subsequent handling by a small army of additional writers, each one specifically directed to beef up action scenes, to polish dialogue, to throw in some romance" (p. 32). The 1998 asteroid thriller *Armageddon* had eight different writers contributing to various portions of the script, all coming onto the project after the initial script had been developed by Jonathan Hensleigh and sold to producer Jerry Bruckheimer, and after the director and star had been hired. Tony Gilroy (*Devil's Advocate*) did a major rewrite on the first 15 pages of the script, with additional help from Paul Attanasio (*Quiz Show*, *Donnie Brasco*) and Jeffrey Abrams (*Regarding Henry*, *Forever Young*). Abrams then took the script and focused on the back stories of the individual driller-spacemen, and did additional scene work. Ann Biderman (*Smilla's Sense of Snow*) then rewrote the portions of the script relating to the romance between Ben Affleck and Liv Tyler, and also did work on the father-daughter conflict between Tyler and Bruce Willis. Shane Salerno edited and revised several of the action sequences, as Scott Rosenberg (*Beautiful Girls*, *Con Air*) wrote punchy humorous lines for Steve Buscemi and Ben Affleck. Robert Towne—perhaps Hollywood's most famous script doctor, with his fame originating in his credits as the writer of *Chinatown*, *Shampoo*, and others—then rewrote some of the more serious lines in the script that emphasized the world's potential elimination at the hands of the asteroid. During this process, Hensleigh, the original writer, served as a coordinator, collecting the pages of these many writers and cutting and pasting them together.

About 40 elite writers make their careers out of such script work. And there's nothing new to such a system; in the studio system of the 1930s and 1940s, writers were narrowly specialized, with some focusing on plot structure, and others filling in the dialogue. Hollywood emphasizes collaboration because it believes that the group process will generate a more creative product than a single writer working alone.

Computer-Assisted Writing

Aspiring Hollywood screenwriters can purchase the software package *Final Draft* to help them write; the product's motto is "Just add words" (www.finaldraft.com [accessed 2/19/04]). As of July 2005, more than 200,000 copies had been sold. And it's not just for aspiring amateurs; it's been used to write many successful and well-known movies, including *American Beauty* (1999) and *The Usual Suspects* (1995). *Final Draft* has been endorsed by Hollywood insiders from director Oliver Stone to actor Tom Hanks.

What can writing software do for you, if you still have to "just add words"? Of course, it does the usual formatting and spell-checking associated with any word processor, but in addition, *Final Draft* actually supports and guides the creative process of the writer. For example, it contains an intelligent "expert problem solver" that suggests a three-act plot structure, and provides tools to enforce that structure; it supports writers by marking whether a problem is one of plot, character, or structure. Reports can be generated that collect all of a character's lines. It remembers character names, scene headings, and transitions. A "Scene Navigator" supports editing of scene descriptions and action shots. And *Final Draft* supports the collaborative script writing that's so common in movies and television, keeping track of who changed a line and when.

Other software packages also focus on supporting the creative core of the writing process. *Dramatica* provides "story development paths" and "structural templates for creating scenes or chapters" in novels, screenplays, and short stories (www.dramatica.com [accessed 7/29/05]). A "Story Guide" prompts the aspiring author with questions that lead the author from a basic concept all the way to a completed text. One question the software asks is:

"At the end of your story, you want the audience to see your Main Character as having:" and then presents a multiple-choice list of items including "Changed," "Remained Steadfast," and "Skip this question for now." A "Story Engine" allows a small change in the dramatic structure to automatically update related plot elements elsewhere in the story. In their marketing literature, the company shows what the story engine for *The Great Gatsby* would look like: under "Plot Dynamics," the driver is "decision," the limit is "optionlock," the outcome is "failure." Other categories are "Character Dynamics" and "Thematic Choices." A "Character Builder" suggests archetypical characters and lists of personality traits, and can suggest what two characters' relationship should look once you've chosen their traits.

When authors wrote stories with quill pens, no one thought that the pen was a collaborator in the author's creativity; it was just a tool. When typewriters became widespread, they too were considered to be passive, transparent tools. But a software package like *Dramatica* somehow seems to be more than just a tool; it seems to cross a line into being a virtual collaborator. To explain this sort of computer-assisted creativity, we need to know a lot about the software, and we need to know a lot about the step-by-step creative process. We can't explain this creativity just by looking inside the writer's head.

Hypertext and the Audience

The mantra of the so-called postmodern school of literary criticism is that readers create their own texts. The writer is not in control of the readers' response. Prior to postmodernism, the text was thought to be the printed letters on the physical pages of the book—in other words, a visible created product. The author was the creator, and the reader was a passive consumer. Today's postmodernists argue that the writer and reader work collaboratively to creatively generate the meaning of the work. The pages of the book are not the created product; after all, they're static and lifeless. The act of reading is performative; the book provides a framework for the reading experience, but doesn't determine that experience. Readers bring books to life through the creative act of reading.

Postmodernism comes to life in a new genre of literature that has been made possible by the personal computer—the hypertext novel (Kakutani, 1997). The computer makes possible any organizational structure for a text; it no longer has to be linear, with one page following the other until the back cover is reached. In a hypertext, each virtual "page" is stored in its own computer file, and the pages are linked according to the author's sense of what story fragments might possibly be connected to what others. When a reader finishes a page, he or she is presented with on-screen buttons that branch in multiple narrative directions. Hypertext fiction has no beginning, middle, or end; the reader chooses where to enter and exit the story, and how to move through the story. After two decades of outsider cult status, hypertext gained a form of establishment legitimacy when several such novels were reviewed in *The New York Review of Books* in 2002 (Parks, 2002).

The hypertext author creates a world, a virtual environment something like a role-playing video game. Many hypertext novels take advantage of the multimedia capabilities of the computer screen, and include graphics and images alongside the text. The author's role is diminished because the reader participates actively in the construction of his or her reading experience.

For almost two decades, fans of hypertext fiction have predicted "a future in which traditional narratives would become obsolete, and discrete, self-contained books would also give way to vast interlinked electronic networks" (Kakutani, 1997, p. 41). In fact, there's no reason why each virtual page has to be written by the same author; in the late 1990s, "chain fiction" was invented, in which different segments of the hypertext are written by different authors (Kakutani, 1997, p. 41). These multivocal works make more clear than ever the collaborative nature of writing—collaborations including not only isolated creative geniuses that we used to call "writers," but now directly including readers in the creative collaborative process. As Mark Taylor and Esa Saarinen (1994) wrote, "No hypertext is the product of a single author who is its creative origin or heroic architect. To the contrary, in the hypertextual network, all authorship is joint authorship and all production is co-production. Every writer is a reader and all reading is writing" (p. 6).

What Lasts: Posthumous Publication

After the death of a well-known and respected writer, what factors play a role in the posthumous development of a reputation? Our individualist myth would have us say it's the work itself. We think that good work will eventually be recognized for its worth. In contrast, the sociocultural approach would argue that reputation is determined by the cooperative evaluation of the art world.

Posthumous publication is a tried-and-true way of keeping a deceased writer in the public eye. For example, there have been as many books published by writer Raymond Carver after his death as during his lifetime. Virginia Woolf's works have been published far more after her death, because her letters and diaries were released by her estate and eventually filled up over 30 volumes.

Some writers try to plan ahead for their career after death: Henry James rewrote his own books to be re-released after his death, and Norman Mailer left plans for an anthology of his greatest works that was released after his death. One way to influence history's opinion is to pick a good biographer. An official biographer is granted privileged access to original documents like letters and draft manuscripts, and other writers are forbidden to see such materials. These careful plans don't always work like the author might have hoped. Robert Frost selected his friend Lawrence Thompson as his biographer, but Thompson changed his opinion of Frost even before he'd passed on. Thomas Hardy chose a devious way to control his posthumous reputation: he secretly wrote his own biography and instructed his wife to release it under her name after his death.

Another common way to control your future reputation is by selectively destroying your files and papers, so that only the most flattering stuff remains. Writers often establish exclusive arrangements for storage of their papers, negotiating the best deals with university libraries across the country. Saul Bellow has his papers at the University of Chicago; Toni Morrison's are at Princeton. Writers frequently spend years of their retirement selecting and ordering the materials. Their final creative act is the creation of their future reputation.

Some writers go to an extreme, burning every last paper in the attempt to prevent future generations from looking past the published work itself. After all, they reason, "During my lifetime I released exactly what I wanted published, and that's my gift to posterity; if I'd wanted my private papers released, I could have done so during my own lifetime and benefited from royalties on sales." Franz Kafka famously instructed his friend Max Brod to burn all his work "even to the last page"; in the end, Brod could not bring himself to carry out the instruction. Critics and readers are grateful the manuscripts exist, but that they do is Brod's choice and not Kafka's. Some executors make these selection decisions on their own. Ted Hughes, widower of Sylvia Plath, destroyed the last volume of her diary after her 1963 suicide, intending to protect their two children from further anguish. Lord Byron's friends burned his X-rated memoirs, fearing a scandal should they ever be printed.

Fans and relatives of deceased writers do all they can to build up a writer's reputation. Usually, the writer's spouse or another family member becomes the official executor of the estate, and has complete control over the writer's letters, diaries, and manuscripts. The executor makes all of the above decisions— what will be published posthumously, who'll be the official biographer, where the archives will be stored. Without the executor's permission, the archival materials can't be quoted.

We can't explain historical reputation by looking only at the work, or only at the writer's personality. Reputation is collaboratively managed and it emerges from a sociocultural process.

The Domain of Writing

> There are three rules for writing a novel. Unfortunately, no
> one knows what they are.
> —*W. Somerset Maugham* (1874–1965)
> (*quoted in Byrne, 1996, 3:490*)

One of the most valuable insights of the sociocultural approach is that you can't create in a vacuum. In chapter 8, we learned that the domain of culture is like the air that supports the wings of a flying bird; even though the bird might curse the wind because its friction slows her down, without the wind there could be no flight. In chapter 7, we learned that creativity always takes place in a domain. The best metaphor for the domain is everyday language. You can't talk at all unless you've learned a language—the vocabulary, syntax, and idioms that you share with the other members of your culture. But just because you're all using the same language, it doesn't mean that you can never talk creatively. In the same way, the conventions of a creative domain enable the possibility of creativity.

The writers interviewed by Csikszentmihalyi (1996) all emphasize the importance of immersing themselves in the domain of the word. Writers, it seems, read more voraciously than anyone else. Many writing teachers say that their single most important piece of advice is to read constantly.

Can one be an "outsider writer"? It seems a contradiction in terms. After all, the definition of an outsider artist is someone who doesn't follow the conventions of a domain, but all writers follow the conventions of the language they use, the conventions of word meanings and grammar. The closest we could come to outsider writing would be a self-taught person who didn't actively participate in the field of creative writing. In 2002, Henry Louis Gates reported that he had purchased, at auction, the manuscript of a novel called *The Bondwoman's Narrative*, written by the slave Hannah Crafts in 1850 (Crafts, 2002; Gates, 2002). Prior to the Civil War there was an entire genre of slave narratives that were published and widely read; *Uncle Tom's Cabin* is the most famous. But this was the first original, pre-edited manuscript ever discovered. Crafts was an African American slave when she wrote the novel, and it was lost, unread, in storage for over a century.

Slaves were forbidden to read and write, so Crafts certainly qualifies as being self-taught. And by being on the margins of society, Crafts seems to meet many of the other criteria now associated with outsiders. But even this apparently "outside" writer did not generate a completely novel, unconventional text. Gates's analysis of the novel revealed that it was, if anything, even more conventional than most novels of the time, and that it borrowed heavily from popular and widely available fiction of the era. For example, throughout Crafts's novel, there are entire passages lifted verbatim from several of Charles Dickens's novels (researchers have discovered that her master's library contained three of Dickens's novels). And the themes, characters, and events in the novel closely follow other popular fiction of the day.

This example suggests that there can never be an outsider writer. Paradoxically, the more outside you are, the more conventional your writing will be. Our creativity myth often leads us to believe that writers are more naive, more self-taught, more inspired than they actually are. And many writers, editors, and publicists are only too happy to oblige us in our mythical belief. Writers always work in a sociocultural system, collaborating with members of the field, working with the conventions of the domain.

Thought Experiments

- How often do you revise when you write?
- Do you write better at some times of the day than others?
- Do you prepare an outline before you start to write?
- Have you ever edited or been edited? What was it like? Did it improve the final product?
- Have you ever written poetry or fiction? Why? Did anyone read it?

Suggested Readings

Csikszentmihalyi, M. (1996). *Creativity: Flow and the psychology of discovery and invention.* New York: HarperCollins. See especially chapter 10.

Eliot, V. (1971). *T. S. Eliot The waste land: A facsimile and transcript of the original drafts including the annotations of Ezra Pound.* New York: Harcourt Brace Jovanovich.

Kakutani, M. (1997, September 28). Never-ending saga. *The New York Times Magazine,* 40–41.

Lamott, A. (1994). *Bird by bird: Some instructions on writing and life.* New York: Pantheon Books.

Max, D. T. (1998, August 9). The Carver chronicles. *The New York Times Magazine,* 34–40, 51, 56–57.

Pritzker, S., & Runco, M. A. (1997). The creative decision-making process in group situation comedy writing. In R. K. Sawyer (Ed.), *Creativity in performance* (pp. 115–141). Norwood, NJ: Ablex.

CHAPTER 12

Music

All art constantly aspires towards the condition of music.
—*Walter Pater (1873/1986, p. 86)*

Many people think that jazz musicians play whatever comes into their heads in a burst of unconstrained inspiration. But even the freest improviser improvises within a musical tradition, and before you can improvise you have to learn that tradition (Alperson, 1984; Berliner, 1994). Young jazz musicians become aware of the structures and conventions of their domain through close listening. For example, they often listen to famous albums and copy the performances note for note. This helps them to develop a personal repertoire of phrases; sometimes, young improvisers sound just like the famous musician they've been copying. Trumpet players sound like Miles Davis or Wynton Marsalis; saxophonists like Coleman Hawkins or John Coltrane. No doubt, it takes a high level of skill to sound like a famous musician. But that's only the first step in a lifetime of learning how to play jazz.

Listening and practicing at home is an important part of learning jazz. But young musicians who have wonderful technique on their instruments, who can play extremely fast and flawlessly, often tend to be poor improvisers, because they haven't yet learned how to communicate musically with the ensemble. Musicians can't learn jazz by playing at home alone. To get really good, a musician has to attend uncountable jam sessions, and play in many different beginner bands.

The late 20th century experienced an incredible flowering of musical creativity. In the 1950s popular music genres were limited pretty much to jazz and rock 'n' roll. Even in the 1970s, record stores had perhaps three or four sections: classical, rock, jazz, or rhythm and blues. But by the 1990s, your run-of-the-mill mall music store had 20, 30, or more genres available, from reggae to world music to metal to trip hop. With the development of the underground genre of electronica, boundaries between genres began to fall; in electronica, computer-savvy producers use digital sampling to combine a century of American pop music in a single song.

Popular music has more in common with jazz than it does with high-status classical music. Like jazz, pop music is often improvised and performance oriented, composers are not valorized as the sole creators of the tradition, and scores are rarely written down for later performance. Cultural critics from Theodor Adorno to Alan Bloom have attacked popular music from across the ideological spectrum—Marxism in Adorno's case, conservative American values in Bloom's case. But these criticisms are rarely more than snobbish prejudice, derived from the ethnocentric assumption that European classical music is the standard of quality.

In this chapter, I'll explore musical creativity by comparing composition and performance. Explanations of musical creativity tend to emphasize one at the expense of the other. Our creativity myths do a better job of explaining composition; we can easily imagine a composer alone in a room, working in a fever of half-crazed hard work, the lone genius of our romantic myth. It's harder to make the myths work with performance, because performance is deeply social, with an audience and co-performers. We've learned throughout this book that our creativity myths have influenced creativity researchers as much as they have everyone else, and that may be why creativity researchers have focused on the creativity of composition, rather than the creativity of performance (Sawyer, 1997a). To explain performance creativity, we need the sociocultural approach. And once you realize how performance creativity works, you see that composition, too, requires a sociocultural explanation.

It's too simple to say that all pop music is improvised and all classical music is composed. For example, in a review of a performance by jazz pianist Ray Bryant, Hollenberg (1978) noted that his solos on two successive nights were note-for-note identical, and wrote: "Some of the freest sounding pieces of the evening were the most mechanical" (p. 42). Bryant is not the only musician to use precomposed solos. Many famous jazz improvisers have occasionally repeated solos note for note, including Jelly Roll Morton, several of Duke Ellington's soloists, and Oscar Peterson (Brown, 1981).

How could a composed piece sound more free and spontaneous than pieces that actually are improvised? Famous European composers including Bach and Beethoven were legendary improvisers. Many of them wrote compositions that were designed to sound like improvisations. These pieces are called "fantasias" or "impromptus," and Bach's fantasias are thought to be pretty close to written-out improvisations. Paradoxically, it takes a lot of compositional effort to create a work that sounds improvised.

Even more so than in jazz, many rock and pop performers compose their solos in advance. Unlike jazz, with a subculture that valorizes pure improvisation, rock lead guitarists don't mind admitting that they compose their solos. In interviews in *Guitar Magazine*, precomposed solos were often published, in detailed musical notation, alongside the interview. Like a Bach fantasia, even though the solos are composed, they sound improvised because they're composed according to the conventions of improvisation.

Composition

It's been said that different composers have different creative styles. Some of them are said to compose in quick bursts, without any preparation or revision, so that the compositional process is essentially like an improvisation. Mozart and Schubert are often said to have composed in this manner. However, this common observation is a Romantic-era myth, without supporting historical evidence. In the last chapter we learned that Romantic poets like Coleridge made up stories about how they created their poems so that their creative process would seem consistent with the creativity myths of the day. In the 19th century, composers and their fans made up similar stories. For example, since the 1960s scholars have known that Mozart's creative process was controlled by a consistently practical approach to the business aspects of music; his manuscripts show evidence of careful editing, revision, and hard work (Sloboda, 1985, pp. 112–114).

Almost all famous composers engage in long periods of preparation and frequent revision. Brahms took 20 years to write his first symphony. Max Bruch's Violin Concerto no. 1 in G Minor, his most popular work, was rewritten almost 10 times between 1864 and 1868, including revisions after its first public performance (Schiavo, 2001). Like all creativity, musical composition is 99% hard work and only 1% inspiration, and that 1% is sprinkled throughout the creative process in frequent mini-insights that are always embedded in the conscious hard work under way. Great music is rarely created in a Romantic burst of inspiration—not even European art music.

As we've learned in prior chapters, the European fine arts traditions tend to be the most receptive to our creativity myths. Like painting or poetry, classical music composition seems at first glance to be an activity that is done in private, by a solitary genius. And again, this is why creativity researchers, like other Americans, first think of these genres when they try to explain musical creativity. But if we want to develop a scientific explanation of musical creativity, we can't limit our study to European classical music. A true explanation of creativity must be able to explain all creativity, and most important, the genres of musical creativity that are most widespread and most influential in our lives. In the following sections, I'll talk about the way composition *really* happens in today's music. You'll see that it has little in common with the Hollywood image of Mozart as fictionalized in the movie *Amadeus*, writing in his sickbed in a fever of inspired creativity.

Composition in the Recording Studio

In the latter half of the 20th century, the most significant burst of musical creativity was in the pop arena—jazz, rock, soul, rhythm and blues, disco, and country. These songs aren't composed by solitary artists, and they're not written down. Instead, they're created as a work in progress by the entire band, working collaboratively in the studio. The member of the band who is credited as the writer of the song typically does no more than suggest the melodic line for the voice, the overall chord structure of the song, and the general style or genre of the piece. He or she presents that to the band, and then the individual musicians are expected to create parts for their own instruments. Their first attempts are then critically discussed by all of the band members, as musicians offer suggestions to one another.

Every musician who's experienced the tedious business of the studio knows how much hard work it is. Very few music fans are aware of the collaborative studio work that results in a popular music recording. However, a few bands have such strong cult followings that fans illegally acquire studio tapes—which contain conversation among band members, aborted first performances, warts and all—and actively trade the tapes with like-minded fans. Some widely bootlegged bands include the Grateful Dead, Bob Dylan, and the Beatles. Of course, the bootleg copies are illegal; but without being able to stop the phenomenon, record companies sometimes respond by formally releasing the most widely copied bootleg tapes on CD. In 1975, Columbia released *The Basement Tapes* with private rehearsal tapes of Bob Dylan that had been circulating for six years; in 1996 The Beatles released the six-disc *Anthology* that contained over eight hours of material, including long-circulated bootleg favorites (Kozinn, 1997).

Bootlegs provide important insights into musical creativity because we can hear how the band experimented with other versions of each song. Some of these are radically different from the version that was eventually released to the public. A pop hit becomes so embedded in a fan's brain that it seems almost a sacrilege to imagine that even a single note could have been any different. That's why bootleg recordings provide an important perspective; they make us aware of the selection processes that bands and producers go through as they decide what gets released to the public. The bootlegs make it clear that a band experiments with many different versions of a song, and may have many potentially final and releasable versions, yet, they must select only one to release. The selection process is collaborative and collective, sociocultural rather than psychological.

In fact, many finished songs are never released because there's no room left on the album or because the producer or record company decides that they won't sell enough copies to earn back the costs of production. In June 2002, the CD *A Cellar Full of Motown* was released, containing 40 fully formed singles recorded in the 1960s at the legendary Motown studio in Detroit. Although these singles were polished and ready to go, they were never released because producer Berry Gordy and the rest of the staff felt they were not as good as the other songs that were released, and they didn't want to flood the market with too many new songs in any given year. Motown under Berry Gordy recorded many more singles than it could ever hope to successfully market. Although this might seem inefficient, it provided him with a pool of material to choose from, and he believed that this would ultimately result in more hits. When I listen to these long-lost songs today, they sound not only stylistically similar, but also equal in quality to the Top 40 Motown hits that we all know so well, the ones that were released instead.

How were these 40 singles selected for the CD from the stacks of basement tapes? To explain the selection, we have to look beyond the individual tastes of record company executives. For years, many of these singles had been illegally copied and widely traded among cult fans, particularly in the northern part of England, which had a network of clubs known as the "Northern Soul" scene. The Northern Soul scene was its own field, which created a new domain of 1960s soul recordings that had never been officially sold. Like much of pop culture, the initial selection was done not by the powerful gatekeepers, but by a collective grassroots emergent process. The record company made sure that these cult favorites were on the CD, because they hoped that the underground scene would buy the new recordings. The selection process that picked these 40 singles was truly a distributed, social, collective process.

Electronica

Perhaps the most significant new musical genre of the 1990s was the underground genre known as "techno" or "electronica." Both are umbrella terms that uncomfortably cover a wide range of very different sounding styles of music, and like many cultish underground scenes, insiders have created a dizzying number of terms for subgenres: house, deep house, ambient, trip hop, drum and bass. What they all share isn't so much the formal features of the music, but their method of composition.

Our mental image of a pop music composer is a pianist trying out different melodies on the keyboard, or a guitarist strumming different chords to see what sounds good. But many electronica composers don't play musical instruments, and can't even read music. How can such a person create music? Electronica artists do it by digitally recording, or "sampling" segments of already recorded music, building up a personal library of interesting samples on their computers' hard drives, and then using computer software to repeat the samples in loops, overlaying multiple tracks to create a polyphonic blend of sounds.

The most admired electronica songs are those that bring together the most unlikely combinations of musical genres, blending samples of 1930s field-hand chants with 1950s tiki lounge, with a sprinkling of 1960s pop orchestra swells. Electronica artist Moby, who has perhaps enjoyed the greatest popular success of any such artist, said, "I want to have the broadest possible sonic palette to draw on when I'm composing music. I wanted to hear pop records, dance records, classical records. . . . On my records, I'm the composer and the musician and the engineer, but also a plagiarist and thief" (quoted in Marzorati, 2002, p. 35). Moby typically creates over 100 songs for each of his CDs, even though he knows that no more than 15 or 20 could possibly fit (Marzorati, 2002). Like Motown, he creates many more songs than the market could support, and this means that a lot of his creativity is applied at the evaluation stage.

The contrast with our contemporary image of the pop musician could not be greater. Since the 1960s, our culture has placed a high value on a musician's authenticity. Through the 1950s, vocalists recorded songs by nameless writers that were selected by their producers. But in the 1960s this changed. Audiences began to insist that musicians write their own songs, and they wanted each song to talk about a musician's personal experience. And it went without saying that musicians would play their own instruments live, and not use any previously recorded material. Many electronica artists reject this model as obsolete. As Moby put it, "What's stranger at this point in time, given the technology and all, than a band where everybody plays one instrument, and you get one kind of music, song after song, album after album?" (quoted in Marzorati, 2002, p. 36).

Electronica composers begin by first collecting a large library of sounds—typically from other albums, but also from news reports, training films, or everyday sounds like fire alarms and cement mixers. These are all digitized and stored in a computer, and the compositional process then involves listening to and thinking about which might sound good together, and experimenting using multitrack computer sound studio software. The creative process begins to seem more like fiction writing, because writers keep notebooks and write every idea that pops into their heads—one paragraph or one character sketch at a time—and later blend and combine these bits to construct a complex story.

Tribute Bands

Popular songs act as an everyday soundtrack for each new generation of high school and college students. But they aren't compositions in the classical music sense. The creators don't write the songs down on music paper and then hand them out to the members of the band. Instead, they're created through collaborative, performative, improvisational processes during rehearsals. Bootleg tapes or CDs, if they exist, can provide the aficionado with a window onto this collaborative compositional process. But once the master tape is finished and hundreds of thousands of CDs are manufactured and sold, the song becomes a fixed product; if anything even more invariant than a Beethoven score.

Bands that perform the famous songs of successful bands are called cover bands or tribute bands. Their goal is to perform, live, a song that has been composed by another band, and to have their performance sound as much like the recorded composition as possible. Some bands spawn more tribute bands than others; there are probably more Grateful Dead tribute bands than for every other band combined. Other widely covered bands include Guns N' Roses and Rush.

Tribute bands get little respect from serious music critics; they seem to be nothing more than wanna-be rock stars, basking in reflected glory. Some may ask, "Why don't they write their own songs and perform them instead?" But they're doing the same thing as a modern symphony orchestra performing a written composition by Beethoven or Brahms. No one thinks to ask, "Why is the orchestra performing a song written by someone else? Why doesn't each city's orchestra write its own new music?" The most common answer would probably be that it's OK to replicate Beethoven's music because it is uniquely brilliant, but it's not OK to replicate late-20th-century pop music because it's not worthy. But we can't accept these subjective judgments as scientific explanations. When a band called Paradise City performs a Guns N' Roses song (Klosterman, 2002), it's a modern version of the St. Louis Symphony performing Beethoven's Ninth.

One clear difference is how the song is stored for history. Hundreds of years ago, there was no audio recording or multitrack studio technology. Composers had to create a written score using musical notation because it was the only way to preserve a song for posterity. Modern pop music instead takes advantage of recording technology and uses the sound studio itself to compose the song. You no longer need a score because the sound recording preserves the original composition more accurately than a written score ever could.

The Audience As Collaborator

An interactive orchestral work, 3D Music, was written specifically for the Internet. It "plays" very much like a videogame (http://www.braunarts.com/ 3dmusic/ [accessed 7/29/05]). The work has seven "spaces" or virtual environments, and the "player/listener" chooses which spaces to enter and when. Each space has its own composed section. The player hears different music depending on where his or her on-screen character is, and which direction the player is moving to and from. You can't sit back and passively listen to this performance; you have to actively participate in its creation. Listening to 3D Music is more like playing a videogame than sitting quietly and letting the music wash over you. Listeners (or "users"?) interact with the music just like readers interact with the hypertext novels that we learned about in chapter 11. When a composer shares control over a work's structure with the listener, our traditional notions of a composition as a fixed created product is challenged. With 3D Music, there is no authentic, authoritative version of the work. Each time it's heard, it's different, and every occasion of performance is equally authoritative.

We don't need to look at advanced computer technology to see audience influence on the compositional creative process; audiences influence musical creation indirectly all the time. For example, much of popular music is created to respond to the demands and tastes of radio listeners and major advertisers. If a radio station attracts more listeners because they like the songs that the radio station is playing, advertisers will pay more money to the station to advertise to those listeners. Country music stations, in particular, are big business. They're money-making machines, with the money coming from big advertisers. Country has been the top radio format in the United States since the late 1990s; around 20% of all radio stations play country. Yet most of country's classic artists and styles—bluegrass, country and western, western swing—are never heard on these stations. Even after the bluegrass soundtrack to the 2002 film *O Brother, Where Art Thou?* won a Grammy award, the songs on it weren't played on country stations. Why not?

Anyone paying attention to country radio's changes over the last 10 or 20 years has probably noticed that the songs are no longer about drinking and fast women—topics for men—but they are instead songs about sassy women, telling off their no-good men. The explanation for this shift starts not with the musicians, but with the major advertisers. The companies that pay for advertising time on country radio stations are the people who really control what gets played on country radio. In a sense, they're the creators of contemporary country. And "contemporary country radio is targeting young adult females," said

Paul Allen, the executive director of the Country Radio Broadcasters, a trade association (quoted in Strauss, 2002, p. AR31). It's a soundtrack for suburban soccer moms, a desirable audience for consumer household goods producers such as Procter & Gamble. Young adult females influence 90% of all of the buying decisions in the household, and they haven't yet made up their minds which brands they like best. The audience research company Arbitron issued a report recently on what women want from country radio: they want family-friendly, upbeat, optimistic songs. And what radio executive won't give it to them, when their major advertisers are reading the same Arbitron report?

Unlike some other musical genres—like alternative rock or rap—country songs are still produced by an assembly-line process that has its roots in post-war Nashville. Songs are written by anonymous writers; then star singers, together with their managers, search through these for a potential hit. Given this creative collaborative process—where singers are not associated with specific themes, and they're not expected to be singing about their own personal experiences—it's easy for artists to shift their songs to suit shifts in consumer taste. Country radio is a microcosm of today's entertainment industry, showing us how the mass audience collectively contributes to the creative process.

Performance

> There is in principle no difference between the performance of
> a modern orchestra or chorus and people sitting around a
> campfire and singing to the strumming of a guitar or a
> congregation singing hymns under the leadership of the
> organ. And there is no difference in principle between the
> performance of a string quartet and the improvisations at a
> jam session of accomplished jazz players.
> —*Alfred Schutz* (*1964, p. 177*)

To explain performance, we have to focus on the creative process rather than the created product. Composition is a creative activity that results in a created product, like a musical score or a studio recording; performance is temporary, and exists only while the band's playing. As we learned in chapter 3, the first wave of creativity research focused on created products and creative personalities, and this led to a neglect of performance. In chapter 4, we learned that the 1970s cognitive psychologists shifted the focus to the creative process, but they continued to focus on the process of creating products, leading to sequential stage theories that don't explain performance very well. In the 1980s and 1990s, the sociocultural approach shifted the focus to processes of performance, and for the first time, we can begin to explain performance creativity.

In the European fine art tradition, performers aren't supposed to be creative; European classical music composers hate it when performers interpret their works creatively. Igor Stravinsky spoke for all composers when he stated his expectations: "Only through the performer is the listener brought in contact with the musical work. In order that the public may know what a work is like and what its value is, the public must first be assured of the merit of the person who presents the work to it and of the conformity of that presentation to the composer's will" (Stravinsky, 1947, pp. 132–133). According to Stravinsky, performers must be modest, and remove their own individuality from the performance; their job is to communicate another creator's vision faithfully, not to be creative themselves. Because our culture equates creativity and novelty, it's not surprising that we don't think performers are as creative as composers.

If the ideal performer is a transparent window to the mind of the creator, then with modern recording and computer technology, who needs the performer at all? A composer can easily create his work in a computer program that will synthetically produce all of the necessary sounds, and he can record the composition on a CD on his own computer. Some contemporary composers do this, but most still write in the old-fashioned way—generating scores that will be performed later by specialists in instrumental performance. Even European classical music composers still prefer to have their music performed by real, live musicians. This suggests that Stravinsky's view is a bit extreme, that many composers believe that the variation of human performance is an important part of musical creativity.

Our prototype of the mythic composer is one of the three B's: Beethoven, Bach, or Brahms. These composers wrote scores that specified every note to be played, and added instructions for how to perform the notes, indicating which passages should be played louder, which notes should stand out, and when the tempo should speed up or slow down. Over historical time, the amount of detail specified in a composer's score has changed dramatically. Many of the most famous piano composers performed their own works during their lifetimes. Chopin was a famous virtuoso performer, and during his lifetime, it wasn't quite the same to hear another pianist play a work by Chopin. Think back to that time, and imagine you're a very good amateur pianist, and you've purchased the published score of a Chopin piece. But then you attend one of his concerts and you discover that he plays it differently than it's written. Which version would you say was the right one—the one you bought two years before, or the live version performed by the composer himself? Your answer depends on whether you value performance or composition more.

Today's virtuoso performers are rarely composers; instead, they perform compositions by others. If a piano composer doesn't perform her own works, we don't think she's less creative, because we associate the creativity with the composing, not the performing. In our creativity myth, the creation of the work is where the action is, and the performance is simply an execution of the work. But there've been many time periods and genres of music when the composer didn't specify in such detail what the performer was supposed to do. Virtuoso performers from the Renaissance through the 19th century embellished and improvised on the composer's score (Dart, 1967; Reese, 1959). In those days, the composer contributed a lesser percentage to the final performance, and more of the creativity came from the performer. Many 20th century composers in the European tradition, including John Cage and Karlheinz Stockhausen, have re-introduced elements of improvisation into their works.

Perhaps the most important example of performance creativity is found in jazz. Miles Davis is credited as the composer of many of the songs on the seminal 1959 album *Kind of Blue*. But the song "Freddie the Freeloader," for example, is only the barest outline of a performance, and was composed to provide the performers with a framework on which to improvise. In general, the jazz community doesn't defer to the composer or to the original version when deciding how to perform a classic jazz standard. Rather, jazz performers are expected to contribute so much to the piece that the original piece may become almost unrecognizable. Needless to say, such license would constitute sacrilege in a symphony hall today—even though 200 years ago, an audience in the same hall might have rightly been outraged if the famous guest pianist did not improvise during the performance.

Flow

Musical performance is a complex skill that takes years of training and rehearsal to master. Talented performers seek out the flow state, a state of heightened awareness, when they're fully focused on the act of performing (Csikszentmihalyi, 1990b). In the flow state, performers can lose track of time and feel themselves fully absorbed in the music. These are peak experiences, in the humanist psychology originated by Carl Rogers and Abraham Maslow; we seek them out because they're fulfilling in their own right, not because of any external rewards that may come from engaging in the activity. Performers get into a flow state because group creativity is challenging; they have to listen to other performers while they're performing, and integrate their partners' actions into their own unfolding activity, while at the same time acting within the conventions of the genre.

These difficult tasks can't be managed or directed consciously; group performance involves a complex interaction between the performer's conscious and unconscious minds. Just like the writers that I quoted in the last chapter, musicians skillfully balance unconscious inspiration with conscious hard work and editing. But where writers can usually separate the inspiration and the editing stages of their creative process, performers always experience both creative "stages" simultaneously; while performing they're consciously directing their actions, and also acting in a heightened state of consciousness in which the conscious mind seems removed from the process, and their action seems to come from a deeper place. This tension is perhaps most exaggerated in improvisational performance, as described by this jazz saxophonist:

> I find what I'm playing is sometimes conscious, sometimes subconscious, sometimes it just comes out and I play it; sometimes I hear it in my head before I play it, and it's like chasing after it, like chasing after a piece of paper that's being blown across the street; I hear it in my head, and grab onto it, and follow it; but sometimes it just comes out, it falls out of my mouth. . . . When you start a solo, you're still in thinking mode; it takes a while to get yourself out of thinking mode . . . and you start giving yourself a little line to follow along, and you start following along that line, and if it's a productive thought, way of expressing yourself, you keep following it, and after a while it's like getting farther and farther into your mind, a way of burrowing in; and if you find the right thread to start with, intellectually, and keep following it, feeling it, you can turn it into something. (quoted in Sawyer, 2003)

Improv performers minimize the role of the intellectual, conscious mind during performance. Yet they realize that some conscious awareness is always essential: they must create while aware of the other performers and the conventions, etiquette, and expectations of the genre: "It's all a matter of listening to the people you're playing with. . . . This is a real difficulty—you have to be able to divide your senses, but still keep it coherent so you can play, so you still have that one thought running through your head of saying something, playing something, at the same time you've got to be listening to what the drummer is doing" (quoted in Sawyer, 2003). There's a constant tension between the performer's conscious and unconscious during performance, and each performer has to balance the tension from moment to moment. Performers say it's like riding a wave; too much of the conscious mind will slow you down and you'll slip off the back of the wave, dead in the water. But too much of the unconscious mind will make you crash over the edge.

Idealist theories can't explain performance creativity; we need an action theory, because all of the creativity occurs in the moment. The staged psychological models of chapter 4 can't explain performance creativity, because there don't seem to be distinct insight and evaluation stages in group creativity. Evaluation has to happen, in part, at the unconscious ideation stage; otherwise, the conscious evaluation stage would be overwhelmed, unable to properly filter the large number of musical ideas. During musical improvisation new ideas come from both the conscious and the unconscious, and new ideas are also evaluated by both the conscious and the unconscious.

Improvisation As Conversation

Group jazz performance is perhaps the most well-known improvisational performance form in American culture. Each performance begins with a song, more or less arranged in advance, and quickly progresses to group improvisation, where each musician takes a turn improvising a solo on the initial song form. During her solo, the soloist is the primary improviser; the remainder of the group is expected to direct their improvisations so that they support her by reinforcing her creative ideas or suggesting new ideas to stimulate her playing.

Monson's 1996 book *Saying Something* analyzed many such examples, along with transcribed musical notation that demonstrated in wonderful detail how musicians converse in a jazz improvisation. Monson described an interview with drummer Ralph Peterson in which she played a tape of a live performance of Peterson's composition "Princess" with pianist Geri Allen and bassist Essiet Okon Essiet. During Allen's solo, Peterson's drum accompaniment was very dense, and there were several instances in which Allen and Peterson traded ideas with each other. Monson and Peterson sat together and listened closely to the tape. Monson recognized that one of the conversational exchanges seemed to be based on the distinctive, catchy pattern from Dizzy Gillespie's famous performance of "Salt Peanuts," and noted this to Peterson. He replied:

> Yeah! "Salt Peanuts" and "Looney Tunes"—kind of a combination of the two. [Drummer] Art Blakey has a thing he plays. It's like: [he sings a rhythmic phrase from the song]. And [pianist] Geri played: [he sings Allen's standard response]. So I played the second half of the Art Blakey phrase: [he sings the second part of Blakey's drum pattern]. (Monson, 1996, p. 77)

Geri Allen immediately recognized the musical quotation from her performances with Blakey, and then responded with her usual response, indicating that she recognized and appreciated Peterson's communication (musical transcripts can be found in Monson, 1996, pp. 78–79). As in this example, musical communication in jazz depends on all of the musicians knowing the jazz language extremely well—not only the notes of the songs, but even knowing how a certain performer typically plays a certain song with a specific other performer. Peterson then told Monson:

> But you see what happens is, a lot of times when you get into a musical conversation, one person in the group will state an idea or the beginning of an idea and another person will *complete* the idea or their interpretation of the same idea, how they hear it. So the conversation happens in fragments and comes from different parts, different voices. (Monson, 1996, p. 78)

At many points in group improvisation, rather than develop their own musical ideas or start a completely new idea, each musician continues in the spirit or mood established by the prior players (Berliner, 1994, pp. 369–370). Rufus Reid told Paul Berliner how he tries to weave in the prior soloist's ideas into his own solo, but not always in an obvious way, and not always by direct quotation; he said it was more interesting to elaborate on the prior idea. In the musical conversation of jazz, as in a good everyday conversation, players borrow material from the previous phrase and then build on it.

Once we realize that performance creativity is like a collaborative conversation, we see that it's not created by any one of the performers. The individualist approach can partially explain what's going on, but it can't provide the complete explanation of group creativity. To explain group creativity, we need a sociocultural approach that analyzes collaboration, interaction, and group dynamics.

Group Creativity

Becker (2000) described the "etiquette" of improvisation, drawing an analogy between musical interaction and the informal and implicit rules of good social conduct. Sometimes the etiquette specifies opposed goals that are in tension. For example, jazz is democratic music, and all musicians should have the freedom to express themselves. But at the same time, players depend on one another and have to rein in their individual freedom for the good of the group.

When one performer introduces a new idea, the other performers evaluate it immediately, determining whether or not the performance will shift to incorporate the proposed new idea. The evaluation of new musical ideas is a collaborative process. Referring to a musical conversation between a trumpet and bass, bassist Richard Davis commented:

> Sometimes you might put a idea in that you think is good and nobody takes to it. . . . And then sometimes you might put an idea in that your incentive or motivation is not to influence but it does influence. (Monson, 1996, p. 88)

Composed music has a more constraining structure that the musicians must follow, but no notational system is capable of completely determining the final performance. All composed music depends on highly trained performers, capable of interpreting the notation in the proper manner. Even in composed musical performance, group creativity is necessary to an effective performance, because a score underdetermines performance.

When Peter Weeks studied chamber orchestra rehearsals, he discovered that even classical music groups have to improvisationally coordinate several aspects of the performance: the initial tempo of the piece; the rate to slow down the tempo in a ritardando, a passage in which the composer has indicated that the tempo should slow down; and the relative durations of the fermata, a mark on the score that indicates that a note should be held for an indeterminate length of time (Weeks, 1990, 1996). This is what Schutz (1964) meant when he compared an orchestra to a campfire sing-along—both of them require group interaction and collective creativity. That's why we need the sociocultural approach to explain musical creativity, and even to explain composed, classical music performance.

The Language of Music

Both composition and performance would be impossible if all of the musicians didn't share a common language—the language of music. We can't talk without talking in some language, and we can't create without being creative in some domain. Music is a language, too, and it couldn't exist at all without conventions. The conventions of music are so taken for granted that we don't often think about them. To begin with the most basic level, all musical notes are grouped into octaves; octaves have 12 equal tones; chords are formed in major, minor, and dominant sevenths. Over the last several centuries, a system of music notation developed in Europe to represent this 12-tone system on the page, and the widespread acceptance of the same notational conventions allows music composed anywhere to be played by musicians trained anywhere. All musicians play one of a standard set of instruments; these instruments are manufactured and can be purchased easily, teachers for the instruments can be found in almost any city, and books of technique are published for the aspiring instrumentalist.

We'd never say an instrumentalist isn't creative simply because he's playing an instrument that has been played before, or that a composer isn't creative because she uses a scale that many others have already used. We don't expect every aspect of a creative work to be novel. All creative works liberally draw on shared conventions, and that fact alone doesn't make us question the creativity of the work (see chapter 7). Many of the most important conventions in a creative genre are so deeply rooted that they're second nature to creators and audiences, and aren't noticed until someone points them out.

The importance of these conventions, like many aspects of taken-for-granted culture, only becomes clear when we experience another musical culture, with a different set of musical conventions. In fact, composer Harry Partch (1949) is legendary for creating a completely new musical culture by breaking all of these taken-for-granted conventions. Partch began by creating a new scale, with 42 equal tones instead of the 12 equal tones of the standard Western scale. Then he developed his own form of musical notation for this scale. Only then could he begin to compose in this completely novel musical language. So far so good. But choosing to discard such deeply shared conventions had major repercussions. Most important, most Western musical instruments cannot play these so-called "microtones," so Partch had to invent completely new instruments, and he had to build them himself because no manufacturer was interested in making instruments that no one knew how to play.

Yet even after creating the musical language, composing the music, and building the instruments, Partch's music still could not be performed, because no musicians knew how to read the music or play the instruments. Partch himself had to train musicians, or else had to convince some musicians to train themselves.

Partch's compositions were only performed a few times. Before they could be performed, Partch had to spend a year in advance of the performance teaching an orchestra's worth of people how to read his notation and play his instruments. For example, at Mills College, California, Partch visited from July 1951 through February 1953, with a performance scheduled in March of 1952. In the fall, interested students volunteered, and began by building the instruments, which he'd already invented, under his direction. In the winter, he taught them his notational system and they learned to play the instruments. In the spring, they rehearsed enough compositions to fill up a two-hour performance. This entire year of effort culminated in a final performance at the end of the spring semester.

Partch's efforts no doubt qualify as radically novel. He not only created music in an existing language, he created a new language. But this high level of novelty comes with a price: the loss of the appropriateness of the created products. There are CDs of Partch's performances available in many university music libraries (although almost never at the local music store) and most listeners find it, shall we say, an acquired taste. Partch's efforts didn't result in the creation of a new domain of music. And, even if they had, that domain would quickly take on all of the conventional properties of the 12-tone Western music that Partch rejected—standard notation, instruments, and training. It's unrealistic to expect every new generation of composers to create a completely new musical language, new instruments, and newly trained musicians, and to expect the economy to respond by building factories for a whole new set of invented instruments. Like all creativity, musical creativity depends on a shared system of creative conventions, and no one can create music without first internalizing the rules and conventions of the domain.

The Social Nature of Musical Creativity

In this chapter we've learned that musical creativity is fundamentally social. Performance is more social than composition, but even composition is a lot more social than we usually realize. Cognitive psychologists who study music have examined how chords and melodies are represented in the brain, or how performers make split-second decisions during performance (Sloboda, 1988). But as we've seen in this chapter, the most important aspects of musical creativity occur outside of the head of the musician: they occur in musical conversations and in interactions between musicians. This is obvious when we consider improvisational forms of music like American jazz. The social nature of music is a little easier to ignore for people who focus only on European art music, with its detailed scores, its conducted orchestras, and its rigid division of labor between the composer and the performer.

As with the other domains of creativity examined in part 4, we can only explain our bias toward composition and European genres of music by first understanding how our culture's conceptions of creativity influence the ways that we think about creativity. Why haven't creativity researchers, for example, studied electronica or tribute bands? Because they don't fit in with our creativity myths. Electronica is music created by people who don't play instruments, created out of bits and pieces that were composed and performed by someone else. In our creativity myth, this is plagiarism or theft; after all, our myth would have us believe that every creator originates everything new with every creation. But if that were true, then how can we listen to a recording we've never heard before, and almost instantly know the time period in which it was recorded? How could we look at an unfamiliar painting from the last 500 years and be able to tell within 10 years or so when it was painted? And I've argued that a tribute band is, objectively speaking, not that different from a modern symphony orchestra. They both perform songs that someone else originally wrote and performed, and they try to do it exactly the same way. Yet creativity researchers have spent a lot of energy studying orchestral musicians while ignoring tribute band musicians. Orchestra musicians might be a lot more creative, but we don't know that because we haven't compared them scientifically, I think the bottom line is that creativity researchers have been culturally biased toward European genres of high art. It's the same reason that so much study has been dedicated to fine art painting, while researchers have neglected cartoons, advertisements, movies, and videogames.

There's no longer any excuse for creativity research to retain antiquated attitudes toward the arts, attitudes that subtly reinforce cultural myths or that place special value on high-status art forms. After all, the art world itself abandoned such attitudes decades ago (see chapter 10), and Americans have already voted with their entertainment dollars. A science of creativity must be judged on how well it explains the most widespread and most active creative domains, not on how well it explains the high-status genres of a privileged few. And ultimately, the sociocultural explanation of creativity that works so well to explain popular music and performance leads to a better explanation of the fine arts too.

Thought Experiments

- Do you like any of the same music as your parents?
- Do your friends like the same bands that you do? If not, does this ever cause any problems?
- Do you prefer to listen to live music or recorded music? Why do you think that is?
- Do you have any friends who compose music? If so, does it sound completely original, or does it sound something like some other musician?
- Have you ever been to a symphony concert? Did you feel as if you had trouble understanding the music? What types of people were in the audi-

ence? Were they different types of persons from those you might see at a stadium concert?

- Have you ever been such a fan of a band that you listened to bootleg tapes or studio or rehearsal recordings? What did you learn about the band from those readings?

Suggested Readings

Becker, H. (2000). The etiquette of improvisation. *Mind, Culture, and Activity, 7*(3), 171–176.

Klosterman, C. (2002, March 17). The pretenders. *The New York Times Magazine,* 54–57.

Marzorati, G. (2002, March 17). All by himself. *The New York Times Magazine,* 32–37, 68–70.

Sawyer, R. K. (2003). *Group creativity: Music, theater, collaboration.* Mahwah, NJ: Erlbaum. See especially chapter 2.

Schutz, A. (1964). Making music together: A study in social relationships. In A. Brodessen (Ed.), *Collected papers, Volume 2: Studies in social theory* (pp. 159–178). The Hague, Netherlands: Martinus Nijhoff.

Weeks, P. (1990). Musical time as a practical accomplishment: A change in tempo. *Human Studies, 13,* 323–359.

CHAPTER 13

Acting

> Anyone interested in processes in the natural world would be very rewarded by a study of theatre conditions. His discoveries would be far more applicable to general society than the study of bees or ants.
>
> —*Director Peter Brook (1968, p. 99)*

In 1992 and 1993, I was the pianist for one of Chicago's most popular improvisational comedy groups. Three times every weekend, Off-Off-Campus would perform to a packed house of laughing fans. Along with the eight actors and the director, I arrived at the theater an hour early for the loud and vigorous warm-up exercises. They exercised in a small circle, watching and listening closely to one another. All of the exercises were group activities, helping the group communicate instantly and think as a unit, building a group mind.

I began each show by playing an up-tempo blues on the piano, as the stage lights came on and the actors ran to the stage, pumped with adrenaline. The show always began with a game of Freeze Tag. First, one of the actors introduced the show and asked members of the audience to shout out suggestions, asking for a location or a starting line of dialogue. Two performers then used this suggestion to begin an improvised scene. The actors accompanied their dialogue with exaggerated gestures and broad physical movements. The audience was told to shout "Freeze!" whenever they thought the actors were in interesting physical positions. Whenever anyone shouted "Freeze!" the actors stopped talking and immediately froze in whatever body position they happened to be in. A third actor then walked up to these two and tapped one of them on the shoulder. The tapped actor left the stage. The third actor then copied that body position, and began a completely different scene with her first line of dialogue, justifying their body positions but interpreting them in a new way.

Later in the show, the actors advanced to more experimental improvisations. They might perform a child's fairy tale chosen by the audience, in a series of different genres—ranging from science fiction to *Charlie's Angels* to opera— also shouted out by the audience. They might perform the Entrances and Exits game, where the audience chooses a word for each actor and during the scene's dialogue, whenever an actor's special word is spoken, that actor must enter or leave the scene. All of these skits are fully improvised. The cast doesn't prepare anything in rehearsal; they never repeat lines, even lines that get a huge laugh. That's because the actors value pure improvisation, where no one on stage knows what will happen next. No single actor takes on a director's role and guides the performance; the dialogue and the plot emerge from group collaboration.

Off-Off-Campus is based at the University of Chicago, where modern improv theater was invented in the 1950s. In 1955, a group of former students got together and formed an alternative theater group they called The Compass Players. The group's new style of improvisational theater, with its social commentary and biting satire, quickly caught on among the intellectual and artsy crowd in the university neighborhood. In 1959, many of the same actors started the Second City Theater, a legendary group that spread the improv style around the country.

In the 1980s and 1990s, improvisational theater grew dramatically in Chicago and in other cities. Now there's a wide variety of improvisation, ranging from short games like Freeze Tag that start from one or two audience suggestions, to the more experimental long-form style. In long-form improv, the ensemble asks for an audience suggestion and then begins to improvise a one-act play that lasts 30 to 60 minutes without interruption. Long-form improv is less focused on comedy than games like Freeze Tag; it focuses instead on character and plot development. These performances often are so good that many audience members assume there's a script. But just like Off-Off-Campus, the actors work hard to avoid repeating even a single line from another night.

It's no accident that improv theater was created in the 1950s, because postwar American culture placed a high value on spontaneity in the arts, not only in theater, but also in jazz, poetry, and painting (Belgrad, 1998; Sawyer, 2000). Improv theater takes the emphasis on spontaneity to an extreme; the actors have to respond instantly, speaking the first line of dialogue that comes into their heads. Pausing to analyze would cause too much delay in the performance. Only by immediately speaking the first thought can a natural-sounding dialogue be sustained.

As we saw in chapter 10, the visual arts have been heavily influenced by the creative potential of performance art, resulting in installation-specific pieces and multimedia works that integrate video images or taped sounds. *The New York Times* critic Michael Kimmelman wrote in 1998, "Art today often seems to aspire to the conditions of theater and film" (p. 32). Performance may be the dominant form of creativity in contemporary U.S. society. More so than ever before, explaining creativity requires us to explain performance creativity and its place among the arts.

Oral Traditions

The current predominance of scripted theater makes it hard to imagine a time when *all* performance was improvised. But of course, this was the case at the beginning of human culture, when writing systems hadn't yet been developed. The idea that a playwright would write down a script for later performance is a relatively recent innovation in human history. Long before the invention of writing, human societies had musical and ritual performances, oral traditions that were passed from one generation to the next.

Oral traditions vary from one performance to the next. Every performance of a North Carolina tall tale or an Appalachian fiddle tune is a little different. Contemporary anthropologists, who study verbal ritual performance around the world, have documented variations even in the most sacred rituals. For example, in many performance traditions only experienced elders have acquired the skills required to speak at important rituals. But even after a lifetime of performing prayers, incantations, and sermons, they still repeat the ritual text a little differently each time. Folklorists initially viewed this as an annoying problem; their goal was to write down the correct version of the story or ritual, but each time they observed a performance, it was different.

In the 1970s, some anthropologists began to accept that oral traditions are not repeated verbatim, like the performances of a literate culture. These researchers began to study the improvisational creativity of the performer, and began to emphasize the ways that folklore was a living, practiced tradition. These new perspectives have changed the way we look at early European theater. They've driven home the importance of a previously neglected fact: Until at least the late medieval period, many European actors remained illiterate. Some scholars, for example, believe that Shakespeare did not write scripts, but rather taught his actors their parts orally. Scholars argue that the scripts we have today are transcriptions of actual performances, done from memory by someone in Shakespeare's group (Delbanco, 2002).

Modern theater is often traced to a popular form of entertainment called the *commedia dell'arte*, a partially improvised genre of plays originating in 16th-century Italy and thriving for the next 200 years throughout Europe. No one has ever found a script for a *commedia dell'arte* performance. Instead, what historians have found are rough outlines of plot, with brief descriptions of the characters. The actors could easily memorize these rough outlines, called *scenarios*, but all of the dialogue was improvised in front of the audience. The success of a *commedia dell'arte* performance depended on the ensemble's improvisational creativity.

Literacy became more widespread in Europe during the same years that improvisation was fading out of our performance tradition. Over the 200-year period that *commedia dell'arte* was popular, literacy became much more common among actors, and the scenarios developed into more highly scripted plays. By the 19th century, this form of early improvisation had been largely replaced by scripted theater.

It wouldn't be until 1955 that improvisation returned to the theater scene. Chicago inspired an improvisation revolution in modern theater that has influenced directors, playwrights, and actor training. Chicago-style improvisation is widely considered to be America's single most important contribution to world theater. For example, British director Mike Leigh has used improvisation to develop plays since the mid-1960s. He later shifted to movie producing, and his innovative technique led to several award-winning and popular movies. For example, his 1996 film *Secrets and Lies* won the Palme D'Or award at the Cannes Film Festival.

In 1997, the *New York Times* reported that "participatory theater"—a form of improvisation that relies heavily on audience participation—had become so popular that it had become mainstream (Marks, 1997). The granddaddy of this genre, performed since 1987 in New York, is *Tony 'n' Tina's Wedding*, a show that recreates a church wedding and reception where the audience participates in the wedding as guests. In the play *Tamara*, which played in New York City in the late 1980s, the action occurred simultaneously in several rooms, and the audience members chose a character to follow around (Caudle, 1991, p. 49). These performances are partially improvised within an overall predetermined structure. In spite of commercial success, participatory theater doesn't get much respect from the theater community. This bias grows straight out of our creativity myths that the real creativity is in creating the script; a composed creative product generated by a single lone genius.

Performing Scripted Plays

> [The actor] may get his ideas obviously from the author, in the
> same way that a painter who paints a certain object in nature is
> receiving his ideas and impressions from that object, but what
> he does is dependent intrinsically on his own creative capacity.
> —*Director Lee Strasberg (1960, p. 83)*

In scripted theater, the actors don't have to improvise the words. But the actors still have to deliver the lines so that they sound like natural human dialogue. For example, when one actor stops speaking and the next one starts, the two actors have to make the transition sound natural, and this requires collaboration; the performers have to be in tune. They have to monitor the other performers' actions at the same time that they continue their own performances. As they hear or see what the other performers are doing, they immediately respond by altering their own actions. They implicitly and subconsciously communicate with subtle facial expressions and gestures (Caudle, 1991, pp. 50–51).

The dialogue written in a script isn't exactly like everyday conversation. For example, theater director Brian K. Crow (1988) transcribed everyday conversation (see figure 13.1) using the techniques of conversation analysis. Note in particular the detailed representation of pauses, overlaps, and subtle changes in pitch and volume.

Normal scripts don't have this much detail. Actors have to decide where to pause, and how long each pause should be; whether there should be speaker overlap at various points in the dialogue; and how to deliver each line—which words to emphasize, and with what tone of voice. When you see a transcript like figure 13.1, you realize how much information is left out of the typical script. Everything that is put back in by the actors involves acting creativity. And although a lot of those decisions are made in rehearsal, many of them are made improvisationally every night, on stage, in front of the audience.

To teach actors how to make their dialogue sound natural, a few directors and playwrights have used detailed transcripts like figure 13.1 to generate their scripts. This style of theater is called everyday life performance (Hopper, 1993; Stucky, 1988, 1993). Crow used detailed transcripts of everyday dialogues to create *Conversation Pieces: An Empirical Comedy* in 1987, a production in which actors performed transcripts like figure 13.1 exactly as written (Crow, 1988). This removes a lot of actor creativity, but it's a useful exercise for teaching actors how much creativity a normal script requires. All of the unwritten aspects of the dialogue have to be improvised by the actors, and the improvisation is collaboratively managed by all actors.

K: That was last <u>night</u>
J: That's what I <u>said</u> last night
    (4.0)
K: Well I—
      [
J: Getting to know you
K: ((laughs))
J: You'll ac<u>cept</u> everything but you <u>do</u> nothing
K: Wo:::::
          [
J: No: that's not true
K: Everybody's that way in certain instances (.) are they not?
J: Not <u>me</u>:, =
K: = Not <u>you</u>:, oh no
              [
J: ((laugh)) Wonderful me
                  [
K: It's your turn—It's your turn to
    get the tea
    Oh:: no (.) <u>I</u> did it six <u>months</u> ago it's
    <u>your</u> turn
        [
J: ((laughs))
          [
K: heheh
J: No

FIGURE 13.1. Transcript of conversation that was performed by a theater group exactly as it was originally spoken. The punctuation marks indicate pitch changes, volume, emphasis, and overlapping speech, which the actors were required to copy exactly. Reprinted from *TDR/The Drama Review*, 32:3, 23–54 T119–Fall 1988. Bryan K. Crow "Conversational Performance and the Performance of Conversation." With permission of New York University and the Massachusetts Institute of Technology. Copyright © 1988.

The Creativity of the Actor

> Outstanding actors like all real artists have some mysterious
> psychic chemistry, half conscious and yet three-quarters hidden
> . . . that enables them to develop their vision and their art.
> —*Peter Brook (1968, p. 29)*

Psychological studies of performance creativity are rare. Partly this is because acting is an ensemble art form, and it's hard to isolate the creative contribution of any one actor (Sawyer, 2003). But it's also due to the all-too-common belief that performance is not creative, but is just execution and interpretation (Kogan, 2002). A few studies of acting creativity have identified three stages: preparation, rehearsal, and performance (Blunt, 1966; Nemiro, 1997). *Preparation* is when the actor learns the basics of acting through academic training, observing other actors in theater and in films, and observing people interacting in everyday life. The preparation stage includes some solitary activities, but for the most part actor training is social and collaborative.

The second stage, *rehearsal,* involves at least five activities:

1. Identifying something in the character that the actor can relate to
2. Using personal experiences as substitutes for the character's feelings
3. Discovering the character's objectives
4. Creating a physical persona for the character—how the character walks and moves
5. Studying the script to learn what the other characters think about the character

The rehearsal stage is mostly collaborative; although actors spend some time alone to memorize their lines, most rehearsal is done with the rest of the cast.

The third and final stage, *performance,* is the most collaborative of all. Performance involves at least five activities:

1. Focusing on the moment—what has just happened and how the character would perceive the situation at that moment, with no knowledge of how the rest of the play unfolds
2. Adjusting to other actors
3. Interacting with the audience
4. Keeping the concentration and energy level high
5. Improving the performance and keeping it fresh over repeated performances

The performance stage is what the audience sees; this is the most important to acting creativity. In improvisational performance, preparation and rehearsal don't play much of a role; almost the entire creative process occurs on stage, in front of a live audience.

Personality

> The most important thing about an actor is his sincerity. If he can fake that, he's made.
> —*Comedian George Burns (quoted in Wilson, 1985, p. 70)*

Using conventional measures of creative ability, first-wave personality psychologists long ago discovered that performing artists score higher than control groups, suggesting that performers are not simply interpreters with no creativity of their own (Lang & Ryba, 1976; Mackler & Shontz, 1965; Torrance & Khatena, 1969). In one study of actors' personality traits (Hammond & Edelmann, 1991a), the variables that distinguished the professional actors from the nonactors included:

- The actors were more privately self-conscious.
- The actors were less attentive to social comparison information.
- The actors were more honest.
- The actors were less socially anxious.
- The actors were less shy.
- The actors were more sociable.
- The actors were more sensitive to the expressive behavior of other people.

These findings are statistically significant, but as with most creativity-trait research, the effect sizes are minor. As a result, these findings don't necessarily help us to explain any specific individual's creativity, in any specific production. To explain acting creativity, we need to use the sociocultural approach to analyze the collaborations of group creativity.

The Flow of Performance

Many actors believe that their performance is much better during public performance than in rehearsal (Konijn, 1991, p. 63). Social psychologists have known for decades that performance often improves in the presence of an audience; they call this *social facilitation* (Guerin, 1993). Konijn (1991) found that actors' heart rates were higher during public performance than rehearsal, indicating an elevated stress level, but the public performances were rated more highly by the actors and by expert observers, suggesting that an increased stress level improves performance. This may be why good actors welcome stage fright; it's good for performers to experience a little stress, because it increases the quality of the performance (Wilson, 1985). But there's an interesting twist: Although social facilitation studies show that an audience can facilitate performance on an easy task, they also show that an audience can reduce performance on a difficult one (Geen, 1989). This paradox can be explained by Csikszentmihalyi's theory of flow, which proposes that individuals experience a flow state when the challenges of the task are perfectly matched to their own level of skill (see chapter 3). Actors are faced with a task that would be too challenging for most of us, but they've mastered the skills necessary to perform the task. They don't experience flow in a rehearsal because that's not challenging enough. They have to seek out the additional pressure of live performance.

Expressing Emotion

A particularly important ability in performing a script is the believable communication of emotion. In 20th-century realist theater, playwrights closely focused on interpersonal relationships, and many of these involve strong emotions—dysfunctional families, alcoholism, or abusive relationships. The pioneering work of director and teacher Konstantin Stanislavsky (1863–1938) is often associated with this emotionally expressive style of acting.

It's a common belief that actors can't play emotions that they haven't experienced themselves. The idea that acting is a reliving of past emotional states is generally associated with Stanislavsky's (1936, 1962) psychological realism. Qualitative and quantitative studies have provided some evidence for this: Actors who perform conventional scripted theater develop complex psychological relationships with their characters. In a series of studies in Romania, Neaçsu (Marcus & Neaçsu, 1972; Neacsu, 1972) found that actors who had a higher capacity for reliving emotional states performed more effectively. Performing certain characters can be cathartic, allowing an actor to work out a personal dilemma through the character, or to get out certain feelings: "In a show once . . . I cried for an hour and a half on stage. Well I was never more happy-go-lucky than during the run of that show 'cause I got it all out" (quoted in Nemiro, 1997, p. 235).

But this catharsis can go too far; many actors fear taking on too much of a character's identity, and worry that they'll lose themselves in the character: "To give a really brilliant performance you have to get so close to that character that you get scared. But you can't lose yourself in it" (quoted in Nemiro, 1997, p. 235). Some actors avoid roles that involve portraying emotions that would be too painful. One actor playing the part of Jesus in a play, for example, was uncomfortable because he kept comparing his own behavior to the goodness of Jesus, and another actor playing in *Death of a Salesman* cried every night from genuine depression (Fisher & Fisher, 1981, p. 156). Some actors say that during the run of a play, they find it hard to keep their character out of their everyday life. In 1989, *The Guardian* reported the case of an established British actor who was removed from his role as Hamlet after he began to talk of the "demons" in the role, and began to see his father in the ghost (Hammond & Edelmann, 1991b, p. 26).

The emotional power of acting inspired the form of therapy known as *psychodrama*, originated by the Viennese theater director J. L. Moreno in the 1920s

(Moreno, 1977). The rationale for psychodrama is that people may change their attitudes simply by playing a certain role. In psychodrama, the therapist works with a group of patients. At any given time, one of the patients is the center of the drama, and is encouraged to improvise his own character, performing critical events from childhood or from his or her current situation. The other patients in the group then improvise the other characters in the situation. Moreno's innovations have become widespread in many forms of therapy, including role-playing and assertiveness training.

Yet it's too simplistic to propose that actors are carried away by their characters. As director Peter Brook reported, "The actor himself is hardly ever scarred by his efforts. Any actor in his dressing-room after playing a tremendous, horrifying role is relaxed and glowing" (Brook 1968, p. 136). In fact, a contrary school of acting theory holds that the actor should be in complete control on stage and should not actually *feel* emotion but only *convey* emotion. This school of thought predated Stanislavsky and is often associated with French essayist Denis Diderot's famous essay *Paradox of the Comedian* (1773/1936). Diderot argued that emotionality interfered with effective acting: "Extreme emotionality results in mediocre actors; mediocre emotionality results in most bad actors; and the absolute absence of emotionality results in sublime actors" (p. 259, my translation). After all, Diderot reasoned, if an actor had a high degree of emotionality he would be unpredictable from night to night. For example, he might be exceptional on opening night, but by the third night his inner inspiration would have dried up. In contrast, the more intellectual, in-control actor would improve from night to night, as he reflected on each night's performance, and progressively gained more insight into the character. Diderot's approach returned in the mid-20th century with Brecht's argument that the actor should play his or her character with distance (Konijn, 1991).

The Creativity of the Ensemble

Theater is an ensemble art. Explaining theater creativity requires a sociocultural approach, because the explanation has to be based in the interpersonal dynamics among the actors. Focusing only on the inner mental states of the individual performers will miss the most fundamental aspects of performance creativity: the emergence of a unique performance from the unpredictable and always changing interactions among performers on stage.

If every group used a script like the one in figure 13.1, there would be a lot less variability from night to night. But theater is not about predictability. Groups attain their best performances by staying in a zone between complete predictability and being out of control. Improvisational actors have to be the most highly attuned to this zone. They can't just develop the scene in a conventional way, because that would be boring. But they also can't do something so radical that it just doesn't make sense, surprising all of the other actors and puzzling the audience. The challenge of staying in this improvisation zone leads to a flow experience, a peak mental state that performers get when they are in a particularly effective performance (Sawyer, 2001a).

But improvisation's unpredictability makes it a risky way to attain flow. It doesn't always happen, even in a group of talented, well-trained performers. Many improvising actors talk about both the high they get from a good improvisation, and the terror they feel when a performance is not going well. The unpredictability of group creativity can be frightening because failure is public. If a painter fails, he or she can paint over the canvas; a writer can crumple up the paper and throw it away. But imagine if writers had to publish every single one of their manuscripts—that's the situation improv actors find themselves in every night. Mark Gordon, a director of and actor in The Compass Players said, "It always felt to me like taking your pants off in front of an audience. A little terrifying" (quoted in Sweet, 1978, p. 110). Ted Flicker, director of the first St. Louis Compass and founder of the New York group The Premise, said, "Unless you've actually tasted what improvising in front of an audience feels like, you can't *imagine* the horror of it" (quoted in Sweet, 1978, p. 162). Up to a certain point, this fear can contribute to the potential for a flow experience. But once it crosses a certain threshold, the actor moves from the flow zone into the anxiety zone.

The flow state that comes from a successful performance is "something like a drug," which is also the title of a book about the improvisational Theatresports league (Foreman & Martini, 1995). Improvisers keep doing it, in spite of the lack of money and fame relative to conventional theater, television, and movies, because of the high they get from the flow experience. Comparing improvisation to conventional theater, Andrew Duncan felt that the flow experience was much greater in improvisation. After leaving Second City in 1963, he said that "I really missed that kind of company—the community, working together, respect. . . . They were intense moments in your life that had meaning" (quoted in Sweet, 1978, p. 61).

Even if the individual performers are prepared and focused, a good group performance doesn't always emerge, because there are simply too many intangible factors that can't be known until the performance begins. For example, a group may be in group flow even when the performers don't realize it. Improvisational musicians and actors alike often describe the experience of walking off of the stage at the end of the night, feeling that the performance had been really bad, and then hearing later that the audience had found it to be a stellar performance. Pete Gardner described how the improvisers always valued shows in which everything connected well, but "the audiences absolutely love the shows where there was a mass confusion." He described an experience where one friend compared a slick show with a confused show, explicitly noting that the confused and messy show was "so much better" (Sawyer, 2003, p. 46). Inversely, most group performers can tell a story of at least one night's performance that they thought was particularly good, but later as they were discussing the performance with knowledgeable, trusted colleagues who had been in the audience, they discovered that it was not one of their best.

Many Chicago improvisers refer to group flow using the term *groupmind*. Group flow helps the individual actors reach their own internal flow state. Comedian Jim Belushi famously said that the high that comes from a group performance was "better than sex" (Seham, 2001, p. 64). Actor Alan Alda referred to this state, saying, "You're actually tuned into something that's inside the actor's mind and there's a kind of mental music that's played and that everybody shares" (quoted in Sweet, 1978, p. 326). Improv actors often speak of group flow as "a state of unselfconscious awareness in which every individual action seems to be the right one and the group works with apparent perfect synchronicity" (Seham, 2001, p. 64). No one actor can make this happen single-handedly; it requires a very special collaboration. The ensemble has to let it emerge from a group creative process.

Interaction Between Actors and Audience

Peter Brook (1968) described a touring performance of *King Lear* by the Royal Shakespeare Company in the 1960s. The tour began by passing through Europe. Brook reported that "the best performances lay between Budapest and Moscow" (p. 21) and that the audience profoundly influenced the cast, even though their mastery of the English language was not great. Yet, their experience of life under communism prepared them to connect with the play's difficult themes. The actors were in peak performance and became progressively more excited as they finished the European portion of the tour and then moved to the United States. Yet after a few weeks in the United States, the spirit had gone out of the company. Brook reported that "it was the relation with the audience that had changed. . . . This audience was composed largely of people who were not interested in the play; people who came for all the conventional reasons—because it was a social event, because their wives insisted, and so on" (p. 22). The actors modified their performances in an attempt to engage this different type of audience, but with limited success.

Performers feed off of a good audience, and it leads the performers to rise to the best of their ability. Audiences can even affect specific moment-to-moment performance decisions. In a theater performance, an unexpected audience chuckle might lead the actors to pause a split-second to let the laughter play out and die down, and they might exaggerate the next similar line by the same character, whereas on another night, an audience might not respond at that moment and the performance would be unaffected. In an improv comedy performance, a laughing audience lets the cast know they're performing well, but if there's no laughter, the cast knows they need to change something, perhaps to take the character and story development in another direction.

When other audience members react, whether with laughter, fear, or sadness, we're more likely to experience that emotion or reaction as well. This group phenomenon is called *emotional contagion* (Hatfield, Cacioppo, & Rapson, 1994). This happens a lot with laughter and applause, and the larger the audience, the more extreme the effects. Examples include the extreme emotions that spread through the crowd at a sports event or a stadium concert. To understand the role of the audience, we need a sociocultural approach that explains group dynamics and communication.

The Creative Process Made Visible

Most creativity research has focused on product creativity instead of performance (Sawyer, 1997a, 2003). In scientific disciplines, creative products include theories, experimental results, and journal articles; in the arts, products include paintings, sculptures, and musical scores. In product creativity, the creative process results in a finished, fixed product. In product creativity, the creative process usually takes place in isolation, in a studio or a laboratory. It can take months or years before the final product is completed. The creator has unlimited opportunities for revision, and doesn't have to release the product until he or she is ready.

Scientists have discovered that only an action theory can explain creativity. Creativity doesn't happen all in the head, as the idealist theory would have it; it happens during the hard work of execution. That's why explaining creativity requires a focus on the creative process. No creative process is ever completely predictable; there's always some improvisation. A painter constantly responds to his canvas and oils as he's painting. Each step of the painting changes the artist's conception of what he's doing—the first part of a painting often leads to a new insight about what to do next. Fiction writers constantly interact with the story as they write. A character or a plot line frequently emerges from the pen unexpectedly, and an experienced writer will respond and follow that new thread, in an essentially improvisational fashion. Improvisation is most essential in stage performance because, unlike the painter or the writer, performers don't have an opportunity to revise their work. The improvisations of the painter can be painted over or discarded, and the writer has the power of a word processor to generate the next draft. But the improvisations that occur on stage are exposed to the audience. As a result, the audience gets to see the creative process in action, sharing not only in every unexpected inspiration but also in those disappointing attempts that fail. Fans of the popular improvisational rock band the Grateful Dead had a rule of thumb: You have to go to five concerts to be assured of getting one really inspired performance. Even the most famous artists often destroy or paint over a significant number of their canvases, and these aborted attempts are generally lost to history. But actors can never take back a bad night.

We can't explain improvisational creativity unless we focus on the collaboration and the emergence of the group. And studying improv can provide valuable insights into all creativity, because collaboration is important in all creative domains. In modern scientific research, these collaborations range from the group work that goes on in the laboratory to informal conversations over late-night coffee. The creative interactions of an improv theater group are much easier to study, since the analyst can hear and transcribe how this interaction affects each actor's creative process. Performance is the creative process made visible.

Of all the world's cultures, modern European performance traditions have been the least receptive to improvisation. And this bias against improvisation is found in both the theater and musical communities. Improvisation has often been considered to be a less refined "popular" or "folk" genre. Because most creativity researchers are also European, they've tended to focus on these more highly valued performance genres. As psychologist Donald MacKinnon—the director of the influential Berkeley IPAR studies of creativity in the 1950s—once said, creativity researchers have tended to study people too much like themselves. They're people who share the values of academic, university researchers, "the theoretical and aesthetic" (MacKinnon, 1987, p. 121). For example, in Professor Csikszentmihalyi's (1996) Creativity in Later Life study, about half of the approximately 90 subjects interviewed held positions as university professors.

Our creativity myths are deeply embedded in our culture, so deeply embedded that they've interfered with our scientific progress in the explanation of creativity. These myths have led us to neglect performance creativity, even though it, of all of the types of creativity, provides us with the best window onto the collaboration and improvisation of the creative process. But thanks to sociocultural science, we now know that many of these myths are false. We now know how these myths originated in deeply held cultural beliefs and attitudes that are unique to European cultures. And we now know that creativity is fundamentally social and collaborative, that it involves preparation, training, and hard work, and that the process is more important than the product or the personality. By explaining performance, we can ultimately better explain all creativity.

Thought Experiments

- Have you and your friends ever had a special catchphrase or saying that no one outside your group understood? Do you remember how it originated? Was it one person's idea, or did it emerge collaboratively?
- Have you ever seen more than one production of the same play? How were they different?
- Have you ever seen more than one performance of the same production, with the same actors and stage set? How were they different?
- The next time you're in a religious setting, think about the performative elements of the ritual. Don't focus only on the religious officials; also examine what the audience is doing.
- The next time you're at a sports event, think about the performative elements of the event. Don't focus only on the team players; also examine the coaches, the cheerleaders, and the fans.

Suggested Readings

Crow, B. K. (1988). Conversational performance and the performance of conversation. *TDR, 32*(3), 23–54.

Hammond, J., & Edelmann, R. J. (1991a). The act of being: Personality characteristics of professional actors, amateur actors and non-actors. In G. D. Wilson (Ed.), *Psychology and performing arts* (pp. 123–131). Amsterdam: Swets & Zeitlinger.

Konijn, E. A. (1991). What's on between the actor and his audience? Empirical analysis of emotion processes in the theatre. In G. D. Wilson (Ed.), *Psychology and performing arts* (pp. 59–73). Amsterdam: Swets & Zeitlinger.

Nemiro, J. (1997). Interpretive artists: A qualitative exploration of the creative process of actors. *Creativity Research Journal, 10*(2 & 3), 229–239.

Sawyer, R. K. (2003). *Group creativity: Music, theater, collaboration.* Mahwah, NJ: Erlbaum.

Sawyer, R. K. (1998). The interdisciplinary study of creativity in performance. *Creativity Research Journal, 11*(1), 11–19.

Strasberg, L. (1960). On acting. In J. D. Summerfield & L. Thatch (Eds.), *The creative mind and method: Exploring the nature of creativeness in American arts, sciences, and professions* (pp. 83–87). Austin: University of Texas Press.

⸺ INTERLUDE 4

Goodbye to Our Creativity Myths

In all of the chapters of part 4, we've seen that explaining creativity requires us to give up our creativity myths. Our culture's creativity myths tell us that creativity is a burst of inspiration from a lone genius; that a person working alone is always more creative than a group; and that social conventions and expectations always interfere with creativity. These creativity myths are modern versions of the ancient idealist theory of philosophy, which states that the most important part of creativity is having an idea, and that the execution of the idea to make an actual artwork is not that important.

But all of these myths quickly fall apart when we examine the lived reality of creativity. In part 4, we've learned that creativity is not a burst of inspiration but is mostly conscious hard work. Scientific studies of creativity have killed the idealist theory forever. Instead, to explain creativity we need an action theory, a theory that explains how the process of doing a work results in the product. We've learned that instead of a single moment of insight, most created products result from hard work peppered with mini-insights, and that these mini-insights don't seem that mysterious in the context of the preceding hard work. We've learned that creativity is almost never a solitary activity but that it's fundamentally social and collaborative. We've learned that the audience and the viewers play key roles in the creative process.

The sociocultural approach gives us the ability to explain the social, collaborative hard work of creativity. The sociocultural approach explains the process of creativity in addition to the personality of the creator. Prior to 1980, the first wave of creativity research took an individualist approach and tried to explain creativity by studying individual creators. In part 4, we've learned again and again why this couldn't have worked, because in many ways, the individualist approach is based on our creativity myths.

In part 5, we'll turn to two types of everyday creativity: scientific creativity and business innovation. In fact, scientific creativity and business innovation are even more deeply social and collaborative than the types of artistic creativity we explained in part 4. And in the final chapter, we'll bring all of these findings together to learn how we can increase our own creativity in everyday life.

Part V

Everyday Creativity

CHAPTER 14

Science

> The greatest collective work of art of the twentieth century.
> —*Jacob Bronowski (1973, p. 328), referring to physics*

Are scientists really creative? After all, you might think that scientists simply discover truths by looking at the world; though of course, by using some very fancy equipment. The astrophysicist Subrahmanyan Chandrasekhar said that when he discovered a new fact, it appeared to him to be something "that had always been there and that I had chanced to pick up" (quoted in Farmelo, 2002a, pp. xi–xii). If a good scientific theory is just an accurate reflection of reality, then a good scientist is one whose theories directly copy reality (Barrow, 2000). And it goes without saying that copying is not creative.

However, this "copy theory" of science is wrong. The copy theory was famously argued by a group of mid-20th century philosophers known as logical empiricists.[1] To an empiricist, science is a game of deduction: taking observations from experience and using them to derive statements about regularities in nature. However, when scholars began to study how scientists actually work, it turned out that empiricism and deduction weren't very good explanations. Beginning with Karl Popper just after World War II, continuing with the influential analyses of science of Thomas Kuhn, through today's studies of scientific laboratories by Bruno Latour and Karin Knorr-Cetina, we now know that scientific theories can't be derived in any simple or mechanical way from observations.

There are two main reasons why logical empiricism doesn't explain science. First, it turns out that the observed data usually fit with more than one theory.

One theory might seem at first to be better at explaining certain observations, but the match is always a matter of degree, and sometimes one can't be sure. A theory that seems better in one year might later turn out to have been the result of a measurement error. Because data underdetermine theory, it takes creativity to bring together all of the competing theories and all of the potentially relevant data and come up with a framework that best explains the data. Jonas Salk, the developer of the first successful vaccine against polio in 1955, described his creative process in such terms: "I recognize patterns that become integrated and synthesized and I see meaning, and it's the interpretation of meaning, of what I see in these patterns." He described his moments of insight as seeing "an unfolding, as if a poem or a painting or a story or a concept begins to take form" (quoted in Csikszentmihalyi, 1996, p. 287).

Second, scientists don't always proceed by deduction; they often proceed by *induction*, starting from a theory and then designing an experiment to see if the theory is supported by reality. A classic example is Albert Einstein's general theory of relativity. Einstein had a hunch that the force of gravity warped the very structure of space and time, a very difficult concept to grasp. The general theory was not deduced from observation; when Einstein first proposed the theory it was just a clever speculation with no supporting data. But Einstein's theory was so appealing in its own right that scientists decided to take the time to test it.

If space really were curved by the gravity of a large planet or a big star, then faraway stars would seem to shift their position a very tiny bit when they were near a planet in the sky, because light from those stars would change direction as it passed through the warped space near that planet. With really good measuring instruments, scientists would be able to measure whether or not the observed position of a distant star really did shift when its light rays had to pass by another big object on the way to earth. But there was a complicating factor: Even Newton's older theory predicted that gravity would cause light rays to bend. In 1916, Einstein used his theory to predict that the degree of light shift would be about twice that predicted by Newtonian physics. This provided a way to experimentally check the theory.

Given the measuring equipment of that time, the sun was the only body large enough to create an effect big enough that the difference between the two theories' predictions could be measured accurately. But most of the time, the sun's light made it impossible to see faraway stars behind it. The best opportunity to see these faraway stars came with the 1919 solar eclipse, when the moon would block the sun's light, allowing the stars behind it to be seen and measured. A team of British physicists led by Arthur Eddington traveled to the island of Principe, off the coast of West Africa, where they knew they'd have the best view. Eddington already believed in Einstein's theory and he was well known in Britain as an advocate of general relativity. When Eddington returned, he claimed that his observations supported Einstein's prediction, and he convinced the scientific community that general relativity was correct.

However, in the 1980s historians discovered that Eddington did not get conclusive evidence; he doctored his results. In fact, scientists now know that there was no way Eddington could have successfully measured the light shift with the primitive equipment that he had available. For example, in 1962 a much better equipped British team tried to reproduce Eddington's findings. The expedition ended in failure, and the team concluded that the method was too difficult to work (Waller, 2002, pp. 48–63). Einstein's theory of general relativity turned out to be right, so this episode didn't slow the course of science. But the story shows that Einstein wasn't just copying reality when he created his theory. When scientists use induction instead of deduction, they are undeniably creative.

The Creative Scientist

> Very often the successful scientist must simultaneously display
> the characteristics of the traditionalist and of the iconoclast.
> —*Thomas S. Kuhn* (1959/1963)

Like creative personalities in general, creative scientists tend to have strong self-confidence and self-reliance, often seeming egocentric and stubborn. The famous Harvard biologist E. O. Wilson emphasized persistence and ambition, "a desire to control," and the ability "to tolerate strong rivals" (quoted in Csikszentmihalyi, 1996, p. 269). These scientists have a strong intrinsic motivation that helps them work for years on a problem. Many successful creative scientists report feeling "chosen" to be scientists in adolescence, long before they had any opportunity to prove themselves in a scientific discipline.

Great Analogies in Science

Scientific discoveries often emerge from analogies. Historians of science have noted hundreds of analogies used by scientists (Holyoak & Thagard, 1995, p. 185). One of the most famous examples is Kekulé's discovery of the molecular structure of benzene. In the benzene molecule, the atoms combine together to form a circle of bonds. Kekulé famously reported falling half asleep and experiencing a daydream in which he imagined the atoms forming into snakelike chains, and then saw one of the snakes biting its own tail. He awoke with a start and immediately realized that benzene was a ring-shaped molecule.[2]

A second famous example involves magnets. By 1600 magnets had been discovered, and their properties were increasingly understood. One of the magnet experts, William Gilbert, studied the behavior of compasses—then already widely used—and also the behavior of other magnets. Gilbert then had the idea that the planet earth was a giant magnet. Analogical thinking led Gilbert to create this theory because the earth shares many properties with magnets. In fact, we now know that Gilbert was right: the earth is indeed a giant magnet.

In a third famous example, Christiaan Huygens, in his 1678 *Treatise on Light*, used an analogy between light and sound in support of his wave theory of light. Because sound traveled in waves, and light and sound shared some properties, Huygens hypothesized that light was a wave. For more than a century, this theory was shunted aside in favor of Newton's particle theory of light, but it was revived in the early 19th century by Thomas Young and Augustin Fresnel. The fact that light diffracts was suggested by observing that both sound and water waves go around corners. The wave analogy also suggested that light from two pinholes would exhibit interference, just like water waves do. Young's landmark experiments demonstrated this to be the case. Twenty-first-century quantum physics now holds to a hybrid theory in which light is both particle and wave, a "wavicle" as some physicists say.

Cognitive psychologists have learned quite a bit about how the mind thinks about analogies. They say that the phenomenon being explained is the *target*, and the metaphorical comparison is the *source*. There are two mental steps required to have an analogical insight: First, an appropriate source has to be selected, and then the source has to be matched up with the target. Psychologists have focused on answering two questions: Given a target problem or domain, how can a good source be found? And given a possible source, how can it be applied to better understand the target?

In answer to the first question, some scientists report noticing a source while they are working on a target problem. This can only happen if the scientist has already internalized a large database of potential sources—from deep experience in this domain, from work in other domains, or from life experience. Other scientists report first noticing a good source of analogy, and then noticing a target problem that they've been working on a long time.

In answer to the second question, the scientist must be able to construct representations of both the source and the target that make useful comparisons easy. This requires creative work, because the scientist has to reframe both the source and the target, emphasizing those features of each that make them most receptive to comparison. After all, the source and the target are never exactly alike. Typically, creative manipulation is required before the analogy can be made to work (Holyoak & Thagard, 1995). Kekulé's source was the snake eating its tail. He'd probably never encountered such a snake on any wooded trail, but nonetheless his mind was able to creatively construct the image.

Different analogies have different strengths and weaknesses, and it takes creativity to pick a the most appropriate one for the situation. When students think of the flow of electricity in a wire using an analogy with water flowing through pipes, they perform well on battery problems. But when they think of electricity as a crowd of people moving through a narrow corridor (with each person representing one electron), they do better on resistor problems (Gentner & Gentner, 1983).

Because many creative insights result from analogy, the psychology of analogical thinking can help us to explain creativity. This exciting line of research is continuing, and promises to add to our explanation of creativity.

Multiple Simultaneous Projects

In chapter 3, we learned that creative individuals often engage in networks of enterprise, multiple overlapping simultaneous projects. Depending on the scientific field, a project can take anywhere from three months to three years or more, as it moves through preliminary pilot study, grant writing, experimental design, theoretical literature review, implementation of the experiment and gathering of data, analysis and interpretation of the results, and writing up the results for submission to a journal. Most practicing scientists schedule multiple projects so that during any given week, each of the projects will be in a different stage of development. While writing up the results of one project for a journal, another project is in the laboratory, and yet another is in the conceptual stage with theoretical speculation and library research on prior studies. A network of enterprises increases the likelihood of cross-fertilization across projects, and many of the most important insights happen when two different projects come together unexpectedly.

This kind of multitasking is supported by the modern system of apprenticeship in scientific laboratories, where each research professor is assigned several PhD students to work as research assistants. Each distinct project is parceled out to different graduate students, and they handle the day-to-day nitty-gritty details of the project. The professor acts as a project leader, managing the overall structure of each project, checking to make sure the schedule isn't excessively delayed, offering expertise to get past unexpected complications.

Successful scientists have learned how to structure their workday for maximum creativity. They shift from one project to another based on what they do most effectively at a given time of day. Original, new, and conceptual work, problem-finding work, is best done first thing in the morning. Many scientists also schedule their writing in the morning, because this involves creative conceptualization. Scientists tend to schedule the concrete, hands-on laboratory work for late morning and after lunch. Finally, many scientists report that they schedule some idle time in the late afternoon, after the concrete phase of hard work, perhaps taking a walk around campus or going for a cup of coffee. They've learned from experience that valuable insights often emerge when they get some distance from the work. Scientists then close the day by returning to writing and conceptual work, often continuing to work long after dinner.

Aesthetics and Science

> It is more important to have beauty in one's equations than to have them fit experiment.
> —*Physicist Paul Dirac, winner of a Nobel Prize in Physics in 1933 (1963, p. 47)*

The most creative scientists are the ones who are especially good at formulating and asking new questions. The most significant new scientific ideas, the ones that result in major revolutions, tend to be the result of a problem-finding process (Csikszentmihalyi & Sawyer, 1995), and it's here that science requires immense creativity.

In many scientific doctoral programs, graduate students aren't expected to come up with their own research questions. That's the responsibility of the advising professor, whose years of experience make him or her particularly good at finding problems. Even when graduate students have a pretty good idea of the kind of work they're interested in, they still need a lot of guidance on how to ask the right kind of question, and how to focus their research. In almost all graduate programs, a professors' most common difficulty is teaching their doctoral students how to formulate and focus their questions appropriately (e.g., Novak & Gowin, 1984 on education doctoral programs).

How do scientists come up with good questions? Many scientists say they use aesthetic beauty rather than cold rationality. Physicists took Einstein's general theory seriously because it was beautiful. Even though there was no data to support it, its beauty made it seem likely to be true. Like a great work of art, a beautiful equation is universal, simple, and has an undeniable purity and power (Farmelo, 2002a). Like great poems, equations have order; hierarchical structure; simplicity and complexity in balance, pattern, and rhythm; and symmetry (Flannery, 1991). Poems and great equations are both powerful because they pack as much meaning as possible into a small space. $E = mc^2$ is enormously powerful in part because it is so simple.

Poems and great equations both act as stimuli that later can result in a wide range of unpredictable and unexpected elaborations. Each reader responds to and interprets a poem in a new way, and the poet can't control the reader's response. In a similar fashion, a great equation has repercussions through subsequent history that its discoverer could not have foreseen. Scientific equations are not as fixed and unyielding as you might think; they're often reinterpreted in light of later discoveries and theoretical developments. Scientists have changed their interpretations of some of Einstein's and Dirac's most famous equations over the years, and Einstein's theory of relativity has developed far beyond what he imagined when he first presented his simple equation (Weinberg, 2002).

Of course, there are differences. Whereas poetry only works in a given language, scientific equations are universal. Whereas poets value ambiguity and intentionally leave many things unsaid, scientists intend their equations to communicate a single logical meaning. And perhaps most important, beauty in science can be misleading; the history of science is filled with discarded theories that seemed beautiful but turned out to be wrong. Einstein devoted his later career to the search for a unified field theory; because the idea was beautiful, he was convinced it was right. But no unified field theory has yet been found. Einstein rejected Heisenberg's uncertainty principle, famously saying, "God does not play dice" with the universe. But now the uncertainty principle is accepted as correct by all working physicists.

The Creativity of Science

The logical empiricists explained science as a passive observation of the world, involving the development of logical propositions that correspond to observation. They thought of science as a body of knowledge. But research from the 1960s onward studied science as a set of practices that scientists engage in in laboratory settings. It's a subtle shift in emphasis—from knowledge itself to the ways that knowledge is generated—but it allowed us to explain scientific creativity in a new way. Scholars of scientific creativity have begun to closely examine what actually happens in laboratories, and in many cases, they've been able to document the emergence of new creative insights.

Most science involves slow, methodical work, with mini-insights occurring every day. There isn't much evidence for a "burst of genius" view of creativity. Instead, scholars have discovered that scientific progress is a cooperative group effort, involving the distribution of labor and small but important contributions from each of a team of professionals.

Scientific discovery happens largely through intensive social interaction in laboratories and universities, not through isolated bursts of insight by a few great individuals. Most scientific creativity occurs in groups; the mythical image of the lone scientist working quietly into the night is a dated historical image from the 19th century. A typical scientific research team includes members with differing levels of experience—professors, postdoctoral students, and graduate students—and with different specialty backgrounds.

The historian of science Mara Beller (1999) uncovered the social processes that led to some of the key discoveries of early-twentieth-century quantum physics. Through a close analysis of the month-by-month interactions of the Copenhagen group, and analyses of multiple successive drafts of their most influential publications, she showed that some of the most important scientific papers of the 20th century, although formally authored by a single person, actually reveal the influence and collaboration of a circle of 10 or more scientists, each working at the cutting edge of scientific knowledge, and all of them in constant communication. For example, Heisenberg's initial formulation of his famous uncertainty principle was developed in part in response to two physicists, Sentfleben and Campbell, who are now relatively unknown. It takes a very close reading of Heisenberg's papers, and a thorough knowledge of the group's collaborations, to detect these influences. Beller applied the same analysis to Bohr's legendary Como lecture, showing that the lecture juxtaposes several coexisting arguments, each addressed to a different theorist and focusing on a different issue. When we learn such facts, we realize that science is often a collaborative dialogue among a close-knit community, even when only one person's name appears on the final publication.

This leads to a big problem with the Nobel Prizes for science: How does one determine who deserves recognition for a given discovery or theory? No more than three scientists can receive the Nobel Prize at a time. But like the Copenhagen group, most of today's scientific advances are the result of cumulative, collaborative work by many scientists. For example, the 2002 Nobel Prize in physics was awarded to Dr. Raymond Davis Jr. and Dr. Masatoshi Koshiba for their work on solar neutrinos. Because of the three-scientist limit, the Nobel Foundation left out many other scientists who played significant roles in developing the theory of solar neutrinos: John Bahcall, Vladimir Gribov, Bruno Pontecorvo, Stanislav Mikheyev, Alexei Smirnov, Lincoln Wolfenstein, and the leaders of the Sudbury Neutrino Observatory in Canada (Johnson, 2002). The basic problem is that the Nobels assume an obsolete vision of science as resulting from solitary work, when in fact, each great work of science is created by a collaboration, by an entire field of coauthors. Our 19th-century conceptions of creativity have become embedded in institutions—like the Nobel Prize—that make it even harder for us to realize the sociocultural nature of creativity.

Myths of Genius

We like to think that geniuses are often ahead of their time. But in chapter 2, we learned that this almost never happens, and that most of the stories people tell about misunderstood geniuses are inaccurate myths. For example, many biologists will tell you that an obscure Moravian monk named Gregor Mendel accidentally discovered modern genetics in 1865, and that his work was ignored for 35 years before being rediscovered in 1900 and serving as the foundation of the new science of genetics. On the 100th anniversary of the date, in April 1965, British evolutionist Sir Gavin de Beer declared: "It is not often possible to pinpoint the origin of a whole new branch of science accurately in time and place. . . . But genetics is an exception, for it owes its origins to one man, Gregor Mendel, who expounded its basic principles at Brno on 8 February and 8 March 1865" (quoted in Waller, 2002, p. 133).

But this story is false (Brannigan, 1981, pp. 89–119; Waller, 2002, pp. 132–158). An examination of what really happened shows that Mendel was working on a completely different problem—a now discredited theory that new species result from hybridization—and he and his colleagues agreed that his work had failed to prove the theory. Although Mendel deserves credit for being one of the first to observe the ratios that helped later scientists discover genes and inheritance, many of the ideas now associated with Mendel were already widely accepted before he published his now famous paper. Contrary to the myth, his findings were not ignored and not misunderstood; he reported them at two scientific conferences, and they were well received, although they weren't considered that radical. Mendel was not a "Mendelian" in the modern usage of the term, and he didn't realize the significance of the ratios to evolutionary theory. But today's scientists attribute ideas to his 1865 papers that Mendel didn't actually have, and in fact, was incapable of having given the state of science at that time.

The conventional story is false. But it survives because it fits in so well with our creativity myths. Stories like Mendel's seem at first glance to support our individualist myths, but on further examination, we find that the real explanation is sociocultural, and we have to become aware of our creativity myths to realize why we believed the inaccurate version in the first place.

The Construction of Scientific Genius

Scientific work depends on a staff of graduate students. Otherwise, the simultaneous execution of multiple projects would not be possible. And if a scientist can't attract the best young graduate research assistants to her laboratory, her ideas will fade in importance. It isn't enough to simply have great ideas. You also have to be able to convince young people that they will be able to make a living and have a career by following in your footsteps.

But to maintain all of these students, a professor has to have money to pay their salaries and benefits, and to pay for the lab space and supplies to run the experiments. Successful scientists have to know how to compete for and win grants, how to budget and allocate funds, and how to manage a team of diverse individuals. Many prominent scientists say they face a difficult balancing act: The more energy they devote to these managerial tasks, the less time they have available to do real science. The size of the research team that surrounds each scientist is a result not of any individual traits of that scientist but of the nature of the scientific work in that domain, the number of graduate students choosing to enter that field, and the amount of research funding available from government and private industry.

Not all brilliant scientists become chief scientists with their own laboratories. Leading a lab requires immense administrative and leadership skills, and some good scientists are too withdrawn from social life to manage such a career. Only a scientist with the right lab, filled with the right kind of staff help, has any hope of becoming known as a genius, because the system of scientific knowledge attributes to the chief scientist the collective products of the entire lab. Mukerji's study of oceanographic lab teams (1996) showed how the collective group work of the team is ultimately attributed to the chief scientist. The chief scientist becomes "larger than life, more brilliant than any individual could be" (Mukerji, 1996, p. 274). Because the chief scientist seems to be the creator of an entire group's product, this process reinforces his stature and makes him seem ever more superhuman. However, the chief scientist only seems great because he's expressing the thoughts of the group.[3]

Why would members of a group prefer to have the leader get credit for their innovations, rather than have the truth of collective authorship be known? Mukerji identified several social and organizational reasons. For example, sole authorship by an identified genius makes the results of the team's work more readily accepted by the scientific community, because such a creation has more authority. It fits in more readily with the cultural ideology because it's easier for our individualist culture to attribute ideas to individuals (Kasof, 1995; Markus & Kitayama, 1991). Building up the greatness of the chief scientist also gives the team's collective actions a singular identity, which is psychologically satisfying, much as the British enjoy having a king or queen to personify the national identity. The great scientist is two people in one. Of course, she's a brilliant scientist and is essential to the lab team. But she's also the social and collective face of the lab, and this second social role is the one that other scientists see in publications and conference talks. Many young researchers enter science hoping to be trained by a true genius who's doing important and significant work, and once in a lab, they naturally tend to engage in practices that reinforce the rightness of their life choice.

For all these reasons, it's in the team's collective interests to pump up the genius of the chief scientist. When one person gets credit for an entire team's work, it's not surprising that she seems superhuman and uniquely creative. Again, we find that it takes a sociocultural approach to look beneath the surface of first appearances, both to explain how scientific creativity really works—collectively and collaboratively—and to explain why we continue to believe the inaccurate mythical version of individual creativity.

Citation Patterns

Scientific fields aren't democratic. A few scientists generate the great majority of the output, and a small number of published papers receives the great majority of citations from other papers.

Output. In 1955, Wayne Dennis found that in many different scientific fields, including linguistics, geriatrics, and chemistry, the top 10% of the most prolific researchers generated half of all published work, and the 50% of the least productive researchers generated only about 15% of all published work (Dennis, 1955). Dennis's database did not include those scientists who never published anything at all, yet some studies suggest that about half of all PhDs from top universities never publish anything (Bloom, 1963).

It turns out that these patterns of productivity follow one of two laws known as the Price law and the Lotka law. According to the Price law, if k represents the total number of contributors to a given field, then *square root(k)* will be the predicted number of contributors who will generate half of all contributions (Price, 1963, p. 46). This results in a highly skewed distribution, one that's more skewed as the discipline grows bigger. In a discipline with 100 members, 10 individuals generate half of all output. According to the Lotka law, if n is the number of published papers, and $f(n)$ is the number of scientists publishing those papers, then $f(n)$ will be inversely proportional to n^2, with a proportionality constant that varies with each discipline (Lotka, 1926).

In fact, a multi-agent computer simulation of a scientific discipline has recently been developed by the sociologist of science Nigel Gilbert (1997) using a new computer technology that simulates each of the members of the group and their interactions. Gilbert programmed a small number of simple rules for how each new paper would be generated and which existing papers it would cite, then ran the simulation for 1,000 iterations. He found that the simulation reproduced the emergent macro features of Lotka's law that have been documented in real scientific disciplines (see figure 14.1).

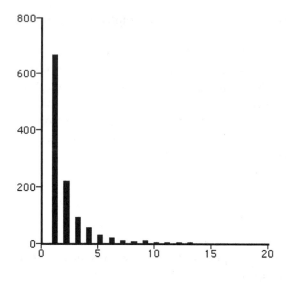

FIGURE 14.1. The number of scientific papers per author, predicted by a computer simulation, closely follows Lotka's Law. Reprinted from *Sociological Research Online*, 2(2). Gilbert 1997, with permission of *Sociological Research Online*, www.socresonline.org.uk.

These findings seem odd when you consider that most personality traits are normally distributed in the population, according to the famous bell curve (see figure 14.2). In fact, the productivity curve in figure 14.1 can't be explained by psychology at all; it's a sociological phenomenon. Access to top jobs at good universities and access to large research grants is limited. Having success early on is a predictor of future success, because it increases the likelihood that future grants will be successful, and that competitive job offers will be forthcoming. At the other extreme, those who start their careers slowly wind up at unknown colleges, teaching large introductory courses to undergraduates, and end up never having time to do the research that would gain them recognition and allow them to move to a more research-focused university (Allison, 1980).

Citations. We've just seen that productivity varies dramatically from one scientist to another. But how do we know that the most productive scientist is

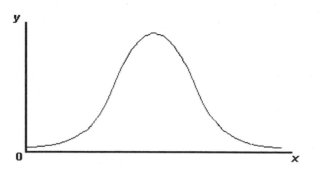

FIGURE 14.2. Normal distribution (by author.)

the most creative? Maybe those highly productive individuals are generating a lot of worthless articles. To test this, researchers have examined citation patterns: which papers cite which other papers in their references. In some scientific disciplines, this information has been stored in computer databases for several decades, allowing for the first time in history a rigorous quantitative analysis of citation patterns across time.

In fact, it turns out that the distribution of citations is even more elitist than the distribution of productivity (see table 14.1). The graph of paper rank by citations follows an inverse power law[4] that results in a Zipf distribution: the kth most popular paper has $(N/k)^{1/(u-1)}$ citations. Remarkably, the curve for all scientific disciplines is identical.[5] Such patterns are not unique to creativity. Zipf's law does an equally good job of explaining such diverse phenomena as the size of traffic jams, the network of connections among Web sites, income distributions, and the population distributions of major cities (Simon, 1957).

Scientific domains all show skewed distributions of productivity, reputation, and success. To explain scientific creativity, we need to understand how these patterns play out in scientific domains. But an individualist approach can't explain the distribution; it's almost impossible that individual talent varies as much as the citation pattern does. The explanation for these distributions can only be found by using sociocultural approaches to examine properties of the domain and the field.

Collaboration in Science

> Science is a very gregarious business. . . . You want to be all the time talking with people . . . it's only by interacting with other people in the building that you get anything interesting done.
> —*Physicist Freeman Dyson (quoted*
> *in Csikszentmihalyi & Sawyer, 1995, p. 347)*

TABLE 14.1 The Number of Papers Receiving
Each Number of Citations (from Redner, 2002)

Number of papers	Citations
1 paper	8,907 citations
64 papers	> 1000
282 papers	> 500
2,103 papers	> 200
633,391 papers	Less than 10
368,110	No citations

> Science is rooted in conversations.
> —*Physicist Werner Heisenberg* (*1971, p. vii*)

Many scientists report having key insights while engaged in discussion with colleagues—both those working the same area, and those working in radically different spheres of human inquiry. Top scientists realize that scientific creativity depends on conversations, and they do all that they can to create more collaborative connections. In the days before the Internet, biologist George Klein created a worldwide network of like-minded intellectuals, held together with old-fashioned letters and stamps. After decades of such networking, Klein became a clearinghouse of ideas from physicists to poets, passing on letters to others he knew would be interested. The files of his correspondence take up dozens of cabinets near his office (Csikszentmihalyi, 1996, p. 277). Jonas Salk, the inventor of the polio vaccine, was inspired to create the Salk Institute for Biological Studies in La Jolla, California, as a forum where diverse interdisciplinary perspectives could come together in everyday hallway discussions: "I can see this done in the form of a collective mind. . . . In this kind of interaction each person helps the others see what they see" (quoted in Csikszentmihalyi, 1996, pp. 284–285).

To study these collaborative conversations, the psychologist Kevin Dunbar chose four of the top laboratories in molecular biology, and then spent a year in each of them (Dunbar, 1995, 1997). He chose 19 scientific research projects to focus on, and observed a total of 23 scientists in the four labs: four senior scientists, each in charge of one of the labs; 12 postdoctoral fellows, five graduate students, and two technicians. By videotaping weekly lab meetings, he discovered that the lab meeting is often the moment when important new ideas and concepts are generated. The lab meetings are attended by all members of the research team: the senior scientist, postdoctoral fellows, graduate students, and technicians. At the typical meeting, one of the team members presents some data from a recent study, and other members ask questions and propose new follow-up experiments. This question-and-answer session often leads the presenting scientist to reconceptualize his or her ideas; in some cases, totally new concepts are generated. The interaction in these meetings is like any other collaborative conversation; it is a spontaneous, improvisational give and take.

Watching a lab meeting allows us to see the creative process at work. Because the scientists talk out loud during the meetings, the videotape provides an external record of their creative process. Dunbar found distributed reasoning in laboratory groups. For example, different members of a group might reason about different stages of an experiment—hypothesis, methodology, and interpretation of results. Dunbar found that during lab meetings, theoretical interpretations of data, known as inductions, made by one scientist were often challenged by the others. Most people have a hard time generating alternative inductions from data, but in a group setting, each person proposes his or her own induction, creating a collaborative situation in which alternative explanations can be contrasted. The distributed reasoning of a scientific team makes the group smarter than the sum of its individual participants. Dunbar also counted the number of inductions and deductions that were *shared*—that had one premise provided by one person, and another premise provided by a different person. He found that 30% of all inductions and deductions were shared, created by a collaborative process. When he interviewed members of the research team months later, they'd already forgotten where the ideas came from. If it weren't for Dunbar and his video camera, the truly social origin of these creative ideas would be lost forever. And as we've already learned, it's usually the chief scientist who gets the credit for these collaborative insights.

Multiple Discovery

Sociological studies of scientific creativity have long downplayed psychological factors, preferring to identify the social properties associated with creations. Sociologists argue that creativity can be analyzed as a sociological-historical process. There's empirical evidence to support this, found in the phenomenon of *multiple discovery*, when two or more independent research teams come up with the same discovery at about the same time, even though they're not in contact and are unaware of each other's work. Historians and sociologists of science have identified hundreds of such cases (Merton, 1961). Classic examples of multiple discovery include:

- The development of calculus by both Newton and Leibniz;
- The prediction of the planet Neptune before it was observed, by both Adams and LeVerrier;
- The formulation of the law of the conservation of energy by Mayer, Helmholtz, and Joule;
- The production of oxygen by both Scheele and Priestley;
- The proposal of a theory of evolution through natural selection by both Darwin and Wallace;
- The invention of the telephone by both Bell and Gray.

Multiple discovery seems to provide evidence that an individual-level analysis can't explain creativity. Sociologists argue that with multiple discoveries, the discovery should be attributed to collective properties of the scientific discipline rather than to psychological processes in any individual scientist. Because the source of the scientific advance must lie outside any one individual and rest in the broader scientific community, we need to explain these discoveries at a group level of analysis.

Conclusion

The most influential and significant scientists are immensely creative. And although their creativity can be partially explained by their internal psychology, we can explain more about scientific creativity by also examining broader social patterns. Most scientific discoveries emerge from highly collaborative laboratory teams. Scientific disciplines are broadly cooperative systems of work. And using a sociocultural approach, we've learned that social forces conspire to reinforce the genius myth of creativity. Research teams have several incentives to falsely encourage the outside world to believe that the chief scientist had all of the key insights, even though actual research reveals that in most cases these insights collaboratively emerge from teamwork.

Two hundred years ago, when science was dominated by gentleman amateurs, it may have been possible to attribute creative advances to solitary, towering intellects. (It may have been, but don't forget that most of our well-known stories about historical scientists exaggerate the creativity myths, and distort the historical record.) But in today's era of big science, when laboratories require millions of dollars every year to pay the salaries of research teams of ten scientists or more, no scientist works alone. Today's scientists realize as well as anyone else that science is a deeply collaborative activity. Sociocultural scientists have analyzed scientific work and have found that creative insights emerge from collaboration. Scientific creativity is both a psychological and a social process, and explaining scientific creativity requires a sociocultural approach.

Thought Experiments

- You've probably heard of Albert Einstein, but you probably don't know the details of any of the theories that he's famous for. Then how do you know he's so brilliant?
- Imagine that you're in charge of government funding of scientific research. What percentage of that money would you devote to the following areas? Physics, biology, the sociology of poverty and schooling, the mental processes studied by psychology. Do you think the government's current allocation of funds is similar to your own?

- How is scientific creativity different from artistic creativity? How is it the same?
- I hope I've convinced you that scientists are creative, after all. But you might still think that artists are more creative than scientists. Do you? Why or why not?

Suggested Readings

Beller, M. (1999). *Quantum dialogue: The making of a revolution.* Chicago: The University of Chicago Press.

Dunbar, K. (1997). How scientists think: On-line creativity and conceptual change in science. In T. B. Ward, S. M. Smith, & J. Vaid (Eds.), *Creative thought: An investigation of conceptual structures and processes* (pp. 461–493). Washington, DC: American Psychological Association.

Farmelo, G. (Ed.). (2002b). *It must be beautiful: Great equations of modern science.* London: Granta Books.

Holyoak, K. J., & Thagard, P. (1995). *Mental leaps: Analogy in creative thought.* Cambridge: MIT Press.

Merton, R. K. (1961). Singletons and multiples in scientific discovery: A chapter in the sociology of science. *Proceedings of the American Philosophical Society, 105*(5), 470–486.

Mukerji, C. (1996). The collective construction of scientific genius. In Y. Engeström & D. Middleton (Eds.), *Cognition and communication at work* (pp. 257–278). New York: Cambridge University Press.

Waller, J. (2002). *Einstein's luck: The truth behind some of the greatest scientific discoveries.* New York: Oxford University Press. See especially pages 32–63.

Notes

1. Also sometimes called logical positivists.

2. This story is often repeated, but there is no evidence it's true. And in fact, historians of science have uncovered a lot of evidence suggesting that it's probably false (Schaffer, 1994). Kekulé didn't report this story until decades after his paper suggesting the ring structure for benzene. And in fact, Kekulé got the structure wrong: he thought the ring was composed of six hydrogen atoms, when in fact it's six carbon atoms. The correct carbon structure was discovered by Adolf Claus although it's often retrospectively attributed to Kekulé (Schaffer, 1994). It's all an example of how a questionable story persists because it fits in well with our creativity myths (see chapter 2).

3. Schaffer (1994) also documents several historical examples of collaborative discoveries being retrospectively attributed to solitary individuals, and suggests several reasons why scientific communities "make up discovery."

4. In an inverse power law, when both axes are transformed to a logarithmic scale, the curve declines linearly.

5. Identical if the number of citations for each paper is divided by the average number of citations for all papers in the discipline, and the paper rank is divided by the total number of papers (Redner, 2002).

CHAPTER 15

Business Creativity

> This process of Creative Destruction is the essential fact about
> capitalism. It is what capitalism consists in and what every
> capitalist concern has got to live in.
> —*Economist Joseph Schumpeter (1942/1975, p. 83)*

According to the famous economist Joseph Schumpeter, creativity is the core of capitalism. New innovations displace the old, often leading to radical transformations, and creative destruction. Creative destruction, with rapid advances in technology, was a fact of life in the United States in the late 20th century. And by the end of the 20th century, creativity had become the key factor driving the U.S. economy (Florida, 2002).

Management scientists have discovered that you can't explain business creativity using a strictly individualist approach. To explain any case of important innovation, we need to examine teamwork and collaboration, overall organizational structures and culture, and contextual factors such as the market and the regulatory climate. Management scientists have demonstrated what executives intuitively know: that organizational creativity occurs in complex social systems.

One of the most well-known recent examples of technological innovation is the Windows operating system.[1] Who created it? Many people will answer by saying that the Microsoft corporation created Windows. Microsoft released its Windows 3.1 operating system in 1990.

But the minority of computer users who are devoted to the Apple Macintosh tell a different story. They know that the most distinctive features of

Windows—its graphical user interface, or GUI—appeared years earlier in the Macintosh. The Apple Macintosh was the first successful consumer computer to have a GUI with windows, menus, and a mouse pointing device, and it was released years before Microsoft Windows, in 1984.

However, Apple didn't create Windows either. The critical creative ideas that we associate today with Windows were first created in the 1960s and 1970s. An early version a GUI was first thought up all the way back in 1945 by Vannevar Bush, who called his invention the memex. In the 1950s, Douglas C. Engelbart explored Bush's idea while working for the Advanced Research Project Agency (ARPA) of the Department of Defense. When this funding ran out, Engelbart and his team of engineers moved to a cutting-edge research facility that Xerox founded in 1970 known as the Palo Alto Research Center, or PARC for short.

Up to the 1970s, the key ideas for windows had remained in the research laboratory. But in 1973, Xerox PARC put these ideas together and released the world's first personal computer: the Alto (see figure 15.1). The Alto had windows and a mouse-controlled cursor. It used a laser printer—a radical new technology also developed at PARC—and you could connect several Altos

FIGURE 15.1. The Alto Computer, created by the Xerox Palo Alto Research Center in the 1970s, was the first windows-and-mouse computer. With permission of Smithsonian Institution, image no. 90-2234.

using a network known as Ethernet, also developed at PARC. This was a highly influential computer, far ahead of its time; today, almost every office uses laser printers and Ethernet. But Xerox chose not to market the Alto because it would have cost the customer 40 thousand dollars. In 1981, Xerox released a less expensive version, the Star, for 16 thousand dollars, but the market had already settled on much cheaper personal computers like the Apple II, and the Star failed to sell.

Steven Jobs, Apple's founder and CEO, was given a couple of tours of Xerox PARC in 1979, and he was inspired by windows technology. He instructed his developers to get to work on a similar type of computer, and by 1981, Apple had hired about 15 of the Xerox developers to work on two graphical user interfaces: the Lisa and the Macintosh.[2]

The Lisa and Macintosh teams worked pretty much independently, and they sometimes duplicated each other's innovations, resulting in multiple discoveries. The engineers sometimes chose different solutions for the same problem. For example, where the Mac had a mouse for cursor control, the Lisa used a touch-sensitive pad next to the keyboard. The Lisa was released first, in January 1983, but at 10 thousand dollars it was too expensive for average consumers, and was doomed like the Alto and the Star. The Macintosh (commonly referred to thereafter as a "Mac") was released at an affordable price in 1984, and the rest is history.

Apple invited Microsoft developers in-house between 1981 and 1984, during the development of the Mac, because Microsoft developers were writing application software for the Mac. Microsoft liked the Mac operating system and offered to pay a licensing fee to use it. When Apple refused, Microsoft announced the creation of Windows in 1983 (although the first version would not be released until August 1987).

Knowing that Xerox PARC developed the first windows computer still doesn't explain how Windows was created. What we know today as the Microsoft Windows GUI is a conglomeration of many mini-insights that originated in university research labs. The first interface that used direct manipulation of graphic objects was the influential Sketchpad system, which was the topic of Ivan Sutherland's 1963 MIT Ph.D. thesis. Sketchpad contained many features that later became central to windows operating systems: icons, a way to select icons by pointing, and the ability to move them by clicking, moving, and clicking again in the new location. David Canfield Smith first used the term "icon" for screen objects in his 1975 Stanford Ph.D. thesis on Pygmalion. Smith later became one of the team members who designed the Xerox Star. Each of the mini-insights that together make up the graphical user interface emerged from a collaborative team of individuals, and tracing sole authorship is nearly impossible (see table 15.1).

TABLE 15.1 Source of Invention of Various Components of the Windows Graphical User Interface

Invention	Year	Project name	Person/Group
Screen pointer (lightpen touching screen)	1963	Sketchpad	Ivan Sutherland
Pointing device, now with on-screen pointer	mid-1970s	Doug Englebart	SRI
Mouse (an upside-down trackball)	1963 (?)	Doug Englebart	SRI
Cursor changes that show system status (arrow to egg timer)	mid-1970s	William Newman	Xerox PARC
Menus	mid-1970s	Learning Research Group (LRG)	Xerox PARC
Pop-up menus	mid-1970s	Ingalls (LRG)	Xerox PARC
Pull-down menus	1983	Lisa	Apple
Disabling (graying) of inactive menu items	Uncertain. Lisa (1983) or Ed Anson (1980) or Xerox PARC (1982)		
Menu bar	1983	Lisa	Apple
Scroll bars	mid-1970s	LRG	Xerox PARC
Radio buttons	mid-1970s	Kaehler (LRG)	Xerox PARC
Check boxes	mid-1970s	LRG (?)	Xerox PARC
Drag and drop movement of icons	1984 (?)	Jeff Raskin	Macintosh

Table 15.1 is only an approximation. No one knows exactly which research group first came up with each of these ideas, and the origins of many of them are contested. It seems likely that many of the ideas were cases of multiple discovery. After all, it's not that big of a leap of insight to look at radio buttons and think of extending the idea to check boxes. But even if these attributions are correct, it doesn't provide much support to the individualist view of creativity, because most of these creative innovations emerged from an entire research team: the Lisa project at Apple, for example, or the Learning Research Group (LRG) at Xerox PARC. And even the innovations that are attributed to specific people—like the idea of turning a trackball upside down to create a mouse—occurred in collaborative contexts, and it's probably unfair to give all of the credit to any one individual.

Many of these creative innovations build on each other. For example, the first screen pointer was a light pen; it had to touch the screen to work. Because the pointer was physically touching the screen, there was no need for a pointer icon to be displayed on the screen. In the 1970s, researchers at Xerox PARC took this idea and elaborated it. They realized that a trackball could be used instead of a light pen, but because the ball didn't actually touch the screen, a pointer had to be placed on the screen to indicate the current position. The insight for the mouse was that the trackball could be placed on the bottom of a small box, and that the box's movement would cause the trackball to move because of friction with a rubber mousepad. Each of these creative insights was a small, incremental elaboration on a preceding series of insights. The idea for a mouse that would control an on-screen cursor did not appear suddenly, full grown, in a burst of insight in 1975. It was a rather small extension of a long series of mini-insights extending back at least to 1963.

The history of the windows GUI provides us with several insights into business creativity.

Each innovation builds incrementally on a long history of prior innovations. Creative products that the consumer sees, that are successful in the market, rarely spring to life full grown. The consumer rarely sees the long historical path of small, incremental mini-insights that accumulate to result in the emergence of the final product.

Innovations emerge from collaborative teams. Although a single person may become associated with a specific idea, it's hard to imagine that person having that idea apart from the hard work, in close intimate quarters, of a dedicated team of like-minded individuals. And most innovative products require many insights, each of them coming from a different team member (Evans & Sims, 1997; Wicklund, 1989).

Multiple discovery is common. In the words of MIT Media Lab cofounder Nicholas Negroponte, "innovation is inefficient" (2003, p. 34). There were several organizations each developing graphical user interfaces—two separate teams within Apple, and even more teams within Xerox PARC—and many critical ideas emerged in multiple teams independently, or by drawing on ideas that predated all of those groups.

There is frequent interaction among the teams. Members of a team occasionally visit and view what is being done by another team. And key employees frequently transfer allegiances, taking their expertise from one team to another (Tuomi, 2002).

A product's success depends on broad contextual factors. How much does it cost? Who and what sort of person can afford it? Is it compatible with other products and practices that are already embedded? How well is it marketed?

Innovation emerges from a complex social and organizational system. We can't explain business creativity without a sociocultural explanation of the complex organization from which innovation emerges. We have to understand not only the individual team members' creative processes but also the nature of teamwork and collaboration, and the roles played by organizational structure and market forces (Grønhaug & Kaufmann, 1988; King & Anderson, 1995).

Innovation Versus Creativity

> History proves that great inventions are never, and great
> discoveries seldom, the work of any one mind. Every great
> invention is either an aggregate of minor inventions or the
> final step of the progression.
>
> —*Mel Rhodes* (*1961, p. 309*)

In a sphere of activity far removed from the mainstream of creativity research, a huge group of highly paid professionals has spent decades poring over the arcane details of creativity and innovation. Who could these neglected creativity scholars be? They are the lawyers connected with the field of intellectual property rights. Many of these scholars believe that a strong patent office, and a legal system with the power to protect intellectual property so that creators are rewarded for their work, has been a major factor contributing to creativity in the United States.

The United States Patent and Trademark Office Web site tells us what it takes for an innovation to be patentable:

> Any new and useful process, machine, manufacture, or composition of matter, or any new and useful improvement thereof (from http://www. uspto.gov/web/offices/pac/doc/general/what.htm [accessed 7/29/05).

This definition emphasizes the two components of the sociocultural definition of creativity: a product that is both "new and useful," both novel and appropriate to some domain of activity. The patent office Web site even provides a helpful elaboration of what "useful" means:

> The term "useful" in this connection refers to the condition that the subject matter has a useful purpose and also includes operativeness, that is, a machine which will not operate to perform the intended purpose would not be called useful, and therefore would not be granted a patent.

The statutory definition of what can be patented has been elaborated and refined through decades of case law, common law, and patent office regulations and practices. As a result, the definition of invention may be the most rigorous definition in the entire field of creativity (Huber, 1998).

In Washington, D.C., on October 16, 2002, the United States Patent and Trademark Office celebrated its 200th anniversary by bringing together 37 members of the National Inventors Hall of Fame. They hold hundreds of patents. The White House Office of Science and Technology Policy has estimated that 52% of the nation's growth since World War II has come through invention (Leary, 2002). The United States Patent and Trademark Office awards 3,500 new patents each week; every year, it receives 326,000 patent applications; and in over two centuries, it has granted more than 6.3 million U.S. patents. These large numbers qualify the office as one of the world's greatest experts on creative innovation.

Innovation is not simply the creation of something new. In the development of the Windows GUI, many people created new technologies in the 1960s and 1970s that didn't become viable products until they all came together in the Apple Macintosh in 1984. Innovation involves both the creation of a new idea, and the implementation, dissemination, and adoption of that idea by an organization (West, 2002, 2003). Often the original insight changes significantly as it is executed, so much that it is essentially reinvented (Grønhaug & Kaufmann, 1988). Explaining these processes requires a sociocultural approach that focuses not only on the individual who originates the idea but the entire organizational system, and the complex social and interactional processes that result in implementation, dissemination, and adoption.

The Frisbee flying disk is a case in point. Arthur "Spud" Melin, the founder and president of the Wham-O toy company, was said to be the creator of the Frisbee. And indeed, Wham-O held the patent for the plastic flying disk. But Melin didn't invent the Frisbee. After all, flying disks have ancient Greek roots, and most of us have heard of the discus throw of the Olympics. But the Frisbee that we all know and love originated in the Frisbie Pie, made in Bridgeport, Connecticut, from 1871 to 1958 at a bakery not far from Yale University. Yale students apparently ate a lot of Frisbie Pies in the first half of the 20th century, and afterward, they tossed around the empty metal tins using the now familiar flick of the wrist.

In 1948, a Los Angeles building inspector, Fred Morrison, had the idea that if the pie tins were made of the new material known as plastic, they might fly better. In an attempt to cash in on a postwar UFO craze, he sold it as the Pluto Platter for a couple of years before selling the idea to Melin at Wham-O. Wham-O began production in 1957, and didn't have much success selling the Pluto Platter at first. But sometime just before 1960, Wham-O cofounder Richard Knerr visited a series of Ivy League colleges and found that students were still throwing pie tins to each other, and calling it "Frisbie-ing." Knerr's inspiration was to change the name from Pluto Platter to Frisbee, and this superficial change was enough for the flying platter to piggyback onto the existing college fad.

So who invented the Frisbee? Not Knerr, who only changed the name. Not Melin, who bought Morrison's patent. Not Morrison, because he simply co-opted a fad that emerged from a group of Yale students, a fad that was a collective group phenomenon. And not William Russell Frisbie, who just wanted to make pies. Just like Windows, the Frisbee was not created in a sudden burst of genius; rather, it emerged from a complex system of social and historical connections, with many individuals playing key roles (Shulman, 2002).

Many novel consumer products are, like the Frisbee, clever appropriations of fads that emerge from youth culture. Since hip-hop culture became mainstream in the 1980s, fashion companies have looked to the street to identify collective, emergent trend waves that they could then ride. A new category of professional—the "cool hunter"—was an expert in scouting the hippest urban neighborhoods and identifying the new, emergent styles that were just on the edge of breaking out into nationwide trends. By July 2002, however, cool hunting had provided corporations with very few marketing successes, and marketing consultant Irma Zandl pronounced that "cool hunting is totally over" (Ferla, 2002, p. ST6). Whether or not cool hunting is in or out, corporations were creating new products from emergent youth culture trends before the 1980s and 1990s, and they'll continue to do so in the future. As with the Frisbee, it's impossible to attribute these creative products to a single individual; rather, the product emerged out of a collective culture, and only after it had emerged from the social group was it later recognized to be a potentially marketable product.

Cultural Differences in Innovation

Through the 1970s and the 1980s, Americans often looked to the Japanese economy with envy. Japanese companies were achieving market penetration in a wide range of industries traditionally dominated by American companies: automobiles, consumer electronics, steel. Although Japan had an older image as the land of conformity and imitation, it was Japan that gave the world the Sony Walkman and the VCR.

But all things go in cycles. With the extended slump in the Japanese economy that began in the early 1990s, the "lost decade," Japan has engaged in a serious bout of self-examination, and many Japanese themselves now believe that their culture is too focused on consensus and conformity, and that this prevents the innovation necessary to bring the Japanese economy out of its slump. With the

U.S. economy thriving during Japan's lost decade, many Japanese focused on the innovative power of the United States.

Anthropologists have long stereotyped the United States as individualist and the Japanese as collectivist (see chapter 8). Many other Asian countries are also said to be collectivist, and leaders in other Asian countries have similar concerns about innovation and creativity. After Japan's lost decade, business leaders there began to think that a more individualist cultural style might lead to increased innovation. The thinking was that a culture that values connections, consensus, conformity, and rule making will be risk-averse. For example, a famous Japanese saying goes: "The nail that sticks up gets hammered down." The Japanese have even named the problem "Big Company Disease," with its symptoms being a bloated bureaucracy, endless meetings, and complex and seemingly unnecessary management practices.

But how can one executive change something as long-standing and entrenched as a cultural value system that prizes consensus and connection? It may seem impossible, but some corporations are trying by developing programs, hiring consultants, or sending their professionals to Silicon Valley. Yet, results have been mixed; culture is extremely resistant to change. For example, the Toshiba corporation introduced flexible working hours in 1994, focusing on its most creative employees. In fact, the employees didn't even have to come into the office as long as they got their work done. But three years later in 1997, most of these people continued to come into the office during regular working hours, and very little had changed.

Individualist and collectivist attitudes affect each person's creative style. Japanese managers prefer a bustling environment when thinking about ideas, whereas Europeans prefer to be alone (Geschka, 1993). Europeans expect stimulation from lectures, seminars, and conferences, whereas Japanese go to the city center and visit bookshops, supermarkets, and theaters. In the preliminary phases of idea generation, European managers talk with internal and external experts and colleagues in the same area; Japanese managers talk with private acquaintances of the same age, regardless of their area. These findings are preliminary but intriguing. Certainly, more cross-cultural research along these lines will be necessary for a complete explanation of creativity.

Innovation As Evolution

Inspired by evolutionary metaphors (see chapter 5), a group of creativity scholars known as The Epistemology Group met several times in England between 1994 and 1997 to explore how technological innovation is like biological evolution (Ziman, 2000). Evolutionary concepts have been applied to cultural development in an interdisciplinary field of study known as *memetics* (e.g., Dennett, 1995). To some degree, this is common sense. After all, the business press routinely talks about new technologies in biological terms, referring to "market niche," and using terms such as "fitness," "survival," and "symbiotic."

New products aren't created by individual minds; they emerge unpredictably from a complex network of organizations and markets. Evolution explains how biological complexity emerges with no designer, and the evolutionary metaphor works best at the social and organizational levels of analysis. Once an individual has an idea, that idea enters a marketplace, an ecosystem of competing ideas. Corporate executives have many new ideas to choose from, but no single executive is in complete control, because business organizations are themselves sociocultural systems that behave in unpredictable ways, and some ideas might fit better with the organization's ecology than others. And once an idea is turned into a product and marketed, it enters the sociocultural system of the marketplace, where it has to compete with other products. The outcome of market competition is not designed; technological developments emerge unpredictably.

New technologies often have unintended effects. When the Defense Department funded the ARPANET in the 1960s and 1970s—the network that we all now know as the Internet—their purpose in networking the large mainframe computers at Defense Department research sites was to allow resources to be shared. These mainframe computers were expensive, and the Defense Department thought they could buy fewer computers if users at each location could run programs on less-busy computers at other locations.

By the early 1970s, ARPANET had developed a single standard for transferring files between computers. Ray Tomlinson, a developer at Bolt, Beranek and Newman, an ARPANET contractor, realized that users at different computers could send messages to one another, with each message being transferred as a small file. He wrote the program off-duty and unofficially shared it with a few colleagues. Tomlinson's mail program caught on like wildfire. By 1973 75% of all network traffic was e-mail, and this was a complete surprise to the experts who had planned and funded the ARPANET. They hadn't even included email in their original design for the network, and Tomlinson's program wasn't an officially authorized project. In fact, through most of the 1970s the Defense Department viewed email as an illegitimate use of expensive computer resources, but they tolerated it because they hoped it would lead more research sites to join the network.

So who created e-mail? Although it wouldn't have been possible without the ARPANET, the network's creators did not create email. And although Tomlinson created the program that supported email, that would not have been possible without the network. And the idea might have been lost to history if researchers across the country hadn't started using it, each person making his or her own decision. The dissemination and success of the innovation was a distributed, emergent, social phenomenon, not planned, organized, or even predicted by anyone. And in this, innovation is like evolution: design without a designer, creativity without a creator.

New products are created by complex social organizations, not by single people, and the selection of products is accomplished by an even more complex organization: the market. The evolutionary metaphor requires us to focus on multiple levels of analysis, combining individualist and contextualist approaches.

Individual Approaches

The correlation between IQ and job performance isn't very high. IQ predicts less than 10% of job performance. One reason that personality trait measures don't do very well at predicting job performance is that these sorts of tests measure a person's performance in isolation, whereas in the real world, everything that we do involves working with other people, and collaborative teamwork ability isn't measured by traditional tests. Wagner and Sternberg (1986) called this practical ability *tacit knowledge*, and they've developed new tests to measure it. Although intriguing, the jury is still out on how well their tests correlate with work performance. But Wagner and Sternberg have found that these scores are not correlated with other measures of intelligence.

Given our culture's individualist myth of creativity, we generally think that the social and cultural context can only be a constraint to creativity. One interview study of corporate engineers found that they almost always associated the context with interference and inhibition (Talbot, 1993). When these engineers think about context at all, they think about how their boss doesn't like novelty or overrides their decisions, about how information doesn't flow freely, or how other departments aren't willing to cooperate. They also complain about short-term managerial thinking, rigid hierarchical structures, or overly tight financial controls. It's not surprising that these engineers associate context with constraint, because in our culture's mythical view of creativity, that's the only role that context is allowed to play. It's much more difficult for us to realize the supporting, enabling, and enhancing role that contexts play in creativity, because those functions don't have a place in our creativity myth.

In the 1950s and 1960s—the first wave of creativity research—it was thought that the most creative organization would be the one that least interfered with individual autonomy (Rockefeller Brothers Fund, 1958). This was consistent both with a fear of a society filled with "organization men," and with the individualist personality focus of creativity research (see chapter 3). However, contemporary research has demonstrated that companies that focus on individual talent—a trendy approach in the 1990s—tend to fail. No company was more sold on freeing individualist talent than Enron, for example, and Enron's failings can be directly tied to its focus on "the talent myth" (Gladwell, 2002). The problem is that such a focus leads one to believe that an organization's creativity is a simple additive function of the creativity of its employees. But in real corporations, the organization's creativity is a complex and emergent property, depending not only on the employees but also on the structures that organize them, and the joint practices that they engage in together (King & Anderson, 1995). Organizational creativity isn't additive, and that's why you can't make your company more creative simply by hiring more creative people. As Gladwell (2002) wrote, "The talent myth assumes that people make organizations smart. More often than not, it's the other way around" (p. 32). Several successful organizations, such as Southwest Airlines, Wal-Mart, and Procter & Gamble, hire ordinary people from midlevel universities rather than the top students from Harvard's business school. Their organizational systems explain their creativity and success. The sociocultural approach is required to explain how such companies can be more innovative than companies full of the best and the brightest.

Improvisation and Collaboration in Business

The last 30 years have seen a huge growth in research on organizational innovation (Grønhaug & Kaufmann, 1988; King & Anderson, 1995; West & Farr, 1990), but only in the 1990s did this research focus closely on the work team. This recent shift is critical, because most business innovations originate in teams (Evans & Sims, 1997). It's intriguing that many of these scholars compare successful, innovative teams to improvising jazz groups (Eisenberg, 1990; Kao, 1996; Miner, Bassoff, & Moorman, 2001; Weick, 2001). In both a jazz group and a successful work team, the members play off of one another, with each person's contributions inspiring the others to raise the bar and think of new ideas. Together, the improvising business team creates a novel, emergent product, both unpredictable and yet more suitable to the problem than what any one team member could have developed alone.

The best knowledge workers available today are people who love this form of creative, improvisational interaction (Eisenberg, 1990). Companies that create an improvisational work environment will be better able to attract these critical professionals, and better able to retain them. The lessons for management are subtle and profound; the best manager is one who can create an environment in which free collaborative improvisation can flourish, and this requires an almost Zen-like ability to control without controlling. As is written in the Tao Te Ching,

> The existence of the leader who is wise is barely known to those he leads. He acts without unnecessary speech, so that the people say, "It happened of its own accord." (Rosenthal, 2003, Section 17)

Many business leaders believe that collaboration, openness, and a lack of hierarchy and rigidity are the keys to business creativity. In the early years of this new century, the Mattel toy corporation launched Project Platypus, a series of efforts designed to unleash employee creativity. Mattel identifies 15 to 20 employees from different departments of the company, and then moves them to a new temporary office for three months of creativity training that focuses on collaboration and innovation. Platypus is designed to facilitate group bonding, and a more collaborative design process, in contrast to the traditional engineering approach of "baton passing" where a project moves from designer, to model maker, to development, to manufacturing (Bannon, 2002).

In business, the bottom line is what the whole organization creates collectively. There might be a lot of creative employees, but if they work in a stifling organizational structure they won't innovate. We can't explain business creativity by looking inside the heads of the smartest employees. We need an approach that explains group dynamics and creative collaboration, organizational structures and corporate cultures, and market penetration and dissemination.

Thought Experiments

- Have you ever been a member of a collaborative team? Why were you working together instead of separately? Can you recall an example of a problem solution or an insight that emerged from the group?
- Have you worked in a large organization, whether corporate or nonprofit? What procedures and practices were you taught? Do you know where those procedures and practices came from? Of the things you had to know to do your work in this organization, were there some that no one taught you, that you had to learn on your own? Of the things that you were taught, how many of them were written down in an official book of corporate procedures?

- Tomorrow, make a note of the creative technological products that you use throughout the day—the washing machine, the computer, the telephone, the automobile. Try to imagine a time before they existed, and see if you can imagine what insights could lead to that product's invention.

Suggested Readings

Csikszentmihalyi, M., & Sawyer, R. K. (1995). Creative insight: The social dimension of a solitary moment. In R. J. Sternberg & J. E. Davidson (Eds.), *The nature of insight* (pp. 329–363). Cambridge: MIT Press.

Fairtlough, G. (2000). The organization of innovative enterprises. In J. Ziman (Ed.), *Technological innovation as an evolutionary process* (pp. 267–277). New York: Cambridge.

Geschka, H. (1993). The development and assessment of creative thinking techniques: A German perspective. In S. G. Isaksen, M. C. Murdock, R. L. Firestien, & D. J. Treffinger (Eds.), *Nurturing and developing creativity: The emergence of a discipline* (pp. 215–236). Norwood, NJ: Ablex.

Gladwell, M. (2002, July 22). The talent myth. *The New Yorker*, 28–33.

Kao, J. (1996). *Jamming: The art and discipline of business creativity.* New York: HarperCollins.

Notes

1. The following narrative is taken from a variety of sources including: http://www.mark13.org/articles/wimp/siegman.html, accessed 7/29/05; from messages posted by Oliver Steele in March 1988; http://www.mackido.com/Interface/ui-_horn1.html, accessed 7/29/05; by Bruce Horn, who worked in the LRG of Xerox PARC from 1973 to 1981, and then worked at Apple from 1981 to 1984; http://www.h-net.org/~mac/lore2html, accessed 7/29/05; by Jeff Raskin, who began working at Apple in 1978 but had frequently visited Xerox PARC in the mid 1970s. (All sites accessed 2/19/04.)

2. This history may overstate the linearity of influence; Jeff Raskin began to work at Apple in 1978 and became a founding member of the MacIntosh team, and although he was aware of the developments at Xerox PARC, he also noted that many of their ideas predated Xerox, as well; for example, he cited his own 1967 thesis on graphic user interfaces. And a lot of the Macintosh and Lisa operating systems had been developed even before Jobs visited PARC in 1979.

CHAPTER 16

How to Be More Creative

The first goal of this book is to explain creativity, drawing on the latest science provided by the sociocultural approach. But a second goal is to use this new scientific research to learn how we can be more creative. While reading the chapters of this book, you've probably already had mini-insights about how you can use these findings in your own creative activities. In this chapter, I bring our exploration to a close by telling you how the science of human innovation can help you be more creative in your own life.

I began this book by critically examining our own cultural conceptions about creativity (chapter 2). I showed how our creativity myths influence our perceptions of creativity. Before we can learn how to be more creative, we first have to understand what creativity is. If we didn't first understand that some of our unexamined assumptions are creativity myths, we'd be sure to get the wrong idea about how to increase our creativity.

These creativity myths focus on the individual and ignore social and cultural context. But we've learned that explaining creativity requires both individualist and contextualist approaches, an interdisciplinary strategy called the sociocultural approach. The sciences of sociology, anthropology, and history balance out the picture provided by psychology. In the many chapters of parts 4 and 5, I used the sociocultural approach to give you the latest scientific explanation of creativity.

Most of us express our creativity by taking care of the simple tasks of everyday life. Some are creative parents; others are creative at the small talk of everyday conversation. Creative parenting involves many small everyday skills; some parents are creative at instructing and teaching their children, whereas others might be able to plan the week's menu and cook all the meals with a uniquely creative style. In all these examples, we see that everyday creativity involves performance. The creativity occurs while we're doing a task, and as we're performing the task we have to improvise through it, responding moment by moment to the changing needs of the situation. Everyday creativity is improvisational, and that's why it's different from what most creativity researchers have studied: creativity that results in a finished product.

There's a growing body of research into the creativity of performance—as I've described in chapters 12 and 13—and if we want to be more creative in everyday life, we can turn to this research. Studies of musical and theater performance, for example, reveal how people can be creative simply by enacting a role, even when there's no finished product at the end of the performance. These studies tell us:

1. Everyday creativity is collaborative;
2. Everyday creativity is improvised;
3. Everyday creativity can't be planned in advance, or carefully revised before execution;
4. Everyday creativity emerges unpredictably from a group of people;
5. Everyday creativity depends on shared cultural knowledge;
6. In everyday creativity, the process is the product.

Everyday creativity isn't about the isolated individual and his or her special genius thought processes. It's about social encounters, and it happens more in the action of execution than in thinking or planning.

In this chapter, I begin by summarizing some of the most popular creativity training techniques. I then talk about advice books in the humanistic or "new age" tradition. It turns out that some training courses and advice books accept the creativity myths that we know are false. I conclude by providing sociocultural advice for how to be more creative.

Creativity Training

In the 1950s, Sidney Parnes and E. Paul Torrance disagreed with their colleagues: They were among the few psychologists who thought creativity could be taught (Parnes, 1993). Most personality psychologists thought that creativity was like IQ: It was fixed at birth and it couldn't be deliberately increased. The 1955 Utah

Conference (see chapter 3) focused on the "identification of creative scientific talent," not on enhancing creativity. At the third Utah Conference in 1959, Torrance and Parnes reported some results that showed that creativity training could work. As a result, the name of future conferences was changed to the "Identification *and Development* of Creative Scientific Talent" (Parnes, 1993, p. 472). By 1972, Torrance looked back at two decades of research and found 142 studies showing that training could enhance creativity (Torrance, 1972).

If creativity can be taught, then corporate executives get very interested. After all, innovation is the holy grail of today's modern corporation. That's why many of the people offering advice about how to be more creative are highly paid management consultants. Some of the most well-known creativity consultants are trained by the Lego Group AG, the Danish parent of the company that makes the world-famous children's toys. Management consultants are trained to use Lego blocks in "Serious Play" workshops with executives. It may be hard to imagine a middle-aged man with white shirt and tie playing with Legos, but the idea is becoming widespread, and some very large and serious companies have hired these consultants, including Nokia, Daimler-Chrysler, Ikea, and Alcatel. "Legos work because they let executives visualize abstract concepts like 'value chain' or 'process engineering' by actually building their interpretations of them," said Kimberly Jaussi (quoted in Gullapalli, 2002, p. B1). The Lego corporation didn't originate the idea of using Legos to teach corporations creativity; several management consulting firms had been doing it for years, including the IDEO corporation of Palo Alto, California, and the Center for Creative Leadership in Greensboro, North Carolina. As we've seen over and over again, many creations are emergent group phenomena, and the idea of using Legos for corporate creativity consulting didn't come in a moment of insight at Lego corporate headquarters. It was an emergent collective phenomenon.

These offbeat approaches to creativity training were a product of the 1990s dot-com era, when small start-ups were more receptive to unusual approaches than were large, established old-industry corporations. Consulting firms used not only Legos but also Etch A Sketches, Play-Doh, Slinkys, dramatic improvisation, painting, and singing. IDEO's training sessions had executives make hats, houses, and other objects out of wood blocks, rubber bands, and Legos (Gullapalli, 2002). The Center for Creative Leadership mixed Lego work with Tinkertoys and dominoes. The 1990s emphasis on innovation led to the casual dress of the workplace because companies believed that employees would be more creative if they were allowed to express themselves freely in their personal appearance.

But creativity consulting didn't start in the dot-com era; creativity consulting for business has been around since at least the 1970s. For example, in Europe,

Tudor Rickards held workshops for executives at the Manchester Business School in 1971, and Horst Geschka began to study corporate creativity at the Battelle Institute in Frankfurt in 1970 (Geschka, 1993). In the 1970s, these researchers moved out of the ivory tower and tried to use the psychological research of the day (chapters 3 and 4) to develop practical, hands-on creativity training for business.

One popular training method is *morphological synthesis*. Team members list the important dimensions of an object and the range of possible attributes for each dimension, and then consider novel combinations of them. Or they divide a complex problem into its elements, and then identify possible solutions for each element and explore all the possible combinations of the different solutions. Because of all the possible combinations, this method can generate lots of potential solutions. The biggest problem with morphological synthesis is identifying the right breakdown of the problem into its elements. This can itself take creativity, but the method can't work until you've already broken down these elements first. That's why morphological techniques are most effective for well-structured problems, and they work better for problem-solving types of creativity.

Perhaps the most popular training method is *brainstorming*, when a group free-associates while withholding criticism. Brainstorming was developed by the advertising executive Alex F. Osborn, who popularized the technique in his 1953 book *Applied Imagination*. Osborn's technique became so widely used that the word is now a part of the English language. *Synectics* is an elaboration of brainstorming that focuses on using analogies as catalysts for creativity (Gordon, 1961). Synectics teaches groups to use three types of analogies: direct analogies that compare parallel facts; personal analogies that ask people to imagine themselves as another animal or thing; and compressed conflicts that are contradictory terms like "joyous pain." *Brainwriting* is an extension of brainstorming that involves writing ideas down on paper, in order to both keep a better record of all the ideas, and also to reduce potentially negative group effects. *Method 635* is a brainwriting method in which a group of six people each generates three ideas and writes them on a sheet of paper, and then passes each sheet five times, with each person adding new ideas to each sheet each of the five times. A typical Method 635 session takes about five minutes. Method 635 is particularly good at generating names or slogans (Geschka, 1993).

The most elaborate development of brainstorming is Creative Problem Solving (CPS), developed by the International Center for Studies in Creativity, a group founded by Alex F. Osborn in the 1950s in Buffalo, New York (Isaksen, Dorval, & Treffinger, 1994, 2000; Isaksen & Treffinger, 1985; Treffinger, Isaksen, & Dorval, 1994).[1] The CPS method as developed by Osborn, Parnes, and their colleagues is based on three broad recommendations (see figure 16.1):

CPS FRAMEWORK

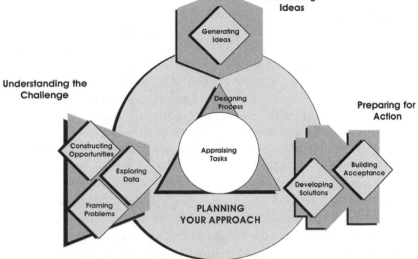

FIGURE 16.1. The six stages of creative problem solving proposed by The Creative Problem Solving Group. Reproduced by permission. CPS Version 6.1™is jointly owned by The Creative Problem Solving Group, Inc. and The Center for Creative Learning, Inc.: Source: Isaksen, S. G., Dorval, K. B., Treffinger, D. J. (2000). *Creative Approaches to Problem Solving: A Framework for Change.* Dubuque, Iowa: Kendall/ Hunt. Figure 2.2, page 37.

1. In the early stages, focus on *generating* (creative or divergent thinking). Aim for quantity of ideas rather than quality; defer judgment; and look for connections among these emerging ideas. When analyzing and choosing among ideas, shift to *focusing* (critical or convergent thinking). At this point, it's time to consider both positives and negatives, and to be more explicit about your opinions.

2. There are three components and six stages to the creative process: understanding the problem or challenge (three stages), generating ideas (one stage), and preparing for action (two stages).

3. Each of the six stages has both a generating (divergent thinking) and a focusing (convergent thinking) component. The three stages within "understanding the challenge" are constructing opportunities, exploring data, and framing problems. There's a single stage for "generating ideas," the classic "brainstorming" stage. And there are two stages in "preparing for action," developing solutions and building acceptance.[2]

Many other advice books also emphasize that creativity occurs in stages, and that divergent thinking has to come first, followed by convergent thinking (e.g., Perkins, 2000). These stages are derived from the cognitive psychological approaches to creativity that we reviewed in chapter 4.

Unfortunately, there's almost no solid experimental evidence that any of these methods work (cf. Feldhusen & Goh, 1995; Stein, 1993; Weisberg, 1986). For example, studies have repeatedly shown that brainstorming groups come up with fewer ideas than the same number of isolated individuals, working separately (Larey & Paulus, 1999; Mullen, Johnson, Salas, 1991). Yet the belief that groups are more creative than isolated individuals is so widespread that it has been termed the "illusion of group effectivity" (Nijstad, Diehl, & Stroebe, 2003). However, some newer studies have shown that certain kinds of groups, structured in just the right ways, can be more creative than isolated individuals (Paulus & Nijstad, 2003). These confusing findings may simply reflect the fact that it's so hard to develop a test to measure creativity, and therefore hard to measure whether creativity has increased or not. For example, most evaluations of brainstorming measure divergent thinking—the number of ideas that the group generates—even though researchers have found no evidence that divergent thinking is correlated with useful creative output (see chapter 3, page 45). Scholars still disagree on which training methods are the best, whether any of them work at all, and how we should test their effectiveness (Nickerson, 1999).

The sociocultural approach to creativity reveals some problems with the most common training programs.

First, many training programs assume that creativity is an individual process or ability, whereas we've seen that much of creativity emerges from complex social and organizational systems. And even though brainstorming is a group activity, it tends to focus on enhancing the creativity of the individuals in the group (Hennessey, 2003); it doesn't require fundamental changes to organizational structure and culture. Increasing the creativity of the employees in a company won't necessarily increase the creativity of the company; rather, a new organizational structure or culture may be necessary, and the creativity training methods reviewed above focus instead on the individuals.

Second, many training programs assume that creativity is a universally applicable, domain-general ability, when we've seen that most culturally significant creativity is domain specific (Baer, 1993). Creativity requires a person to become an extremely knowledgeable expert in his or her domain of activity. Creativity-training programs rarely instruct individuals to learn more about what has come before, even though the bulk of research suggests that this knowledge is a prerequisite for creativity.

Third, high levels of creative performance require a high level of commitment and dedication, a level that is not likely to develop unless the individual finds the task intrinsically motivating. Yet very few of these training programs emphasize the importance of commitment, hard work, and intrinsic motivation.

Fourth, many training programs emphasize the moment of creative insight as the critical feature of creativity, when most of the research suggests that insight plays a very small part in creative works. Rather, creative products result from long, complex, involved processes incorporating networks of people and long periods of hard work, during which many independent but connected mini-insights take place. Yet creativity training rarely instructs people in how to schedule and design an extended project so as to encourage and then incorporate these many sequential, incremental small insights.

Given all of what we know about the explanation of creativity, why do many training programs continue in these scientifically incorrect ways? It's because of our cultural conceptions of creativity (chapter 2). Many creativity training programs are the way they are because they reinforce our culture's myths about creativity (Weisberg, 1986). We believe that the moment of insight is critical, so creativity consultants give us what we want: they teach us how to have more insights. But creativity researchers know that insight plays a small part, if any, in creative products. We believe that creativity is a domain-general ability or process, and creativity consultants treat it that way, too, teaching creativity as a set of domain-general processes and abilities rather than teaching individuals to become experts in their domain. We believe that the main reason we aren't creative is because of constraints and limitations in the environment, and creativity advice always associates contextual factors with limitations to creativity, rather than pointing to the large body of research showing that contextual factors are essential to creativity. We believe that creativity is a product of an individual mind, and creativity consultants focus on enhancing individual creative ability rather than changing the culture and the organization.

Creativity research shows that creativity is hard work; creativity is usually an incremental step beyond what has come before; creativity often emerges from a team, not a solitary individual; and increasing creativity often requires substantive organizational change.

Humanistic Psychology and the New Age

It is ironic that our scientific objectivism about genius is mingled with a strong remnant of what looks like religious faith. The fact is that we cannot bring ourselves to renounce

> the dream of the superhuman . . . the post-Enlightenment
> guise of artistic or scientific genius.
> —*Marjorie Garber, 2002, p. 72*

Many advice books say that the highest level of creativity is shown in how one lives one's life. The visualization guru Shakti Gawain (1979/1982) wrote that "my life is my greatest work of art" (p. 123). Such perspectives are grounded in the 1950s humanistic psychology of Abraham Maslow and Carl Rogers, who emphasized the importance of becoming self-actualized. One's spiritual life is the ultimate creative product, and the ultimate in creativity is the process of becoming vibrant, alive, and self-actualized. Julia Cameron, author of the 1992 book *The Artist's Way*, said, "I simply wrote down the precepts of divine intervention in our lives the moment we engage our creativity and, through that, engage our Great Creator" (2002, p. 4). New Age adherents often claim that they're conduits for a deeper creativity that originates in a spiritual source. As we learned in chapter 2, this conception of creativity goes back at least to the time of the ancient Greeks.

New Age perspectives emphasize process rather than product; creativity is a spiritual practice, not a way to generate useful products. The association of process and creativity emerged during the 1960s (in the art world) and the 1970s (in cognitive psychology). The New Age movement itself emerged during the 1970s, so it's not surprising that its assumptions about creativity reflect the general beliefs of our culture at that time.

New Age conceptions of creativity draw on psychoanalytic and spiritual conceptions of the unconscious, the importance of dreams, and the Jungian notions of archetypes. Many New Age writings draw from amateur anthropological studies that trot out the ethnocentric stereotypes of a century ago: that primitive peoples or children are more pure and are less corrupted by convention and civilization. These beliefs about creativity are hard to square with the scientific findings we've learned about in this book. And in fact, they're not that new either. As we saw in chapter 2, these conceptions of creativity originated in the 19th-century Romantic era.

In the New Age approach, people are advised "to practice art as a means of awakening" (Cushman, 1992, p. 58). The goal isn't to increase the quality and marketability of the finished product, since thinking about the final product can interfere with the spiritual effectiveness of the practice. New Age conceptions of creativity are found in many art education classes, including drawing, writing, acting, and music. Anne Cushman (1992) signed up for one of each type of class in the San Francisco area and found some common themes in all of the classes:

- Trust your intuition, honor your initial impulses.
- Stay in the present, forget about your plan, and stay attuned to the moment.
- Don't cross out or paint over, even if you change your mind.
- Create boldly, without afterthoughts or regret.
- Focus on the process, not the product.
- Create for the sheer pleasure of doing it.
- Don't analyze the result, because this isn't psychotherapy.
- Special talent is not required, and in fact technique can get in the way.
- Practice and persevere.

The question of the quality of the finished product is irrelevant; anything generated "with a profound consciousness or with total awareness is artful" (performance artist Ruth Zaporah, quoted in Cushman, 1992, p. 59).

But of course, many of us are interested in increasing the quality of our created products. Art school students hope to generate works that will be sold and displayed in museums, and writing workshop students want to be published. Executives want their corporations to develop innovations that can be successfully marketed. But even if your eventual goal is to create a useful and marketable product, New Age instructors would argue that you should still begin your work in this process-focused, non-goal-directed way. There'll be time for critical reflection and editing later. Writing instructor Natalie Goldberg told Cushman that aspiring writers shouldn't move on to this editing stage for at least two years (quoted in Cushman, 1992, p. 60).

New Age advice has some scientific support in Teresa Amabile's research on intrinsic motivation, and Mike Csikszentmihalyi's research on flow (chapter 3). These psychologists have discovered that most creativity occurs when a person is in a flow state. And New Age advice is effective at helping a person attain a flow state.

In addition, the best of these books do a good job of dismissing some common creativity myths:

Only special geniuses are creative. This myth has been proved wrong by decades of research in cognitive psychology. In chapter 4, we learned that creative processes are based in the same mental processes that every human holds.

Creativity is only found in the arts. Creativity is required in all walks of life, not only in painting and poetry. In part 5, I explored the creativity of science and business. Creativity is also important in everyday life—in everyday small talk, parenting, teaching, and in being a good friend (Sawyer, 2001a).

Creativity is only found in crazy people. The myth of the madness of creativity is incredibly resilient, despite decades of research debunking any connection \(see chapter 5).

At the same time, a lot of New Age advice perpetuates other creativity myths. "How to be an artist" (Sark, 1989) is based on the myth that children are more creative than adults. If we build a perfect fort with blankets, perhaps that will put us in a childlike mindset and make us more creative. Much of Cushman's (1992) collected advice is straight out of the 19th-century Romantic-era beliefs that creativity originates in a pure inner nature, unconscious or divine, that exists prior to convention and society. But now we've learned that many of these myths have no basis in scientific research.

When you read a creativity advice book, you need to be watch out, because many of them perpetuate one of the following creativity myths.

Creativity Is Fun

The flow state of peak experience is extremely positive and self-actualizing, but it would be misleading to describe it as "fun." Creativity isn't easy or peaceful. Although creators are often in a flow state, they have to train for years and work hard to get there. And they have to constantly accept new challenges to keep themselves in the flow state; they never let themselves get too comfortable. The same activities that put a creative person in flow often seem either deathly boring or incredibly stressful to the rest of us.

Creativity Is a Burst of Inspiration

Creativity is not a sudden burst of inspiration, a gift from above, or a divine moment. Rather, creativity is a long, extended process over time, in which many small, mini-insights occur throughout the work day. These mini-insights emerge directly from the hard daily work of the task, and then are immediately integrated into the ongoing work of the project. Larger insights occasionally occur, but always in the context of hard work. And most of the highly publicized stories of insight aren't true. It turns out that historians (and sometimes creators themselves) often embellish the story to make it fit better into our cultural myth of creativity, in the same way that Coleridge made up the story about how the poem "Kubla Khan" came to him suddenly in an opium-induced haze (see chapter 11). Creative people also believe in many of their culture's myths about creativity, and they know, at least subconsciously, that if their stories better match our culture's conceptions of creativity, they'll be more likely to be judged creative.

Creativity Is an Individual Trait

Creativity isn't just a property of individuals, it's also a property of social groups. Modern creativity is more like an improvising jazz ensemble or like the development of the Windows operating system than like a poet writing in solitude. But it's hard for our individualist culture to accept this, and creative domains are often structured so that the credit for an entire group's work goes to one person. For example, Thomas Edison gets credit for all of the inventions generated by his 14-man skunk works; senior scientists get credit for the scientific advances generated by their teams of 10 or 20 scientists; movie directors get credit for a critical success even though a movie involves the creative efforts of over 100 people. For a variety of complex sociological reasons explained throughout this book, the members of a team often benefit from assigning all of the credit to the team leader, even though they have to deny their own creative role in the process (see chapter 14).

Individual creativity is more likely to occur in collaborative groups than in solitude. It's no accident that jazz musicians play better in groups and in front of live audiences than they do alone at home or in group rehearsal with no audience. Creators in all fields of life report their most significant insights emerging from collaborations (John-Steiner, 2000).

Creativity is a social phenomenon, involving variation and selection at multiple overlapping levels of analysis. What movies are selected as the best in a given year? Even before a movie is made, what about the group processes that determine which movie ideas are funded and produced? Once a movie is distributed, what group of experts decides which ones are the best, and how do they do it? How do these decisions relate to the box office, the majority vote of the ticket-buying public? And even these decisions are temporally and historically bounded; the movies that won awards 50 years ago often are not the movies that have stood the test of time. What are the historical processes that determine which movies are judged to be the classics, that deserve to be shown to each new generation?

Creativity Is the Rejection
of Convention

In fact, for the most part, creativity accepts and builds on convention. There's a small component of novelty in most creative products, but it's always smaller than we think at the time. With 50 or 100 years' distance, almost everything being created today will sound and look the same, even though to us it seems like an incredible variety.

It wasn't freedom from social constraint that resulted in Einstein, Michelangelo, or Shakespeare. Most social systems have vested interests in the status quo, and true creative novelty is often perceived to be dangerous to those in positions of power. As a result, what creative people might really need is not the feel-good message of humanistic psychology, but rather the thick skin and big ego advocated by existentialist Salvatore Maddi (Maddi, 1975, p. 182). Of course, this kind of person doesn't sound very nice, and what Maddi advocated doesn't fit with our cultural conceptions about creativity as the pure and good expression of the self-actualized individual.

Sociocultural Advice
for Creativity

Throughout this book, we've seen that explaining creativity requires a sociocultural approach, because creativity is a collaborative group enterprise. We have to consider not only individual psychology but also social and cultural context. But this raises big problems for those of us who want to be more creative. It's hard enough to change our own cognitive processes and personality, but who has any hope of changing the whole society, or redefining cultural values and attitudes? Throughout history, from time to time, a few remarkable people have managed to change an entire society or culture. But the odds are long, and many more have tried and failed.

Fortunately, you don't have to change the world to be creative. The sociocultural approach emphasizes synergy among person, domain, and field. You might not be able to change your creative domain, but you can leave your domain for another one. And when you're ready to increase your personal creativity, you can be much more effective if you've studied the domain and field that you're working in. The sociocultural approach recommends that you evaluate your domain and field and ask yourself: Does this domain and field, at this point in history, need someone like me?

Choose a Domain That's
Right for You

Domains that are widely accessible are more likely to experience creativity. In some cultures and historical periods, elites restricted access to the domain; only a certain privileged class of people could participate. Think back to the Middle Ages, when all knowledge was written in Latin but very few Europeans spoke or read Latin. Books were rare and expensive. As a result, many creative domains were inaccessible to the great majority of the population. Now that Western countries have near-universal literacy, and books are relatively inexpensive, creative domains are accessible to just about anyone.

Some domains are fairly advanced and most of the important problems are well known to everyone. Knowledge in the domain is well organized and well structured. If you prefer a problem-finding style of creativity, then you're likely to be frustrated in such a domain, because it needs problem solvers. Problem-finding people are better off in domains where the most important issues are unresolved, where conventions and rules are not rigidly specified, where no one even knows where to start. These tend to be relatively new areas of activity, installation art in the 1970s, or personal computer software in the 1980s, or electronic music in the 1990s. If you prefer a problem-finding style of creativity, you'll need to keep a broad watch on the society, looking for the next new thing.

In contrast, if you prefer a problem-solving style, then you'll probably be happier in a mature domain that has been around a while. In such a domain, there are textbooks, college courses, and doctoral programs. There's probably a national association and a national conference dedicated to this one special domain. The questions are well known and the criteria for judging work are objective; everyone will know it when you come up with something new. Many people prefer the certainty of such domains; in the more ambiguous problem-finding domains, the criteria for creativity are ill defined, and there may be subjective differences of opinion in what counts as good work.

Choose a Field That's
Right for You

A field is more likely to experience creativity if it has formal systems of training, with teachers, mentors, and experts who can pass on the domain of known knowledge.

A field is more likely to experience creativity if it has systems in place where potentially creative young people can be identified and selected by older members of the field, and if mentor-apprentice relationships are common (Hooker, Nakamura, & Csikszentmihalyi, 2003). Newcomers to a field need experienced guidance to learn about all of the aspects of the domain that are orally transmitted, not written down in books.

A field is more likely to experience creativity if it provides opportunities for newcomers to work in the domain. Talented young people won't choose a career if there are no job opportunities, or if the field only accepts older people.

You can increase your chances of creativity by making sure you're working in a field that fits your personality and work style. Some fields are very large, and require a lot of networking to stay involved and connected. That's fine if you're an extrovert, but a more introverted person might be intimidated by having to deal with 5,000 people at the annual conference. Introverts might be more comfortable in smaller fields.

In domains like math, if you have the right answer it doesn't matter whether or not people like you; the answer speaks for itself. The field becomes more important in those domains where the criteria aren't well defined, because then success requires your active involvement in the field. If you don't like dealing with people, if you don't like selling yourself, then you should be working in a domain with very explicit and objective criteria for judging works, like mathematics or theoretical physics. That way, the work will speak for itself. If you don't mind marketing and networking, then a domain that's more vague and less well defined might be fine for you.

Turn Your Gaze Outward Instead of Inward

Begin by becoming aware of the field that you're working in. Talk to people working in the area. Get to know the top people, who's in and who's out. Find out what cities and what universities are known as centers of creative work.

Examine the structure of the field—the gatekeepers, intermediaries, the art world—and see where you can best fit. Try to place yourself in an area where you'll be given opportunities for choice and discovery. Try to find a senior person to be your mentor.

Find out how the selection process works. Who decides what creative products are selected as useful and appropriate? What is the step-by-step procedure that they use to decide? Are decisions made without knowing the name of the work's creator, or do the gatekeepers know who they're judging? All of this information will help you to negotiate your entry into the field.

Market Yourself

Don't assume that if you build a better mousetrap, the world will beat a path to your door. The most successful creative people are very good at introducing their ideas to the field. They know who the key people are, and they know how the selection process works. They know how their new product is likely to be perceived by the field, because they've spent so much time becoming familiar with the field. They know which aspects of their idea to emphasize and which to leave unstated.

Don't Try to Become Creative in General; Focus on One Domain

Try out as many domains as possible. Start with something you enjoy and then branch out from there. Choose a domain that you like and that you won't mind spending years internalizing. Take the time to build basic skills in that domain, take classes, go to graduate school, read a lot of books, listen to the experts. Expect to spend several years paying your dues before you can be truly creative; be patient yet alert to opportunity.

Be Intrinsically Motivated

Don't expect to be creative if your goal is to become rich and famous. Creativity almost always results from intrinsic motivation; from people who work in an area just because they love the activity itself, not because of the eventual payoff. Choose an area that you are passionate about. Creative breakthroughs take years of hard work, and you won't be able to stay the course if you love the endpoint but not the process. It's often said that even the sexiest careers involve only 10% fun stuff, with the remaining 90% being work that most people would find tedious. The most creative people are the ones who choose a career in which they actually enjoy that 90%.

Don't Get Comfortable

The flow state of peak experience tends to occur when your skills are matched by the challenges of the task. If you find that your work is becoming easier as your experience and skill level increases, then don't just sit back and get comfortable. Instead, find a way to increase the challenges facing you. Seek out new projects, move to a new company, make a lateral move, change careers.

Balance Out Your Personality

Many creative people have what seem to be contradictory personalities; they can work at both ends of the personality spectrum. They're both masculine and feminine; they're both introverted and extroverted. They have a full range of personality styles, and they can shift to suit the situation. You can increase your odds for creativity if you broaden your personality range. For example, if you're extroverted, then work at developing the introverted side of your personality. If you're abstract and theoretical in style, then start a new project that's a little more practical and hands on.

Look For the Most Pressing Problems Facing the Domain

Work at asking good questions. Don't get caught up solving the easy, known problems. If you can't identify good questions, ask more senior experts in the field what they think the key unanswered questions are. Most of them will be happy to share, because they tend to have more good questions than they have time to answer.

Collaborate

Develop a network of close colleagues that you can discuss ideas with.
 Share your ideas with like-minded colleagues.
 Schedule time for free-wheeling, unstructured discussion without a specific goal.
 Listen for the creative insight that emerges from the group, rather than trying to push your own ideas on everyone.

Don't Worry About Who Gets Credit

Many of us are afraid to collaborate because we want to make sure we get the proper credit for the work that we do. We may worry that other group members won't carry their weight, or that they'll take credit for an idea that we originally had. But if you hold back during collaboration, saving your idea for later when you can present it as your own, you're hurting yourself. Ultimately, your own idea won't be as good as it would have been if it had gone through the collaborative process.

One problem is our system of copyright and patent law, which attributes each creation to a specific individual or corporation. Recent extensions of copyright far beyond the original time period envisioned by Congress are stifling our culture's creativity.[3] Fair use provisions are becoming increasingly limited, and that too is stifling creativity. These laws are based on obsolete myths about creativity—that it's the unique possession of a single individual, and that every component of a creative product is completely novel. But most creative products are collaboratively created, and most of them are built out of existing ideas and components.

Use Creative Work Habits

Work hard. Spend long hours working on a task. Expect to work more than 40 hours a week, sometimes much more. Don't give up easily. Expect important creative breakthroughs to come in small mini-insights while you're doing the work.

Multitask. Work on more than one project at a time. If the work isn't flowing, then shift gears and move on to another project for a while, then come back to the first project later.

Take time off. Creative people work harder than other people, but paradoxically, they also take more time off. Mini-insights often come during a period of idle time that immediately follows a period of hard work. In fact, creative people seem to sleep longer hours than average (Csikszentmihalyi, 1996, pp. 351–355). People who work 365 days a year and never take vacation rarely realize their creative potential.

Be Confident and Take Risks

Timidity, anxiety, and fear always get in the way of creativity. Many creative people seem to others to be arrogant or to have big egos, because they have immense self-confidence that allows them to take risks. Once you have a few successes, you'll be more confident. But at first, you'll help yourself get started if you seek out an environment that's supportive of creative thinking. Don't try to start right out in a stiff, unwelcoming environment; wait until later in your career when you've had a few successes.

Being confident isn't the same thing as being naive. Confidence will come from years of preparation in the domain, and from additional years of hard work once you've learned the domain.

To Believe or Not to Believe?

The idea of the lone hunter, or the lone voyager or explorer, who's guided by his principles and is going to get there against all odds, that self-image, as romantic and foolish as many people might consider it, is a very powerful force in making a major scientist.
—E. O. Wilson (*quoted in Csikszentmihalyi, 1996, p. 269*)

It's often been said that a belief doesn't have to be true to be helpful. And it might be helpful to believe in creativity myths even though they aren't true. I personally find myself quite attracted to many of the New Age, spiritualist writings on creativity, even when I know they're misleading. If I'm with my friends on a Friday night, talking about my workweek, I might even use some of that language in explaining how my writing and research went. Of course, if we hope to scientifically explain creativity we can't let ourselves be sidetracked by the myths. But if our goal is to increase our own creativity, it might be helpful to believe in even a false myth. Those advice books might work even if they're wrong.

Most readers of this book live in the United States, the culture most in love with individualist creativity myths. These myths survive because they show us as we like to imagine ourselves—the lone outsider, the rugged individualist, rejecting the stifling conventions of decaying old-world society. It almost sounds like an old cowboy movie. And of course, the myths are half true—creativity often starts with the individual.

But the sociocultural approach is just as positive and life affirming. It views us as social, collaborative beings. After all, the things that distinguish us from the animals are language, communication, and creativity—all fundamentally social. We are truly social animals. Together, we've created amazing things no one person could have done alone; the institutions of modern government, economy, and science are all collective, emergent phenomena. The sociocultural explanation of creativity is the only approach that can explain these collective social creations. And as our society becomes progressively more advanced and complex, creativity increasingly looks more like an emergent social process than like an individual thought process.

Thought Experiments

- As you've read this book, what are the connections that you've made with your own creative experience?
- What lessons do you think are most likely to help you be creative in the future?
- Do you think you'd be more creative if you gave up our creativity myths, or if you held onto them?

Suggested Readings

Cushman, A. (1992, March/April). Are you creative? *Utne Reader,* 52–60.
Chapter 14 of: Csikszentmihalyi, M. (1996). *Creativity: Flow and the psychology of discovery and invention.* New York: HarperCollins.
Feldhusen, J. F., & Goh, B. E. (1995). Assessing and accessing creativity: An integrative review of theory, research, and development. *Creativity Research Journal, 8*(3), 231–247.
Garber, M. (2002, December). Our genius problem. *The Atlantic Monthly,* 64–72.

Notes

1. The group's original name was the Creative Education Foundation. It was based at the University of Buffalo from 1954 to 1967, when it then moved to its current home at Buffalo State. The group received its current name in 2002.

2. Prior to their inclusion in Isaksen, Dorval, & Treffinger, 2000, the six stages were known as mess finding, data finding, problem finding, idea finding, solution finding, and acceptance finding.

3. See Boynton, 2004. Most scholars are opposed to the Sonny Bono Copyright Term Extension Act of 1998, which extended copyright protection an additional 20 years beyond the current term of 50 years after the author's death (in the case of corporate

authors, the current term is 75 years from publication). Formal statements in opposition have been made by copyright and intellectual property law professors (http://homepages.law.asu.edu/~dkarjala/OpposingCopyrightExtension/legmats/1998Statement.html, accessed 7/29/05) and by the American Association of University Professors (http://homepages.law.asu.edu/~dkarjala/OpposingCopyrightExtension/letters/aaup-01.html, accessed 7/29/05).

EPILOGUE

In the last few decades, we've seen a huge growth in the scientific understanding of creativity. Creativity research attracts an increasing number of scholars, and they continue to discover new findings every year. More and more of these scientists use the sociocultural approach, combining individualist and contextualist approaches. In chapter 12 on music, for example, we examined not only the creativity of the composer, isolated at his piano, but also the group creativity of improvising jazz ensembles. In chapter 13 on acting, we considered not only the creativity of the actor but also how the audience influences the performance. And in chapter 11 on writing, we examined the key roles played by editors, friends, and colleagues.

But creativity research is still in its infancy. For example, in psychology—where most of these studies take place—there are no professorships in creativity, and before this book there was no textbook for a college course in creativity. Creativity scholars haven't yet formed the disciplinary organizations that would efficiently spread new knowledge and research; there's no national conference for creativity scholars, no Internet newsgroup, no Web site.

Part of the reason for this marginal status is that the sociocultural approach is interdisciplinary, and most of the scientific community focuses on only one discipline at a time. Reality is organized into levels, ranging from small units—like genes and neurons—up to increasingly complex systems such as human beings, groups, societies, and cultures. Psychology studies the individual's creative process; sociology studies the complex networks and institutions that support and evaluate individual creativity. Each discipline has its own strengths

315

and weaknesses. Psychology is pretty good at helping us understand individual creativity, but doesn't do such a good job of explaining why one historical period displays a burst of creative output, when 100 years earlier, nothing much was happening. Anthropology is good at explaining why conceptions of creativity are different in different cultures, and why individuals manifest their creativity in different ways across the globe, but it doesn't explain individual differences within cultures very well.

For a complex phenomenon like creativity, a complete understanding requires us to develop explanations at individual, social, and cultural levels. We need to understand relationships between individuals and contexts: how conventions emerge from groups of people, and how people are influenced by the conventions of a domain. Since the 1990s, scientists have increasingly focused their research on the study of complex, multi-leveled social phenomena (Sawyer, 2001b, 2005). It turns out that nature is filled with examples of complex phenomena that require explanations at multiple levels of analysis, because the behavior of many systems in nature is unpredictably emergent from the interactions of the system's parts. The design of an ant colony emerges from the tiny decisions of thousands of ants; the decisions made by a human brain emerge from millions of neurons firing; a new social phenomenon emerges from the mini-insights of hundreds of people working together.

Emergence comes into play whenever scientists are trying to understand phenomena that require explanation at multiple levels of analysis. For example, scientists who study the mind and brain generally agree that although human behavior is rooted in the neurons and synapses of the brain, that brain has emergent properties that may be impossible to identify even if you know everything about neurons. Even though a creative insight is nothing more than a bunch of neurons firing, scientists agree that because of emergence, we will always need the higher-level explanations of psychology.

In the same way, even though creative groups are nothing more than the people in them, because of social emergence we often need sociocultural explanations. Social emergence is the opposite of the case where one smart, creative person imposes her will on the group; instead, it results from the social processes of collaboration. For example, the collective creativity of an improvised jazz performance can't be explained by psychology alone. Even if we knew everything there was to know about the mental makeup of each musician, we'd still have trouble predicting the emergence of the group's improvisation, because there are so many possibilities for change at each moment. If a musician delays her next melodic phrase by even a second, it could have unexpected effects on the performance. As with all complex systems, small differences can balloon into large effects.

In chapter 8, we learned that of all the world's cultures, Americans are the most individualist. And when it comes to the study of social phenomena, Americans tend to fall back on their cultural belief that the individual is primary, and this belief leads us to assume that we can explain everything about creativity in terms of individual personalities and decisions. But this belief leads us to ignore other types of creativity—the creativity of a jazz ensemble generating a brilliant group improvisation, the creativity of a scientific field as individual scientists contribute successive mini-insights, the creativity of an economy as new industries emerge through creative destruction. These are all examples of creative emergence, and a complete science of creativity should be able to explain all of them.

This is the potential of the sociocultural approach. Today, we have the scientific explanation of creativity within our grasp.

REFERENCES

Abbott, B. (1964). *The world of Atget*. New York: Horizon Press.

Abra, J. (1994). Collaboration in creative work: An initiative for investigation. *Creativity Research Journal*, *7*(1), 1–20.

Abrams, M. H. (1953). *The mirror and the lamp: Romantic theory and the critical tradition*. New York: Norton.

Abrams, M. H. (1984). *The correspondent breeze: Essays on English romanticism*. New York: Norton.

Ades, D., Forge, A., & Durham, A. (1985). *Francis Bacon*. London: Thames & Hudson.

Alajouanine, T. (1948). Aphasia and artistic realization. *Brain*, *71*, 229–241.

Alperson, P. (1984). On musical improvisation. *Journal of Aesthetics and Art Criticism*, *43*, 17–29.

Alter, J. B. (1984). A factor analysis of new and standardized instruments to measure the creative potential and high-energy action preference of performing arts students: A preliminary investigation. *Personality and Individual Differences*, *5*(6), 693–699.

Amabile, T. M. (1982). Social psychology of creativity: A consensual assessment technique. *Journal of Personality and Social Psychology*, *43*(5), 997–1013.

Amabile, T. (1983). *The social psychology of creativity*. New York: Springer-Verlag.

Amabile, T. (1996). *Creativity in context: Update to the social psychology of creativity* (2nd ed.). Boulder, CO: Westview Press.

Anderson, F. E. (1976). Esthetic evaluations and art involvement in Australia. *Studies in Art Education*, *17*, 33–43.

Andreasen, N. C. (1987). Creativity and mental illness: Prevalence rates in writers and their first-degree relatives. *American Journal of Psychiatry*, *144*(10), 1288–1292.

319

Ardery, J. S. (1998). *The temptation: Edgar Tolson and the genesis of twentieth-century folk art*. Chapel Hill, NC: University of North Carolina Press.

Arieti, S. (1976). *Creativity: The magic synthesis*. New York: Basic Books.

Arnold, W. N. (1992). *Vincent van Gogh: Chemicals, crisis, and creativity*. Boston: Birkhaüser.

Arnold, W. N. (2002, March 22). *Vincent van Gogh: Chemicals, crisis, and creativity*, Talk given at Washington University Department of Psychology, St. Louis, MO.

Augusta, A. (1842). *Sketch of the analytical engine invented by Charles Babbage, by L. F. Menabrea, with notes by the translator, Ada Augusta*. Retrieved June 3, 2000, from http://www.fourmilab.ch/babbage/sketch.html.

Bacon, F. (1868). *The works of Francis Bacon* (Vol. 12). (James Spedding, Robert Leslie Ellis, & Douglas Denon Heath, Eds.). London: Longman.

Baer, J. (1993). *Creativity and divergent thinking: A task-specific approach*. Hillsdale, NJ: Erlbaum.

Bain, A. (1977). *The senses and the intellect*. Washington, DC: University Publications of America. (Original work published 1855)

Bannon, L. (2002, June 7). Project Platypus: Mattel's answer to toy innovation: Workers "play" with ideas to unleash creativity. *Wall Street Journal*, p. E1.

Barnett, H. G. (1953). *Innovation*. New York: McGraw-Hill.

Barron, F. (1963). The disposition toward originality. In C. W. Taylor & F. Barron (Eds.), *Scientific creativity: Its recognition and development* (pp. 139–152). New York: Wiley.

Barron, F. (1972). *Artists in the making*. New York: Seminar Press.

Barron, F., & Harrington, D. M. (1981). Creativity, intelligence, and personality. *Annual Review of Psychology, 32*, 439–476.

Barron, F., & Welsh, G. S. (1952). Artistic perception as a possible factor in personality style: Its measurement by a figure preference test. *Journal of Psychology, 33*, 199–203.

Barrow, J. D. (2000). *The universe that discovered itself*. New York: Oxford University Press.

Bartlett, J. (1955). *Familiar quotations: A collection of passages, phrases, and proverbs traced to their sources in ancient and modern literature*. Boston: Little, Brown.

Baudelaire, C. (1964). *The painter of modern life, and other essays* (Jonathan Mayne, Trans.). London: Phaidon. (Original work published 1863.)

Baxandall, M. (1972). *Painting and experience in fifteenth century Italy*. New York: Oxford University Press.

Becker, G. (2000–2001). The association of creativity and psychopathology: Its cultural-historical origins. *Creativity Research Journal, 13*(1), 45–53.

Becker, H. (1982). *Art worlds*. Berkeley and Los Angeles: University of California Press.

Becker, H. (2000). The etiquette of improvisation. *Mind, Culture, and Activity, 7*(3), 171–176.

Beittel, K. R. (1972). *Mind and context in the art of drawing*. New York: Holt, Rinehart & Winston.

Beittel, K. R., & Burkhart, R. C. (1963). Strategies of spontaneous, divergent, and academic art students. *Studies in Art Education, 5,* 20–40.

Belgrad, D. (1998). *The culture of spontaneity: Improvisation and the arts in postwar America.* Chicago: University of Chicago Press.

Beller, M. (1999). *Quantum dialogue: The making of a revolution.* Chicago: The University of Chicago Press.

Bennett, W. (1980, January–February). Providing for posterity. *Harvard Magazine, 82,* 13–16.

Bennetts, L. (1986, October 18). Alda stars in televised M*A*S*H seminar. *The New York Times,* p. A11.

Bennis, W., & Biederman, P. W. (1997). *Organizing genius: The secrets of creative collaboration.* Reading, MA: Addison-Wesley.

Berliner, P. (1994). *Thinking in jazz: The infinite art of improvisation.* Chicago: University of Chicago Press.

Berlyne, D. E. (1971). *Aesthetics and psychobiology.* New York: Appleton-Century-Crofts.

Berman, K. B. (2003). Transformation to transcendence: The creativity of performance through the eyes of classical musicians. *Unpublished manuscript, University of Connecticut.*

Bever, T., & Chiarello, R. (1974). Cerebral dominance in musicians and nonmusicians. *Science, 185,* 137–139.

Biebuyck, D. (1973). *The Lega: Art, initiation and moral philosophy.* Berkeley and Los Angeles: University of California Press.

Black, D. (2000). Dreams of pure sociology. *Sociological Theory, 18*(3), 343–367.

Bloom, B. S. (1963). Report on creativity research by the examiner's office of the University of Chicago. In C. W. Taylor & F. Barron (Eds.), *Scientific creativity* (pp. 251–264). New York: Wiley.

Blunt, J. (1966). *The composite art of acting.* New York: Macmillan.

Boden, M. (1991) *The creative mind: Myths and mechanisms.* New York: Basic Books.

Boden, M. A. (1999). Computer models of creativity. In R. J. Sternberg (Ed.), *The handbook of creativity* (pp. 351–372). New York: Cambridge University Press.

Bourdieu, P. (1979/1984). *Distinction: A social critique of the judgement of taste.* Cambridge, MA: Harvard University Press. (Originally published in 1979 by Les Éditions de Minuit, Paris, as *La Distinction: Critique sociale du jugement.*)

Bourdieu, P. (1993). *Fields of cultural production.* New York: Columbia University Press.

Bowles, S. (2003, June 20). Fans use their muscle to shape the movie. *USA Today,* pp. A1, A2.

Boynton, R. S. (2004, January 25). The tyranny of copyright? *The New York Times Magazine,* pp. 40–45.

Bransford, J. D., Brown, A. L., & Cocking, R. R. (Eds.). (1999). *How people learn: Brain, mind, experience, and school.* Washington, DC: National Academy Press.

Brannigan, A. (1981). *The social basis of scientific discoveries.* New York: Cambridge University Press.

Bronowski, J. (1973). *The ascent of man.* Boston: Little, Brown.

Brook, P. (1968). *The empty space.* New York: Atheneum.

Brown, R. (1981). How improvised is jazz improvisation? *Jazz Research Papers, 1,* 22–32.

Bruner, E. M. (1993). Epilogue: Creative persona and the problem of authenticity. In S. Lavie, K. Narayan, & R. Rosaldo (Eds.), *Creativity/anthropology* (pp. 321–334). Ithaca, NY: Cornell University Press.

Budick, A. (2002, March 15). Creedmoor, creatively: Patients let artistic juices flow in QMA exhibit. *Newsday,* p. B3.

Byrne, R. (1996). *The 2,548 best things anybody ever said.* New York: Galahad Books.

Cameron, J. (1992). *The artist's way: A spiritual path to higher creativity.* Los Angeles: Jeremy P. Tarcher.

Cameron, J. (2002). *Walking in this world: The practical art of creativity.* New York: Penguin Putnam.

Campbell, D. T. (1960). Blind variation and selective retention in scientific discovery. *Psychological Review, 67,* 380–400.

Candy, L. (1999). *COSTART Project Artists Survey Report: Preliminary Results* (LUTCHI: C&CRS Research Report, Loughborough University). Retrieved January 20, 2004, from http://research.it.uts.edu.au/creative/ccrs/costart/doc/overview.rtf].

Candy, L. (2002). Defining interaction. In L. Candy & E. Edmonds (Eds.), *Explorations in art and technology* (pp. 261–266). Berlin: Springer.

Candy, L., & Edmonds, E. (Eds.). (2002). *Explorations in art and technology.* Berlin: Springer.

Carroll, J. (1995). *Evolution and literary theory.* Columbia: University of Missouri Press.

Cattell, R. B. (1971). *Abilities: Their structure, growth, and action.* Boston: Houghton Mifflin.

Caudle, F. M. (1991). An ecological view of social perception: Implications for theatrical performance. In G. D. Wilson (Ed.), *Psychology and performing arts* (pp. 45–57). Amsterdam: Swets & Zeitlinger.

Chapman, A. J., & Williams, A. R. (1976). Prestige effects and aesthetic experiences: Adolescents' reactions to music. *British Journal of Social and Clinical Psychology, 15,* 61–72.

Charlton, J. (1980). *The writer's quotation book: A literary companion.* New York: Barnes & Noble Books.

Child, I. L. (1968, December). The experts and the bridge of judgment that crosses every cultural gap. *Psychology Today,* 25–29.

Cohen, H. (1999). A self-defining game for one player. In L. Candy & E. Edmonds (Eds.), *Creativity & cognition: Proceedings of the third creativity & cognition conference* (p. 14). New York: ACM Press.

Cole, J. R., & Cole, S. (1972). The Ortega hypothesis. *Science, 178,* 368–375.

Cole, J. R., & Cole, S. (1973). *Social stratification in science.* Chicago: University of Chicago Press.

Collingwood, R. G. (1938). *The principles of art.* New York: Oxford University Press.

Comte, A. (1854). *The positive philosophy of Auguste Comte* (Harriet Martineau, Trans.). New York: D. Appleton. (Original work published in six volumes, from 1830 to 1842.)

Cooper, E. (1991). A critique of six measures for assessing creativity. *The Journal of Creative Behavior, 25*(3), 194–204.

Copland, A. (1952). *Music and imagination.* Cambridge, MA: Harvard University Press.

Cornock, S., & Edmonds, E. A. (1973). The creative process where the artist is amplified or superseded by the computer. *Leonardo,* volume 6, 11–16.

Cox, C. (1926). *The early mental traits of three hundred geniuses.* Stanford, CA: Stanford University Press.

Crafts, H. (2002). *The bondwoman's narrative* (Henry Louis Gates, Jr., editor). New York: Warner Books.

Crain, C. (2001, October). The artistic animal. *Lingua Franca,* 28–37.

Crow, B. K. (1988). Conversational performance and the performance of conversation. *TDR, 32*(3), 23–54.

Crozier, W. R., & Chapman, A. (1981). Aesthetic preferences: Prestige and social class. In D. O'Hare (Ed.), *Psychology and the arts* (pp. 242–278). Brighton, Sussex, England: Harvester Press.

Csikszentmihalyi, M. (1965). *Artistic problems and their solutions: An exploration of creativity in the arts.* Unpublished doctoral thesis, University of Chicago, Chicago.

Csikszentmihalyi, M. (1988a). Motivation and creativity: Toward a synthesis of structural and energistic approaches to cognition. *New Ideas in Psychology, 6*(2), 159–176.

Csikszentmihalyi, M. (1988b). Society, culture, and person: A systems view of creativity. In R. J. Sternberg (Ed.), *The nature of creativity* (pp. 325–339). New York: Cambridge University Press.

Csikszentmihalyi, M. (1990a). The domain of creativity. In M. A. Runco & R. S. Albert (Eds.), *Theories of creativity* (pp. 190–212). Newbury Park, CA: Sage.

Csikszentmihalyi, M. (1990b). *Flow: The psychology of optimal experience.* New York: HarperCollins.

Csikszentmihalyi, M. (1996). *Creativity: Flow and the psychology of discovery and invention.* New York: HarperCollins.

Csikszentmihalyi, M. (1999). Implications of a systems perspective for the study of creativity. In R. J. Sternberg (Ed.), *The handbook of creativity* (pp. 313–335). New York: Cambridge University Press.

Csikszentmihalyi, M., & Getzels, J. W. (1988). Creativity and problem finding in art. In F. H. Farley & R. W. Neperud (Eds.), *The foundations of aesthetics, art & art education* (pp. 91–116). New York: Praeger.

Csikszentmihalyi, M., & Sawyer, R. K. (1995). Creative insight: The social dimension of a solitary moment. In R. J. Sternberg & J. E. Davidson (Eds.), *The nature of insight* (pp. 329–363). Cambridge: MIT Press.

Cushman, A. (1992, March/April). Are you creative? *Utne Reader*, 52–60.

Damasio, A. R. (2001). Some notes on brain, imagination, and creativity. In K. H. Pfenninger & V. R. Shubik (Eds.), *The origins of creativity* (pp. 59–68). New York: Oxford University Press.

Dart, T. (1967). *The interpretation of music* (4th ed.). London: Hutchinson.

Delbanco, N. (2002, July). In praise of imitation. *Harper's Magazine*, 57–63.

Dennett, D. (1995). *Darwin's Dangerous Idea: Evolution and the meanings of life*. New York: Simon & Schuster.

Dennis, W. (1955). Variations in productivity among creative workers. *Scientific Monthly, 79*, 180–183.

Dennis, W. (1958). The age decrement in outstanding scientific contributions: Fact or artifact? *American Psychologist, 13*, 457–460.

Dennis, W. (1966). Creative productivity between the ages of 20 and 80 years. *Journal of Gerontology, 21*, 1–8.

Denoyelle, F. (2002, June, July, August). Photographie: Les voies de la reconnaissance. *Sciences Humaines, 37*, 41–43.

DePalma, A. (1992, June 17). Hard sell for top universities: Finding new chiefs. *The New York Times*, p. B11.

Deppman, J., Ferrer, D., & Groden, M. (Eds.). (2004). *Genetic criticism: Texts and avant-textes*. Philadelphia: University of Pennsylvania Press.

Devereux, G. (1961). Art and mythology. In B. Kaplan (Ed.), *Studying personality cross-culturally* (pp. 361–386). Evanston, IL: Row, Peterson.

Dewey, J. (1934). *Art as experience*. New York: Perigree Books.

Diderot, D. (1936). Paradoxe sur le Comédien. In F. C. Green (Ed.), *Diderot's writings on the theatre* (pp. 249–317). New York: Cambridge University Press. (Original work published 1773.)

Dimaggio, O., & Useem, M. (1978). Social class and arts consumption: The origins and consequences of class differences in exposure to the arts in America. *Theory and Society, 5*, 141–161.

Dirac, P. (1963). The evolution of the physicist's picture of nature. *Scientific American, 208*(5), 45–53.

Dissanayake, E. (1988). *What is art for?* Seattle: University of Washington.

Domino, G. (1970). Identification of potentially creative persons using the adjective check list. *Journal of Consulting and Clinical Psychology, 35*, 48–51.

Donnat, O. (2002, June, July, August). Entre passade et passion: Les amateurs. *Sciences Humaines, 37*, 70–73.

Dunbar, K. (1995). How scientists really reason: Scientific reasoning in real-world laboratories. In R. J. Sternberg & J. E. Davidson (Eds.), *The nature of insight* (pp. 365–395). Cambridge: MIT Press.

Dunbar, K. (1997). How scientists think: On-line creativity and conceptual change in science. In T. B. Ward, S. M. Smith, & J. Vaid (Eds.), *Creative thought: An investigation of conceptual structures and processes* (pp. 461–493). Washington, DC: American Psychological Association.

Dunbar, K. (1999). How scientists build models: Invivo science as a window on the scientific mind. In L. Magnani, N. Nersessian, & P. Thagard (Eds.), *Model-based reasoning in scientific discovery* (pp. 89–98). New York: Plenum Press.

Dutton, D. (2001). What is genius? *Philosophy and Literature, 25*, 181–196.

Ebert, R. (1997, October 22). Film, the snubbed art. *The New York Times,* p. A23.

Edwards, B. (1979). *Drawing on the right side of the brain: A course in enhancing creativity and artistic confidence.* Los Angeles: J. P. Tarcher.

Einstein, A., & Infeld, L. (1938). *The evolution of physics.* New York: Simon & Schuster.

Eisenberg, E. M. (1990). Jamming: Transcendence through organizing. *Communication Research, 17*(2), 139–164.

Eisenberger, R., & Cameron, J. (1996). Detrimental effects of reward: Reality or myth? *American Psychologist, 51*(11), 1153–1166.

Eliot, T. S. (1971). *T. S. Eliot The waste land: A facsimile and transcript of the original drafts including the annotations of Ezra Pound.* New York: Harcourt Brace Jovanovich.

Elkins, J. (2001). *Why art cannot be taught: A handbook for art students.* Urbana: University of Illinois Press.

Ellis, H. (1904). *A study in British genius.* London: Hurst & Blackett.

Elman, J. L., Bates, E. A., Johnson, M. H., Karmiloff-Smith, A., Parisi, D., & Plunkett, K. (1996). *Rethinking innateness: A connectionist perspective on development.* Cambridge: MIT Press.

Engell, J. (1981). *The creative imagination: Enlightenment to romanticism.* Cambridge, MA: Harvard University Press.

Epstein, J. S. (Ed.). (1994). *Adolescents and their music: If it's too loud, you're too old.* New York: Garland Publishing.

Evans, K. B., & Sims, H. P., Jr. (1997). Mining for innovation: The conceptual underpinnings, history and diffusion of self-directed work teams. In C. L. Cooper & S. E. Jackson (Eds.), *Creating tomorrow's organizations: A handbook for future research in organizational behavior* (pp. 269–291). New York: Wiley.

Eysenck, M. W. (1990). Creativity. In M. W. Eysenck (Ed.), *The Blackwell dictionary of cognitive psychology* (pp. 86–87). Oxford, England: Basil Blackwell.

Eysenck, H. (1995). *Genius: The natural history of creativity.* New York: Cambridge University Press.

Fairtlough, G. (2000). The organization of innovative enterprises. In J. Ziman (Ed.), *Technological innovation as an evolutionary process* (pp. 267–277). New York: Cambridge University Press.

Farmelo, G. (2002a). Foreword: It must be beautiful. In G. Farmelo (Ed.), *It must be beautiful: Great equations of modern science* (pp. ix–xvi). London: Granta Books.

Farmelo, G. (Ed.). (2002b). *It must be beautiful: Great equations of modern science.* London: Granta Books.

Farnsworth, P. R. (1969). *The social psychology of music* (2nd ed.). Ames: Iowa State University Press.

Feist, G. J. (1998). A meta-analysis of personality in scientific and artistic creativity. *Personality and Social Psychology Review, 2*(4), 290–309.

Feist, G. J., & Runco, M. A. (1993). Trends in the creativity literature: An analysis of research in the *The Journal of Creative Behavior* (1967–1989). *Creativity Research Journal, 6*(3), 271–286.

Feldhusen, J. F., & Goh, B. E. (1995). Assessing and accessing creativity: An integrative review of theory, research, and development. *Creativity Research Journal, 8*(3), 231–247.

Feldman, D. H. (1974). Universal to unique. In S. Rosner & L. E. Abt (Eds.), *Essays in creativity* (pp. 45–85). Croton-on-Hudson, NY: North River Press.

Feldman, D. H. (1980). *Beyond universals in cognitive development.* Norwood, NJ: Ablex.

Feldman, D. H., Csikszentmihalyi, M., & Gardner, H. (1994). *Changing the world: A framework for the study of creativity.* Westport, CT: Praeger.

Ferla, R. L. (2002, July 7). Once hot, now not, hunters of cool are in a freeze. *The New York Times,* p. ST6.

Fineberg, J. D. (1997). *The innocent eye: Children's art and the modern artist.* Princeton, NJ: Princeton University Press.

Fineberg, J. (Ed.). (1998). *Discovering child art: Essays on childhood, primitivism and modernism.* Princeton, NJ: Princeton University Press.

Finke, R. A., Ward, T. B., & Smith, S. M. (1992). *Creative cognition: Theory, research, and applications.* Cambridge: MIT Press.

Fish, S. (1980). *Is there a text in this class? The authority of interpretive communities.* Cambridge, MA: Harvard University Press.

Fisher, S., & Fisher, R. L. (1981). *Pretend the world is funny and forever: A psychological analysis of comedians, clowns, and actors.* Hillsdale, NJ: Erlbaum.

Fiske, A. P., Kitayama, S., Markus, H. R., & Nisbett, R. E. (1998). The cultural matrix of social psychology. In D. T. Gilbert, S. T. Fiske, & G. Lindzey (Eds.), *The handbook of social psychology* (pp. 915–981). New York: McGraw-Hill.

Flannery, M. C. (1991). Science and aesthetics: A partnership for science education. *Science Education, 75*(5), 577–593.

Flavell, J. H., & Draguns, J. (1957). A microgenetic approach to perception and thought. *Psychological Bulletin, 54*(3), 197–217.

Florida, R. (2002). *The rise of the creative class and how it's transforming work, life, community and everyday life.* New York: Basic Books.

Foreman, K., & Martini, C. (1995). *Something like a drug: An unauthorized oral history of theatresports.* Calgary, AB, Canada: Red Deer Press.

Forge, A. (1967). The Abelam artist. In M. Freedman (Ed.), *Social organization: Essays presented to Raymond Firth* (pp. 65–84). London: Frank Cass & Co.

Freud, S. (1989). Creative writers and day-dreaming. In P. Gay (Ed.), *The Freud reader* (pp. 436–443). New York: Norton. (Paper originally presented December 6, 1907).

Freud, S. (1966). *Introductory lectures on psycho-analysis* (James Strachey, Trans.). New York: Norton. (Original work published 1917.)

Friedman, R. A. (2002, June 4). Connecting depression and artistry. *The New York Times*, p. D6.

Friend, T. (1998, September 14). Copy cats. *The New Yorker*, 51–57.

Frith, S. (1978). *The sociology of rock.* London: Constable.

Fry, E. F. (Ed.). (1970). *On the future of art.* New York: Viking.

Galenson, D. W. (2001). *Painting outside the lines: Patterns of creativity in modern art.* Cambridge, MA: Harvard University Press.

Galton, F. (1962). *Hereditary genius: An inquiry into its laws and consequences.* Cleveland: Meridian Books. (Original work published 1869.)

Galton, F. (1874). *English men of science.* London: Macmillan.

Garber, M. (2002, December). Our genius problem. *The Atlantic Monthly*, 64–72.

Gardner, H. (1973). *The arts and human development: A psychological study of the artistic process.* New York: Wiley.

Gardner, H. (1975). *The shattered mind.* New York: Knopf.

Gardner, H. (1983). *Frames of mind: The theory of multiple intelligences.* New York: Basic Books.

Gardner, H. (1993). *Creating minds.* New York: Basic Books.

Gardner, H. (2001). Creators: Multiple intelligences. In K. H. Pfenninger & V. R. Shubik (Eds.), *The origins of creativity* (pp. 117–143). New York: Oxford University Press.

Gates, H. L. (2002, February 18). The fugitive. *The New Yorker*, 104.

Gawain, S. (1982). *Creative visualization.* New York: Bantam. (Original work published by Whatever Publishing, March 1979).

Gazzaniga, M. (1970). *The bisected brain.* New York: Appleton-Century-Crofts.

Gedo, J. E. (1996). *The artist & the emotional world: Creativity and personality.* New York: Columbia University Press.

Geen, R. G. (1989). Alternative conceptions of social facilitation. In P. B. Paulus (Ed.), *Psychology of group influence* (2nd ed., pp. 15–51). Hillsdale, NJ: Erlbaum.

Geertz, C. (1973). *The interpretation of cultures.* New York: Basic Books. (Original work published 1966).

Gentner, D., & Gentner, D. R. (1983). Flowing waters or teeming crowds: Mental models of electricity. In D. Gentner & A. L. Stevens (Eds.), *Mental models* (pp. 99–129). Mahwah, NJ: Erlbaum.

Geraghty, M. (1997, January 31). Art schools change admissions policies to place more emphasis on academics. *The Chronicle of Higher Education*, A27–A28.

Gerard, A. (1966). *An essay on genius.* Munich: Fink Verlag. (Original work published 1774.)

Gerbrands, A. A. (1967). *Wow-Ipits: Eight Asmat carvers of New Guinea.* The Hague, Netherlands: Mouton.

Geschka, H. (1993). The development and assessment of creative thinking techniques: A German perspective. In S. G. Isaksen, M. C. Murdock, R. L. Firestien, & D. J. Treffinger (Eds.), *Nurturing and developing creativity: The emergence of a discipline* (pp. 215–236). Norwood, NJ: Ablex.

Getzels, J. W. (1964). Creative thinking, problem-solving, and instruction. In E. R. Hilgard (Ed.), *Theories of learning and instruction* (pp. 240–267). Chicago: University of Chicago Press.

Getzels, J. W. (1987). Creativity, intelligence, and problem finding: Retrospect and prospect. In S. G. Isaksen (Ed.), *Frontiers of creativity research* (pp. 88–102). Buffalo, NY: Bearly.

Getzels, J. W., & Csikszentmihalyi, M. (1976). *The creative vision.* New York: Wiley.

Getzels, J. W., & Jackson, P. W. (1962). *Creativity and intelligence: Explorations with gifted students.* New York: Wiley.

Gilbert, N. (1997). A simulation of the structure of academic science. *Sociological Research Online, 2*(2). Retrieved 7/29/05, from http://www.socresonline.org.uk/socresonline/2/2/3.html.

Gladwell, M. (2002, July 22). The talent myth. *The New Yorker,* 28–33.

Goertzel, M. G., Goertzel, V., & Goertzel, T. G. (1978). *Three hundred eminent personalities.* San Francisco: Jossey-Bass.

Goldberg, N. (1986). *Writing down the bones: Freeing the writer within.* Boston: Shambala.

Goldwater, R. (1967). *Primitivism in modern art.* Cambridge, MA: Harvard University Press. (Original work published 1938.)

Golomb, C. (2002). *Child art in context: A cultural and comparative perspective.* Washington, DC: APA Press.

Gordon, W. J. J. (1961). *Synectics: The development of creative capacity.* New York: Harper.

Gough, H. G., & Heilbrun, A. B. (1965). *The adjective checklist manual.* Palo Alto, CA: Consulting Psychologists Press.

Graburn, N. H. H. (Ed.). (1976). *Ethnic and tourist arts.* Berkeley and Los Angeles: University of California Press.

Green, G. S. (1981). A test of the Ortega hypothesis in criminology. *Criminology, 19,* 45–52.

Greenberg, C. (1996, April 14). The Jackson Pollock market soars. *The New York Times Magazine,* 115–116. (Originally published in the April 16, 1961, issue.)

Grønhaug, K., & Kaufmann, G. (Eds.). (1988). *Innovation: A cross-disciplinary perspective.* Oslo, Norway: Norwegian University Press.

Gruber, H. E. (1974). *Darwin on man: A psychological study of scientific creativity.* Chicago: University of Chicago Press.

Gruber, H. E. (1988). The evolving systems approach to creative work. *Creativity Research Journal, 1*, 27–51.

Gruber, H. E., & Davis, S. N. (1988). Inching our way up Mount Olympus: The evolving-systems approach to creative thinking. In R. J. Sternberg (Ed.), *The nature of creativity* (pp. 243–270). New York: Cambridge University Press.

Guerin, B. (1993). *Social facilitation.* New York: Cambridge University Press.

Guerrilla Girls. (1998). *The Guerrilla Girls' bedside companion to the history of Western art.* New York: Penguin.

Guilford, J. P. (1950). Creativity. *The American Psychologist, 5*(9), 444–454.

Guilford, J. P. (1967). *The nature of human intelligence.* New York: McGraw-Hill.

Guilford, J. P. (1970). Creativity: Retrospect and prospect. *The Journal of Creative Behavior, 4*(3), 149–168.

Guilford, J. P. (1971). Some misconceptions regarding measurement of creative talents. *The Journal of Creative Behavior, 5*, 77–87.

Gullapalli, D. (2002, August 16). To do: Schedule meeting, play with Legos. *The Wall Street Journal*, p. B1.

Haacke, H. (1975). *Framing and being framed: 7 works 1970–75.* Halifax, NS, Canada: The Press of the Nova Scotia College of Art and Design.

Hadamard, J. (1945). *The psychology of invention in the mathematical field.* Princeton, NJ: Princeton University Press.

Hammond, J., & Edelmann, R. J. (1991a). The act of being: Personality characteristics of professional actors, amateur actors and non-actors. In G. D. Wilson (Ed.), *Psychology and performing arts* (pp. 123–131). Amsterdam: Swets & Zeitlinger.

Hammond, J., & Edelmann, R. J. (1991b). Double identity: The effect of the acting process on the self-perception of professional actors—two case illustrations. In G. D. Wilson (Ed.), *Psychology and performing arts* (pp. 24–44). Amsterdam: Swets & Zeitlinger.

Harris, N. (1966). *The artist in American society: The formative years 1790–1869.* New York: Simon & Schuster.

Hatfield, E., Cacioppo, J. T., & Rapson, R. L. (1994). *Emotional contagion.* New York: Cambridge University Press.

Heinich, N. (1993). *Du peintre a l'artiste.* Paris: Minuit.

Heisenberg, W. (1971). *Physics and beyond.* New York: Harper & Row.

Helmstadter, G. C. (1972). The Barron-Welsh art scale. In O. K. Buros (Ed.), *The seventh mental measurements yearbook* (pp. 82–84). Highland Park, NJ: Gryphon Press.

Henderson, M. (2003, February 17). "Genetic changes" triggered man's artistic abilities. *London Times.*

Hennessey, B. A. (2003). Is the social psychology of creativity really social? Moving beyond a focus on the individual. In P. B. Paulus & B. A. Nijstad (Eds.), *Group creativity: Innovation through collaboration* (pp. 181–201). New York: Oxford.

Henshilwood, C. S., d'Errico, F., Yates, R., Jacobs, Z., Tribolo, C., Duller, G. A. T., et al. (2002). Emergence of modern human behavior: Middle stone age engravings from South Africa. *Science, 295*(5558), 1278–1280.

Herrnstein, R. J., & Murray, C. (1994). *The bell curve: Intelligence and class structure in American life.* New York: Free Press.

Hill, R. (1978, July). Dozens of uses for Velcro fasteners. *Popular Science, 213,* 110–112.

Hill, K. G., & Amabile, T. M. (1993). A social psychological perspective on creativity: Intrinsic motivation and creativity in the classroom and workplace. In S. G. Isaksen, M. C. Murdock, R. L. Firestien, & D. J. Treffinger (Eds.), *Understanding and recognizing creativity: The emergence of a discipline* (pp. 400–432). Norwood, NJ: Ablex.

Hollenberg, D. (1978). Performance review: Ran Blake/Ray Bryant trio. *Downbeat, 45*(10), 40–42.

Holyoak, K. J., & Thagard, P. (1995). *Mental leaps: Analogy in creative thought.* Cambridge: MIT Press.

Honour, H., & Fleming, J. (1999). *World history of art* (5th ed.). London: Lawrence King.

Hooker, C., Nakamura, J., & Csikszentmihalyi, M. (2003). The group as mentor: Social capital and the systems model of creativity. In P. B. Paulus & B. A. Nijstad (Eds.), *Group creativity: Innovation through collaboration* (pp. 225–244). New York: Oxford.

Hoppe, K. D. (1988). Hemispheric specialization and creativity. *Psychiatric Clinics of North America, 11*(3), 303–315.

Hopper, R. (1993). Conversational dramatism and everyday life performance. *Text and Performance Quarterly, 13,* 181–183.

Huang, G. T. (2003, May). Machining melodies. *Technology Review,* p. 26.

Huber, J. C. (1998). Invention and inventivity as a special kind of creativity, with implications for general creativity. *The Journal of Creative Behavior, 32*(1), 58–72.

Hughes, R. (1984). The rise of Andy Warhol. In B. Wallis (Ed.), *Art after modernism: Rethinking representation* (pp. 45–58). New York: New Museum of Contemporary Art/David Godine.

Hulbert, A. (2003). *Raising America: Experts, parents, and a century of advice about children.* New York: Knopf.

Isaksen, S. G., Dorval, K. B., & Treffinger, D. J. (1994). *Creative approaches to problem solving: A framework for change.* Buffalo, NY: Creative Problem Solving Group.

Isaksen, S. G., Dorval, K. B., & Treffinger, D. J. (2000). *Creative approaches to problem solving: A framework for change* (2nd ed.). Buffalo, NY: Creative Problem Solving Group.

Isaksen, S. G., & Treffinger, D. J. (1985). *Creative problem solving: The basic course.* Buffalo, NY: Bearly.

Iser, W. (1978). *The act of reading: A theory of aesthetic response.* Baltimore: Johns Hopkins University Press.

James, W. (1880). Great men, great thoughts, and the environment. *The Atlantic Monthly, 46*(276), 441–459.

Jamison, K. R. (1993). *Touched with fire: Manic-depressive illness and the artistic temperament.* New York: Free Press.

Jamison, K. R. (1995, February). Manic-depressive illness and creativity. *Scientific American,* 62–67.

John-Steiner, V. (1985). *Notebooks of the mind: Explorations of thinking.* Albuquerque: University of New Mexico Press.

John-Steiner, V. (2000). *Creative collaboration.* New York: Oxford.

Johnson, G. (1997, November 11). Undiscovered Bach? No, a computer wrote it. *The New York Times,* pp. B9, B10.

Johnson, G. (2002, October 13). Oil and water: Why prizes and science don't mix. *The New York Times,* Section 4 [Week in Review], p. 3.

Juda, A. (1953). *Höchstbegabung: Ihre Erbverhältnisse sowie ihre Beziehungen zu psychischen Anomalien.* Munich: Urban & Schwarzenberg.

Kaeppler, A. L. (1987). Spontaneous choreography: Improvisation in Polynesian dance. *Yearbook for Traditional Music, 19,* 13–22.

Kakutani, M. (1997, September 28). Never-ending saga. *The New York Times Magazine,* 40–41.

Kakutani, M. (1998, March 1). Portrait of the artist as a focus group. *The New York Times Sunday Magazine,* 26.

Kant, I. (1900). *Critique of pure reason* (J. M. D. Meiklejohn, Trans.). New York: Colonial Press. (Original work published 1781.)

Kao, J. (1996). *Jamming: The art and discipline of business creativity.* New York: HarperCollins.

Kaplan, R., & Kaplan, S. (1989). *The experience of nature: A psychological perspective.* New York: Cambridge University Press.

Kasof, J. (1995). Explaining creativity: The attributional perspective. *Creativity Research Journal, 8*(4), 311–366.

Kaufmann, G. (1988). Problem solving and creativity. In K. Grønhaug & G. Kaufmann (Eds.), *Innovation: A cross-disciplinary perspective* (pp. 87–137). Oslo, Norway: Norwegian University Press.

Kavolis, V. (1968). *Artistic expression: A sociological analysis.* Ithaca, NY: Cornell University Press.

Kelley, T. (2001). *The art of innovation: Lessons in creativity from IDEO, America's leading design firm.* New York: Doubleday.

Kimmelman, M. (1998, August 9). Installation art moves in, moves on. *The New York Times,* Section 2, pp. 1, 32.

Kimmelman, M. (2003, April 6). The Dia generation. *The New York Times Magazine,* 30–37, 58, 61, 72, 76–77.

King, N., & Anderson, N. (1995). *Innovation and change in organizations.* London: Routledge.

Kirton, M. J. (1988). Adaptors and innovators: Problem solvers in organizations. In

K. Grønhaug & G. Kaufmann (Eds.), *Innovation: A cross-disciplinary perspective* (pp. 65–85). Oslo, Norway: Norwegian University Press.

Klahr, D. (2000). *Exploring science: The cognition and development of discovery processes.* Cambridge: MIT Press.

Klahr, D., & Simon, H. A. (1999). Studies of scientific discovery: Complementary approaches and convergent findings. *Psychological Bulletin, 125*(5), 524–543.

Klein, R. G., & Edgar, B. (2002). *The dawn of human culture.* New York: Wiley.

Klosterman, C. (2002, March 17). The pretenders. *The New York Times Magazine,* 54–57.

Koestler, A. (1964). *The act of creation.* New York: Macmillan.

Kogan, N. (2002). Careers in the performing arts: A psychological perspective. *Creativity Research Journal, 14*(1), 1–16.

Konijn, E. A. (1991). What's on between the actor and his audience? Empirical analysis of emotion processes in the theatre. In G. D. Wilson (Ed.), *Psychology and performing arts* (pp. 59–73). Amsterdam: Swets & Zeitlinger.

Kozinn, A. (1997, October 8). Bootlegging as a public service: No, this isn't a joke. *The New York Times,* p. B2.

Kris, E. (1952). *Psychoanalytic explorations in art.* New York: International Universities Press.

Kuhn, A. (1925). *Lovis Corinth.* Berlin: Im Propyläen-Verlag.

Kuhn, T. S. (1963). The essential tension: Tradition and innovation in scientific research. In C. W. Taylor & F. Barron (Eds.), *Scientific creativity: Its recognition and development* (pp. 341–354). New York: Wiley. (From a paper presented at the third Utah conference on creativity in 1959.)

Kuper, A. (1988). *The invention of primitive society.* London: Routledge.

Lamott, A. (1994). *Bird by bird: Some instructions on writing and life.* New York: Pantheon Books.

Lang, R. J., & Ryba, K. A. (1976). The identification of some creative thinking parameters common to the artistic and musical personality. *British Journal of Educational Psychology, 46,* 267–279.

Lange-Eichbaum, W. (1932). *The problem of genius.* New York: Macmillan. (Original work published 1930)

Larey, T. S., & Paulus, P. B. (1999). Group preference and convergent tendencies in small groups: A content analysis of group brainstorming performance. *Creativity Research Journal, 12*(3), 175–184.

Layton, R. (1991). *The anthropology of art* (2nd ed.). New York: Cambridge.

Leary, W. E. (2002, October 22). The inquiring minds behind 200 years of inventions. *The New York Times,* p. F4.

Lehman, H. C. (1953). *Age and achievement.* Princeton, NJ: Princeton University Press.

Lenat, D. B. (1977). The ubiquity of discovery. *Artificial Intelligence, 9,* 257–286.

Lenat, D. B. (1983). The role of heuristics in learning by discovery: Three case studies.

In R. S. Michalski, J. G. Carbonell, & T. M. Mitchell (Eds.), *Machine learning: An artificial intelligence approach* (pp. 243–306). Palo Alto, CA: Tioga.

Lorblanchet, M. (2002, June, July, August). L'art des premiers hommes: Entretien avec Michal Lorblanchet. *Sciences Humaines, 37*, 8–11.

Lord, A. B. (1960). *The singer of tales.* New York: Cambridge University Press.

Lotka, A. J. (1926). The frequency distribution of scientific productivity. *Journal of the Washington Academy of Sciences, 16*, 317–323.

Ludwig, A. M. (1992). Creative achievement and psychopathology: Comparison among professions. *American Journal of Psychotherapy, 46*(3), 330–356.

Ludwig, A. M. (1995). *The price of greatness: Resolving the creativity and madness controversy.* New York: The Guilford Press.

MacKinnon, D. W. (1962). The nature and nurture of creative talent. *American Psychologist, 17*(7), 484–495.

MacKinnon, D. W. (1978). What makes a person creative? In D. W. MacKinnon (Ed.), *In search of human effectiveness* (pp. 178–186). New York: Universe Books. (Originally published in *Saturday Review*, Feb. 10, 1962, pp. 15–17, 69)

MacKinnon, D. W. (1978). *In search of human effectiveness.* Buffalo, NY: Creative Education Foundation.

MacKinnon, D. W. (1987). Some critical issues for future research in creativity. In S. G. Isaksen (Ed.), *Frontiers of creativity research* (pp. 119–130). Buffalo, NY: Bearly.

Mackler, B., & Shontz, F. C. (1965). Life style and creativity: An empirical investigation. *Perceptual and Motor Skills, 20*, 873–896.

Mackworth, N. H. (1965). Originality. *American Psychologist, 20*, 51–66.

Maddi, S. R. (1975). The strenuousness of the creative life. In I. A. Taylor & J. W. Getzels (Eds.), *Perspectives in creativity* (pp. 173–190). Chicago: Aldine.

Maduro, R. (1976). *Artistic creativity in a Brahmin painter community.* Berkeley, CA: Center for South and Southeast Asian Studies.

Malevich, K. S. (1968). On new systems in art. In T. Anderson (Ed.), *Essays on art 1915–1933* (pp. 83–117). London: Rapp & Whiting. (Original work published 1919)

Mann, P. H. (1969). *The romantic novel: A survey of reading habits.* London: Mills & Boon.

Marcus, S., & Neaçsu, G. (1972). La structure psychologique du talent dramatique. *Revue Roumaine des Sciences Sociales, Série de Psychologie, 16*(2), 133–149.

Marcuse, H. (1970). Art as a form of reality. In E. F. Fry (Ed.), *On the future of art* (pp. 123–134). New York: Viking.

Marks, P. (1997, April 22). When the audience joins the cast. *The New York Times*, pp. B1, B7.

Markus, H. R., & Kitayama, S. (1991). Culture and the self: Implications for cognition, emotion, and motivation. *Psychological Review, 98*(2), 224–253.

Martindale, A. (1972). *The rise of the artist in the middle ages and early renaissance.* London: Thames & Hudson.

Martindale, C. (1990). *The clockwork muse: The predictability of artistic change*. New York: Basic Books.

Marzorati, G. (2002, March 17). All by himself. *The New York Times Magazine*, 32–37, 68–70.

Maslow, A. H. (1954). *Motivation and personality*. New York: Harper & Row.

Max, D. T. (1998, August 9). The Carver chronicles. *The New York Times Magazine*, 34–40, 51, 56–57.

McCorduck, P. (1991). *Aaron's code: Meta-art, artificial intelligence, and the work of Harold Cohen*. New York: Freeman.

McLurkin, J. (2002). *The swarm orchestra: Temporal synchronization and spatial division of labor for large swarms of autonomous robots*. Retrieved June 26, 2003, from http://www.swiss.ai.mit.edu/projects/amorphous/6.978/final-papers/jamesm-final.pdf.

Mednick, S. A. (1962). The associative basis of the creative process. *Psychological Review, 69*(3), 220–232.

Mednick, S. A., & Mednick, M. T. (1967). *Remote associates test examiner's manual*. Boston: Houghton Mifflin.

Meehan, J. (1976). *The metanovel: Writing stories by computer*. Unpublished doctoral dissertation, Yale University, New Haven, CT.

Meehan, J. (1981). TALE-SPIN. In R. C. Schank & C. J. Riesbeck (Eds.), *Inside computer understanding: Five programs plus miniatures* (pp. 197–226). Mahwah, NJ: Erlbaum.

Menand, L. (1998, February 9). What is "art"? *The New Yorker*, 39–41.

Merton, R. K. (1961). Singletons and multiples in scientific discovery: A chapter in the sociology of science. *Proceedings of the American Philosophical Society, 105*(5), 470–486.

Michael, W. B., Rosenthal, B. G., & DeCamp, M. A. (1949). An experimental investigation of prestige-suggestion for two types of literary material. *Journal of Psychology, 28*, 303–323.

Miner, A. S., Bassoff, P., & Moorman, C. (2001). Organizational improvisation and learning: A field study. *Administrative Science Quarterly, 46*, 304–337.

Mittler, C. A. (1976). An instructional strategy designed to overcome the adverse effects of established student attitudes toward works of art. *Studies in Art Education, 17*, 13–31.

Monson, I. (1996). *Saying something: Jazz improvisation and interaction*. Chicago: University of Chicago Press.

Moore, H. (1985). Notes on sculpture. In B. Ghiselin (Ed.), *The creative process: A symposium* (pp. 68–73). Berkeley and Los Angeles: University of California Press. (Original work published 1952)

Moore, M. (1985). The relationship between the originality of essays and variables in the problem-discovery process: A study of creative and non-creative middle school students. *Research in the Teaching of English, 19*, 84–95.

Morelli, G. A., Rogoff, B., Oppenheim, D., & Goldsmith, D. (1992). Cultural variation in infants' sleeping arrangements: Questions of independence. *Developmental Psychology, 28*(4), 604–613.

Moreno, J. L. (1977). *Psychodrama* (3 vols.). Beacon, NY: Beacon House.

Mukerji, C. (1996). The collective construction of scientific genius. In Y. Engeström & D. Middleton (Eds.), *Cognition and communication at work* (pp. 257–278). New York: Cambridge University Press.

Mullen, B., Johnson, C., & Salas, E. (1991). Productivity loss in brainstorming groups: A meta-analytic integration. *Basic and Applied Social Psychology, 12*(1), 3–23.

Mumford, M. D. (1995). Situational influences on creative achievement: Attributions or interactions? *Creativity Research Journal, 8*(4), 405–412.

Nagel, E. (1961). *The structure of science: Problems in the logic of scientific explanation.* New York: Harcourt, Brace & World.

Nakamura, J., & Csikszentmihalyi, M. (2003). Creativity in later life. In R. K. Sawyer et al., *Creativity and development* (pp. 186–216). New York: Oxford.

Neaçsu, G. (1972). L'Unité de la transposition et de l'expressivité: Indice fondamental du talent scénique. *Revue Roumaine des Sciences Sociales, Série de Psychologie, 16*(1), 3–15.

Negroponte, N. (2003, February). Creating a culture of ideas. *Technology Review,* 34–35.

Nemiro, J. (1997). Interpretive artists: A qualitative exploration of the creative process of actors. *Creativity Research Journal, 10*(2 & 3), 229–239.

Newhall, B. (1964). *The history of photography.* New York: Museum of Modern Art.

Nicholls, J. G. (1972). Creativity in the person who will never produce anything original and useful: The concept of creativity as a normally distributed trait. *American Psychologist, 27,* 717–727.

Nickerson, R. S. (1999). Enhancing creativity. In R. J. Sternberg (Ed.), *The handbook of creativity* (pp. 392–430). New York: Cambridge University Press.

Nijstad, B. A., Diehl, M., & Stroebe, W. (2003). Cognitive stimulation and interference in idea-generating groups. In P. B. Paulus & B. A. Nijstad (Eds.), *Group creativity: Innovation through collaboration* (pp. 137–159). New York: Oxford.

Novak, J. D., & Gowin, D. B. (1984). *Learning how to learn.* New York: Cambridge University Press.

Olson, D. R., & Torrance, N. (Eds.). (1996). *The handbook of education and human development: New models of learning, teaching, and schooling.* Cambridge: Blackwell.

Ornstein, R. E. (1972). *The psychology of consciousness.* San Francisco: W. H. Freeman.

Ornstein, R. (1997). *The right mind: Making sense of the hemispheres.* New York: Harcourt Brace.

Oromaner, M. (1985). The Ortega hypothesis and influential articles in American sociology. *Scientometrics, 7,* 3–10.

Ortega y Gasset, J. (1932). *The revolt of the masses* (Anthony Kerrigan, Trans.). New York: Norton.

Osborn, A. F. (1953). *Applied imagination.* Buffalo, NY: Creative Education Foundation Press.

Over, R. (1982). The durability of scientific reputation. *Journal of the History of the Behavioral Sciences, 18,* 53–61.

Ox, J. (2002). The color organ and collaboration. In L. Candy & E. Edmonds (Eds.), *Explorations in art and technology* (pp. 211–218). Berlin: Springer.

Parks, T. (2002, October 24). Tales told by the computer. *The New York Review of Books,* 49–51.

Parnes, S. J. (1993). A glance backward and forward. In S. G. Isaksen, M. C. Murdock, R. L. Firestien, & D. J. Treffinger (Eds.), *Understanding and recognizing creativity: The emergence of a discipline* (pp. 471–474). Norwood, NJ: Ablex.

Parnes, S. J., & Harding, H. F. (1962). Preface. In S. J. Parnes & H. F. Harding (Eds.), *A source book for creative thinking* (pp. v–viii). New York: Scribner's.

Partch, H. (1949). *Genesis of a music.* Madison: University of Wisconsin Press.

Pater, W. (1986). *The Renaissance: Studies in art and poetry* (Adam Phillips, Ed.). New York: Oxford University Press. (Original work published 1873)

Paulus, P. B., & Nijstad, B. A. (2003). *Group creativity: Innovation through collaboration.* New York: Oxford.

Peiry, L. (2001). *Art brut: Dubuffet and the origins of outsider art.* London: Thames & Hudson.

Perkins, D. (2000). *The Eureka effect: The art and logic of breakthrough thinking.* New York: Norton.

Pfeiffer, J. E. (1982). *The creative explosion: An inquiry into the origins of art and religion.* New York: Harper & Row.

Pfenninger, K. H., & Shubik, V. R. (2001). Insights into the foundations of creativity: A synthesis. In K. H. Pfenninger & V. R. Shubik (Eds.), *The origins of creativity* (pp. 213–236). New York: Oxford University Press.

Piirto, J. (1999). A survey of psychological studies in creativity. In A. S. Fishkin, B. Cramond, & P. Olszewski-Kubilius (Eds.), *Investigating creativity in youth: Research and methods* (pp. 27–48). Cresskill, NJ: Hampton.

Pinker, S. (2002). *The blank slate: The modern denial of human nature.* New York: Viking.

Planck, M. (1949). *Scientific autobiography and other papers* (Frank Gaynor, Trans.). New York: Philosophical Library.

Pound, E. (1954). A retrospect. In T. S. Eliot (Ed.), *Literary essays of Ezra Pound* (pp. 3–14). London: Faber & Faber.

Price, D. (1963). *Little science, big science.* New York: Columbia University Press.

Price, D. (1965). Networks of scientific papers. *Science, 149,* 510–515.

Prinzhorn, H. (1972). *Artistry of the mentally ill.* New York: Springer.

Pritzker, S., & Runco, M. A. (1997). The creative decision-making process in group situation comedy writing. In R. K. Sawyer (Ed.), *Creativity in performance* (pp. 115–141). Norwood, NJ: Ablex.

Purser, R. E., & Montuori, A. (2003). *In search of creativity: Beyond individualism and collectivism.* Retrieved 7/29/05 from http://online.sfsu.edu/~rpurser/revised/pages/CREATIVITYwam.htm.

Quetelet, A. (1969). *A treatise on man and the development of his faculties.* Gainesville, FL: Scholars' facsimiles and reprints. (A facsimile reproduction of the English translation of the 1835 French original)

Radway, J. A. (1991). *Reading the romance: Women, patriarchy, and popular literature.* (2nd ed.). Chapel Hill: University of North Carolina Press. (Original work published 1984)

Raina, M. K. (1993). Ethnocentric confines in creativity research. In S. G. Isaksen, M. C. Murdock, R. L. Firestien, & D. J. Treffinger (Eds.), *Understanding and recognizing creativity: The emergence of a discipline* (pp. 435–453). Norwood, NJ: Ablex.

Raina, M. K. (1999). Cross-cultural differences. In M. A. Runco & S. R. Pritzker (Eds.), *Encyclopedia of creativity, Volume 1* (pp. 453–464). San Diego, CA: Academic Press.

Raskin, E. (1936). Comparison of scientific and literary ability: A biographical study of eminent scientists and men of letters of the nineteenth century. *Journal of Abnormal and Social Psychology, 31*(1), 20–35.

Ray, D. J., & Blaker, A. A. (1967). *Eskimo masks: Art and ceremony.* Seattle: University of Washington Press.

Redner, S. (2002, November 13). *The statistical mechanics of popularity.* Paper presented at the Department of Physics colloquium, Washington University, St. Louis, MO.

Reese, G. (1959). *Music in the Renaissance.* (Rev. ed.). New York: Norton.

Reichardt, J. (1971). *The computer in art.* London, United Kingdom: Studio Vista.

Restak, R. (1993). The creative brain. In J. Brockman (Ed.), *Creativity: The reality club 4* (pp. 164–175). New York: Simon & Schuster.

Reznikoff, M., Domino, G., Bridges, C., & Honeyman, M. (1973). Creative abilities in identical and fraternal twins. *Behavior Genetics, 3*(4), 365–377.

Rhodes, M. (1961). An analysis of creativity. *Phi Delta Kappan, 42*(7), 305–310.

Robertson, Z. (1991). Dreams, creativity and the problems of performers. In G. D. Wilson (Ed.), *Psychology and performing arts* (pp. 191–197). Amsterdam: Swets & Zeitlinger.

Rockefeller Brothers Fund. (1958). *The pursuit of excellence: Education and the future of America; panel report V of the Special Studies Project.* Garden City, NY: Doubleday.

Roe, A. (1952a). *The making of a scientist.* New York: Dodd, Mead.

Roe, A. (1952b). The psychologist examines 64 eminent scientists. *Scientific American, 187*(5), 21–25.

Roe, A. (1972). Patterns in productivity of scientists. *Science, 176,* 940–941.

Rogers, C. R. (1954). Toward a theory of creativity. *ETC: A review of general semantics, 11*(4), 249–260.

Rogers, C. R. (1961). *On becoming a person: A therapist's view of psychotherapy.* Boston: Houghton-Mifflin.

Rogers, E. M. (1962). *Diffusion of innovations*. New York: Free Press of Glencoe.

Rosaldo, R., Lavie, S., & Narayan, K. (1993). Introduction: Creativity in anthropology. In S. Lavie, K. Narayan, & R. Rosaldo (Eds.), *Creativity/anthropology* (pp. 1–8). Ithaca, NY: Cornell University Press.

Rose, A. R. (1969). Four interviews. *Arts Magazine, 43*(4).

Rosengren, K. E. (1985). Time and literary fame. *Poetics, 14,* 157–172.

Rosenthal, S. (2003). *Tao Te Ching* [Electronic version]. Retrieved March 24, 2003, from http://www.clas.ufl.edu/users/gthursby/taoism/ttcstan3.htm#5.

Rosner, S., & Abt, L. E. (1974). Conclusions. In S. Rosner & L. E. Abt (Eds.), *Essays in creativity* (pp. 191–200). Croton-on-Hudson, NY: North River Press.

Ross, B. M. (1976). Preferences for nonrepresentational drawings by Navaho and other children. *Journal of Cross-Cultural Psychology, 7,* 145–156.

Rothenberg, A. (1979). *The emerging goddess: The creative process in art, science, and other fields*. Chicago: University of Chicago Press.

Rothenberg, A. (1990). *Creativity and madness: New findings and old stereotypes*. Baltimore: Johns Hopkins University Press.

Rothstein, E. (1997, October 26). Where a democracy and its money have no place. *The New York Times*, pp. AR1, 39.

Rowe, J., & Partridge, D. (1993). Creativity: A survey of AI approaches. *Artificial Intelligence Review, 7,* 43–70.

Rubin, D. C. (1995). *Memory in oral traditions: The cognitive psychology of epic, ballads, and counting-out rhymes*. New York: Oxford University Press.

Runco, M. A., & Albert, R. S. (1986). The threshold theory regarding creativity and intelligence: An empirical test with gifted and nongifted children. *The Creative Child and Adult Quarterly, 2*(4), 213–218.

Sacks, O. (1970). *The man who mistook his wife for a hat*. New York: Harper Collins.

Sante, L. (1998, January 4). They know what we like. *The New York Times Book Review*, 8.

Sass, L. (1992). *Madness and modernism: Insanity in the light of modern art, literature, and thought*. New York: Basic Books.

Sass, L. A. (2000–2001). Schizophrenia, modernism, and the "creative imagination": On creativity and psychopathology. *Creativity Research Journal, 13*(1), 55–74.

Sawyer, R. K. (1993). He blinded me with science: Review of Colin Martindale, *The clockwork muse: The predictability of artistic change. Creativity Research Journal, 6,* 461–464.

Sawyer, R. K. (Ed.). (1997a). *Creativity in performance*. Greenwich, CT: Ablex.

Sawyer, R. K. (1997b). *Pretend play as improvisation: Conversation in the preschool classroom*. Mahwah, NJ: Erlbaum.

Sawyer, R. K. (1998). The interdisciplinary study of creativity in performance. *Creativity Research Journal, 11*(1), 11–19.

Sawyer, R. K. (2000). Improvisation and the creative process: Dewey, Collingwood, and the aesthetics of spontaneity. *Journal of Aesthetics and Art Criticism, 58*(2), 149–161.

Sawyer, R. K. (2001a). *Creating conversations: Improvisation in everyday discourse.* Cresskill, NJ: Hampton Press.

Sawyer, R. K. (2001b). Emergence in sociology: Contemporary philosophy of mind and some implications for sociological theory. *American Journal of Sociology, 107*(3), 551–585.

Sawyer, R. K. (2003). *Group creativity: Music, theater, collaboration.* Mahwah, NJ: Erlbaum.

Sawyer, R. K. (2005). *Social emergence: Societies as complex systems.* New York: Cambridge.

Sawyer, R. K., John-Steiner, V., Moran, S., Sternberg, R., Feldman, D. H., Csikszentmihalyi, M., et al. (2003). *Creativity and development.* New York: Oxford.

Schaefer, C. E., & Anastasi, A. (1968). A biographical inventory for identifying creativity in adolescent boys. *Journal of Applied Psychology, 52*, 42–48.

Schaffer, S. (1994). Making up discovery. In M. A. Boden (Ed.), *Dimensions of creativity* (pp. 13–51). Cambridge: MIT Press.

Schiavo, P. (2001, Fall). Comments: Wolfgang Amadeus Mozart. *St. Louis Symphony Orchestra Stagebill,* 24b–24c.

Schneider, E. (1953). *Coleridge, opium, and Kubla Khan.* Chicago: University of Chicago Press.

Schooler, C. (1972). Birth order effects: Not here, not now! *Psychological Bulletin, 78*, 161–175.

Schuessler, J. (1999, December/January). The visionary company: Call it what you will, outsider art is making its mark. *Lingua Franca,* 48–58.

Schumpeter, J. (1975). *Capitalism, socialism, and democracy.* New York: Harper. (Original work published 1942)

Schutz, A. (1964). Making music together: A study in social relationships. In A. Brodessen (Ed.), *Collected papers, Volume 2: Studies in social theory* (pp. 159–178). The Hague, Netherlands: Martinus Nijhoff.

Seabrook, J. (1997, January 6). Why is the force still with us? *The New Yorker,* 40–53.

Seham, A. E. (2001). *Whose improv is it anyway? Beyond Second City.* Jackson: University Press of Mississippi.

Seifert, C. M., Meyer, D. E., Davidson, N., Patalano, A. L., & Yaniv, I. (1995). Demystification of cognitive insight: Opportunistic assimilation and the prepared-mind perspective. In R. J. Sternberg & J. E. Davidson (Eds.), *The nature of insight* (pp. 65–124). Cambridge: MIT Press.

Selfe, L. (1977). *Nadia: A case of extraordinary drawing ability in an autistic child.* New York: Academic Press.

Shelley, P. B. (1901). *The complete poetical works of Shelley* (George Edward Woodberry, Ed.). Boston: Houghton Mifflin.

Shelley, P. B. (1965). *A defence of poetry.* Indianapolis: Bobbs-Merrill.

Shostak, M. (1993). The creative individual in the world of the !Kung San. In S. Lavie,

K. Narayan, & R. Rosaldo (Eds.), *Creativity/anthropology* (pp. 54–69). Ithaca, NY: Cornell University Press.

Shulman, S. (2002, October). Frisbee's marketing wind. *Technology Review*, 75.

Silver, H. R. (1981). Calculating risks: The socio-economic foundations of aesthetic innovations in an Ashanti carving community. *Ethnology, 20*, 101–114.

Simon, H. A. (1957). *Models of man, social and rational.* New York: Wiley.

Simon, H. A. (1988). Creativity and motivation: A response to Csikszentmihalyi. *New Ideas in Psychology, 6*(2), 177–181.

Simonton, D. K. (1976). Biographical determinants of achieved eminence: A multivariate approach to the Cox data. *Journal of Personality and Social Psychology, 33*, 218–226.

Simonton, D. K. (1984). *Genius, creativity, and leadership.* Cambridge, MA: Harvard University Press.

Simonton, D. K. (1988a). Creativity, leadership, and chance. In R. J. Sternberg (Ed.), *The nature of creativity* (pp. 386–426). New York: Cambridge University Press.

Simonton, D. K. (1988b). *Scientific genius: A psychology of science.* New York: Cambridge University Press.

Simonton, D. K. (1994). *Greatness: Who makes history and why.* New York: Guilford.

Simonton, D. K. (1997a). Creative productivity: A predictive and explanatory model of career trajectories and landmarks. *Psychological Review, 104*(1), 66–89.

Simonton, D. K. (1997b). Creativity in personality, developmental, and social psychology: Any links with cognitive psychology? In T. B. Ward, S. M. Smith, & J. Vaid (Eds.), *Creative thought: An investigation of conceptual structures and processes* (pp. 309–324). Washington, DC: American Psychological Association.

Simonton, D. K. (1999a). Creativity from a historiometric perspective. In R. J. Sternberg (Ed.), *The handbook of creativity* (pp. 116–133). New York: Cambridge University Press.

Simonton, D. K. (1999b). *Origins of genius: Darwinian perspectives on creativity.* New York: Oxford University Press.

Simonton, D. K. (2004). Group artistic creativity: Creative clusters and cinematic success in feature films. *Journal of Applied Social Psychology, 34*(7), 1494–1520.

Skinner, B. F. (1968). *The technology of teaching.* New York: Appleton-Century-Crofts.

Skinner, B. F. (1972). A lecture on "having" a poem. In B. F. Skinner (Ed.), *Cumulative record: A selection of papers* (pp. 345–355). New York: Appleton-Century-Crofts.

Slivka, R. (1971, October). Laugh-in in clay. *Craft Horizons, 31*, 39–47, 63.

Sloboda, J. A. (1985). *The musical mind: The cognitive psychology of music.* New York: Oxford.

Sloboda, J. (Ed.). (1988). *Generative processes in music.* New York: Oxford.

Smith, L. P. (1961). Four words: Romantic, originality, creative, genius, *S. P. E. Tracts, I–XX, Vol. I* (pp. 521–566). London: Oxford University Press.

Souriau, P. (1881). *Theorie de l'invention.* Paris: Librairie Hachette.

Sperry, R. W., Gazzaniga, M. S., & Bogen, J. E. (1969). Interhemispheric relationships:

The neocortical commissures; syndromes of hemispheric disconnection. In P. J. Vinken & G. W. Bruyn (Eds.), *Disorders of speech, perception, and symbolic behaviour* (pp. 273–290). New York: Wiley Interscience.

Springer, S. P., & Deutsch, G. (1981). *Left brain, right brain.* San Francisco: W. H. Freeman.

Stanislavsky, K. (1936). *An actor prepares.* New York: Theatre Arts Books.

Stanislavsky, K. (1962). *Building a character.* New York: Theatre Arts Books.

Starko, A. J. (1999). Problem finding: A key to creative productivity. In A. S. Fishkin, B. Cramond, & P. Olszewski-Kubilius (Eds.), *Investigating creativity in youth: Research and methods* (pp. 75–96). Cresskill, NJ: Hampton.

Stein, M. I. (1963). Creativity in a free society. *Educational horizons, 41,* 115–130. (Reprinted with minor changes from the October 1961 issue of *Graduate Comment* at Wayne State University, Detroit, MI).

Stein, M. I. (1967). Creativity and culture. In R. L. Mooney & T. A. Razik (Eds.), *Explorations in creativity* (pp. 109–119). New York: Harper & Row.

Stein, M. I. (1974). *Stimulating creativity, Volume 1: Individual procedures.* San Francisco: Academic Press.

Stein, M. I. (1987). Creativity research at the crossroads: A 1985 perspective. In S. G. Isaksen (Ed.), *Frontiers of creativity research: Beyond the basics* (pp. 417–427). Buffalo, NY: Beary.

Stein, M. I. (1993). The olden days: Better, worse, does it matter? In S. G. Isaksen, M. C. Murdock, R. L. Firestien, & D. J. Treffinger (Eds.), *Understanding and recognizing creativity: The emergence of a discipline* (pp. 477–491). Norwood, NJ: Ablex.

Steinberg, L. (1972). *Other criteria: Confrontations with twentieth-century art.* New York: Oxford.

Steiner, W. (1996, March 10). In love with the myth of the "outsider." *The New York Times,* pp. H45, H48.

Sternberg, R. (1985). *Beyond IQ: A triarchic theory of human intelligence.* New York: Cambridge University Press.

Sternberg, R. J. (Ed.). (1999). *Handbook of creativity.* New York: Cambridge University Press.

Sternberg, R. J., & Dess, N. K. (2001). Creativity for the new millennium. *American Psychologist, 56*(4), 332.

Sternberg, R. J., & Lubart, T. (1991). An investment theory of creativity and its development. *Human Development, 34,* 1–31.

Storr, A. (1972). *The dynamics of creation.* New York: Atheneum.

Strasberg, L. (1960). On acting. In J. D. Summerfield & L. Thatch (Eds.), *The creative mind and method: Exploring the nature of creativeness in American arts, sciences, and professions* (pp. 83–87). Austin: University of Texas Press.

Strauss, N. (2002, March 24). The country music country radio ignores. *The New York Times,* pp. AR1, AR31.

Stravinsky, I. (1947). *The poetics of music.* Cambridge, MA: Harvard University Press.

Stucky, N. (1988). Unnatural acts: Performing natural conversation. *Literature in Performance, 8*(2), 28–39.

Stucky, N. (1993). Toward an aesthetics of natural performance. *Text and Performance Quarterly, 13,* 168–180.

Sulloway, F. (1996). *Born to rebel: Birth order, family dynamics, and creative lives.* New York: Pantheon Books.

Sweet, J. (1978). *Something wonderful right away: An oral history of the Second City & the Compass Players.* New York: Avon Books.

Talbot, R. J. (1993). Creativity in the organizational context: Implications for training. In S. G. Isaksen, M. C. Murdock, R. L. Firestien, & D. J. Treffinger (Eds.), *Nurturing and developing creativity: The emergence of a discipline* (pp. 177–215). Norwood, NJ: Ablex.

Tardif, T. Z., & Sternberg, R. J. (1988). What do we know about creativity? In R. J. Sternberg (Ed.), *The nature of creativity* (pp. 429–440). New York: Cambridge University Press.

Taylor, C. W. (1962). A tentative description of the creative individual. In S. J. Parnes & H. F. Harding (Eds.), *A source book for creative thinking* (pp. 169–184). New York: Scribner's.

Taylor, C. W. (Ed.). (1964). *Creativity: Progress and potential.* New York: McGraw-Hill.

Taylor, C. W., & Barron, F. (Eds.). (1963). *Scientific creativity: Its recognition and development.* New York: Wiley.

Taylor, D. W., Berry, P. C., & Block, C. H. (1958). Does group participation when using brainstorming facilitate or inhibit creative thinking? *Administrative Science Quarterly, 3*(1), 23–47.

Taylor, M. C., & Saarinen, E. (1994). *Imagologies: Media philosophy.* London: Routledge.

Tomkins, C. (2002a, April 15). Can art be taught? *The New Yorker,* 44.

Tomkins, C. (2002b, August 5). Man of steel. *The New Yorker,* 52–63.

Tonelli, G. (1973). Genius from the renaissance to 1770. In P. P. Wiener (Ed.), *Dictionary of the history of ideas* (pp. 293–298). New York: Scribner's.

Torrance, E. P. (1962). *Guiding creative talent.* Englewood Cliffs, NJ: Prentice-Hall.

Torrance, E. P. (1965). *Rewarding creative behavior: Experiments in classroom creativity.* Englewood Cliffs, NJ: Prentice-Hall.

Torrance, E. P. (1972). Can we teach children to think creatively? *The Journal of Creative Behavior, 6,* 114–143.

Torrance, E. P. (1974). *Torrance tests of creative thinking: Norms-technical manual.* Princeton, NJ: Personnel Press/Ginn.

Torrance, E. P., & Khatena, J. (1969). Originality of imagery in identifying creative talent in music. *The Gifted Child Quarterly, 13,* 3–8.

Treffinger, D. J. (1986). Research on creativity. *The Gifted Child Quarterly, 30*(1), 15–19.

Treffinger, D. J., Isaksen, S. G., & Dorval, K. B. (1994). *Creative problem solving: An introduction* (Rev. ed.). Sarasota, FL: Center for Creative Learning.

Triandis, H. C. (1995). *Individualism & collectivism.* Boulder, CO: Westview Press.

Trollope, A. (1989). *Anthony Trollope: An illustrated autobiography.* Wolfeboro, NH: Alan Sutton. (Original work published 1883)

Tuomi, I. (2002). Networks of innovation: Change and meaning in the age of the Internet. New York: Oxford University Press.

Turner, V. (1969). *The ritual process.* Harmondsworth, United Kingdom: Penguin Books.

Turner, S. R. (1994). *The creative process: A computer model of storytelling and creativity.* Mahwah, NJ: Erlbaum.

Tylor, E. B. (1889). *Primitive culture: Researches into the development of mythology, philosophy, religion, language, art, and custom.* New York: Holt. (Original work published 1871)

Vandenberg, S. G. (Ed.). (1968). *Progress in human behavior genetics.* Baltimore: Johns Hopkins Press.

Varnedoe, K., & Gopnik, A. (1990). *High & low: Modern art, popular culture.* New York: Museum of Modern Art.

Veblen, T. (1919). The intellectual preeminence of Jews in modern Europe. *Political Science Quarterly, 34,* 33–42.

Vinacke, W. E. (1952). *The psychology of thinking.* New York: McGraw-Hill.

Vygotsky, L. S. (1971). *The psychology of art.* Cambridge: MIT Press.

Wagner, R. K., & Sternberg, R. J. (1986). Tacit knowledge and intelligence in the everyday world. In R. J. Sternberg & R. K. Wagner (Eds.), *Practical intelligence: Nature and origins of competence in the everyday world* (pp. 51–83). New York: Cambridge University Press.

Wakefield, J. F. (1991). The outlook for creativity tests. *The Journal of Creative Behavior, 25*(3), 184–193.

Wallach, A. (1997, October 12). Is it art? Is it good? And who says so? *The New York Times,* p. AR36.

Wallach, M. A. (1971). *The intelligence/creativity distinction.* New York: General Learning Press.

Wallach, M. A. (1988). Creativity and talent. In K. Grønhaug & G. Kaufmann (Eds.), *Innovation: A cross-disciplinary perspective* (pp. 13–27). Oslo, Norway: Norwegian University Press.

Wallach, M. A., & Kogan, N. (1965). *Modes of thinking in young children: A study of the creativity-intelligence distinction.* New York: Holt, Rinehart & Winston.

Waller, J. (2002). *Einstein's luck: The truth behind some of the greatest scientific discoveries.* New York: Oxford University Press.

Ward, T. B. (2001). Creative cognition, conceptual combination, and the creative writing of Stephen R. Donaldson. *American Psychologist, 56*(4), 350–354.

Ward, T. B., Smith, S. M., & Vaid, J. (1997a). Conceptual structures and processes in creative thought. In T. B. Ward, S. M. Smith, & J. Vaid (Eds.), *Creative thought: An investigation of conceptual structures and processes* (pp. 1–27). Washington, DC: American Psychological Association.

Ward, T. B., Smith, S. M., & Vaid, J. (Eds.). (1997b). *Creative thought: An investigation of conceptual structures and processes.* Washington, DC: American Psychological Association.

Warrington, E. K., James, M., & Kinsbourne, M. (1966). Drawing disability in relation to laterality of cerebral lesion. *Brain, 89,* 53–82.

Weeks, P. (1990). Musical time as a practical accomplishment: A change in tempo. *Human Studies, 13,* 323–359.

Weeks, P. (1996). Synchrony lost, synchrony regained: The achievement of musical coordination. *Human Studies, 19,* 199–228.

Weick, K. E. (2001). *Making sense of the organization.* London: Blackwell.

Weiner, R. P. (2000). *Creativity & beyond: Cultures, values, and change.* Albany: State University of New York Press.

Weisberg, R. W. (1986). *Creativity: Genius and other myths.* New York: Freeman.

Weisberg, R. W. (1988). Problem solving and creativity. In R. J. Sternberg (Ed.), *The nature of creativity* (pp. 148–176). New York: Cambridge University Press.

Weisberg, R. W. (1993). *Creativity: Beyond the myth of genius.* New York: Freeman.

Weinberg, S. (2002). Afterword: How great equations survive. In G. Farmelo (Ed.), *It must be beautiful: Great equations of modern science* (pp. 253–257). London: Granta Books.

Wenzel, M. (1972). *House decoration in Nubia.* London: Duckworth.

Wertheimer, M. (1945). *Productive thinking.* New York: Harper.

West, M. A. (2002) Sparkling fountains or stagnant ponds: An integrative model of creativity and innovation implementation in works groups. *Applied Psychology: An International Review, 51*(3), 355–424.

West, M. A., & Farr. J. L. (Eds.). (1990) *Innovation and creativity at work: Psychological and organizational strategies.* New York: Wiley.

West, M. A. (2003). Innovation implementation in work teams. In P. B. Paulus & B. A. Nijstad (Eds.), *Group creativity: Innovation through collaboration* (pp. 245–276). New York: Oxford.

White, E. W. (1966). *Stravinsky: The composer and his works.* Berkeley and Los Angeles: University of California Press.

Whyte, W. H. (1956). *The organization man.* New York: Simon & Schuster.

Wicklund, R. A. (1989). The appropriation of ideas. In P. B. Paulus (Ed.), *Psychology of group influence* (2nd ed., pp. 393–423). Hillsdale, NJ: Erlbaum.

Wilford, J. N. (2002, February 26). When humans became human. *The New York Times,* pp. D1, D5.

Wilkinson, A. (2002, May 27). Moody toons: The king of the cartoon network. *The New Yorker*, 76–81.

Wilson, G. (1985). *The psychology of the performing arts*. London: Croom Helm.

Winner, E. (1982). *Invented worlds: The psychology of the arts*. Cambridge, MA: Harvard University Press.

Wisniewski, E. J. (1997). Conceptual combination: Possibilities and esthetics. In T. B. Ward, S. M. Smith, & J. Vaid (Eds.), *Creative thought: An investigation of conceptual structures and processes* (pp. 51–81). Washington, DC: American Psychological Association.

Wittkower, R., & Wittkower, M. (1963). *Born under Saturn*. London: Shenval.

Wolf, J. (1998, August 23). The blockbuster script factory. *The New York Times Magazine*, 32–35.

Wordsworth, W. (1957). *Wordsworth's preface to lyrical ballads* (W. J. B. Owen, Ed.). Copenhagen, Denmark: Rosenkilde and Bagger. (Original work published 1800)

Wypijewski, J. (Ed.). (1997). *Painting by numbers: Komar and Melamid's scientific guide to art*. New York: Farrar, Straus & Giroux.

Yuasa, M. (1974). The shifting center of scientific activity in the west: From the 16th to the 20th century. In N. Shigeru, D. L. Swain, & Y. Eri (Eds.), *Science and society in modern Japan* (pp. 81–103). Tokyo: Tokyo University Press.

Zaimov, K., Kitov, D., & Kolev, N. (1969). Aphasie chez un peintre. *Encephale, 68*, 377–417.

Zhao, H., & Jiang, G. (1986). Life-span and precocity of scientists. *Scientometrics, 9*, 27–36.

Ziman, J. M. (Ed.). (2000). *Technological innovation as an evolutionary process*. New York: Cambridge University Press.

INDEX